CONTEMPORARY ISSUES IN CRIMINAL JUSTICE

CONTEMPORARY ISSUES IN CRIMINAL JUSTICE

SECOND EDITION

Edited by Szde Yu

cognella
SAN DIEGO

Bassim Hamadeh, CEO and Publisher
Carrie Montoya, Manager, Revisions and Author Care
Kaela Martin, Project Editor
Christian Berk, Production Editor
Emely Villavicencio, Senior Graphic Designer
Alexa Lucido, Licensing Manager
Natalie Piccotti, Director of Marketing
Kassie Graves, Vice President of Editorial
Jamie Giganti, Director of Academic Publishing

Printed in the United States of America.

cognella® | ACADEMIC PUBLISHING
3970 Sorrento Valley Blvd., Ste. 500, San Diego, CA 92121

CONTENTS

INTRODUCTION

This is a book aimed to instigate discussions about some, regrettably not all, contemporary issues in criminal justice. Several previously published articles have been chosen for this anthology, and each relates to the specific chapter's topic. Although they are organized into eight chapters, these issues could very well be connected or correlated with one another. Readers are encouraged to gain informed opinions regarding each topic and, at the end, develop a comprehensive understanding on what the criminal justice system is facing and how the system is or is not working. Given the limited space in one book, it was impracticable to include all valuable articles. Hence, readers should find external sources to further enrich their knowledge on the discussion topic broached in each chapter.

This book starts with a discussion about the death penalty. By starting with a topic familiar to most people, it sets the tone about the kind of discussion intended. It is not a discussion about choosing sides. Rather, it should be a discussion about critical thinking and reality. What do we believe? What is the practical goal? What is really happening? What is going to happen? What is the cost? These critical but crucial questions apply to all topics in the ensuing chapters. In chapter 2, "Police Conduct," a controversial topic is addressed. It is worth discussing precisely because it is controversial. It should be noted there is a difference between police misconduct and police conduct, but they both deserve discussion. The topic of the delicate balance between privacy and security, as discussed in chapter 3, is of interest and is also related to police conduct. How much should we allow the police to invade privacy in the name of security? In chapter 4, another delicate issue is brought to attention: mental illness. Mental illness has been either stigmatized due to ignorance or blindly downplayed due to political correctness. Nevertheless, it is a worsening problem currently threatening the criminal justice system and society, which warrants an honest look. In chapter 5, hate crime is discussed, as recently we see an increasing trend of hate being manifested while hiding behind some self-righteous rhetoric. Hate is a complex subject, much more than simply a right-or-wrong dichotomy. Likewise, racial disparity is also much more complicated than the system simply being racist. It is discussed in chapter 6. Actually, most criminal justice issues are more complex than a choice between two answers, but when it comes to the war on drugs, very few can deny it is a failure. This is not to say we must be soft on drugs now, but our current drug policies indeed need to be reviewed and reflected on. Chapter 7 addresses why drug policies need to be more sensible and goal oriented instead of ideology based. One of the undesirable effects of the drug war is mass incarceration, which is the center of discussion in chapter 8.

As mentioned, there are other informative or educational articles related to each topic out there, and this anthology cannot include all of them. This book serves as an instigator of an educated discussion on an advanced level. Therefore, this book is most suitable to be used for upper-level criminal justice courses where students are expected to integrate knowledge so as to form a full understanding. However, it is also beneficial for those who do not have pre-established opinions about these issues and simply wish to know what contemporary issues our criminal justice system is facing. This second edition replaces some articles in the previous edition and proposes new discussion questions to fit the contemporary backdrop of our society.

CHAPTER 1

The Death Penalty

Introduction

The death penalty has been a topic open to debate for decades. Like many other ideological debates, no matter how long people argue about it, there never seems to be an ultimate conclusion regarding whose view is correct. This is how ideology works. It entails no right or wrong answer. It simply reflects different worldviews, and people tend to believe their view is the correct one. It takes an open mind to appreciate the opposing view. It is important to note that appreciation is not the same as agreement. It means you can appreciate an argument without the need to agree with it first.

As far as the death penalty is concerned, after all these years of debate, advocates on both sides have proposed some arguments worth our consideration. The pros and cons are frequently listed and discussed in criminal justice textbooks. Among the pros, retribution seems to resonate with many people's ideology because it seems only fair to ask the wrongdoer to pay a price for the harm inflicted on the victim. If the victim is dead, the offender should be dead as well. This so-called "just desert" model has always been a popular concept embraced by the ones who support the death penalty. Deterrence is another argument that ostensibly appeals to common sense. Most people want to avoid punishment. When death is the outcome, it makes sense to expect such punishment will exert great deterrence. Despite the lack of empirical evidence, it has been observed that many people, including criminal justice students and scholars, still believe in this deterrent effect. This is another thing about ideology. Once we believe something because it "makes sense" it is usually hard to challenge this belief regardless of what research finds. Further, it is not uncommon to hear people say they support the death penalty because they do not want to spend too much money keeping criminals alive in prison. If this is really the reason they support the death penalty, they should switch sides, because the cost associated with a death penalty case is typically much higher than locking up the criminal in prison for life. This cost-saving argument actually favors the abolition of the death penalty.

In addition to cost saving, some abolitionists have been arguing that taking a human life is immoral no matter who is doing it. Violence begets violence. When the government kills, it sends a message that says killing is okay, which contradicts the purpose of deterrence. Some abolitionists also see the death penalty as a cruel and unusual punishment, which violates the constitutional rights protected by the Eighth Amendment. However, arguments like these are ideological in essence because not everyone sees things in the same way and the definitions of "immoral" and "cruel" are just too vague to convince people who simply do not have the same worldview. A more pragmatic argument against the death penalty is regarding wrongful conviction. Wrongful conviction is not a myth. It has happened and it will continue to happen in the criminal justice system. While advanced technologies are helpful in determining legal guilt, they are not without flaws, especially when combined with human error. No one can guarantee that an innocent person will never be sent to death row. It is true that the possibility of executing an innocent person cannot be ruled out. Nevertheless, does it mean we ought to abolish the death penalty entirely because of this possibility, even for those cases where there is no doubt over who committed the crime? This would be another ideological question that entails no right or wrong answers.

In this chapter, you will read two articles about the death penalty. The first article, "Crime and the Death Penalty," addresses how ideology affects our opinions. Instead of engaging in another debate, this article provides an in-depth understanding on the ideological differences between liberals and conservatives and explains how such differences lead to different views on crime and the death penalty. The author argues the death penalty is a major dividing line between liberals and conservatives. Although this dichotomy could be somewhat oversimplified, this article nonetheless offers a refreshing angle, as it presents a chance to appreciate and understand where the opposing view originates. The second article, "The Problem of Explanation: Understanding the Scandal of Judicial Override in Capital Cases" illustrates the arbitrary nature of the death penalty through a thorough analysis on court decisions in capital cases. It is not necessarily calling for abolition. Rather, it raises some good questions about whether the death penalty is really serving justice as advertised. Again, you do not need to agree with the conclusion to appreciate a reasonable argument.

Crime and the Death Penalty

George Lakoff

No topic draws a clearer line between liberals and conservatives than that of violent crime. Strict Father morality sees the cure for violent crime simply as strict punishment. This derives from the Strict Father model of the family that demands that disobedience must be punished, preferably in a painful fashion with an instrument like a belt or a rod. It assumes the Morality of Reward and Punishment, which says that punishment is the moral alternative. And it also assumes a behaviorist theory of human nature that says punishment will work to eliminate violence.

In addition, conservatives claim that violent crime has been the result of "permissive" childrearing practices. They claim that violent crime in later life is caused by a lack of strict discipline at home, a lack of painful corporal punishment in response to disobedience. A mother's nurturance without a father's discipline, they imply, produces antisocial, uninhibited, violent children with no respect for law. Conservatives, using this reasoning, attribute the rise in violent crime to the corresponding decline in the presence of fathers in American homes, due to divorce and illegitimacy. The assumption is that a father would administer strict discipline, with painful corporal punishment for disobedience, and that this would teach children to behave and to grow up as law-abiding, self-reliant citizens.

The Nurturant Parent model of the family makes exactly the opposite claim. It says that children are best socialized and taught responsibility through a nurturant upbringing where discipline is maintained through loving, respectful, and firm interactions and a constant attention to mutual responsibilities and explanations. Painful corporal punishment, the nurturant model says, does just the opposite of what it is intended to do. It teaches violence and violence begets violence. Children who are made to submit through pain to the will of a parent are taught to make others submit to them through their use of violent methods. Correspondingly, neglect has a similar effect. Neglect is a lack of the nurturance in which discipline comes out of loving, responsible interactions. Neglect is thus a form of violence, a denial of needed nurturance.

Liberals respond that violence among fatherless children living in high-crime districts is a result of one or more of the following: (1) mothers who act like abusive strict fathers, administering corporal punishment for disobedience and berating their children; (2) mothers who are neglectful; or (3) social causes, such as poverty or peer pressure. Liberals further argue that mothers who are abusive or neglectful were abused or neglected themselves. The long-term cure for violent crime, liberals argue, is (1) nurturant environments in which there are no neglectful or abusive strict-parent models and (2) the reduction or elimination of poverty by the provision of job training and jobs. From the liberal perspective, what the conservatives are suggesting would just increase violence.

Advocates of nurturant–parent child-rearing practices cite research indicating that strict-father families and corporal punishment contribute importantly to delinquency and violence in later life. [...]

Gun Control

Liberal support for gun control is a consequence of the nurturant parent's view of painful corporal punishment—that it contributes to a cycle of violence. Guns are not intended just for target practice or sport. They are intended to hurt or kill people. The very presence of a gun evokes scenarios in which guns are used. These scenarios (self-defense, retribution, or revenge) all share the property that violent punishment is seen as the natural response to wrongdoing. That very idea, the Nurturant Parent model claims, leads to further violence. And further violence with guns means more killing.

Conservatives' support for the right to bear arms—even the right to bear machine guns—comes from Strict Father morality, which says that it is the responsibility of everyone to protect himself as well as he can and it is the responsibility of the Strict Father to protect his family. Guns are seen as the individual's form of protection in a hostile world and they are symbolic of the male role as family protector. They are an instrument of moral strength and a symbol of the power of the Strict Father. As such, they also uphold the moral order. There is thus a very good reason why it is conservatives who support the right to bear arms at a time when conservatives are down in general on rights as liberals have defined them, e.g., the right to a decent standard of living, the right to an education, and the like.

There is also a good reason why very impassioned opposition to gun control often goes with survivalism. Survivalism is about self-reliance through self-discipline, the hallmark of Strict Father morality. And there is a good reason why those who are impassioned about the right to bear arms and about survivalism are also against the income tax. As we have seen, opposition to taxation fits Strict Father morality. And there is a reason why advocates of the right to bear arms are often violently anticommunist. The Strict Father model provides the link between the protective function of the father and the principle of the Morality of Reward and Punishment, the very basis of all morality in the Strict Father model.

This is by no means to say that all conservatives are gun nuts, survivalists, antitax activists, and strong anticommunists. But there is a good reason why those values fit together and why people with those values tend to be conservatives.

Crime

Why do conservatives believe in spending money to build more prisons, and in tougher sentencing laws even for nonviolent offenders. Why do they support the Three-Strikes-and-You're-Out law, mandating twenty-five-year-to-life sentences for repeat nonviolent as well as violent offenders? Why do they do so in the face of evidence that having more people in prison does not reduce crime?

The state of Minnesota's Kids First program, which stresses day care, education, and community involvement, has succeeded in crime prevention at a much lower cost than running prisons. Why has this model not been supported by conservatives?

The answer comes out of Strict Father morality, in which the Moral Strength system of metaphors is primary, with Moral Self-Interest right behind it. Strict Father morality thus includes Retribution, Moral Strength, Moral Self-Interest, and Moral Essence. Retribution sees punishment as defining justice. The priority of Moral Strength entails that a show of strength is the best protection against evil. It is a consequence of Moral Self-Interest that people act in their own self-interest hence, people will commit crimes if it is in their interest (that is, if punishment is lenient) and won't commit crimes if it is not in their interest (if punishment is harsh). And according to Moral Essence, past behavior is a guide to essential character and essential character predicts future behavior. Therefore, a repeat offender has a bad character, which means he's likely to commit crimes again. To protect the public, he should be imprisoned for a long time.

By Strict Father morality, harsh prison terms for criminals and life imprisonment for repeat offenders are the only moral options. Programs like Minnesota's Kids First are social programs and are, as such, immoral to conservatives for reasons given above. The conservative arguments are moral arguments, not practical arguments. Statistics about which policies do or do not actually reduce crime rates do not count in a morality-based discourse.

Liberals, following Nurturant Parent morality, point to Minnesota's Kids First as an argument that prevention programs can reduce crime, while pointing to statistics indicating that putting people in prison does not. Liberals see crime as having social causes—poverty, unemployment, alienation, and lack of caring and community—and argue that social programs are needed to address those social causes. Conservatives don't believe in social causes of crime or in any other social causes. Let's consider why.

Class and Social Causes

Conservatives tend not to use explanations based on the concepts of class and social causes, nor do they recommend policy based on those notions. Why? Liberals use these concepts all the time, in providing explanations and in formulating and justifying policy. Again, why? What is it about the difference between liberals and conservatives that makes these concepts sensible to one, but not to the other?

Think for a moment about how the notions of class and social forces are used. Class structure comes with the notion of an upper class with wealth and power that wants to maintain its privileges; a lower class—the cheap labor of the upper class—held down and kept subservient to the upper class; and a middle class caught in between—aspiring to the upper class and afraid of falling into the lower class, but also depending on the cheap labor of the lower class. Social forces are usually postulated to account for the failure of certain lower-class groups to succeed, to gain access to wealth and power. People in the lower class can get caught in the system and be unable to rise. Such a social arrangement is seen by liberals as unfair. It is a social injustice.

According to this picture, the upper and middle classes could not maintain their current lifestyles without the cheap—and often difficult and demeaning—labor of the lower class: picking vegetables, working in fast-food places, cleaning houses, collecting garbage. In this picture, the upper classes owe a lot to the lower class—much more than they are paying. Social justice demands that the lower class be paid more, live under better conditions, and be given maximal opportunities to work their way out of poverty, opportunities for education and job training, for example.

This picture is usually supplied as a justification for government to do something to help out the people at the bottom, at least to provide for their basic needs and to give them enough education and job training to allow them to do a bit better. It is also used to explain the rage and violence of lower-class people against the system that "imprisons" them socially and economically. It is the class structure and the social forces holding it in place that does the "imprisoning."

Concepts like "class" and "social and economic forces" and "social and economic imprisonment" fit naturally into a liberal worldview. For liberals, the essence of America is nurturance, part of which is helping those who need help. People who are "trapped" by social and economic forces need help to "escape." The metaphorical Nurturant Parent—the government—has a duty to help change the social and economic system that traps people. By this logic, the problem is in the society, not in the people innocently "trapped." If social and economic forces are responsible, then other social and economic forces must be brought to bear to break the "trap."

This whole picture is simply inconsistent with Strict Father morality and the conservative worldview it defines. In that worldview, the class hierarchy is simply a ladder, there to be climbed by anybody with the talent and self-discipline to climb it. Whether or not you climb the ladder of wealth and privilege is only a matter of whether you have the moral strength, character, and inherent talent to do so. Because explanations for success or failure give priority to Moral Strength and Moral Essence, explanations in terms of social forces and class make no sense. They are only seen as excuses for lack of talent, laziness, or some other form of moral weakness. In such a worldview, the concept of social justice does not make sense. If the poor are selling their labor to the rich, then it is the labor market and the labor market alone that determines what that labor is worth. Labor, in this metaphor, is a commodity like any other commodity, and its value is not inherent but determined by what people are willing to pay in exchange for it. The Morality of Reward and Punishment, which requires that all markets be free markets, demands this. Any other arrangement would be immoral and threaten the very moral foundations of society. It is for this reason that conservatives are against the minimum wage, while liberals, in the name of a bare minimum of social justice, support it.

To conservatives, the existence of a wealthy class simply makes real the Morality of Reward and Punishment, the basis of all morality. It is not wrong, not something to be corrected, for the wealthy to seek further privilege. It is natural and moral, a guarantee that the Morality of Reward and Punishment continues to work. Crucial to this is what conservatives see as the essence of America—the Ladder of Success myth. As long as free enterprise flourishes and anyone with enough self-discipline and imagination can become an entrepreneur, the Morality of Reward and Punishment will hold and all will be well.

The logic of conservatism locates so-called "social" problems within people, not within society. For this reason, it would make no sense to conservatives to use class and social forces as forms of explanation and justification for social policy.

Nature and Nurture

The term "nurture" has two related senses, one having to do with nurturance (nurture-1) and the other with environmentally determined rather than genetically determined factors in human development (nurture-2), as in the opposition between "nature" and "nurture." Nurturance is certainly an environmentally determined factor, and it leads liberals to look almost exclusively at environmentally determined factors in social and political explanations.

Though Strict Father morality is opposed to the goal of a nurturant society, it is extremely concerned with environmental factors, such as childrearing and the more general use of reward and punishment. But there are other parts of Strict Father morality that are concerned with nature as opposed to nurture-2.

Strict Father morality gives high priority to Moral Essence and the idea that the Moral Order is the *natural* order of dominance. Thus, there is a strain in conservatism that uses nature, as well as environmentally determined factors, as a means of explanation for social problems. Conservatives can have it both ways. Unsuccessful people can fail for one of two reasons: because they lack either (1) character (which is environmentally determined) or (2) talent (which is natural). That is why conservatives tend to like books like *The Bell Curve,* while liberals tend not to. *The Bell Curve* provides the second explanation for the economic failure of blacks—lack of talent; but if that can't be proved, there is always lack of character as an explanation.

Preventing Crime

The difference in conservative and liberal moral systems leads to different views of the role of nature and nurture and of the explanatory validity of concepts like class and social forces. To conservatives, any appeal to social forces is always just an excuse for lack of talent (nature) or lack of character (nurture-2). Conservatives therefore don't address crime by looking for social causes. They address crime just the way they would address the refusal of a child to abide by his parents' rules—according to the Morality of Reward and Punishment. Conservatives punish crime, and they assume that if crime is punished harshly enough, it will end, because criminals will have a strong enough disincentive to keep them from committing crimes. If disincentives don't work, then the criminals must be inherently bad—rotten to the core—and should be locked away for life or for a very long time.

Given the central position that the Morality of Reward and Punishment has in the conservative moral system, it is no surprise that conservatives in most cases prefer retribution over restitution as a form of justice, as a way of balancing the moral books. It is therefore no surprise that conservatives are in favor of the death penalty. It is a form of retribution, a life for a life.

Liberals, of course, look at these issues very differently. The primacy of empathy leads to an overriding concern with fairness toward anyone committing a crime (Moral Action Category 1). Given the overwhelming power of the state, any citizen is helpless by comparison unless the rule of law is carried out scrupulously. Great care must be exercised that people accused of crimes be given a fair trial and that their rights as citizens not be overridden by the state. Liberals are acutely aware that the police can abuse their power and act unfairly to get a conviction. This is especially true where the accused is someone who is poor or a member of a minority group. Poor people cannot get as good representation in court as rich people, and members of minority groups are subject to prejudice. Most of the people who have been given the death penalty and are on death row are poor members of minority groups. Overwhelming concerns for empathy and fairness, which grow out of the Nurturant Parent model, lead liberals to have a paramount concern for the abuse of state power.

Conservatives see such a concern as coddling criminals, as caring more about the criminal than the victim. They are puzzled by liberal behavior. If liberals are so concerned about protecting the helpless, why aren't they more concerned about protecting the victims of crime? Why aren't they promoting stricter penalties in the name of protection?

It is not that liberals are not concerned about the victims of crimes. Rather, they disagree about how crime is to be minimized overall. First, the rule of law must be upheld. If the state can act like a criminal, framing innocent people and trampling on the rights of the accused, then all hope for the rule of law is lost. To keep the state and its representatives—the police and the courts—honest, the rights of everyone accused of a crime must be upheld strictly.

Fairness is the issue here. If the legal system is not fair, it will have no legitimacy. Fairness is a consideration that arises, in Nurturant Parent morality, out of concerns for empathy and nurturance for all.

Second, liberals do believe in social causes; they believe that if children are not raised in nurturant environments, they will not learn to behave responsibly toward others. If a gang is the closest thing to a nurturant community a child knows, then he will engage in gang behavior. Thus, the way to best inculcate responsible behavior over the whole society is to provide nurturant environments for as many people as possible. The best long-range approach to fighting crime is to fund programs like Project Head Start, to provide high-quality day care for poor working parents, to provide high-quality education for the poor, and so on. That is why a liberal like Anthony Lewis *(New York Times,* August 8, 1995) is so outraged when he sees conservatives cutting $137 million from Project Head Start and simultaneously giving the military $7 billion more than it said it needed. It costs more than $20,000 a year to house one prisoner for a year—the cost of tuition at an Ivy League college. Liberals argue that, in the long run, it is more effective, a lot cheaper, and a lot better for everyone to fund Project Head Start, day-care centers, and so on. But conservatives believe that there can be no such thing as social causes of crime, that crime is always a matter of individual moral weakness. It follows then that it is silly to spend money on countering nonexistent social causes.

Third, liberals do not believe in the overriding Morality of Reward and Punishment. They do not believe that it is mainly fear of punishment that binds society together and makes people act kindly, responsibly, or at least civilly, toward each other. Liberals believe that it is nurturance that brings this about, that loving and supportive parent-child bonding creates communities in which there are strong social ties. It is not that rewards and punishments are never appropriate, but they are not the basis of morality, nurturance is.

Simply increasing penalties, liberals argue, will not eliminate crime. The death penalty, liberals argue, has been shown not to be a deterrent to murder. Murderers apparently do not do a cost-benefit analysis before killing someone, and so the death penalty does not deter them.

The Death Penalty

The death penalty itself is a major dividing line between liberals and conservatives. Supporters tend to be conservative and opponents tend to be liberal. Nurturant Parent morality militates against the death penalty. The major legal argument given rests on fairness, which, as we have seen, arises in Nurturant Parent morality from considerations of empathy and nurturance. The argument is that the courts do not have a way to guarantee that the death penalty is applied fairly. Prejudice and politics do enter into murder trials. If a person unfairly convicted of murder is executed, then there is no recourse if he is later discovered to have been innocent. Most of the people on death row are poor and black and are unable to afford adequate legal representation, which, it is argued, makes it more likely that they will get the death penalty. The same penalties should apply to all racial and economic groups. If that is not true of the death penalty, the death penalty should not be applied at all.

But liberals' feelings about the death penalty run much deeper than that. Nurturance itself implies a reverence for life, which is a form of the unconditional love of nurturant parents for their children. If the government is conceptualized as a nurturant parent, then it should have such an overwhelming reverence for life itself. The death penalty denies such a reverence for life, and so is inconsistent with the conception of the government as nurturant parent.

In Strict Father morality, the strict father metes out punishment for the wrongdoings of children. The Nation As Family metaphor makes the government into the Big Daddy who is meting out punishment. Are there any limits on the harshness of punishment? The lack of such limits in the family would make it moral for a parent to kill his child in the name of discipline. When parents are abusive, this can happen, and all too frequently does. Infanticide is what the death penalty amounts to in the Nation As Family metaphor. The spectre of the state functioning like a murderously abusive parent is, I believe, what lies behind the constitutional prohibition against cruel and inhuman punishment and behind liberals' abhorrence of the death penalty.

For these reasons, I believe, liberals find the death penalty uncivilized and point out that nations around the world have banned it. It sets a bad example for the state to be engaged in killing people, the worst crime someone could commit. Just as parents can set bad examples, so, according to the Nation As Family metaphor, can the government. Governments should not be in the business of killing people.

Arguments against the death penalty are not just about the death penalty itself. They are emblematic of a broader issue. They are about how the state should be conceptualized and how it should function in general.

The liberal arguments, of course, cannot possibly be persuasive to conservatives. If the very basis of morality is reward and punishment, then in a moral society the way to deal with crime is punishment, an eye for an eye—period. The argument that the death penalty does not deter murder doesn't really matter that much. To conservatives, the death penalty is part of a moral society, in which the Morality of Reward and Punishment rules supreme.

READING 2

The Problem of Explanation

Understanding the Scandal of Judicial Override in Capital Cases

Paul Kaplan, Kerry Dunn, and Shannon Jackson

Deciding to sentence a person to death creates a difficult metaphysical problem for the decider—what Jennifer Culbert (2008) calls "the problem of judgment." Judging whether a person convicted of capital murder should be executed or spared requires a thoughtful decider to think hard about the nature of reality. The decision presents the decider with a string of questions about complex ideas such as intent, causality, justice, state power, the human mind, and the purposes of punishment.

Indeed, as Culbert (2008) shows, the US Supreme Court's about-face from *McGautha* v. *California* (1971) to *Furman* v. *Georgia* (1972) instantiates this metaphysical difficulty. In *McGautha*, the Court validated the idea that judging the worthiness of death or life can only be understood in relation to the matter being judged—and *not* in relation to some external set of "real" or "perfect" rules that are articulable:

> To identify before the fact those characteristics of criminal homicides and their perpetrators which call for the death penalty, and to express those characteristics in language which can be fairly understood and applied by the sentencing authority, appear to be tasks which are beyond present human ability. (*McGautha* v. *California* 402 US 183 (1971); at 204, quoted in Culbert 2008, 18)

Reversing in *Furman*, the Court said that death sentences and executions were arbitrary—or ungoverned by any principles—and thus validated the opposite idea that there is a "real," external authority to which judgment can, and for death sentencing, must, refer. In terms of metaphysics as Culbert sees it, this move by the court mirrored the "error" made by Socrates in his quest for the "real" world of "pure truth" that exists outside the sensual experience of the human "apparent world" (see Culbert 2008, Ch. 1). The metaphysical problem of judgment is to figure out whether there

Paul Kaplan, Kerry Dunn, and Shannon Jackson, "The Problem of Explanation: Understanding the Scandal of Judicial Override in Capital Cases," *Social Justice* vol. 43, no. 1, pp. 23-49.

are "real" external truths that can (and must) govern the thing—life or death in this case—to be judged. In this study, we borrow the phrase—"problem of judgment"—to include its specifically metaphysical meaning, but also to include all the problems listed above.

US law has struggled with this problem since the early 1970s, producing a "Frankenstein's monster" (Zimring 2003) of contradictory jurisprudence that seesaws between the *Furmanian* position of a "two-world metaphysics" with "real" external truths that can give order to death sentencing, and the *McGauthian* position that rejects universality and focuses on the "self-evident-ness" of death sentencing. Along the way, the Court has tried to accommodate many of the vexing issues presented by the problem of judgment that challenge America's death penalty. One especially complex aspect of judgment in the death penalty is the rule that the decider must "weigh and give effect to" aggravation and mitigation before he or she chooses life or death for the defendant (*Penry* v. *Lynaugh* 1989). This requirement is a part of the contemporary death penalty's doctrine of "guided discretion," and is one of the primary reasons why death penalty law is "different" from most other criminal jurisprudence.

A long list of research demonstrates how difficult it is for people to consider aggravation and mitigation.[1] This is not to say that it is difficult for people to assign death sentences—obviously, they regularly do so in the United States. Rather, to weigh and give effect to aggravation and mitigation—to legitimately attack the "problem of judgment"—is probably one of the most difficult challenges any person could ever face. For example, how does someone assess the relative weight of two factors, such as whether a killer raped the victim versus the childhood abuse suffered by the killer? To do so would require the person to ponder the complexity of human motivation, including all the difficult metaphysical categories listed above. Consequentially, the decider is often not up to the task and dismisses half of the moral equation: the mitigation.

This article is partly about the problem of judgment. But it also concerns the problem of explanation. Scholars have observed that human beings tend to interpret reality in terms of meaningful narrative (see Bruner 1991). Especially in cases of violence, harm, or destruction, people resist randomness as an explanation. When something catastrophic occurs, such as murder, most people wish for "an explanation" that involves an agent (see Scarry 1985). Often, the explanation for killings adds up to: "an evil man decided to kill because killing satisfied an evil urge."

But in US law, this simplistic explanation is inadequate because of the role of mitigation in the doctrine of guided discretion. The essence of this doctrine since *Lockett* v. *Ohio* (1978) can be characterized as "anything goes" because of "catchall" provisions in the statutes: "The existence of any other factors in the defendant's background that would mitigate against imposition of the death penalty" (FL 921.141(6)(h); see similar indeterminacy in AL 13A-5-52; DE 429(c)(1)). In our estimation, the rules established by *Lockett* v. *Ohio* (1978) and *Penry* v. *Lynaugh* (1989) require death penalty deciders to actually grapple with deep metaphysical questions. We argue that this should produce more complex and nuanced explanations than the common "evil man" story. The narrative structure of explanations should be temporally longer and should include more points of view. What we call "the problem of explanation" *flows out of* the problem of judgment. We will show below that if deciders fail to deeply contend with the metaphysical problems entailed in their judgment, they likewise fail to explain it.

Judicial Override in Capital Cases

We analyze the intertwined problems of judgment and explanation through a study of judicial override opinions. Of the 32 states that employ capital punishment, three—Alabama, Delaware, and Florida—are unusual in that the trial judge makes the final decision on the death sentence after a sentence recommendation from the jury (rather than ultimately by the jury, as in all other death penalty states). Although the capital statutes of these states have passed constitutional muster, they remain controversial because in 222 cases trial judges have overridden jury recommendations for life and sentenced defendants to death.[2] These states require the judge to write a sentencing opinion that explains his or her findings on aggravation and mitigation (Alabama Code 13A-5-47[d], Delaware 429 (d)(4); Florida Statute § 921.141). In other words, judge-overridden death sentences require something close to an explanation of the judgment. This study analyzes the total population of these opinions to examine the problems of judgment and explanation by tracing the metaphysical, moral, and ideological aspects of what judges say when sentencing persons to death. Along the way, we identify rhetorical techniques, illuminate how judges understand (or fail to understand) mitigation, and argue that the symbolic power of pain overrides other considerations when judges must decide life or death for the offender.

Override statutes create four possible scenarios for sentencing orders: (1) when the jury recommends life and the judge agrees, (2) when the jury recommends death and the judge agrees, (3) when the jury recommends death and the judge disagrees, and (4) when the jury recommends life and the judge disagrees.[3] Although the orders in each scenario are important, we focus on the fourth one because override to death represents a special, antidemocratic form of capital punishment unique to these states, with judges contradicting the voice of the people when assigning death.

Two Frames of Analysis

There are two frames for this study. The first is sociolegal: the sentencing opinions help us to learn more about how post-*Gregg* v. *Georgia* (1976) statutes work and, more broadly, to deepen our understanding of the nature of state power. These sentencing opinions "constitute an official record (albeit selected and partial) of the ways in which the state legitimates and justifies its power to punish" (Daly and Bonhours 2008, 502). In analyzing them, "we ... learn how a judge, as the authorized spokesperson for the state in censuring and sanctioning crime, speaks ... about what is right and wrong social conduct" (p. 502). Override opinions offer a rare moment when the decision-maker is supposed to put in writing a rationale for state-sanctioned killing in top killing states.[4]

We will show that it is impossible to know how most of these judges contend with the problem of judgment because they fail to solve the problem of explanation. As discussed below, explanations offered by most overriders do not illuminate processes of judgment and do not explain why these defendants are sentenced to death.

This sociolegal frame allows us to see the phenomenon of override as a scandal. Almost all overrides are to death; on the rare occasion when judges try to explain their override decisions, their accounts are sparse and tautological. Judges almost never consider mitigation and judges do not see Life Without the Possibility of Parole (LWOP) as a very harsh punishment. They believe that jurors are inherently unqualified to decide life or death and employ curious logic to enable their override decisions. These characteristics of override are scandalous because they produce a picture of state power that is, in a sense, unjustified because it is not explained. Using Weber's classic definition of a modern state—one with a legitimate and justifiable monopoly on power (Weber 1946, 78–79)—we can say that override represents absolute judgment, but does so without justification. Override thus represents only the "power" part of the modern liberal state's contract with its citizens, and not the "justifiable" part. In a subtle but important way, these sentencing orders represent a broken contract between the state and its citizens.

The second frame is metaphysical. Observers of the law know that judges regularly behave scandalously. Unfortunately, it is not surprising that judges use state power to the detriment of marginalized defendants. Analyzing override metaphysically allows us to attempt to explain the legal scandal as follows: in a sense, the Court got it right in *McGautha* because deciders of life or death usually fail to live up to the "two-world" metaphysical demands of *Furman*. Applying well to contemporary judges with the power to override is the Court's 1971 position that the life or death decision at the heart of a capital trial is not governable by understandable external rules. As we show, overriders often rely on the metaphysical power of *pain and suffering* to authorize their decisions. Put another way, overriders *replace* the Court's rules about weighing and giving effect to mitigation with the simple authority of the pain and suffering of the victims and their families. Later, we draw on Culbert (2008) and Scarry (1985) to show how the authority of pain obliterates facts about mitigation and provides overriders with legitimacy that allows them to circumvent the Court's rules about mitigation with little or no explanation.

Previous Research on Override

Scholars have studied how post-*Gregg* guided discretion works primarily by studying juror decision-making. Much of this data comes from the Capital Jury Project (CJP), which examines jurors' decision-making, particularly arbitrariness, in capital cases (Steiner et al. 1999). CJP data have shown that a host of factors influence how juries make capital decisions, including, knowledge of sentencing options (Bowers and Steiner 1999; Eisenberg et al. 2001), (mis) understandings of jury instructions (Eisenberg and Wells 1993), defendant's (lack of) remorse (Eisenberg et al. 1998), premature decision-making (Bowers et al. 1998), perceptions of personal sentencing responsibility (Hoffman 1995), and folk knowledge about punishment (Steiner et al. 1999). This study is similar to the work of CJP to the extent that it analyzes capital judgment. It differs in three important ways: (1) it focuses on the judgment of the state rather than lay persons; (2) it focuses more on explanation of judgment; and (3) it offers a metaphysical explanation for the state's unsatisfying explanations.

Previous research on judicial override has appeared exclusively in law reviews (e.g., Lebowitz 1996) and only infrequently discusses empirical characteristics of the cases (e.g., jurors are less likely to assign death than judges; Radelet 1985). In the only qualitative critique of override, Russell (1994) compares Florida and Alabama, and delineates the legal constructions of judgment and explanation that are meant to guide death in these two states—with the former possessing at least the veneer of a standard for death, and the latter lacking standards. Florida's rule includes what is known as "the *Tedder* standard," which requires the judge to give the jury's recommendation "great weight" and "requires that a trial judge's use of the override rests upon a belief that the majority of the jury did not act reasonably" (Russell 1994, 8). As thin as this standard is, it is more than exists in Alabama. In Alabama's procedure, after a jury finds the defendant guilty of capital murder and then, after a penalty-phase trial, recommends life or death, the judge chooses life or death with the following instruction:

> [T]he trial court shall determine whether the aggravating circumstances it finds to exist outweigh the mitigating circumstances it finds to exist, and in doing so the trial court shall consider the recommendation of the jury contained in its advisory verdict, unless such a verdict has been waived. ... While the jury's recommendation concerning sentence shall be given consideration, it is not binding upon the court. (Code of Ala. § 13A-5-47 [2011])

Russell (1994, 8) observes that this law creates no statutory standard; nor does it refer to any case law standard for guiding judges when deciding life or death. Looking into this statutory void, Russell turns to the actual sentencing memos for some semblance of criteria for death, and finds none, causing her to conclude that the Alabama statute is arbitrary and therefore unconstitutional (p. 8). The US Supreme Court disagreed. In *Harris* v. *Alabama* (1995), the Supreme Court upheld Alabama's statute, ruling that the constitution does not require standards such as *Tedder* or a specific method for weighing aggravation and mitigation (for a discussion, see Maullem 1996).

Override in Florida and Alabama

Florida was the first post-*Furman* state to enact a new statute. Just five months after the decision, it laid the groundwork for guided discretion and launching judicial override. Apart from judicial sentencing, the Florida model resembles the *Gregg* model; it creates a separate post-conviction sentencing hearing, provides a list of aggravating factors that make a case death eligible, and provides immediate judicial review of a death sentence by the Florida Supreme Court. The statute states that the judge, not the jury, makes the final decision, and requires the judge to weigh the aggravating and mitigating circumstances independently of the jury. It does not, however, explain what consideration a judge must give to the jury's advisory sentencing verdict. The

Florida Supreme Court elaborated on this question in *Tedder* v. *State* (1975). In *Tedder*, the trial judge overrode the jury's recommendation of life imprisonment after finding three aggravating and no mitigating circumstances. The Florida Supreme Court reversed the trial court's decision, creating the *Tedder* standard:

> A jury recommendation under our trifurcated death penalty statute should be given *great weight*. In order to sustain a sentence of death following a jury recommendation of life, the facts suggesting a sentence of death should be *so clear and convincing that virtually no reasonable person could differ*. (p. 53, emphasis added)

This creates a presumption in favor of the jury verdict. As a result of *Tedder*, about 75 percent of life-to-death overrides in Florida were overturned on direct appeal (Radelet 2011). The last life-to-death override in Florida was in 1999, although the reasons for this change are unclear (see Radelet 2011, for a discussion). Since 1999, override in the United States has become strictly Alabaman (ibid., 28–29). Florida judges have stopped the practice and there has only been one life-to-death override ever in Delaware. Alabama's current statute dates to 1981. It requires the jury to find the defendant guilty of capital murder and to hear a penalty phase and recommend a sentence to the court, with the court ultimately making a decision (ibid.).

Perhaps the most important fact about Alabama in relation to override is that, unlike in Florida, the judges tasked with deciding death are elected in *partisan* elections (EJI 2011, 14).[5] The potential for arbitrariness under these conditions is obvious enough, and the Equal Justice Initiative has documented a great deal of anecdotal evidence of political influence, including the simple fact that 92 percent of overrides in Alabama are life-to-death (p. 14), with some evidence of higher rates of life-to-death overrides in election years (p. 16), and tough-on-crime rhetoric in judicial ad campaigns (pp. 14–15). Finally, the race effect on capital punishment is so well known that it is unnecessary to amplify on it regarding Alabama. Suffice it to say that the usual suspects are present in the Heart of Dixie: white victims receive special treatment, African Americans are disproportionately represented on death row, and district attorneys and judges are almost all white (p. 18).

Characteristics of the Data

This analysis began by coding all 222 memos and collecting descriptive data from each memo to make general statements about the body of memos. Memos ranged in length from two pages to over 40. Most cases had only one victim, and "multiple victims" was an aggravating factor in just 5 percent of the memos. The most common aggravating factors found by the judge include murder committed during commission of a felony (72 percent), defendant had a prior violent conviction (68 percent), and the murder was especially heinous (61 percent). Data on race was not available in Florida, but analysis of Alabama cases with race data (N=82) revealed facts similar to those in national data. The race of the defendants was about even (49 percent white and 51 percent black), but was disproportionate to the state population (70 percent white,

26 percent black, in the US Census for 2011), while victim data showed a higher valuing of white victims at 77 percent white and 22 percent black. The data on gender of the defendant also reflected national death penalty statistics: all but two defendants in Alabama and Florida were male. National data show that victims in death sentence cases are more likely to be female, but victims were slightly more likely to be male in Florida and female in Alabama. Unanimous jury votes are not required in any of the states, and unanimous jury votes for life constituted only 6 percent of the cases in Alabama. However, 29 percent in Alabama had a strong majority (9–11 jurors) voting for life.

We also tried to assess how much detail judges gave on specific elements of the memos, including the description of the crime, the aggravating and mitigating factors, the weighing process, and the decision to override. In most memos, we found that little detail was given to key elements of the death decision. In Florida, judges provided no or minimal description of the aggravating factors (22 percent), the mitigating factors (53 percent), and the weighing (85 percent) of the cases. In Alabama, judges provided no or minimal description of the aggravators (62 percent), the mitigating factors (68 percent), and the weighing process (81 percent). We flagged memos with significant detail given by judges on the crime, aggravators, mitigators, weighing process, and decision to override as most likely to allow for a deeper analysis of judges' legal and metaphysical struggles. The next section is based on our close reading of these approximately 30 memos.

Death Unexplained

In the standard form, judges' memos briefly introduce the case by summarizing procedural history and facts about the crime. Then the judge delineates the full list of aggravating, statutory, and non-statutory mitigating circumstances (whether they were argued at trial or not), declares whether she believes that each factor exists in the case and whether she considered it, mentions the jury's recommendation, declares that the aggravators outweigh the mitigators, and finally orders the sentence of death.

Most memos offer little to no explanation of the weighing process. In *Alabama* v. *Barnes* (1995), for example, the entire weighing process is described in just one sentence: "The Court rejects the advisory verdict of the jury, and finds that the aggravating circumstances in this case outweigh the mitigating circumstances and that the punishment should be death" (p. 6). The description of the weighing process in *Florida* v. *Pomeranz* (1993), though much longer, is equally devoid of meaning:

> When the aggravating and mitigating circumstances are weighed in a reasoned and deliberate process any reasonable person truly using the weighing process can not conclude there were any reasonably convincing mitigating circumstances established that outweighed the aggravating circumstances enumerated. ... All of the circumstances statutory and non-statutory presented to the jury, when considered in the totality of this Defendant's life and character, can not be considered extenuating or reducing the degree of the Defendant's

> moral culpability for the murder of Mr. Patel; this is the conclusion reached when the evidence presented at both phases of the trial is considered and weighed fairly and deliberately through the Court's own independent and reasoned evaluation and judgment. ... (p. 19)

In both examples, and in almost all of the other memos, we are told that the aggravating factors outweigh the mitigating factors, but not why.

This was also the case in judges' discussions of their decision to override the jury's vote for LWOP. Many of the memos contain boilerplate legal language. In Florida, many judges simply say that "the aggravators outweigh the mitigators and that no reasonable person could differ," thereby satisfying the *Tedder* standard. Judges who do more follow one of three strategies: they compare the case to prior capital cases to find that death is justified, they say their decision was influenced by evidence the jury did not get to see, or they suggest that the jury was incapable because it was confused by emotional defense arguments or the complexity of the case. Sometimes, judges cannot find any rational reason for the jury's life vote. In explaining his override in *Alabama* v. *Sneed* (2006), the judge dismissed the jury's 8–4 vote for life because:

> The Court finds it incomprehensible that a jury would vote for guilt of a person for four counts of capital murder during a kidnapping, robbery, burglary, as well as sexual abuse of the victim—three of the four being for pecuniary gain—then consider the twenty-eight stab wounds, the nine incised wounds, as well as the multiple contusions and lacerations which occurred in and about the face of the victim, then recommend that the person who committed such a heinous, atrocious, and cruel crime should be given life in the penitentiary without the possibility of parole and not the death penalty. (p. 16)

Because the discussions of weighing and the override decision offer so little insight into the explanation of death in all but a few cases, most of our analysis focuses on the discussion of the mitigating and aggravating factors. In the discussion of the individual factors, judges assign weight to the aggravating and mitigating evidence, usually leading to a foregone conclusion that the aggravators clearly outweigh the mitigators when it comes time for weighing. The following subsections show how judges over-weight aggravation and under-weight mitigation.

Overweighting Aggravation

Judges often took great effort to establish heavy aggravation and later used it in the weighing to show that death is the obvious answer. They did this in a number of ways, from arguing that elements of the crime were worse than in normal capital murders, to emphasizing the bad character of the defendant, employing curious logic, and describing in great detail the pain and suffering of the victim.

Worse than Normal

In *Alabama* v. *Killingsworth* (2006, 264), Judge Thomas Jones "afforded more weight than a typical robbery" to this robbery-murder. He believed it was more reckless than "normal" robberies because Killingsworth's codefendant had shot the driver of a fast-moving car with passengers inside, and this codefendant had beaten the wife of the victim after the car was on the side of the road. Although Judge Jones does not explain "typical" robbery-murders, he delineates why he thinks these circumstances are especially bad and "require more weight in aggravation" (p. 265).

Often the result of a "worse than normal" aggravator is the automatic dismissal of mitigation. In *Alabama* v. *Spradley* (2008), the judge declared that she thinks that intentionally killing a person during a robbery is "so vile, and morally and legally reprehensible" (p. 17) that she "finds it very hard to imagine a combination of mitigating circumstances that could fairly outweigh this aggravating circumstance as proven" (p. 17). This statement suggests that this judge was, *a priori*, strongly disinclined to consider *any* mitigation. And while including the phrase "very hard to imagine" preserves the legality of this sentence, the judge's position seems to be out of touch with the Court's requirement for super-due process and "difference" in capital cases, especially relating to mitigation.

Bad to the Bone

Beyond stressing the badness of the crime, judges sometimes also emphasized the badness of the defendant, to the point where it overshadowed even the possibility of mitigation. In *Alabama* v. *Spradley* (2008), the judge makes it clear that the defendant is beyond redemption. Using a strategy discussed further below, she brings aggravating evidence into her discussion of mitigation (including the claim of the defendant's family's that he is a good person at heart):

> Irrespective of how the defendant's family members viewed him, the evidence presented at trial clearly reflected that he is simply a "bad boy to the bone," and is proud of it, as evidenced by his tattoos, which are permanent reminders of his wicked and evil deeds. The evidence further reflected that the defendant did not benefit one bit from all of his Bible studies, and he certainly has not done any good works in the Church. Additionally, there was overwhelming evidence that reflected the defendant was a dope dealer, and that when he was riding around with his kids in his car, he was dealing dope and putting them at risk. Moreover, the evidence reflected that the defendant certainly was not a positive influence or a good role model to his kids when he fought with their mother and beat her in front of them.
>
> Nevertheless, the Court finds the defendant's love and devotion to his family and their love and devotion to him to be a non-statutory mitigating circumstance. However, the court feels this mitigating circumstance should be given extremely minimal weight as the listed attributes are inconsistent with the violent nature of the capital offense. (p. 55)

The evidence of the defendant's bad character presented as aggravating factors and again when discussing mitigating factors is so overwhelming that it outweighs all evidence of good character and affects the weight of mitigating factors.

This memo is striking in its provocative invocation of "gangster" culture. Throughout the order, Judge Bahakel refers to key persons by their apparent street monikers (e.g., a person named Cedric Atkins, known as "See Boo"; another person with the moniker "Big Queet"). She also uses the terms "bitch," "ho," "homeboys," "chillin," and "dope dealer," refers to Spradley's girlfriend as "his baby's mama" (p. 4), and describes Spradley as "a bad boy to the bone" (p. 23). The impression is that the judge is repelled by a dangerous and morally corrupt "gangsta culture" in which human life is worthless:

> Prior to his arrest, Mr. Spradley told his baby's mama, Alisha Renea Booker, that he and a friend had killed a lady because they thought she had some money and she wouldn't give it up. ... When the defendant learned that Ms. Booker had spoken to the police about the murder and robbery, he savagely beat and kicked her and threatened to kill her. This occurred while Ms. Booker was 7 or 8 months pregnant with the defendant's third child. ... After having been arrested, and while in jail, Mr. Spradley told a fellow inmate that he choked "the bitch" (Mrs. Jason) and then killed her because "she didn't have shit." Further, he told the inmate, that he would have killed his baby's mama for talking to the police if she had not been pregnant with his child. (p. 4)

Curious Logic

At least two judges engaged in sleight of hand to increase aggravation. One of the statutory aggravators in all three state statutes is "that the defendant was previously convicted of another capital offense or of a felony involving the use or threat of violence to the person." The commonsense understanding of this provision is: "does the defendant have prior violent convictions," with most judges in this study treating it as such. But a few judges count co-occurring crimes as previous convictions at sentencing. In *Alabama* v. *Evans* (1996)—with two murders occurring during one robbery event—the judge counted each murder as a "previous conviction" for each other murder.

Pain and Suffering

The most common overweighting of aggravation occurred in discussions of evidence of the victim's pain and suffering during the murder. All three states have an aggravating factor of "heinousness" and judges often provided a detailed description of the pain and suffering of the victim to establish heinousness of the crime. In one detailed example, *Florida* v. *Washington* (1992), the defendant was convicted of sexual battery and rape of an elderly woman while he was on work release. The judge spent five pages on the question of heinousness, including graphic details about the crime, information from the autopsy, and a review of definitions of heinous from other cases. He describes the victim's suffering:

> At this point in time, Defendant ... must have literally knelt on the victim's chest with both knees. ... There were 17 separate rib fractures to the victim's chest. ... So, after this victim was battered about, had her teeth ripped out, had her legs pried apart, and the entrance to her vagina torn while her body was entered by the Defendant's penis, he then got on top of her and broke seventeen ribs which caused her great pain. He put his hands around her throat and violently choked her. This brave lady must have continued to struggle causing the bruises to her head as she tried to break free, or else the Defendant pounded her head against the floor to stop her struggle. For at least thirty to forty seconds as she struggled for breath, this Defendant tightened his hands around her so violently he broke the bones and cartilage in her neck. (pp. 4–6)

Here, heinousness is defined by victim suffering, which is established through medical evidence of physical damage and awareness of impending death. In *Washington*, the level of victim suffering, as evidenced by crime scene and autopsy evidence, establishes the heinousness of the crime, while negating the defense argument that Washington did not intend to kill the victim:

> If, as Dr. Merin claims, he chose a weak, older woman to show his strength, manhood, and masculinity, he had already done that. He had already raped her. She was no match for him. He beat her, broke her, and raped her. He could have gone on his way. Even as he kneeled on her chest and her bones broke in seventeen places, he must have known she was not readily going to run after him and tackle him and hold him for the police. She was old and frail. He had disarmed her. But when he then put his hands around her throat and choked the very life out of her, breaking her hyoid bone and the cartilage of her larynx, and kept his hands around her throat for no fewer than thirty seconds and up to three minutes, he did so for one purpose—to kill her. (pp. 19–20)

The harrowing details of the crime overshadow the entire opinion. Again, the judge's discussion of the mitigating evidence is full of aggravating evidence. She finds just one mitigating factor: evidence of good character in the form of a good school record and being an obedient son. Having established heinousness and dismissed most of the mitigating evidence, the judge's explanation of weighing takes just one sentence: "This Court finds the aggravating factors far outweigh the non-statutory mitigating factor, and they do so beyond all reasonable doubt" (p. 20). Having already over-weighted the aggravation and lessened the weight of the mitigation, the judge does not see a reason to say more. Pain and suffering of the victim trumps all possible mitigation.

Underweighting Mitigation

Discussions of mitigation varied from over 15 pages to one sentence. Most cases provide at least some discussion of mitigation, often to negate or dismiss, making the weighing process less complicated. In about 23 percent of cases, judges dismissed all statutory and non-statutory mitigation point by point before getting to the weighing process, thereby making the weighing very simple (see, e.g., *Florida* v. *Herzog* 1981, 4). In this section, we discuss the ways in which the weight of mitigating evidence is reduced, including negating mitigation with aggravation, dismissing the relevance of mitigating evidence and sidestepping the implications of mitigation by relying on the language of individual choice and accountability.

Negating

The concept of "negating" differs slightly from that of "converting" mitigation, in which deciders (typically understood to be jurors) interpret evidence submitted for the purpose of mitigation as aggravation.[6] In negating, the judge does not argue that the mitigator is actually an aggravator, but instead uses negative evidence about the defendant to deny or "lighten" the mitigator. In *Florida* v. *Lewis* (1976), the judge uses his analysis of a statutory mitigator (victim involvement in the crime) as an opportunity to bring in more negative information about the defendant:

> That the victim was a participant in the defendant's conduct or consented to the act:
>
> The evidence showed that the defendant shot the victim a number of times in the head at close range with a shotgun—blowing away portions of his head and causing his instant death. ... There is no mitigating circumstance under this paragraph because the defendant did—by stealth and premeditation—shoot and kill the victim and the same was obviously done without the foreknowledge or consent of the victim. (pp. 5–6)

This mitigating factor was not argued by the defense. The boilerplate format in which judges delineate the entire list of statutory aggravating and mitigating factors gives judges extra opportunity to bring in negative information as they discuss each factor.

In *Washington*, discussed above, the judge comes close to converting mitigation to aggravation as he brings in extensive negative information while discussing the mitigating factor of "mental or emotional disturbance":

> His basic problem is having a weak personality while living in an area where he had to be tough. Thus, Mr. Washington, a weak person, became a "bully" to cope with his real personality. He learned to exploit persons to hide his own weakness. ... He takes what he wants, whether it is money, property, or sex. ... Dr. Merin says he is an opportunist—someone who takes advantage of situations presented to him. And so he did. Our murder victim had the misfortune of leaving her door open, an opportunity too great for this Defendant to ignore. ...
>
> While this court would agree that emotional or psychological problems not reaching the level of statutory mitigating circumstances can be and should be considered non-statutory mitigating circumstances in an appropriate case, and, as suggested by the defense, a "troubled personal life" may give rise to a mitigating circumstance, there is simply no evidence in this case that calls for this conclusion. It will be a sad day if a "bully", and "opportunist", and a "weak personality" that preys on those weaker than he is for his own desires and pleasures, can have this considered mitigation in a death sentence. ... (*State of Florida* v. *Washington* 1992, 17)

This judge goes to great lengths to discuss the defendant's bad character, which could be logical in a sentencing opinion, but perhaps not in the section titled "mitigation." Beyond explaining that the factor was not present because the defendant had a sound mind at the time of the crime, the judge makes the case that the defendant had a criminal mind.

In these examples, the judges used negative information to explain why a particular mitigator does not exist. In other cases, judges find the mitigator, but include negative information in explaining why the mitigator has little or no weight.

In *Alabama* v. *Evans* (1996) the defendant was convicted of robbing and murdering an elderly woman and her four-year-old granddaughter. According to the judge, the facts in this case reveal that the defendant was mentally ill. The judge devotes considerable attention to discussing Evans's bizarre behaviors before the crime—strangely licking his fingers, playing with rocks, and referring to them as family members—and the judge's own knowledge about psychological or psychiatric diagnoses. This judge's understanding of mental illness prompted him to diagnose Evans as suffering from borderline personality disorder and antisocial personality disorder, which the judge believed causes people to be manipulative. Remarkably, this judge claimed that Evans's strange behavior *prior to* the crime was an attempt to set up an insanity defense after he committed the robbery and murders. In all, the judge negates significant evidence of mental problems for the defendant, including evidence from defense experts concerning problems associated with taking Prozac, a claim that Evans was in a fugue state, and a suicide attempt while in custody. The judge decided that Evans's emotional distress was "produced by the defendant's own personality" (p. 24), but that "finding" this to be a mitigator "comes awfully close to making a mitigating circumstance out of the precise fact that the defendant is a vicious and dangerous person" (p. 25). So while he finds the mitigating factor to exist, he lightens its weight on the scale by negating it.

Mitigation is also found, then negated, in *Alabama* v. *Jackson* (1998). The judge begins by reporting the defense's position—that one statutory mitigator (Jackson's young age of 18), and two non-statutory mitigators (that Jackson turned himself in and that he "did not avoid his probation officer after he was declared a delinquent probationer") applied (p. 5). After listing all of the statutory mitigators, the judge rejects them all except for Jackson's young age, which he "finds" as a mitigator, but then undermines it with a treatise on Jackson's physical attributes (6 feet tall, 175 pounds) and criminal history (13 arrests and 5 felony charges throughout his teens). Here we encounter repressive formalism—the "finding that mitigation exists" is a nod toward the liberal state's need for rational and formal rules; the negation of that mitigation is repressive. What is the point of "finding" the mitigation, if that mitigation is totally irrelevant?

These judges are likely concerned over appellate review. To agree that a defendant was 18 when he killed someone "is" mitigation forecloses appellate courts from overturning the conviction because of judicial failure to consider mitigation. At the same time, however, the law lets the judge negate the mitigation he "found." Indeed, the fact that the judge said Jackson's age counted as a mitigator allowed him to negate it. Had Judge Gordon decided that Jackson's age was *not* a mitigating factor because of all the reasons cited in negating it, the case might have been overturned.

Dismissing

In many memos, judges did not explain why they did not give weight to mitigating factors, sometimes exposing a lack of understanding of human behavior and the legal requirement to consider mitigating evidence. In a few cases, judges simply ignored mitigating evidence with no explanation. In *Alabama* v. *Barnes* (1995), for example, the judge finds mitigating factors, including hearing impairment and "borderline mental retardation," but concludes that these factors "make the defendant no less accountable for his actions (p. 4). This declaration explains nothing. The judge does not explain why hearing impairment and borderline mental retardation do not make Barnes less accountable, or why LWOP is not enough accountability.

More commonly, the judge provides some explanation for why mitigating evidence does not exist or should be given no weight. In *Florida* v. *Hansbrough* (1985), the judge provides a lengthy discussion of the statutory and non-statutory mitigating factors, which he dismisses one by one:

> 1. *Early turbulent home life*. The evidence did establish that the Defendant was a product of a broken home and residing with the mother and the father during periods of family break up. Such early turbulent home life is experienced by many, many people in our society and

> under the facts of this case cannot be construed as a mitigating factor in the homicide. ... Kirk Allen Hansbrough was responsible for his own actions and to blame turbulent home life as an approximate cause or mitigating factor is just not supported by the evidence. *He had a loving mother and brothers and sisters raised in the same environment who ... establish as normal, healthy and law abiding citizens.* This factor is not present.
>
> 2. *History of physical abuse and/or neglect.* While there is evidence that the mother and possibly the father inflicted physical abuse or neglect, *it was not inflicted to the extent that such could, in the long run, adversely affect the Defendant to the extent which he wishes the Court to interpret.* Such incidences of physical abuse, according to the evidence, were sparsely administered by the mother. The evidence showed that these actions by the mother were lightly regarded by the Defendant and that they did not physically hurt him.
>
> 3. *History of drug abuse and drug addiction.* Evidence does suggest that the Defendant did abuse drugs and had an addiction, however, such addiction to the extent claimed by the Defendant is not established by the evidence. It is clear that the Defendant has been informed by the local drug rehabilitative program, "Thee Door," that he was not sick enough to be admitted into their program. Doctor's testimony as well as lay witnesses regarding the actions of the Defendant and his drug addiction prior to the homicide *clearly shows that while he had a history of drug abuse and drug addition, it was not to the extent at the time of the homicide that would justify his actions. ... Drug use was a voluntary action by the Defendant.* ... The Court finds this factor to be a consideration but not evidence serious enough to warrant mitigation. ... (pp. 11–12, emphasis added)

This section of *Hansbrough* includes examples of several forms of dismissing mitigation based on evidence of a turbulent home life, physical abuse, and drug addiction. This ignores social science research on the impact of childhood instability and abuse and medical research on addiction (e.g., Khantzian and Albanese 2008). The judge dismisses each piece of mitigating evidence until there is nothing left to weigh.

Similarly, in *Alabama* v. *Killingsworth* (2006), the defendant submitted evidence that his parents were alcoholics, his mother abandoned him at age five, his mother was killed in an accident when he was 11, and that his father neglected him (p. 16). The judge negates these facts by noting that responsible grandparents adopted Killingsworth at age five and that they were model caregivers for the duration of Killingsworth's childhood and adolescence. This view of the mitigation fails to consider the complex impact of early trauma on vulnerable persons. Most mental health professionals would recognize that even when loving and responsible caregivers step in and take over, early trauma (e.g., maternal abandonment and paternal neglect) can have profound lingering effects on the person's well-being. Indeed, this judge seems to be guilty of "selective receptivity" of mitigation evidence; he believes in the beneficial effects of the kindly grandparents, but does not believe in the earlier negative effects of the neglectful biological parents. For this judge, only evidence that favors his desired outcome—death for the defendant—seems to count.

Judges frequently dismiss evidence of mental illness even when it is extensive and compelling. In a case of curious logic to dismiss mitigation (*Alabama* v. *Evans* 1996), the judge argues that the defendant's mental illness "symptoms, and possible causes of the disorders [borderline and antisocial personality disorder], standing alone, are not strong mitigators" (p. 22). Instead, the judge believes that "the disorders themselves carry a great deal more weight" (p. 22). This logic says that the traumas that caused the defendant's disorders are *not* strong mitigation, but that the diagnosis of them is. The judge's argument seems to be that trauma *in and of itself* should not mitigate violent crimes, but if the traumatized person develops an officially recognized disorder, then that disorder itself could be a mitigator. This is like saying that to understand a catastrophic wave that destroyed a village, it is only important to know that what happened was called a tsunami, while ignoring that an earthquake under the sea led to the formation of the tsunami.

Individualism and Choice

A common means for sidestepping mitigating evidence is to rely on the concepts of individual responsibility and choice. As in *Hansbrough,* in *Killingsworth* the judge relies on choice to dismiss mitigating evidence of drug abuse. After conceding that childhood drug and alcohol abuse were mitigating factors, and affording them weight, the judge continues:

> Yet, this weight is tempered by the fact that this drug and alcohol use was voluntary. Regardless of what his parents did, Killingsworth chose to take drugs and drink alcohol. As previously discussed, Killingsworth was even ordered not to use drugs or alcohol while on probation; yet he still chose to do so. ... As a result, while this Court finds that Killingsworth history *[sic]* of drug and alcohol use is mitigating, it gives this factor a minimum weight because voluntary abuse of drugs and alcohol—when a person knows that such use is wrong—cannot outweigh that person's responsibility for murdering an innocent person. (p. 17)

This judge sees no connection between early childhood trauma and adolescent onset of drug and alcohol abuse. This compartmentalization of childhood trauma and later substance abuse evinces either ignorance or cynicism; decades of research on addiction shows a strong connection between "what parents did" and later substance abuse by their children (e.g., Khantzian and Albanese 2008).

"Choosing" is a complex concept that involves some of the metaphysical ideas referenced above (intent, the human mind, etc.) and also challenges us to think about the fundamental problem of individual versus social explanations for acts. We have addressed this topic in detail elsewhere (Dunn and Kaplan 2009), but suffice it to say that we interpret this judge to be operating deeply under the hegemony of individualism. By delinking childhood trauma and adolescent substance abuse and insisting that drug and alcohol abuse is freely "chosen," Judge Jones instantiates an extreme form individualism.

Zero Sum Game

Also in *Killingsworth*, the judge evidently believed that giving the defendant LWOP is the same thing as relieving him of responsibility for murder. The last line of his memo states: "voluntary abuse of drugs and alcohol ... cannot outweigh that person's responsibility for murdering an innocent person" (p. 272). This sentence illuminates this judge's belief that only death—not LWOP—counts as "responsibility" for murder.

Likewise in *Alabama* v. *Sneed* (2006), the court "finds" some mitigation—significant trauma, including the childhood rape of the defendant—but disregards it: "The court finds these non-statutory mitigating factors are entitled to little weight in considering the appropriate sentence to impose in this case" (p. 13). This judge's final comments reveal an understanding of mitigation as "an excuse": "The court does not attribute the defendant's unfortunate upbringing and experiences as excuses for or explanations for his total lack of regard for the life of Mr. Terry as is evident by the defendant's actions in this case" (p. 15). In these two examples, judges make the question of life or death punishment a zero-sum equation—LWOP becomes not an extremely harsh punishment, but a "win" for the defendant that can only be achieved if mitigation "excuses" his actions.

In *Alabama* v. *Evans* (1996), the judge discusses the defense's considerable childhood trauma. His father set his hands on fire, he stabbed himself in the leg, threatened to hang himself at school, and has always been deeply troubled (p. 18). The judge believes that childhood trauma does not count as mitigation to the extent that it should change the defendant's sentence from death to LWOP:

> The Court understands that the defendant's environment had a role in making the defendant what he is. Against the aggravating circumstances enumerated previously, however, the necessity for every person being morally responsible for his or her own actions causes these environmental factors which are offered as mitigation to appear quite weak. There is no question that environment was not kind to Edward Lewis Evans. Nevertheless, what Edward Lewis Evans' natural father and mother did to him does little, in and of themselves, to mitigate what Edward Lewis Evans did to Katie Gates and Ivory Gates. It is dangerous policy for the law to suggest that the very factors that propel a defendant into a life of crime in some way mitigate a defendant's personal responsibility for the criminal activity. The argument that when a bad social environment produces bad people, that fact should in some way mitigate the punishment of these bad people, leads ultimately to the absurd conclusion that only people who come from an impeccable social background deserve the death penalty if they commit capital murder. (pp. 18–19)

This logic is striking in its lack of understanding of the concept of capital mitigation. The whole point of capital mitigation is to claim that "the very factors that propel a defendant into a life of crime in some way mitigate a defendant's personal responsibility for the criminal activity"—but only to the extent that the defendant's culpability requires LWOP. Capital mitigation never claims that persons convicted of capital murder should be set free or be given prison sentences less than LWOP, which is itself an astoundingly harsh punishment that is almost never employed by other advanced democracies in the world.[7]

We have discussed several techniques of dismissing mitigation in isolation, but most memos included multiple techniques. In *Killingsworth*, for example, Judge Jones over-weights the aggravation, dismisses the mitigation, uses the language of responsibility and choice, and compares the case to other cases. We argue that the fundamental key to comprehending their process of judgment is in their understanding of mitigation. Simply put, some judges do not believe that prior trauma is related to later behavior—a basis of most forms of mitigation evidence. For these judges, mitigation has no weight because human agency is all that matters.

Pain and Suffering: A Metaphysical Explanation for the Scandal of Override

As the work of the CJP and this study show, deciders of life or death readily dismiss mitigation, even in cases when the evidence submitted is plentiful and strong. Because only a few of the override orders say anything at all about the reasons for the decision, we cannot know what caused judges in those cases to choose death. However, in orders with some explanation, judges almost always state that the aggravating factors—which are usually related to the suffering of the victim—significantly outweigh whatever mitigation was presented. Several memos indicated that judges use crime scene and autopsy evidence to describe the mental and physical pain of the victim in gruesome detail. In these explanations, "the facts" make it self-evident for the judge that the defendant deserved death. The pain and suffering of the victim *authorize* the judge to override the jury's recommendation for LWOP.

The work of Elaine Scarry can help us to see why. In *The Body in Pain* (1985), "Scarry suggests that the experience of pain generates an experience of agency or, more properly, of being acted upon by an agent" (Culbert 2008, 99). Put another way, "Scarry claims that the [painful] effects of an act experienced in the object imply the presence of a subject who is the source of that act and of those effects" (p. 100). According to Scarry, humans experience pain as *caused* by some agent (even when it is not). Suffering, for human beings, does not feel like it "just happens."

The implication for capital decision-making is that attempts to diminish the agency of the killer by proffering evidence of mitigation will be met with stiff resistance because of the metaphysical power of pain and suffering to amplify the agency of the killer. When the killer actually did cause pain, suffering, and death, evidence of his reduced agency due to some real factor that by all logic should demonstrate diminished autonomy—mental illness, a traumatic social history—is simply very weak in comparison to the "self-evident" metaphysical power of the victim's suffering to, as it were, *put back* agency into the monad of the killer.

As Culbert (2008) argues, the US Supreme Court validated the authority of pain and suffering with its ruling in *Payne* v. *Tennessee* (1991), which authorized victim-impact evidence in capital cases:

> After the Court's ruling in *Payne* v. *Tennessee*, those who must decide what a defendant deserves as punishment in a death penalty case may turn to expressions of pain and suffering as others may once have turned to God or some other absolute, in trust that these expressions will make it possible for them to answer the question, "In the name of what or whom do we judge?" (p. 89)

In terms of metaphysics, this move by the Court is a seesaw toward *McGautha* and away from *Furman* because it signifies a move *inward* to particular cases and away from external rules, where the pain and suffering of the particular victim and his or her family is all that is necessary to authorize death. We can see this move as part of the "Frankenstien's monster" of contradictory capital jurisprudence because it, like *Lockett*, tries to satisfy the law's need for individual treatment of victims and offenders, in tension with the law's need for consistency.

For Culbert, this is an important moment in modern capital jurisprudence because, in a sense, it resolves for the Court the metaphysical problem of "two worlds." It discards the *Furmanian* concern over the "real world" of "universal truths" and valorizes the *McGauthian* preference for the "apparent world" of human sensuality:

> By recognizing pain and suffering as the Law, the hierarchy between the supersensuous and the sensuous is inverted, and the "physical aspect," repudiated by Plato for hindering us in the acquisition of the knowledge of true being, is now taken to be, in Adorno's words, "the only source of whatever hope the mind can have." (p. 110)

We argue that this is probably happening in unexplained or curiously rationalized judicial overrides to death over jury recommendations for life because the power of pain simply erases the need to explain:

> For the Supreme Court, I suggest, pain and suffering give a sense to what otherwise would appear as having no justification or explanation—a law that authorizes partial, imperfect human beings not simply to judge others but to punish some of those others with death. So as no longer to be "like a leaf in the breeze, the plaything of the absurd, of nonsense," the Court appears to have turned anguish and injury into something if not desirable, then something potent, something irresistible. For with the *Payne* decision, the Court makes an absolute of pain and suffering and maintains the legitimacy of a rule of law threatened by uncertainty. (Culbert 2008, 111)

Overriders seem to be similarly "making an absolute" of pain and suffering, and in so doing, obliterating mitigation evidence, even when that evidence shows that the defendant suffered himself, albeit in years past. The immediate pain and suffering of the victim and the victim's family is "absolute" and requires little further explanation. In this sense, contemporary judicial override is metaphysically analogous to the position of the Court over 40 years ago in *McGautha:* the facts of any particular murder are all that matter when deciding the fate of a killer. Following rules based on extraneous "real-world" principles—such as requiring people to "weigh and give effect" to mitigation—appears to be, as the Court said in *McGautha*, "beyond present human ability," at least for judges with the authority to override.

Conclusion

For over 30 years scholars have argued that post-*Furman* sentencing schemes—including override—have failed to live up to their promise of rational death decisions. Most of the evidence on capital sentencing suggests that the arbitrariness disallowed by the Court in 1972 still plagues the death penalty in America. This study suggests that this problem applies to override. Our sociolegal findings demonstrate a scandalous abuse of unexplained state power: in almost all of the sentencing orders, judges say nothing about how they weighed aggravation and mitigation; in the few that do include discussion, mitigation is almost always rejected, ignored, or negated. For the most part, then, we do not know whether judges in these states grapple with the problem of judgment. As for the problem of explanation, they mostly fail. Looking at the big picture of the 222 sentencing orders, there is almost no explanation for the decision to override the local community's choice for life. In the few explanations we see, the explanation is simple: mitigation does not matter. In practice, then, override in these states is unconstitutional because the evidence shows that judges do not consider mitigation.

Acknowledgments: We thank the following individuals for their various forms of assistance with this project (any errors or flaws should be attributed exclusively to us): Bryan Stevenson and Randy Susskind of the Equal Justice Initiative, Sam Kamin, Michael Radalet, and Austin Sarat.

Notes

1. For an overview, see the Capital Jury Project (at *www.albany.edu/scj/13192.php*).
2. It is difficult to know exactly how many capital cases have transpired in Alabama, Florida, and Delaware since 1972. However, by counting persons on death row (630) and executions (145) (Death Penalty Information Center, DPIC, at *www.deathpenaltyinfo.org*) in these states, we arrive at 775 total condemnations in the modern era. For the purpose of comparison to 220 overrides, we can double the number of known condemnations to account for capital trials that went to a penalty phase and resulted in something less than a death sentence: 1,550. This admittedly crude approximation of the number of capital trials in the override states allows us to reasonably speculate that the number of overrides accounts for a significant portion of death sentences.
3. We do not have data for Florida, but know that in Alabama the ratio of death to life overrides is 98–9 (92 percent of overrides are to death) (EJI 2011, 4).
4. Since 1976, Florida has the fifth-highest execution rate and the second-largest death row in the United States, while Alabama has the ninth-highest execution rate and the fifth-largest death row (DPIC).
5. Judges in Florida are chosen in nonpartisan elections; judges in Delaware are appointed.
6. The US Supreme Court succinctly explicated "converting mitigation" in *Penry* v. *Lynaugh* (1989, 319–24): "Penry's mental retardation and history of abuse is thus a two-edged sword: it may diminish his blameworthiness for his crime even as it indicates that there is a probability that he will be dangerous in the future."
7. Anders Breivik, the Norwegian killer of 77 persons in 2011, was sentenced to 21 years in prison, the maximum in that country (*www.pbs.org/newshour/bb/world/july-dec12/othernews_08-24. html*).

References

Bowers, W.J. and B.D. Steiner. 1999. "Death by Default: An Empirical Demonstration of False and Forced Choices in Capital Sentencing." *Texas Law Review* 77(3): 605–717.

Bowers, William J., Marla Sandys, and Benjamin D. Steiner. 1998. "Foreclosed Impartiality Capital Sentencing: Jurors' Predispositions, Guilt Trial Experience, and Premature Decision Making." *Cornell Law Review* 83(6): 1476–556.

Bruner, Jerome. 1991. "The Narrative Construction of Reality." *Critical Inquiry* 18(1): 1–21.

Burnside, Fred B. 1999. "Comment: Dying to Get Elected: A Challenge to the Jury Override." *Wisconsin Law Review* 1017.

Cope, Gerald B. 1993. "Discretionary Review of the Decisions of Intermediate Appellate Courts: A Comparison of Florida's System with Those of the Other States and the Federal System." *Florida Law Review* 45(1): 21–134.

Culbert, Jennifer L. 2008. *Dead Certainty: The Death Penalty and the Problem of Judgment.* Stanford, CA: Stanford University Press.

Daly, Kathleen and Brigitte Bonhours. 2008. "Judicial Censure and Moral Communication to Youth Sex Offenders." *Justice Quarterly* 25(3): 496–522.

Dunn, Kerry and Paul Kaplan. 2009. "The Ironies of Helping: Social Interventions and Executable Subjects." *Law & Society Review* 43(2): 337–68.

Eisenburg, T., S.P. Garvey, and M.T. Wells.

1998. "But Was He Sorry? The Role of Remorse in Capital Sentencing." *Cornell Law Review* 83(6): 1599–637.

2001. "The Deadly Paradox of Capital Jurors." *Southern California Law Review* 74: 371–97.

Eisenburg, T. and M.T. Wells. 1993. "Deadly Confusion: Juror Instructions in Capital Cases." *Cornell Law Review* 79(1): 1–17.

Equal Justice Initiative (EJI). 2011. *The Death Penalty in Alabama: Judge Override.* Report available from the authors.

Erlich, Scott E. 1996. "Comment: The Jury Override: A Blend of Politics and Death." *The American University Law Review* 45: 1403–52.

Forrester, Nathan A. 2003. "Two Views on the Impact of *Ring* v. *Arizona* on Capital Sentencing: Judge Versus Jury: The Continuing Validity of Alabama's Capital Sentencing Regime after *Ring* v. *Arizona*." *Alabama Law Review* 54: 1157–204.

Garvey, Karin E. 1996. "Supreme Court Review: Eighth Amendment—The Constitutionality of the Alabama Capital Sentencing Scheme." *Journal of Criminal Law & Criminology* 86(4): 1411–37.

Hoffman, Joseph L. 1995. "'Where's the Buck?'—Juror Misperception of Sentencing Responsibility in Death Penalty Cases." *Indiana Law Journal* 70: 1137.

Khantzian, Edward J., M.D., and Mark J. Albanese, M.D. 2008. *Understanding Addiction as Self Medication: Finding Hope Behind the Pain.* Lanham, MD: Rowman & Littlefield.

Lafferty, LaTour Rey. 1995. "Florida's Capital Sentencing Jury Override: Whom Should We Trust to Make the Ultimate Decision?" *Florida State University Law Review* 23: 463.

Lebowitz, Neil R. 1996. "*Harris* v. *Alabama*: Standardless Jury Override in Capital Cases Deemed Constitutional." *Maryland Journal of Contemporary Issues* 7: 515.

Maullem, Abe. 1996. "*Harris* v. *Alabama*: Is the Death Penalty in America Entering a Fourth Phase?" *Journal of Legal Legislation* 22: 85.

Mello, Michael. 1991. "The Jurisdiction to Do Justice: Florida's Jury Override and the State Constitution." *Florida State University Law Review* 18(4): 923.

Radelet, Michael L.
1985. "Rejecting the Jury: The Imposition of the Death Penalty in Florida." *UC Davis Law Review* 18: 1409–31.
2011. "Overriding Jury Sentencing Recommendations in Florida Capital Cases: An Update and Possible Half-Requiem." *Michigan State Law Review* 2011: 793–822.

Radelet, Michael and Michael Mello. 1992. "Death-to-Life Overrides: Saving the Resources of the Florida Supreme Court." *Florida State University Law Review* 20: 196.

Richardson, John M. 2004. "Reforming the Jury Override: Protecting Capital Defendants' Rights by Returning to the System's Original Purpose." *The Journal of Criminal Law and Criminology* 94(2): 455–79.

Rossano, Matt J. 2006. "The Religious Mind and the Evolution of Religion." *Review of General Psychology* 10(4): 346–64.

Russell, Katheryn Kenyatta.
1993. *Trial by Jury, Death by Judge: An Empirical and Legal Analysis of Jury Override in Alabama.* Doctoral Dissertation, UMI, Ann Arbor, MI.
1994. "The Constitutionality of Jury Override in Alabama Death Penalty Cases." *Alabama Law Review* 46: 5.

Scarry, Elaine. 1985. *The Body in Pain: The Making and Unmaking of the World.* Oxford, UK: Oxford University Press.

Scheffel, David A. 1997. "*Harris* v. *Alabama*—A Portrait of Deference to the States in Capital Punishment." *Thomas Jefferson Law Review* 19: 39.

Silverstein, Ken. 2001. "The Judge as Lynch Mob." *The American Prospect,* Dec. 19. At *http://prospect.org/article/judge-lynch-mob.*

Steiner, B.D, W.J. Bowers, and A. Sarat. 1999. "Folk Knowledge as Legal Action: Death Penalty Judgments and the Tenet of Early Release in a Culture of Mistrust and Punitiveness." *Law and Society Review* 33(2): 461–505.

Weber, Max. 1946. "Politics as Vocation." In *From Max Weber: Essays in Sociology.* Translated, edited, and introduced by H.H. Gerth and C. Wright Mills, pp. 77–128. New York: Oxford University Press.

Zimring, Franklin E. 2003. *The Contradictions of American Capital Punishment.* Oxford, UK: Oxford University Press.

Override Memos Cited:

State of Alabama v. *Michael Shawn Barnes* CC-94–1401 (1995)
State of Alabama v. *Edward Lewis Evans* CC-95–59 (1996)
State of Alabama v. *Shonelle Andre Jackson* CC-97–2300-WRG (1998)
State of Alabama v. *Jimmy L. Killingsworth, Jr.* CC-2005–009 (2006)
State of Alabama v. *Calvin McMillan* CC-08–476 (2009)
State of Alabama v. *Ulysses Charles Sneed* CC-93–1307.80 (2006)
State of Alabama v. *Montez Spradley* CC-2006–950, CC-2006–951 (2008)
State of Delaware v. *Sadiki Garden*, I.D. No. 9912015068 (2001)

State of Florida v. *Kirk Allen Hansbrough*, CR 84–3951 (1985)
State of Florida v. *Stuart Pomeranz,* CR 92–38 (1993)
State of Florida v. *Anthony Washington,* CR 90–06491 (1992)
State of Florida v. *William Lee Strausser,* CR 92–16860 (1994)
State of Florida v. *George Morris*, CR 86–7626 (1987)
State of Florida v. *Fred Herzog Jr.,* CR 81–4201 (1981)
State of Florida v. *Robert Fieldmore Lewis*, CR 76–1161 (1976)

Cases Cited:

Baldwin v. *Alabama,* 472 US 372 (1985)
Harris v. *Alabama*, 513 US 504 (1995)
Lockett v. *Ohio*, 438 US 586 (1978)
McGautha v. *California* 402 US 183 (1971)
Payne v. *Tennessee* 501 US 808 (1991)
Penry v. *Lynaugh*, 492 US 302 (1989)
Proffitt v. *Florida* 428 US 242 (1976)
Ring v. *Arizona*, 536 US 584 (2002)
Roberts v. *Louisiana* 428 US 153 (1976)
Roper v. *Simmons*, 543 US 551 (2005)
Spaziano v. *Florida* 468 US 447 (1984)
Tedder v. *State* 322 So. 2d 908; 1975 Fla (1975)
State v. *Dixon*, 283 So. 2d 1 (1973)
Woodson v. *North Carolina* 428 US 153 (1976)

CHAPTER 1

Conclusion

The death penalty is inevitably political due to its strong ideological root that often coincides with other political views. No matter which side you believe you are on, it is imperative that you are aware of the reason and that you are willing to test such reason with empirical evidence. It does not mean you need to change your position easily, but an educated and informed person should not resort to ideology as the sole source of opinions. Ideology has a tendency to reduce a complex issue to a simple yes-or-no choice because this is more convenient for the sake of argument. The death penalty is not an issue that renders only two options. It is more than a choice between retention and abolition. Some states, such as Texas, execute their death row inmates every year, while some states have not executed anyone in a long time even though the death penalty technically is an option. For example, Kansas has not executed anyone on death row since 1965. Why not use it if you believe it is the right thing to do? Is it more humane to keep criminals in prison for life while both the criminal and the victim's family are living in agony? Questions like these deserve some consideration before we draw a conclusion about the death penalty.

Discussion Questions

1. Conduct some research on your state's historical use of the death penalty. What has changed in the past fifty years? What factors might have contributed to such changes?
2. Why does the death penalty typically cost more than life in prison? How much more money does it cost?
3. What is your main takeaway after reading these two articles?
4. Conduct research on which states have abolished the death penalty. Do they have higher or lower crime rates, compared to those states still using the death penalty?
5. Find a news story about death row inmates being exonerated by new evidence. How can we prevent this from happening again?

CHAPTER 2

Police Conduct

Introduction

Police conduct has long been subject to scrutiny. It is fair to expect our law enforcement officers and agencies to behave ethically and properly, since they represent authority. We cannot have the authorities abusing power in a democracy. In the old days, when people filed complaints against the police, they often turned into he-said-she-said situations because proof was hard to find. Nowadays, things have changed thanks to the popularity of smartphones. Now, almost anyone can video record an incident or even livestream it for others to see on the Internet. A simple search on Google or YouTube can reveal thousands of such videos. Many police officers have been fired due to videos showing their questionable behavior. These videos, after being broadcast on the media, tend to have a detrimental effect on the public's trust in the police and, therefore, disrupt relations between the police and the public. As a result, the police are facing greater pressure to shape a positive public image in the era of citizen journalism. More and more police agencies are requiring officers to wear body cameras so that they can produce their own videos that document interactions between officers and civilians. These videos have proven helpful, especially when a false accusation is filed against an officer. After all, a video may not tell the whole story. What seems questionable at first may not necessarily attest to police misconduct before the full context can be revealed. Sometimes, the so-called misconduct is simply a different interpretation of the situation.

Among all police conduct, police use of force probably is most likely to be interpreted differently from different perspectives. While the police deem it necessary to use force in some situations, other people might see it as excessive or uncalled for. Some high-profile events have led many people in the society to believe the police are biased against certain groups of people and are more likely to use force on them. Many people attribute this tendency to personal prejudices such as racism. However, a police officer's decision is usually made based on more than just personal belief. Aside from the rules that officers are told to follow, the environment also plays a role in their decision making. More precisely, it is about their perception of the environment. Simply put, if they perceive a neighborhood as dangerous or hostile, police officers will become more sensitive and nervous when they are in this neighborhood. Accordingly, they are prone to interpret a situation negatively in this neighborhood context. It does not matter whether this neighborhood is truly more dangerous or hostile. It is the perception that determines the reaction. While perceptions certainly reflect personal biases, they are affected by many other factors as well, such as crime rates, past experiences, physical appearances, cultural misunderstanding, peer pressure, and so on.

The first article selected for this chapter explains how and why neighborhood context influences police use of force. It looks into structural disadvantages in a neighborhood and how these disadvantages may account for more police use of force. The second article introduces an important concept: police discretion. We all exercise discretion on a daily basis to make various decisions. Police officers are no exception. They have to use discretion to decide what action to take and how far they will go. Poor discretion leads to bad decisions and, therefore, police misconduct. In this article, the author, a former police officer, discusses the mechanisms that might help control police misconduct. After reading these articles, students should be able to better understand, on both structural and personal levels, what contributes to police misconduct and what we can do to curb misconduct before it happens.

READING 3

Why Neighborhood Context May Influence Police Behavior

Zachary R. Hays

Researchers have long studied both the causes of police use of force and the importance of neighborhood context in the explanation of crime, but in the history of both disciplines, rarely have the subjects theoretically or empirically dovetailed. To date, only a handful of inspired researchers have attempted to bring together any concepts or methodologies from the policing and neighborhoods and crime fields to study police use of force within the context of socially disorganized neighborhoods. Moreover, since the reemergence of the social disorganization tradition in the 1980s and 1990s, even the few studies that have actually utilized neighborhood-level contextual measures to predict police officers' use of force, none have specifically used a theoretical framework based on the social disorganization tradition as a whole to explain why officers might use excessive force in disorganized areas. Instead, those few studies that have empirically tested concepts from the tradition have generally conducted variable-driven research that fails to offer any theoretical explanations for their results. Furthermore, even though policing researchers have begun to embrace some of the more advanced multi-level modeling techniques commonly utilized by neighborhoods and crime researchers, none have done so to the full extent of the techniques' capabilities.

Neighborhood Context and Police Use of Force

Only four empirical studies have attempted to examine the relationship between aggregate-level contextual factors and police officers' use of force (Kane 2002; Lawton 2007; Lersch, Bazley, Mieczkowski, and Childs 2008; Terrill and Reisig 2003). Unfortunately, while each of these studies has utilized concepts from the social disorganization tradition, none has actually developed a theoretical framework as a foundation for explaining *why* those concepts should be related to police use of force behavior. Moreover, only one has actually studied neighborhoods, in comparison to alternative levels of aggregation (Terrill and Reisig 2003). Nonetheless, such research provides clues as to which aggregate-level contextual factors might be related to police officers' use of force. Additionally, three of the four (with the exception of Lersch et al. 2008) studies utilized multi-level modeling techniques, and help to demonstrate how research on policing can benefit from a more widespread incorporation of such advanced techniques. Despite such important contributions, however, each of the studies is flawed in some way that makes drawing conclusions about the viability of a social disorganization explanation of police use of force difficult, if not impossible.

In the most recent study to consider neighborhood contextual effects, Lersch and colleagues (2008) empirically tested whether various measures of structural disadvantage could be linked to police officers' use of force in one unidentified city in the Southeastern US. Data for their dependent measure came from official use-of-force report forms (that must be completed any time an officer uses force against a civilian), as reported by the local municipal department's officers. In order to measure neighborhood structural disadvantage, they used census block groups as proxies for neighborhoods and measured the percentage of each tract that was non-white, headed by females with children, and that were either rentals, or vacant.[1] They also controlled for tract-level crime rates (violent and property crimes per 1,000 residents) and the number of active resistance incidents (officer reports of individuals who attempted to physically defeat control efforts or injure officers).

Lersch and colleagues then conducted negative binomial regression analyses (they are the only study of neighborhood context and police use of force not to utilize multi-level modeling techniques) and found that only the number of active resistance incidents and percentage non-white significantly predicted increases in police officers use of force, net of their other controls (although both crime rate measures and percent female-headed households significantly predicted police use of force when the number of active resistance incidents were not included in their models). Subsequently, even though their research is a step in the right direction, their findings provide only partial support for the capacity of social disorganization concepts to explain police use of force.

The study conducted by Lersch and colleagues suffers from a number of noteworthy flaws, however, that should lead shrewd researchers to take their findings with that proverbial grain of salt. First, Lersch and colleagues do not actually use real neighborhoods as their unit of analysis. Census tracts and census tract block-groups are notoriously imprecise estimations

---

1 Although the Lersch and colleagues' (2008) four measures of structural disadvantage are slightly different than those commonly utilized by social disorganization researchers to assess neighborhood levels of poverty, racial/ethnic heterogeneity, and residential instability [...], their measures are generally considered to still be good indicators of the same broad concept that Shaw and McKay (1942) originally envisioned and have been used (primarily as supplements to the standard measures) by other researchers studying neighborhoods and crime (for a review, see Sampson et al. 2002).

of true neighborhoods [...]. Second, the researchers did not conduct a multi-level analysis that would have allowed them to control for individual-level "neighborhood" compositional effects [...]. Finally, although they included measures of structural disadvantage, Lersch and colleagues did not specifically utilize the social disorganization tradition to frame their research, rather they only borrowed one of its concepts. Unfortunately, however, because many concepts from the social disorganization tradition might also be used as measures of the social threat theoretical framework (i.e., researchers could make a pretty compelling argument that percentage non-white, female-headed households, and rental units could all be used to measure the minority populations that pose a threat to the existing social hierarchy), without expressly identifying and laying out their arguments for how they test a specific theoretical framework, their research cannot, and should not, be considered an actual test of the social disorganization tradition.

In a second study empirically linking neighborhood contextual factors and police use of force, Lawton (2007) tested how a variety of individual- and contextual-factors influenced the amount of (legitimate) force police officers used on civilians. Using data from the Philadelphia Police Department in 2002, Lawton conducted a multilevel analysis of individual police-civilian encounters with a number of police district-level controls for violent crime rates and racial heterogeneity (percentage of each police district that was African American). Although Lawton never intended for his police districts to approximate actual neighborhoods, his findings do shed some light on how the effect of aggregate-level predictors on police use of force can vary across geographic space.

Lawton found that district-level violent crime rates were positively related to police officers' use of higher levels of non-lethal force ($p < 0.15$), but only when individual-level factors related to the police-civilian encounter (e.g., officer and civilian race and gender, and civilian behavior during the encounter) were not included in his model. Additionally, he found that racial heterogeneity was negatively related to police use of force, this time net of individual-level encounter controls ($p < 0.15$). As a consequent of the relaxed significance levels that Lawton reported, however, it is once again difficult to draw any firm conclusions from his work.

Nevertheless, like Lersch and colleagues (2008), Lawton's research provides some additional, if not provisional, evidence that racial heterogeneity may be related to police use of force behavior at the aggregate-level. Unfortunately once again, though, because Lawton tested only one concept from the social disorganization tradition, and because he did not specifically use the tradition to frame his research, it is difficult to conclude that his research is truly supportive a social disorganization effect on police use of force, rather than a social threat one. Moreover, because he measured racial heterogeneity at the district-level (rather than the neighborhood-level), it is unlikely that he accurately captured the contextual effect of neighborhoods on police behavior. Despite these reservations in regards to his findings, however, Lawton's study takes a step in the right direction by being one of only two extant studies that test both individual- and aggregate-level predictors of police use of force simultaneously using multi-level modeling techniques.[2]

Kane (2002) takes another step towards legitimizing a potential relationship between neighborhood social disorganization and police officers' use of force. Using two concepts from the social disorganization tradition—concentrated disadvantage and residential instability—Kane attempted to predict variation in police officer misconduct (including, but not specific to, police officers' use of excessive force). He created his concentrated disadvantage and residential mobility variables using U.S. census data in the same fashion as originally constructed by Sampson and colleagues' (1997) measures (see Sampson et al. 1997 for a discussion). He then utilized data from official police records for 75 New York City police precincts, within 20 larger police divisions, between 1975 and 1996 to conduct a multi-level analysis of police misconduct over time. The results of his analyses revealed that both disadvantage and mobility were positively and significantly related to police misconduct at both the precinct- and division-level.

The results of Kane's study provide compelling evidence that aggregate-level concepts related to the social disorganization tradition may truly be related to police officers use of force. Unfortunately, as with both Lersch and colleagues (2008) and Lawton's (2007) studies, Kane's study is simply not a rigorous enough test of the relationship between neighborhood social disorganization and police use of force for a number of reasons. First, although his dependent variable measured police use of excessive force (which is the primary variable of interest for this research), it was actually a scale measure of a number of types of police misconduct, including corruption, administrative policy violations, and drug test failures. Because he did not disaggregate his dependent variable by type of misconduct, it is impossible to determine how well his explanatory variables (including the two concepts from the social disorganization tradition) actually predicted variation in police officers' use of excessive force in particular. Second, like those two other studies, Kane did not actually examine neighborhood-level effects. Instead, he analyzed precinct- and division-level effects and made no effort to discuss how those aggregations might compare to neighborhoods. Thus, even though he found significant effects for concentrated disadvantage and residential mobility (which better measure neighborhood social disorganization than either of the two previously reviewed studies reviewed), his levels of aggregation are a concern. Third, Kane's multi-level analysis did not examine any individual-level predictors of police misconduct. Although he conducted a multi-level analysis, he used two aggregate levels, precincts and divisions, and did not control for any of the individual-level factors that may also influence police misconduct. Finally, while he utilized concepts from the social disorganization tradition, he made no attempt to explain why those concepts should be related to police misconduct. As a consequence, Kane's study, like the ones reviewed above, provides tentative, but by no means definitive, evidence that aggregate-level contextual measures might be related to police use of excessive force.

Finally, in the only piece to specifically claim to examine neighborhood contextual effects, Terrill and Reisig (2003) used observational data from the Project on Policing Neighborhoods

2 See the review of Terrill and Reisig (2003) below.

(POPN) study to examine whether neighborhood concentrated disadvantage influenced the level of force police officers used on crime suspects, net of neighborhood levels of crime and a host of individual-level controls related to police-suspect encounters. The results of their multi-level analysis revealed that police officers were more likely to use higher levels of force on individuals who they encountered in disadvantaged neighborhoods (concentrated disadvantage was measured following the lead of Sampson et al. [1997] as well) as compared to individuals who they encountered in better neighborhoods (i.e., those with lower levels of disadvantage). For the very first time then, Terrill and Reisig were able to specifically demonstrate that *neighborhood* context could in fact predict police officers' use of force.

Unfortunately, just as with the cases of each of the other studies reviewed thus far, there are limitations of Terrill and Reisig's study that must be taken into consideration before any broader conclusions can be drawn. First, the researchers tested only one concept from the social disorganization tradition (concentrated disadvantage), although they do measure it in the same way, and at the same level of aggregation, as other social disorganization researchers commonly do (unlike the three previous studies). And, while they observed a statistically significant relationship ($p < 0.05$), including only one measure of disorganization should still not be considered a rigorous enough test of the relationship between neighborhood social disorganization and police use of force. Second, Terrill and Reisig examined the influence of concentrated disadvantage on only the legitimate use of force by the police. Subsequently, it is still unclear whether or not neighborhood context can specifically predict police officers' use of *excessive* force. Finally, just as the three studies reviewed above failed to do, Terrill and Reisig once again fail to offer any theoretical explanations for why neighborhood context should influence police officers' use of force behaviors. Consequently, even though their study provides the strongest evidence of a relationship between neighborhood context and police use of force thus far, it only begins to address the object of this research, which is to propose and empirically test a social disorganization theory of police use of *excessive* force.

To briefly review, the four primary criticisms of all four studies discussed above were 1) they did actually use the social disorganization tradition as a framework to explain how or the related concepts should have been related to police use of force, 2) they examined only measures of structural disadvantage (but never all three at the same time) and did not consider the effects of any other important social disorganization concepts (i.e., neighborhood social ties and collective efficacy), 3) they did not accurately estimate actual neighborhoods in three of the four studies (with the exception being Terrill and Reisig [2003]), and finally, 4) they failed to use multi-level modeling techniques to their fullest extent which might have allowed them to better distinguish individual-level compositional factors from neighborhood contextual factors.[...] Thus, even though the four studies reviewed above provide some tentative evidence which suggests that aggregate-level contextual factors might viably be used to predict police officers' use of force, the primary objective of this book is to address each of the above criticisms and for the first time reliably demonstrate the viability of a social disorganization theory of police use of force.[3]

3 Only the first criticism is addressed in this chapter (in the following section). [...]

Linking Social Disorganization to Police Use of Force

As the four studies reviewed above perfectly demonstrate, perhaps the most essential condition for convincingly linking neighborhood social disorganization to police officers' use of force is precisely formulating the theoretical mechanisms and/or processes that connect the phenomena. In particular, it is necessary to illustrate exactly how and why police officers working in disorganized neighborhoods might be more inclined to use force—especially excessive levels of force.

[... T]he social disorganization tradition predicts that crime rates will be the highest in neighborhoods where structural disadvantage (poverty, racial/ethnic heterogeneity, and residential instability) leads to a decrease in neighborhood informal social control, social ties, and collective efficacy, rendering those neighborhoods more vulnerable to crime. Increased crime rates might not be the only negative consequence of disorganization, though. In the same way the social disorganization signals to criminals that they will be able to get away with criminal activities (because residents lack the social ties and/or collective efficacy to stop them), it may also signal to police officers that they will be able to get away with the use of excessive force. To exacerbate the issue, the higher crime rates typically found in those neighborhoods should send an even stronger signal to the officers working in those neighborhoods that the residents are incapable of controlling any type of deviant behavior, whether they are criminal acts committed by civilians or the use of excessive force by the police. In order to more fully flesh out the potential processes and mechanisms through which neighborhood social disorganization might lead to police use of excessive force, though, it is useful to discuss the subject in more detail.

The link between neighborhood social disorganization and crime rates is well-established (for a detailed review, see Sampson et al. 2002). In socially disorganized neighborhoods, residents come to rely on formal forms of social control (i.e., the police) more heavily since, by definition, they lack the collective capacity to handle the problems that arise in their neighborhoods on their own. In other words, where high levels of structural disadvantage lead to a loss of social ties and collective efficacy, neighborhood residents lack the means necessary to "police" themselves. Consequently, without these means, it is logical to assume that socially disorganized neighborhoods will have a greater dependence on *formal* forms of social control than neighborhoods that are able to "police" themselves. And, in fact, there has been empirical research which has shown that neighborhood social disorganization is positively and significantly related to calls for police services (Sherman, Gartin, and Buerger 1989; Warner and Pierce 1993).

The fact that socially disorganized neighborhoods come to rely more heavily on the police to resolve their crime problems has multiple implications. First, an increased dependence of neighborhood residents on formal police action may further impair residents' collective capacity to solve problems on their own. That is, if they continuously rely on outside sources of control, they may become dependent on them completely, such that neighborhood residents no longer even consider handling problems informally. Second, while the increased dependence on formal social controls may increase police officers' presence in the neighborhood, it might also send a message to criminals that the neighborhood is vulnerable to victimization any time the police are not present. Consequently, overall rates of crime may not decrease, as criminals simply shift their activities to times and locations when and where the police are not present. Finally, and of most importance for this research, social disorganization, and the lack of collective efficacy in particular, may also signal to police officers that their own deviant behavior, including the use of excessive force, will very likely go unreported and unpunished.

Given this last point, it might be reasonable to question whether police officers actually notice things such as neighborhood social disorganization. That is, will police officers realize not only that they are working in a high crime neighborhood, but also one that has no social ties and/or collective efficacy? And, if they do notice, would they pass such information on to their fellow officers to the extent that overall rates of police use of excessive force would substantially increase? Research has found that police officers do recognize the seriousness of crime problems in the neighborhoods in which they work, and that they do discuss such issues amongst their colleagues (McLaughlin, Johnson, Bowers, Birks, and Pease 2007; Ratcliffe and McCulagh 2001; Rengert 1995). And, even though there has not been any empirical research considering whether police officers discuss things such as neighborhood social disorganization, it seems reasonable that if police officers recognize and discuss the crime problems associated with certain neighborhoods, they should probably also recognize and discuss their use of force in those same neighborhoods, and in particular, how the neighborhood residents responded to it (or, alternatively, how they failed to respond to it).

Based on this reasoning, as police officers come to realize that residents of socially disorganized neighborhoods lack the capacity to informally deal with the crime problems facing their neighborhoods (i.e., without police assistance), they may also realize that those same residents are unable to organize to prevent, deter, and/or bring about punishment for police officers' use of excessive force. Subsequently, if even just one officer proceeded to share such information with his or her fellow officers working in the same neighborhood, an increase in the overall rate of police use of excessive might result. In the end, socially disorganized neighborhoods would then have just one more problem which they could not handle and nowhere else to turn for help, ultimately leaving the residents of those neighborhoods doubly-victimized—both by the criminals who offend in their neighborhoods and by the police officers who were supposed to protect them.

Before proposing the specific research questions and hypotheses that will be focus of this research, however, it is important to understand three points about the arguments presented above. First, research has shown that police officers' use of force, though rare, is more common when dealing with criminals (U.S. Department of Justice 2005). Subsequently, it should be expected that police officers will use more force in socially disorganized neighborhoods as compared to socially organized neighborhoods simply because they deal with more criminals in disorganized neighborhoods and it takes at least some force for officers to arrest those individuals (e.g., handcuffing criminal suspects).

The primary difference between socially organized and socially disorganized neighborhoods may then lie in whether or not the police officers use force on *non*-criminal residents as well. That is, if both criminals *and* non-criminal neighborhood residents of socially disorganized neighborhoods have force used upon them, those neighborhoods should experience relatively greater levels of police use of force than their socially organized counterparts. And, because any unjustified use of force on individuals who have not committed a crime must be considered "excessive," if the police use any force on noncriminal residents of disorganized neighborhoods, those neighborhoods should have greater problems with the police use of excessive force as a whole.[4]

Based on the discussion above, it can therefore be expected that, in addition to the "normal" levels of force police officers use against neighborhood criminals (i.e., the force necessary to effect arrests), the *additional* use of force on *non*-criminal residents should result in socially disorganized neighborhoods experiencing both an increased amount of police use of legitimate force *and* an increased amount of police use of excessive force compared to their socially organized counterparts. Then, on top of the illegitimate, and therefore excessive, use of force on non-criminal residents of socially disorganized neighborhoods, police officers may also be more likely to use more force than is necessary to arrest neighborhood criminals, which must also be considered excessive force. Consequently, in comparison to the residents of socially organized neighborhoods, both the criminal and non-criminal residents of socially disorganized neighborhoods may have much more problems with police officers' use of excessive force.

Second, it is in no way expected that *all* police officers working in socially disorganized neighborhoods will use excessive levels of force. In fact, it should be understood that the vast majority of police officers are *not* expected to use excessive force, even if they realized that they might be able to get away with it. Instead, the basic argument made here is that *some* police officers might realize that their use of force in disorganized neighborhoods was much less likely to gain widespread public attention or result in their formal punishment. Then, even if it was only a few "bad apples" who used more excessive force, the overall rate of police use of excessive force in those neighborhoods would still be expected to increase.

Furthermore, in what would have to be considered a worst case scenario, if a police subculture regarded the use of force as being more justifiable in a broader range of circumstances, then members of that subculture might be expected to use force more often. Research has shown police subcultures to have a very powerful influence over officers' behaviors (Chappell and Piquero 2004; Micucci and Gomme 2005; Skolnick 1966; Terrill, Paoline, and Manning 2003; Waegel 1984a), so if the belief that people living in socially disorganized neighborhoods were more "deserving" of forceful behaviors (as Klinger's ecological theory of police vigor (1997) might contend [...]), then officers might even come to believe that the use of excessive force was also *acceptable* in such neighborhoods. Consequently, if such pro-use-of-force beliefs spread throughout a department, then increased problems of police use of excessive force in disorganized neighborhoods would not be surprising.

---

4 The use of force against some non-criminal individuals may be justified when police officers' must physically control or restrain individuals in altered mental or physical states (e.g., mentally or emotionally unstable, or under the influence of a controlled substance), but who have not committed any crimes. In such cases, if it is for the benefit of the individual, the police officer, or others, any reasonable amount of force necessary to control the situation should not be considered excessive, even if no crime has been committed.

Finally, regardless of why excessive force problems increase in socially disorganized neighborhoods, if officers began using overly excessive levels of force on residents (e.g., used deadly force against a misdemeanor offender), it is not expected that such behaviors go unnoticed or unpunished simply because they occurred in a socially disorganized neighborhood. Rather, the contention is that the "more common" abuses of force (e.g., unnecessary use of handcuffs, pressure holds, pain compliance techniques, impact maneuvers, etc.) would be most likely to increase when police officers realized that neighborhood residents would not do anything to stop them. That is, unless an officer so grossly overstepped his or her use-of-force protocol that it somehow garnered attention from people outside of the neighborhood (e.g., severely beat a child or some other especially vulnerable individual), it would be unlikely that the residents of disorganized neighborhoods could prevent police officers' use of excessive force any more than they could prevent criminal activity.

Thus, for all the reasons discussed above, police officers are expected to use excessive levels of force more often in socially disorganized neighborhoods, where residents do not have the capacity to address the problem (i.e., low levels of social ties and/or collective efficacy), than in more organized neighborhoods. Unfortunately, data do not currently exist that assess police officers' perceptions of neighborhood social disorganization, so it is not yet possible to definitively test this theory. However, simply discovering whether objectively-defined social disorganization, and neighborhood collective efficacy in particular, is related to police use of excessive force is also very important.

Research Questions & Hypotheses

As reviewed earlier in this chapter, a small number of recent empirical studies provide some compelling evidence that aggregate-level contextual factors are related to police use of force behaviors (Kane 2002; Lawton 2007; Lersch et al. 2008; Terrill and Reisig 2003). To date, however, no research has convincingly demonstrated that the social disorganization tradition might be legitimately utilized as a theoretical framework for the study of police officers' use of excessive force. Thus, the primary goal of this book is to answer the broad question—*is neighborhood social disorganization related to police officers' use of excessive force?* Additionally, because most of the recent research testing concepts from the social disorganization tradition have found that the effect of neighborhood social ties (i.e., the systemic model) is not as consistent or powerful as the effect of neighborhood collective efficacy [...], this book more specifically attempts to answer the question—*is neighborhood collective efficacy a better predictor of police use of excessive force than other neighborhood contextual factors such as neighborhood structural disadvantage and social ties?*

In order to answer each of these research questions, it is essential that the relationships between each of the three most prominent concepts from the social disorganization tradition—neighborhood structural disadvantage, social ties, and collective efficacy—and police use of excessive force is examined. Although the latter two concepts are expected to mediate the relationship between the former concept and police officers' excessive force behaviors (as they have been shown to do for crime [...]), it is first necessary to demonstrate that there is a relationship between neighborhood structural disadvantage and police use of force that can be mediated. Thus, the first hypothesis presented and discussed below pertains to the direct relationship between the three contextual factors that measure neighborhood structural disadvantage and police officers' use of excessive force.

Structural Disadvantage

[... S]ocial disorganization researchers understand that Shaw and McKay (1942) did not specifically posit a direct relationship between neighborhood structural disadvantage and crime. Despite this fact, however, the majority of studies testing concepts from the social disorganization tradition have continued to assess the direct effect of the three component measures of structural disadvantage—poverty, racial/ethnic heterogeneity, and residential instability. Following this precedent, the first hypothesis tested in this research predicts that each of the three component measures of structural disadvantage will be positively related to police officers' use of excessive force. Figure 3.1 presents path diagrams for Hypotheses 1a through 1c.

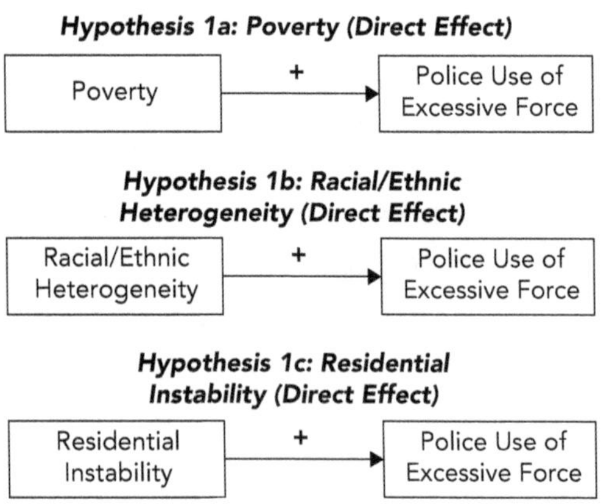

FIGURE 3.1

Systemic Model

Although recent research has begun to question the importance of neighborhood social ties [...], in order to fully test the social disorganization tradition as a framework for explaining police use of excessive force, it is necessary to propose and test a hypothesis based on the systemic model (Bursik and Grasmick 1993; Hunter 1985; Sampson and Groves 1989). And, even though some of that research has also been suggestive of a positive relationship between the number of neighborhood residents' social ties and crime (Bellair 1997; Browning et al. 2004; Patillo-McCoy 1999; Sampson et al. 1997; Wilson 1996), for this research, it is expected that larger social networks should still decrease police use of excessive force. This negative relationship is expected for two reasons. First, as systemic model theorists originally posited, as neighborhood social networks grow, it is expected that more people will care about the well-being of their neighbors, and then be willing to act on their behalf. Second, and most importantly, in the case of police use of excessive force, there should be no reason for neighborhood residents to cover up or shield the offending officers from punishment, as might be the case for well-networked criminals [...]. It is therefore hypothesized that *neighborhood social ties will be negatively related to the police use of excessive force.* Figure 3.2 presents the path diagram for Hypothesis 2a.

In addition to the direct relationship between the two phenomena, neighborhood social ties are also expected to mediate the relationship between neighborhood structural disadvantage

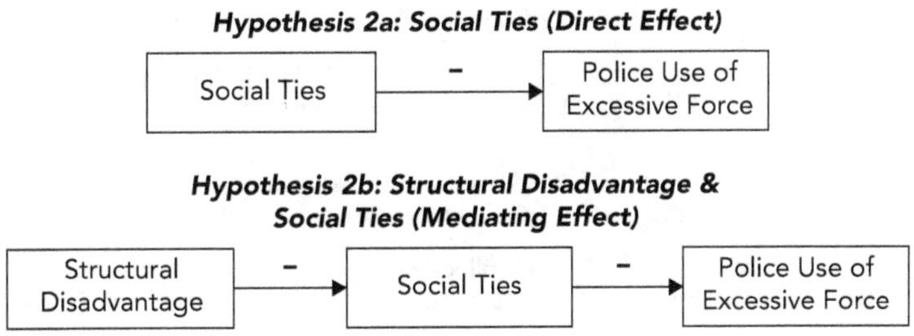

FIGURE 3.2

and police use of excessive force. [... T]he systemic model predicts that structural disadvantage will undermine neighborhood residents' ability to form strong social ties, which will then reduce residents' willingness to watch out for each other, and ultimately lead to an increase in crime rates. In regards to the police use of excessive force, a similar process of events is expected to occur. That is, neighborhood structural disadvantage should decrease the number of social ties among neighborhood residents, which should then lead them to be less likely to watch out, or care, for what happens to their neighbors. Ultimately, this process should result in an increase in police officers' use of excessive force since neighbors will not care about, or at the very least be unwilling to do anything about, incidents in which their neighbors are abused by the police. Thus, Hypothesis 2b states that neighborhood *social ties will mediate the relationship between neighborhood structural disadvantage and police officers' use of excessive force.* Figure 3.2 presents the path diagram for Hypothesis 2b.[5]

Collective Efficacy

The relationship between collective efficacy (Morenoff et al. 2001; Sampson et al. 1999; Sampson et al. 1997) and police officers' use of excessive force is the primary focus of this book. A large body of research has shown that collective efficacy is a strong, robust, predictor of neighborhood crime rates [...]. A similar relationship is expected between collective efficacy and police use of excessive force. Specifically, it is expected that neighborhoods with low social cohesion (i.e., mutual trust and solidarity) and low informal social control (i.e., willingness to intervene for the common good of the neighborhood) will be unable to come together as a group and put a stop to police officers' use of excessive force. The first collective efficacy hypothesis tested in this book therefore states that *neighborhood collective efficacy will be negatively related to police officers' use of excessive force.* Figure 3.3 presents the path diagram for Hypothesis 3a.

---

5 To conserve space, the three components of poverty, racial/ethnic heterogeneity, and residential instability, will be collectively depicted as "structural disadvantage" in the remaining path diagrams. However, as with Hypotheses 1a–1c, the effects of all three components will be analyzed separately in order to determine the individual effects of each component of structural disadvantage on the mediating and dependent variables. Thus, in each of the remaining path diagrams presented in this chapter, it is expected that all three components of structural disadvantage will have the same relationship (directionally) with the variable(s) they are predicting.

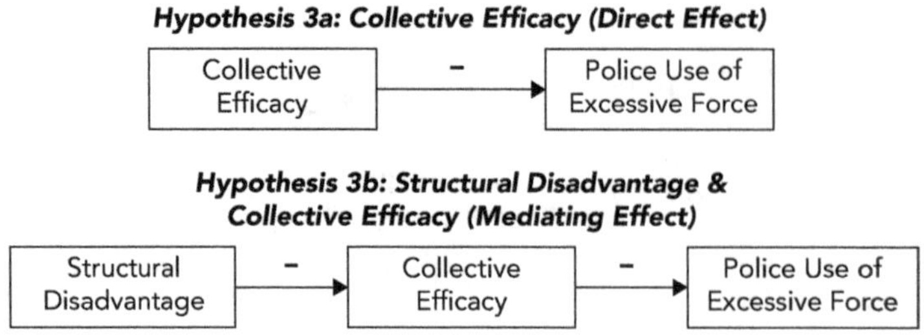

FIGURE 3.3

As with the systemic model discussed above, the level of neighborhood collective efficacy is also expected to mediate the relationship between structural disadvantage and the police use of excessive force. That is, as increases in neighborhood structural disadvantage make it difficult for residents to come together and find a common set of goals and values, they will never come to trust those neighbors to intervene on the behalf of the neighborhood. Ultimately, just as social disorganization researchers believe that this lack of collective efficacy signals to criminals that they can get away with committing crimes, the same processes should also signal to police officers that they too can get away with inappropriate behaviors, including the use of excessive force. Thus, it is also hypothesized that *collective efficacy will mediate the relationship between neighborhood structural disadvantage and police officers' use of excessive force.* Figure 3.3 presents the path diagram for Hypothesis 3b.

Systemic Model vs. Collective Efficacy

While the overall goal of this book is to establish a relationship between neighborhood social disorganization and police officers' use of excessive force, it also seeks to answer the more specific research question—*is neighborhood collective efficacy the best predictor of police use of excessive force, net of other neighborhood contextual factors such as neighborhood structural disadvantage and neighborhood social ties*? Collective efficacy is expected to be the best (i.e., strongest and most robust) predictor of police officers' use of excessive force for two reasons. First, a number of recent empirical tests of the systemic model have suggested that relationship between social ties and criminal activity could actually be both positive and negative (Bellair 1997; Browning et al. 2004; Patillo-McCoy 1999; Sampson et al. 1997; Wilson 1996). Second, in the only extant study to simultaneously examine the effect of social ties and collective efficacy on neighborhood crime rates, Browning and colleagues (2004) found that collective efficacy was the better predictor, net of a series of controls. As a result of these studies, it is likely that collective efficacy may be the best predictor of not only crime rates, but also neighborhood problems with police officers' use of excessive force.[6]

---

6 Although there is some reason to believe that it might (for a discussion see Sampson et al. 1999), collective efficacy is not expected to mediate the relationship between social ties and the police use of excessive force. Instead, for the purposes of this research, the systemic model and the collective efficacy framework are considered to be competing explanations of both crime and police use of excessive force. Subsequently, no hypotheses regarding a mediation effect are tested here. Instead, it is simply expected

To put it more clearly, the mutual trust shared by neighbors to engage in informal social control behaviors (i.e., collective efficacy) is expected to be the most important factor for reducing both problems with crime and problems with police use of excessive force, even in neighborhoods where residents do not know each other well (i.e., do not share close social ties). To wit, Sampson and colleagues once similarly argued that "[collective efficacy] facilitates social control without requiring strong social ties or associations" (Morenoff et al. 2001:250). Accordingly, in neighborhoods where residents trust their neighbors to exercise informal social control when necessary and regardless of the strength of their ties to those neighbors, it is expected that there will be fewer problems not only with crime, but with police use of excessive force as well. The fourth and final hypothesis tested in this research therefore states that *neighborhood collective efficacy will be the strongest and most robust predictor of officers' use of excessive force, net of all the other social disorganization tradition measures.* Figure 3.4 below presents the path diagram for Hypothesis 4.

References

Hypothesis 4: Comparative Effects

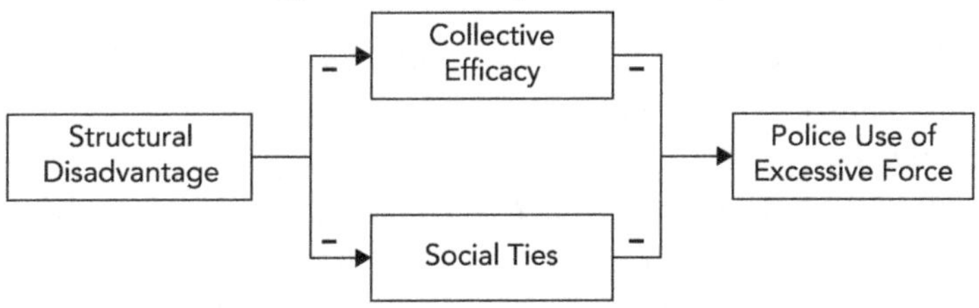

FIGURE 3.4

Bellair, Paul E. 1997. "Social Interaction and Community Crime: Examining the Importance of Neighborhood Networks." *Criminology* 25:677–703.

Browning, Christopher R., Seth L. Feinberg, Robert D. Dietz. 2004. "The Paradox of Social Organization: Networks, Collective Efficacy, and Violent Crime in Urban Neighborhoods." *Social Forces* 83:503–534.

Bursik, Robert J., Jr. 1999. "The Informal Control of Crime through Neighborhood Networks." *Sociological Focus* 32:85–97.

Chappell, Allison T. and Alex R. Piquero. 2004. "Applying Social Learning Theory to Police Misconduct." *Deviant Behavior* 25:89–108.

Hunter, Albert J. 1985. "Private, Parochial and Public School Orders: The Problem of Crime and Incivility in Urban Communities." In G.D. Suttles and M.N. Zald (eds.), *The Challenge of Social*

---

that collective efficacy will be the more powerful and robust predictor of police officers' use of excessive force, net of the effect of neighborhood social ties.

Control: Citizenship and Institution Building in Modern Society, pp. 230–242. Norwood, N.J.: Ablex Publishing.

Kane, Robert J. 2002. "The Social Ecology of Police Misconduct." *Criminology* 40:867–896.

Lawton, Brian A. 2007. "Levels of Nonlethal Force: An Examination of Individual, Situational, and Contextual Factors." *Journal of Research in Crime and Delinquency* 44:163–184.

Lersch, Kim M., Thomas Bazley, Thomas Mieczkowski, and Kristina Childs. 2008. "Police Use of Force and Neighbourhood Characteristics: An Examination of Structural Disadvantage, Crime, and Resistance." *Policing & Society* 18:282–300.

McLaughlin, Lindsay M., Shane D. Johnson, Kate J. Bowers, Dan J. Birks, and Ken Pease. 2007. "Police Perceptions of the Long- and Short-Term Spatial Distribution of Residential Burglary." *International Journal of Police Science and Management* 9:99–111.

Micucci, Anthony J. and Ian M. Gomme. 2005. "American Police and Subcultural Support for the Use of Excessive Force." *Journal of Criminal Justice* 33:487–500.

Morenoff, Jeffrey D., Robert J. Sampson, and Stephen W. Raudenbush. 2001. "Neighborhood Inequality, Collective Efficacy, and the Spatial Dynamics of Urban Violence." *Criminology* 39:517–559.

Patillo-McCoy, Mary. 1999. *Black Picket Fences: Privilege and Peril Among the Black Middle Class.* Chicago, IL: University of Chicago Press.

Rengart, George F. 1995. "Comparing Cognitive Hotspots to Crime Hotspots." In C. Block, M. Daboub, and S. Fregly (eds.), *Crime Analysis through Computer Mapping*, pp. 33–47. Chicago, IL: Police Executive Research Forum.

Sampson, Robert J. and W. Byron Groves. 1989. "Community Structure and Crime: Testing Social Disorganization Theory. *American Journal of Sociology* 94:774–802.

Sampson, Robert J., Jeffrey D. Morenoff, and Felton Earls. 1999. "Beyond Social Capital: Spatial Dynamics of Collective Efficacy for Children." *American Sociological Review* 64:633–660.

Sampson, Robert J., Jeffrey D. Morenoff, and Thomas Gannon-Rowley. 2002. "Assessing 'Neighborhood Effects': Social Processes and New Directions in Research." *Annual Review of Sociology* 28:443–478.

Sampson, Robert J., Stephen W. Raudenbush, and Felton Earls. 1997. "Neighborhoods and Violent Crime: A Multilevel Study of Collective Efficacy." *Science* 277:918–924.

Shaw, Clifford R. Henry D. McKay. 1942. *Juvenile Delinquency in Urban Areas.* Chicago, IL: University of Chicago Press.

Sherman, Lawrence W., Patrick R. Gartin, and Michael E. Buerger. 1989. "Hot Spots of Predatory Crime: Routine Activities and the Criminology of Place." *Criminology* 27:27–56.

Skolnick, Jerome. 1966. *Justice without Trial: Law Enforcement in Democratic Society.* New York, NY: Wiley.

Terrill, William, Eugene A. Paoline, III, and Peter K. Manning. 2003. "Police Culture and Coercion." *Criminology* 41:1003–1034.

Terrill, William and Michael D. Reisig. 2003. "Neighborhood Context and Police Use of Force." *Journal of Research in Crime and Delinquency* 40:291–321.

United States Department of Justice. 2005. *Contacts between Police and the Public: Findings from the 2002 National Survey.* Bureau of Justice Statistics.

Waegel, William B. 1984a. "The Use of Lethal Force by Police: The Effect of Statutory Change." *Crime and Delinquency* 30:121–140.

Warner, Barbara D. and Glenn L. Pierce. 1993. "Reexamining Social Disorganization Theory Using Calls to the Police as a Measure of Crime." *Criminology* 31:493–517.

Wilson, William Julius. 1996. *When Work Disappears: The World of the New Urban Poor.* New York, NY: Vintage Books.

Police Discretion, Police Misconduct, and Mechanisms to Control Police Misconduct

Michael J. Palmiotto

Introduction

Police discretion—the power to take action or not to take action or to arrest or not to arrest—is an important component of police powers and makes the police officer in our society an extremely powerful official. How officers use the discretion allowed them usually determines whether justice is done and whether the law has been applied fairly. Before the mid-1950s, our politicians and police administrators constantly told us that they enforced all laws and investigated all crimes equally. Today, we recognize that it would be impossible for the police to do this.

The major issues concerning the use of police discretion are the abuses that can occur with unchecked police discretion. Police abuses, often referred to as police misconduct, have been a major problem with many police departments in the 1990s and 2000s.

All vocations and professions have their outlaws, and policing is no exception. The police field has its share of officers who violate not only departmental policies and procedures but also the very laws they are to enforce. When a police officer is involved in misconduct, a scandal is created that tarnishes not only the reputation of the police officer but the reputation of the department that employs him or her and, even worse, the image of all police officers.

Since some police officers are involved in misconduct, mechanisms must be put in place to check police misconduct. These mechanisms investigate accusations of police misconduct and attempt to eliminate any police improbity when it is found. They are important not only for police personnel but for the community as well. Police officers following the rules of their department and doing their jobs strongly support mechanisms that punish and, if needed, remove police officers from the force. The community wants to have confidence in its police officers. Community policing cannot be successful without this trust.

Police Discretion

America is a nation of laws. Our laws are passed by the legislative branch of government and enforced by the executive branch. Cox and McCamey write that:

> The law explicitly grants some discretionary powers to police officers and creates a framework within which other discretionary judgments may legitimately be made. It is one measure of the importance of discretion in police work that these are among the first items that become incorporated into the officer's working knowledge of the law.
>
> (2008, 36–37)

Laws are passed to keep the peace and maintain order. Political scientists often claim that the purpose of laws is to "keep the underclass under control" for the benefit of the middle and upper classes. These groups could not remain affluent if chaos and disorder became rampant. Therefore, laws are passed and are enforced, not only for public safety purposes, but also to keep our society functioning well economically.

Individuals in our society, including those responsible for enforcing the law, do not always specifically follow the letter of the law. In addition, legal norms are constantly changing (Aaronson et al. 1984, 4). For example, a few years ago, it was acceptable to discriminate against homosexuals, but today this discrimination would be a violation of the law. Also, several decades ago it could be appropriate behavior to smack a youngster who talked back to a police officer and send him home to his parents, where he could expect to be smacked again. Today, this would be considered misconduct on the police officer's part.

Police discretion is the authority of police to decide how much effort they will apply to enforcing specific laws and which laws they will or will not enforce. According to Reiss (1984), the concept implies several things:

> One is quite simply that an officer who has discretion has the power to choose among alternatives. A second and closely related aspect is that a choice made by an officer in the exercise of his discretion must be permitted by law. A third is that an officer who has discretion exercises individual judgment in making a choice.
>
> (89–90)

Although the police are sworn to enforce all the laws all the time, they enforce only the laws they choose to enforce, and even when they choose to enforce specific laws, they often will enforce these laws only some of the time. In many situations, they will warn, reprimand, or release an individual rather than make an arrest. Often they decide not to arrest for crimes they do not consider to be violent or a serious threat, such as traffic violations, petty gambling offenses, and simple assaults between acquaintances. When the police decide not to arrest someone who qualifies to be arrested, it can be said that they are using discretion.

Joseph Goldstein (1960) argued that full enforcement would be difficult, if not impossible, to achieve. Police officers take an oath on the day they officially are sworn in as police officers that they will uphold and defend the U.S. Constitution, their state constitution, and federal and state laws. They are expected to respect individual rights of all people as outlined with the Bill of Rights of the U.S. Constitution, including the rights of those suspected of committing a criminal offense; to know and follow all the various court decisions establishing legal police procedures; and to protect the due process rights, as guaranteed by the Fifth and Fourteenth Amendments, of everyone that they arrest, search, or interrogate. Given the ambiguities in criminal law and due process boundaries, the conflicts between requirements, the time constraints, and the limitations of personnel and investigative techniques, full enforcement is simply not feasible. Therefore, actual enforcement of the law is inevitably selective enforcement (554–561).

Selective enforcement emphasizes the "spirit of the law" rather than the letter of the law. The unwritten selective enforcement policy of police departments enables police to enforce only the most serious laws and the laws the community wants enforced. Although legislation is written as if full enforcement is expected, lawmakers do not really expect it, and police agencies do not really expect it either. Kenneth Culp Davis (1971) argued that the police should not be expected to enforce all laws when prosecutors do not prosecute all cases. Prosecutors pick and choose what to prosecute, and police officers who observe them soon know what it takes for a prosecutor to take a case to trial. Further, insufficient funds allocated to police departments allow only for selective enforcement. Finally, lawmakers frequently pass laws that are difficult to obtain evidence to enforce (79–97).

The recognition of police discretion can be traced back to the early twentieth century, when the Supreme Court of Michigan, in *Gowan v. Smith*, 122 N.W. 286 (1909), asserted that

> the police commissioner is bound to use the discretion with which he is clothed. ... To enable him to perform the duties imposed upon him by law, he is supplied with certain limited means. It is entirely obvious that he must exercise a sound discretion as to how those means shall be applied for the good of the community.

Although police discretion has been recognized by the courts since the early 1900s, it was not until the late 1950s that the police began to officially claim that officers possess discretion in performing their policing duties. The legitimating of police discretion was aided by an American Bar Association survey on the administration of justice in the mid-1950s. The survey found that criminal laws were frequently used for a variety of purposes other than their specified purposes—for example, to deal with numerous social problems, such as family problems, mental illness, and alcohol abuse. Thus, it was acceptable practice for police officers to use their own judgment about when to arrest and for what purpose (Walker 1993, 10). The 1987 U.S. Supreme Court ruling in *McClesky v. Kemp*, 411 crL 4107, further upheld the use of police discretion. Although police administrations under the professional model of policing have held onto the claim that the police fully enforce all the laws, progressive police administrators and personnel know that selective enforcement is the norm.

Discretion in when and whether to arrest or to use force against an individual places police officers in an extremely significant position in our society. Michael Brown (1988) went so far as to claim that "police discretion—the day to day decisions of policemen—is tantamount to political decision making, for the role of the police is based upon the legitimate use of coercion" (3–4). Brown further argued that

> the police have crucial policymaking powers by virtue of their power to decide which laws will be enforced and when. At issue is not simply the legality of these decisions, but the routine use of the legitimate means of coercion in society. The day-to-day choices of policemen affecting the meaning of law, order, and justice within American society.
>
> (5–6)

Fairness issues necessarily arise when race or class biases influence who is arrested or apprehended and who is not. Kenneth Culp Davis (1971) provides a realistic example:

> A statute, an ordinance, and a police manual all provide that a policeman "shall" arrest all known violators of the law. A policeman lectures a boy from a middle-class neighborhood, but he arrests a boy from the slums, although he knows that both are equally guilty of violating the same statute. Because the evidence against both boys is clear, the policeman's decision is the only one that counts, for the release of the first boy is permanent and the conviction of the second follows almost automatically.
>
> (218)

Further, police discretion can be abused. One common form of abuse is the dispensing of street justice. Street justice occurs when the police believe that someone should be punished for what he or she did or is about to do. The police usually have no qualms about using street justice on an individual who defies their authority or insults them. They feel that if they are to function effectively, they must be in control, and that if they are insulted and allow an individual to get away with it, then they have lost control of the situation. The Rodney King beating by the Los Angeles police officers could be considered an example of street justice. Rodney King gave the police a high-speed chase. He refused to stop when the police were in pursuit. According to police culture, when the police want you to do something, you do it. If you refuse to follow police orders, you may have to pay the price. Rodney King was beaten to teach him a lesson—and also to teach a lesson to the passengers in the vehicle King was driving.

Some police officers see nothing wrong with street justice. They consider it to be a part of their right and duty to teach an individual a lesson. However, when police officers dispense street justice, the individual has been denied due process and judicial review. By using street justice, a police officer has violated the law. Assaulting an individual is a crime, and police officers should not be immune from criminal charges if they have violated the criminal law or denied someone his or her constitutional rights.

The nature of the role assigned to the police by the community may be a factor contributing to the use of street justice:

> Studies of police discretion largely reinforce the view that street decisions to intervene, arrest, use force or issue traffic citations are primarily a function of situational and organizational factors that reflect interpretations of community needs and expectations by police. "Street justice" in this sense is a response to a community mandate that something be done about situations where formal institutions cannot or will not respond for a variety of reasons.
>
> (Sykes 1986, 498)

Sykes argued that the liberal reformers fear police repression and overlook the functional role of "street justice" in creating a sense of community. They choose to emphasize justice defined as due process over the community-based idea of justice as righting a wrong and protecting the physically weak from the powerful. Police accountability remains a problem, and order maintenance continues to create the potential for abuse of power. However, the answer provided by the professional model, which emphasizes the enforcement role, leaves many citizens without the means to civilize their community. The trade-off must be recognized and provides an ongoing moral dilemma in liberal society (507).

The dilemma here is that street justice is used by police officers to enforce the moral code of the community they police but that the use of street justice pushes justice aside.

According to Carl Klockars (1986), the police, for practical reasons, do not use street justice all that frequently. If an individual given street justice has been beaten severely, the police officer has to transport the individual to the emergency room and file a report explaining how the individual received his injuries. Because of the threat of departmental charges and the reactions of the community, which may not know the context of the officer's use of force, street justice is kept to a minimum (515–516)—although this may be hard to believe at a time when publicity has surrounded the Rodney King fiasco and the case of Brooklyn police officers accused of shoving a broom handle up a suspect's rectum. The next section will discuss the various forms of police misconduct in detail.

As Joseph Goldstein (1960) pointed out, police, unlike the other actors within the criminal justice process, generally operate without being seen, so their actions are not reviewed. If police officers assigned to investigate a disturbing event report the complaint as unfounded, in most cases their report will be accepted and not visible to the public. Even the records maintained by the police are usually too incomplete to be used to evaluate nonenforcement decisions (543–553). Because of concerns over fairness issues in police discretion, police abuses of discretionary powers, and the public invisibility of much police practice, many commissions and agencies have recommended that police departments establish rules to guide police discretion. In 1967, the President's Commission on Law Enforcement and Administration of Justice recommended such guidelines, stating that

> in view of the importance, complexity, and delicacy of police work, it is curious that police administrators have seldom attempted to develop and articulate clear policies aimed at guiding or governing the way policemen exercise their discretion on the street.
>
> (103)

In 1973, the National Advisory Commission on Criminal Justice Standards and Goals reiterated this theme. It recommended that

> every police agency should acknowledge the existence of the broad range of administrative and operational discretion that is exercised by all police agencies and individual officers. That acknowledgment should take the form of comprehensive policy statements that publicly establish the limits of discretion, that provide guidelines for its exercise within those limits, and that eliminate discriminatory enforcement of the law.

1. Every police chief executive should have the authority to establish his agency's fundamental objectives and priorities and to implement them through discretionary allocation and control of agency resources. ...
2. Every police chief executive should establish policy that guides the exercise of discretion by police personnel in using arrest alternatives. ...
3. Every police chief executive should establish policy that limits the exercise of discretion by police personnel in conducting investigations, and that provides guidelines for the exercise of discretion within those limits. ...
4. Every police chief executive should establish policy that governs the exercise of discretion by police personnel in providing routine peacekeeping and other police services that, because of their frequent recurrence, lend themselves to the development of a uniform agency response.
5. Every police chief executive should formalize procedures for developing and implementing the foregoing written agency policy.
6. Every police chief executive immediately should adopt inspection and control procedures to insure that officers exercise their discretion in a manner consistent with agency policy. (21–22)

In 1974, the American Bar Association argued that

> police discretion can best be structured and controlled through the process of administrative rule making by police agencies. Police administrators should, therefore, give the highest priority to the formulation of administrative rules governing the exercise of selective enforcement, investigative techniques, and enforcement methods. (8)

Internal rule making gives police agencies a means of limiting the control of external agencies that can regulate police decision making. The courts, state legislatures, city councils, and county commissioners can all influence police policies and discretion. The numerous United States Supreme Court decisions have dictated police policies and have limited police discretion in many situations. State legislatures and city councils have directed the police to arrest the abuser during a domestic violence call. When the police observe or believe that a person has been assaulted by a spouse or live-in companion, they are legally required to make an arrest. This requirement to arrest during a domestic dispute is an example of how the legislative branch has taken away the power of the police to exercise discretionary decision making in certain situations.

Rule making exists to increase predictability, fairness, and efficiency in daily policing activities. It should also contribute to more effective and responsive policing by minimizing procedural errors, improving police–community relations, establishing uniform policy, and centralizing accountability for decision making (Aaronson et al. 1984).

Although rule making has been advocated as a means of controlling police discretion and police behavior, most police departments have not followed the recommendations to implement rule making for the police officers. For the most part, departments initiate rules for their officers as a reaction to predicaments or in response to lawsuits, political pressure, or some other crisis. Rule making by police departments reflects a reactive approach rather than a proactive approach (Walker 1986, 362–363). But when police departments have failed to implement rules to control police discretion, the judicial branch has taken over this function. For example, the United States Supreme Court in *Delaware v. Prouse* has taken a strong stand against random traffic stops by the police. The Supreme Court in 1979 ruled that police officers could not randomly stop motorists without probable cause to suspect crime or illegal activity, to check the driver's license and auto registration (24CrL 3089). In 2000 the United States Supreme Court ruled in Indianapolis v. Edmond that police check points aimed at discovering drugs and other illegal activity are illegal and in violation of the Fourth Amendment rights of citizens (N99–1030).

Enlightened police leaders have realized that when police activities have intruded on the liberty of citizens, policies and procedures are required to give police officers guidance on:

1. The use of physical and deadly force.
2. Arrest and alternatives to arrest.
3. Stopping, questioning, and frisking citizens.
4. The handling of disorders and/or minor nuisances short of arrest.
5. The use of all intrusive investigative techniques including informants, infiltrators, and electronic surveillance.

(Walker 1986, 388–389)

How does police discretion fit into community policing? The community policing philosophy emphasizes a closer police–community working relationship. Traditional, or professional-model, policing requires that police respond to citizen complaints that are telephoned in to a dispatcher. When patrol officers have free time and are not responding to citizen calls or investigating a traffic accident, they are expected to look for crime on their beat—for example, by patrolling areas that are known to have a high rate of burglaries or a high rate of automobile accidents. Under the community policing philosophy, all police officers are community-policing officers. If this concept becomes operationally successful, the use of discretion by patrol officers may be more carefully thought out. As the beat patrol officer and the neighborhood develop a closer working relationship, breaking down barriers and sharing a stake in crime prevention and control, police discretion may become more attuned to community needs, and police misconduct may decrease.

Police Misconduct

According to organizational scholars, most occupations provide their members with the opportunities for behavioral misconduct, and police departments are no exception. Three elements of occupational misconduct are: "(1) opportunity structure and its accompanying techniques of rule violations, (2) socialization through occupational experiences, and (3) reinforcement and encouragement from the occupational peer group, i.e. group support for certain rule violations" (Barker 1977, 356).

The quality of work performance varies considerably from one police department to another. Most police departments employ police officers who generally function in a fair and impartial manner. However, some police officers become involved in police misconduct. Despite the publicity that police misconduct receives, police departments or even state or federal agencies keep few records of misconduct. It is not uncommon for departments to allow officers involved in police misconduct to resign their position rather than to be fired or prosecuted so that both the officers and the department can avoid publicity. In some states, policy agencies that do this may be violating state training standards that certify police officers. By these standards, an officer involved in police misconduct can lose his certification so that he is no longer employable as a police officer. But when a department allows a police officer to resign, this individual can obtain employment in another police department.

When the police are involved in misconduct, or even when the community believes that the police have committed acts of misconduct, the community loses confidence in the police. To obtain and maintain the community's backing, the police must refrain from wrongdoing. The community expects its police officers to be beyond reproach. When the police lose the community's respect and trust, the department cannot be an effective tool in criminal apprehension and in controlling crime. Without the community's support, victims and witnesses will not come forward. This is crucial because victims and witnesses willing to participate in the legal process contribute to the arrest and prosecution of offenders.

Forms of Police Misconduct

Since the formal organization of policing in the United States, police misconduct has inundated police departments. The police in the early decades of the twenty-first century are no closer to removing the misconduct problem than they were in the twentieth century. The police are in a position of authority and power. Their authority can lead to confrontation with citizens who challenge that authority. Often, police–citizen confrontations create the appearance that the police overstep their boundaries. It is important to recognize that the police have the duty to protect the constitutional rights of all citizens. It is not unusual for police officers to be accused of not fulfilling this role (Palmiotto 2001, 32).

Police misconduct may be either a criminal violation or a violation of departmental rules. It may be unethical or amoral without being criminal, and it does not have to result in personal gain, such as monetary rewards. It may be a reflection of the community, the police department, or an individual police officer. Misconduct of police officers include not only lying, protection of illegal activities, accepting of bribes, and theft occurring during investigations (Hyatt 2001, 75) but also the following misconduct actions:

> Sleeping on Duty—Sleeping on duty usually occurs on the midnight shift during slow periods when there are few calls for service. Although this violates police policies, there are officers who attempt to take catnaps during working hours. Some police officers have second jobs and work during the day and need to rest during their midnight tour of duty.
>
> Use of Illegal Drugs—In the modern era of policing, the use of drugs by police officers can be added to the police misconduct list. Police officers who were exposed to drugs growing up and who in all probability experimented with drugs do not necessarily see anything wrong in using drugs. With drugs easily available in our society, it can be expected that some police officers will use illegal drugs.

Police Brutality

Police brutality is an ambiguous term that has had different meanings depending upon who uses it. Does police brutality include verbal abuse? To some people, it does. A number of police actions, including profane and abusive speech, commands to move or go home, field stops and searches, threats, prodding with a nightstick or approaching with a pistol, and the use of "physical force," may be called police brutality (Barker 1986, 71).

Citizens should recognize that police have the right to direct citizens' behavior. For example, if a person is double parked and blocking traffic on a city street, the police officer has the responsibility to require that person to move his or her vehicle. Also, if a group of teenagers are blocking access into a store and intimidating adults from entering the store, the police officer has the right to tell the teenagers to move. In these situations, the police officer should be civil and courteous but should expect the citizen or teenagers to comply with his or her request.

Many citizens are unaware that when police are patrolling their beat they are expected to conduct field stops and searches. The stops are to determine if the person or group stopped has legitimate business in the area. Generally, stops will take place during the evening hours. Citizens not versed in the law may not know that police officers have the legal right to conduct searches to protect themselves or others from potential harm. Whether police misconduct occurs during a field stop or search depends upon the specific situation and the police officer's behavior.

The use of physical force by police officers is not illegal or a violation of a departmental policy if it is justifiable. Every situation where physical force has been used must be judged on its own merit. Generally, acts of police brutality are known only to the police officer and a few witnesses, normally fellow police officers, who observe excessive force being used. Segments of the American population, especially minority members, who have the largest number of brutality complaints against the police, consider police brutality to be more of a serious problem than politicians or police administrators care to admit. Police brutality is usually discovered when the victim of police brutality reports it to police authorities or to other governmental agencies. Most states provide for a state investigative agency to investigate police brutality by local police officers. On the federal level, the Federal Bureau of Investigation has the authority to investigate police misconduct that can be in violation of federal laws.

Today, with the prevalence of video cameras, cases of police brutality can be videotaped and shown later. The videotaping of acts of police brutality is evidence that a specific officer or officers were involved in the use of excessive force. One case in which an act of police brutality was brought to the world by a citizen's videotaping was the beating of Rodney King on March 3, 1991, by Los Angeles police officers. George Holliday, the citizen who videotaped the Rodney King beating, brought the tape to the Los Angeles Police Department, who refused it. Upon the department's refusal, Holliday brought the tape to a local Los Angeles television station, which aired it. Eventually, CNN received a copy of the videotaped beating of Rodney King and gave it national and international coverage.

Another well-publicized case of police brutality took place on August 9, 1997, when a Haitian immigrant, Abner Louima, was taken into custody by police while sitting in a Brooklyn music club. The police took him to the 70th Precinct station house, where they strip-searched him and beat him. A New York City police officer allegedly shoved a toilet plunger into his rectum and then forced the toilet plunger into his mouth, breaking his front tooth. Louima asserted that while this was occurring, the officers taunted him, saying, "That's your shit, nigger," "We're going to teach niggers to respect police officers," and "This is Giuliani time, not Dinkins time" (Farley 1997, 38). Later, Louima recanted these comments. Eventually, Louima was hospitalized after a one and one-half hour ordeal in the station house. His injuries included a ripped bladder and a punctured lower intestine. The New York City police Commissioner Howard Safir called the incident a "horrific crime" and stated "We're going to make sure the perpetrators ... go to jail." He also pointed out that a police officer who had been present had come forward to implicate his colleagues (Farley 1997, 38). One police officer was arrested and charged with sexual assault and sexual abuse, and 12 police officers were transferred, suspended, or demoted to desk duty.

When the public becomes aware of acts of police brutality in incidents such as the Rodney King or Abner Louima cases, they cannot have much confidence that the police will refrain from using excessive force. As acts of police brutality keep coming to the attention of the public before they can forget the last act of brutality brought to their attention, the police forfeit the community's trust more and more. The gap between police and minority communities grows wider or at least cannot be lessened while such inhumane acts are being committed.

Police brutality cannot be condoned. For community policing to be successful, police brutality must be eliminated. Why would citizens want to cooperate with the police when police are abusing community residents? The negative publicity from the Rodney King beating and the Abner Louima abuses will take decades for the police to overcome.

Throughout the 1990s, there have been numerous documented incidents of police brutality in American police departments of all sizes and in all parts of the country, rural and urban. But very little statistical information is available to document the overall extent of police brutality. Obtaining reliable data on police brutality is extremely difficult. To correct this deficiency, the U.S. Congress passed the Violent Crime Control and Law Enforcement Act in 1994, requiring the Attorney General to collect data on the use of excessive force by the police and to publish an annual report of the findings. The President's Commission on Law Enforcement and Administration of Justice (1967) reported in its task force report that physical abuse by police officers was not a serious problem but did exist. Commission researchers observed patrol officers in a number of cities and did observe instances where excessive force was used when none was necessary. Those abused were poor, drunks, sexual deviates, or youngsters considered hoodlums. The key ingredient discovered by the task force members was that those abused had verbally challenged the police officer's authority (181–182). If police officers are willing to use excessive use of force in the presence of the president's task force, what can the community expect when officers are not in the presence of witnesses?

In order to deal with the "use of force" misconduct issue the Community-Oriented Policing Service (COPS) national office with the New England Regional Community Policing Institute developed a curriculum on how to deal with the "use of force" in the community-policing environment. The training program was designed for police chiefs and senior managers with the authority and responsibility for overseeing, reviewing, and revising the department's use of force approaches. This training program makes the assumption that the administrators attending the "use of force" training will have experience in implementing policies, familiarity with internal affairs, and a commitment to community policing. The goal of the attendees for this "use of force" training is to identify and implement "the use of force" model for their department (Sweeney, n.d.).

Specific "use of force" training curriculums that are designed specifically for senior police administrators should go a long way in curtailing police brutality and excessive use of force by police officers.

Corruption

Police corruption is the abuse of police authority to obtain personal gain. This gain may be either monetary or nonmonetary. In committing acts of corruption, police officers gain financially by failing to perform services they are required to perform or by giving services that they should not be giving. Thirty years ago Barker and Wells characterized acts of corruption, which are still valid today, in three ways: "(1) They are forbidden, by some norm, regulation or law, (2) they involve the misuse of the officer's position, and (3) they involve a material gain, no matter how insignificant" (1981, 4).

Police corruption, according to veteran police officers, is always around and comes to life whenever the police department's vigilance subsides. For example, New York City police officers have been charged with selling protection to drug dealers and sometimes trafficking in drugs themselves. A report by the Mollen Commission investigating corruption in the New York City Police Department asserted that the department's internal affairs unit routinely buried corruption cases. The report also stated that police officers routinely made false arrests, tampered with evidence, and perjured themselves in court ("Policing the Police," 1994, 16).

Stoddard (1995) found that the police culture has an informal code that protects police misconduct and tolerates corruption. Recruits are indoctrinated into the police culture and soon come to the realization that they need the support of their fellow police officers, because their personal safety may depend upon a fellow officer being there when they need assistance. Further, recruits quickly learn that they themselves are bound to make mistakes, which may result in violations of departmental policy or criminal law, so that it may be best "not to see anything" if they observe misconduct by other officers.

Corruption has been found in many police departments—among them Atlanta, Miami, Houston, New Orleans, Philadelphia, Savannah (Georgia), and Los Angeles. Further, suburban and rural areas are not free from corruption. For example, a number of rural sheriffs from Georgia have been sent to prison for protecting drug dealers. Scandals involving police officers in corruption cannot benefit the police-community relationship. Police departments must check corruption if they hope to develop a successful community policing program.

Commission of Criminal Acts

A police officer lying in a court of law to obtain a conviction of a suspect has committed a crime. Lying in court has been termed perjury and is considered a criminal offense. Other violations of criminal law by police officers include murder, bank robbery, burglary, domestic violence, child abuse, and rape. In New Orleans, an off-duty police officer committing a robbery killed her partner, who was moonlighting as a security guard. Four Detroit police officers were charged with the murder of a black motorist who was beaten to death. In Galesburg, Illinois, a police officer was charged with bank robbery, and in Chatham County, Georgia, a police officer was caught robbing a convenience store on his own beat. In Wichita, Kansas, a police officer was charged with child molestation. In Savannah, Georgia, a police officer placed his own child in scalding hot water.

Although few police officers commit criminal acts, the few that do create a negative image for all police officers. Police departments must recruit people of integrity and investigate all complaints of improbity. Also, they must be proactive in their investigations and emphasize eliminating not only police crime but all police misconduct.

Mechanisms to Control Police Misconduct

For police misconduct to be controlled, mechanisms must be in place to control police behavior. These mechanisms can be either internal or external to the police agency. There are strong arguments for both approaches. Groups and individuals that distrust the police claim that the police cannot clean their own house, so that outside mechanisms are necessary to control police misconduct. On the other hand, police personnel find it offensive that "outsider" civilians who do not understand police work will be reviewing their behavior. This controversy is a hot topic in policing. If community policing is to be accepted by both the community and the police, this dispute will eventually have to be settled to the satisfaction of both.

Internal Affairs Units

Since the 1950s, midsized and large police departments have established internal affairs units to investigate citizen complaints of police misconduct. The size of an internal affairs unit can range from one officer to several hundred officers. The norm for staffing internal affairs is to have a ranking officer, captain or lieutenant, involved in investigating the conduct of police officers.

The ideal would be for every complaint against a police officer to be investigated impartially. When the internal affairs unit conducts an investigation, it interviews all witnesses and examines all pertinent evidence. The internal affairs unit commander reports directly to the chief of police. A report is made of the unit's findings to the chief, who then makes a decision for the appropriate action to be taken.

Civilian Review Board

The notion of a civilian review board can be traced to the 1930s. A civilian review board is "an independent tribunal of carefully selected outstanding citizens from the community at large" (Bopp and Schultz 1972, 146). Today, civilian review boards are often referred to as civilian oversight of the police. Although there may have been a name change, the two terms have similar meaning.

Every time there is a situation where the police are suspected of police misconduct, we hear the call for implementing a civilian review board if one does not already exist. Many of the same arguments made for a civilian review board in the late 1990s are similar to those made by supporters for civilian review boards in the 1960s and 1970s.

Civilian review boards review citizens' grievances against the police and are made up of only civilians, without any police representative. In 1967, the President's Commission on Law Enforcement and Administration of Justice recommended the adoption of such an external grievance system, stating that

> the primary need is for the development of methods of external control which will serve as an inducement for police to articulate important law enforcement policies and to be willing to have them known, discussed and changed if change is needed.
>
> (32)

Police acceptance of such an external grievance mechanism is a way of showing that their operations are open for inspection. The police can only create doubt and suspicion by rejecting an external grievance mechanism. In keeping with the community policing philosophy, with its emphasis on community–police interaction, it is a friendly gesture on the part of the police to accept civilian review boards, or civilian oversight bodies, as they are referred to today. Civilian oversight bodies have several characteristics in common. First, civilian oversight has been legally approved, either as an amendment to the city charter or by city ordinance. Second, civilian oversight bodies function independently of the police agency (Terrill 1990, 80).

Many of America's largest cities have some type of civilian oversight of police actions. In addition, many of America's midsized cities have adopted civilian oversight boards (Snow 1992, 51). The implementation of civilian oversight bodies does not necessarily mean that the police officer will always be found guilty. In all probability, the police officer will be exonerated. Civilian oversight boards are not in conflict with the community policing philosophy. In fact, civilian oversight boards indicate to the community the seriousness of police intentions to develop alliances and a cooperative spirit. The City of Wichita, Kansas, Police Department, which has a civilian oversight board, rarely has a recommendation of its internal affairs unit overturned by the civilian oversight board.

Civil Liabilities

For the past four decades, the United States Supreme Court has utilized Title 42, Section 1983 of the U.S. Code to control police misconduct. Section 1983 prohibits government employees from using any state law, ordinance, regulation, or custom as a technique to deprive citizens of their constitutional rights. The Court's purpose in establishing Section 1983 has been described as follows:

> As a result of the new structure of law that emerged in the post-Civil War era—and especially of the Fourteenth Amendment, which was its centerpiece—the role of the federal government as a guarantor of basic federal rights against state power was clearly established. Section 1983 opened the federal courts to private citizens, offering a uniquely federal remedy against incursions under the claimed authority of state law upon rights secured by the Constitution and the laws of the nation. ...

The very purpose of Section 1983 was to impose the federal courts between the states and the people, as guardians of the people's federal rights—to protect from unconstitutional action under color of state law, "whether that action be executive, legislative, or judicial" (Nahmond 1986, 4).

Section 1983 of Title 42 of the U.S. Code pertains to procedural remedies rather than substantial remedies. It provides an avenue of redress for violating the federal constitutional rights addressed in the Bill of Rights. In the 1960s, Section 1983 was expanded by the United States Supreme Court to afford the petitioner the right to take action against any person who—under color of law (state law, custom, or usage)—subjects another person to the deprivation of any rights, privileges, or immunities guaranteed by the U.S. Constitution. This means that the Fourth Amendment guarantees against unreasonable searches and seizures are equally applicable to the states via their judicial incorporation into the due process clause of the Fourteenth Amendment.

The Supreme Court of the United States has the authority to enforce the Fourteenth Amendment's provisions against state agents. This includes police officers who in some way fail to act according to their authority or who abuse their authority. The abused citizen, under Section 1983, can file a suit of equality, or other proceedings for redress, for being denied his or her constitutional rights, privileges, and immunities by an official's abuse of his or her position.

The United States Supreme Court concluded that local government officials under Section 1983 could be sued in their official positions for damages and retrospective declaratory and injunctive relief, even though local government may pay. A local government body can be held liable for traditions and customs that are unwritten and practiced by governmental departments or their employees.

When community members become stakeholders in the mission of police officers and have a major interest in crime prevention and control of disorder, a closer relationship between the police and the community can develop. With a police-community partnership, trust and confidence can grow, and fewer complaints will be made concerning police actions.

Summary

Police administrators used to claim that the police fully enforced all laws and investigated all crimes equally. But this has never been true. Full enforcement of the law would be impossible. In reality, selective enforcement is the norm. Police officers assigned to investigate a disturbing event can report the event as unfounded, and, in most cases, their report will be accepted and not visible to the public. Even the records maintained by the police are usually so incomplete that they cannot be used to evaluate nonenforcement decisions.

Although the police are sworn to enforce all the laws all the time, they enforce only the laws they choose to enforce and enforce even these laws only some of the time. In many instances, they warn, reprimand, or release an individual rather than make an arrest. Often, they decide not to arrest for crimes that they do not consider to be violent or a serious threat, such as traffic violations, petty gambling offenses, and simple assaults between acquaintances. In making such decisions, police are using discretion. Police discretion is the authority of police to decide how much effort they will apply to enforcing specific laws and which laws they will or will not enforce. It would be ridiculous to eliminate police discretion. Discretion is crucial to policing. But because it can be abused or applied unfairly, many commissions and agencies have recommended that police departments institute rules and procedures to guide and control the use of police discretion.

The quality of police work performance varies considerably from department to department. Most police departments employ police officers who generally function in a fair and impartial manner, but some police officers become involved in misconduct. Police misconduct is wrongdoing committed by a police officer. It can be either a criminal violation or a violation of departmental rules. It may be unethical or amoral without being criminal. Incidents of police misconduct include commission of criminal acts, corruption, excessive use of force, racism, and denying someone his or her civil rights. Police misconduct has taken place throughout history and still takes place today.

For police misconduct to be controlled, mechanisms must be put in place to control police behavior. These mechanisms can be either internal or external to the police agency. There are strong arguments for both approaches. Groups and individuals that distrust the police claim that the police cannot clean their own house and advocate outside mechanisms to control police misconduct. But some police personnel find it offensive that "outsiders"—civilians who do not understand police work—will be reviewing their behavior. Since the 1950s, midsized and large urban police departments have established internal affairs units to investigate citizen complaints of police misconduct. The size of an internal affairs unit can range from one officer to several hundred officers. The norm for staffing internal affairs is to have a ranking officer, such as a captain or lieutenant, involved in investigating the conduct of police officers.

One external mechanism for controlling police misconduct is civilian review boards. A civilian review board is an independent tribunal of carefully selected outstanding citizens from the community at large who review citizens' grievances against the police. Supporters of civilian review boards recommend that boards be composed of only civilians without any police representative. An additional remedy to check police misconduct is Title 42, Section 1983 of the U.S. Code. Section 1983 prohibits government employees from using any state law, ordinance, regulation, or custom to deprive citizens of their constitutional rights. The United States Supreme Court concluded that local government officials under Section 1983 could be sued in their official positions for damages and retrospective declaratory and injunctive relief, even though local government may pay. A local government can be held liable for traditions and customs that are unwritten and practiced by government departments or their employees.

Key Terms

- Abner Louima
- actual enforcement
- civil liability
- civilian review board
- corruption
- full enforcement
- *Gowan v. Smith*
- internal affairs units
- police brutality
- police misconduct
- Rodney King
- rule making
- selective enforcement
- street justice

Review Questions

1. Explain police discretion.
2. What did the American Bar Association study discover about police discretion?

3. Provide an example of police discretion.
4. What do the terms full and selective enforcement mean?
5. Describe rule making as it pertains to police discretion.
6. Describe the meaning of street justice.
7. What does the term police misconduct mean?
8. Describe the purpose of an internal affairs unit.

References

Aaronson, D.E. et al. 1984. *Public policy and police discretion: Processes of decriminalization.* New York: Clark Boardman.

American Bar Association. 1974. *The urban police function.* Gaithersburg, MD: International Association of Chiefs of Police.

Barker, T. 1977. Peer group support for police occupational deviance. *Criminology* 15(2): 356.

———. 1986. An empirical study of police deviance other than corruption. In *Police deviance* ed. T. Barker and D.L. Carter. Cincinnati, OH: Anderson.

Barker, T. and R.O. Wells. 1981. Police administrators' attitudes toward the definition and control of police deviance. Paper presented at the Academy of Criminal Justice Sciences, Philadelphia.

Bopp, W.J. and D.O. Schultz. 1972. *A short history of American law enforcement.* Springfield, IL: Charles C. Thomas.

Brown, M.K. 1988. *Working the streets: Police discretion and the dilemmas of reform.* New York: Russell Sage Foundation.

Cox, S.M. and W.P. McCamey. 2008. *Introduction to criminal justice*, 5th ed., Durham, NC: Carolina Academic Press.

Davis, K.C. 1971. *Discretionary justice: A preliminary inquiry.* Urbana: University of Illinois Press.

Farley, C.J. 1997. A beating in Brooklyn. *Time*, August 22, p. 38.

Goldstein, J. 1960. Police discretion not to invoke the criminal process: Low-visibility decisions in the administration of justice. *Yale Journal* 69: 543–561.

Hyatt, W.D. 2001. Parameters of police misconduct. In *Police misconduct* ed. M.J. Palmiotto, Upper Saddle River, NJ: Prentice-Hall.

Klockars, C.B. 1986. Street justice: Some micro-moral reservations: Comments on Sykes. *Justice Quarterly* 3(4): 515–516.

Nahmond, S.H. 1986. *Civil rights and civil liberties litigation.* New York: McGraw-Hill.

National Advisory Commission on Criminal Justice Standards and Goals. 1973. *Police.* Washington, DC: Government Printing Office.

Palmiotto, M.J. 2001. Police misconduct: What is it? In *Police misconduct* ed. M.J. Palmiotto, Upper Saddle River: NJ: Prentice-Hall.

Policing the police [editorial] 1994. *New York Times*, May 1, section 4, p. 16.

President's Commission on Law Enforcement and Administration of Justice. 1967. *The challenge of crime in a free society.* Washington, DC: Government Printing Office.

Reiss, A.J. 1984. Consequences of compliance and deterrence models of law enforcement for the exercise of police discretion. *Law and Contemporary Problems* 47 (Autumn): 89.

Snow, R. 1992. Civilian oversight: Plus or minus. *Law and Order* 40(12): 51.

Stoddard, E.R. 1995. The informal "code" of police deviancy: A group approach to "blue-coat crime." In *The police and society: Touchstone readings*, ed. V.K. Kappeler. Prospects Heights, IL: Waveland.

Sweeney, Joan, n.d. "Use of Force Issues in a Community Policing Environment," U.S. Department of Justice: COPS.

Sykes, G. 1986. Street justice: A moral defense of order maintenance policing. *Justice Quarterly* 3: 498–507.

Terrill, R.J. 1990. Alternative perceptions of independence in civilian oversight. *Journal of Police Science and Administration* 17(2): 80.

Walker, S. 1986. Controlling the cops: A legislative approach to police rulemaking. *University of Detroit Law Review* 63: 362–389.

———. 1993. *Taming the system: The control of discretion in criminal justice 1950–1990*. New York: Oxford University Press.

CHAPTER 2

Conclusion

Our society is often polarized in the event of controversial police conduct. Some people tend to assume the police must be in the wrong, since they have not earned a good reputation in the past years, and others tend to become defensive and like to label critics as anti-police. Many times, people have taken sides before the truth is clear. As mentioned in Chapter 1, this is ideology working: we already determine what we want to believe without knowing the whole truth. As normal as this tendency has become, it is bad for making social progress. Police conduct or misconduct should not be a subject of ideological debate. It should be fact-based. If an officer indeed commits a crime or engages in unethical behavior, he or she should be exposed and expelled. On the other hand, if what the officer did was not wrong, he or she deserves respect and recognition for doing his or her job. Certainly, there will be times when the line is blurry. Luckily, we do not need to rush to a conclusion before it gets clear. Police misconduct should never be tolerated. Even if it is not misconduct, all police conduct may still be reviewed and discussed for improvement. There is nothing anti-police about questioning how the police can improve. Transparency and communication are good for building a stronger police force.

Discussion Questions

1. Find a video on the Internet that allegedly shows police misconduct. Share the link to this video, and discuss whether this video is adequate in telling the whole story.
2. What is discretion? How have you used your discretion to make important decisions in your life?
3. Do you consider the neighborhood you are living in a disorganized one? How do you think the police perceive your neighborhood?
4. Look up Eric Garner's death. Do you believe the police in this case did anything wrong? Even if it was not wrong, was there a better way to handle the situation that could have saved Garner's life?
5. Discuss your experience of interacting with the police if any.

CHAPTER 3

Privacy and Security

Introduction

Since the year of 2001, there has been a push for more emphasis on homeland security. In the name of homeland security, the government has justified the need for surveillance and data collection on the people. Noticeably, in most cities, surveillance cameras are installed everywhere. Without a doubt, these cameras have been a tremendous help in criminal investigations. Many crimes have been caught on tape, so to speak. It is easier to find the suspect when you can see what he or she looks like. Moreover, the presence of these cameras serves as a deterrent and possibly prevents some crimes from happening, although there is always a chance these crimes were simply displaced rather than prevented. On the flip side, however, it can be argued that now you are practically being watched everywhere you go. Combined with facial recognition technology, in theory, the government can use surveillance cameras to keep track of your whereabouts if there is a reason to do so.

Perhaps we do not generally have a problem with those surveillance cameras installed in public places. After all, one should expect little privacy when going to public places. However, surveillance can take place in other forms. For example, a law enforcement agency may be wiretapping your phone or monitoring your Internet activity. In the past, common sense would suggest only those who are involved in criminal activities would be subjected to such clandestine surveillance. Nowadays, it is hard to say. It has been proven that the government was or has been monitoring almost everyone to generate big data that will be useful for identifying potential threats in terms of homeland security. Such practice might not be illegal because, in the name of homeland security, some legislation, such as the PATRIOT Act, has made Fourth Amendment rights very flexible, but still it raises concerns regarding citizens' expectation for privacy. To what extent should we give up privacy to ensure security? Is it impossible to keep privacy and achieve security at the same time? These are the questions students should bear in mind when studying privacy issues in criminal justice.

In this chapter, the author of the article uses the case of cell phone location data to illustrate the legal ramifications associated with law enforcement collecting such data. This should help students understand the complexity of the issue, and it also piques the concern about whether the law can catch up with fast-advancing technologies.

The Curious Case of Cell Phone Location Data

Fourth Amendment Doctrine Mash-Up[†]

Monu Bedi

Introduction

The third-party and public disclosure doctrines are longstanding hurdles to Fourth Amendment protection. Federal courts have recently invoked these doctrines to determine whether police can acquire cell phone location data from providers without constitutional scrutiny.[1] These rulings are all over the map. Courts disagree not only on whether location information is constitutionally protected but also if one, both, or neither of these doctrines applies. The Supreme Court has yet to enter the fray. So for now, we are left with muddled results.[2] A major reason for the confusion turns out to rest on a hitherto overlooked tension between the two doctrines. This Essay is the first to raise this issue and, in turn, harmonize these doctrines in the cell phone location data context.[3]

While both doctrines vitiate privacy protection and are often associated together, they rest on unique foundational triggers.[4] The third-party doctrine involves an individual voluntarily disclosing nonpublic information to an actual person or entity. The

---

† This Essay was originally published in the *Northwestern University Law Review Online* on October 29, 2015, 110 NW. U. L. REV. ONLINE 61 (2015), http://scholarlycommons. law.northwestern. edu/cgi/viewcontent.cgi?article=1227&context=nulr_online [http://perma.cc/SX4B-33KG].

1 *See infra* Part III.

2 *See, e.g.*, Orin Kerr, *When and How Will the Supreme Court Enter the Cell-Site Fray?* WASH. POST: THE VOLOKH CONSPIRACY (Aug. 5, 2015), https://www.washingtonpost.com/news/volokh-conspiracy/wp/2015/08/05/when-and-how-will-the-supreme-court-enter-the-cell-site-fray [http://perma.cc/U6YR-VR6Z].

3 This Essay focuses exclusively on constitutional protection without reference to statutory authority or any good faith exception analysis. For an example of such analysis, see generally *id.*

4 *See infra* Sections II.A–B.

Supreme Court has applied this doctrine to statements made to undercover informants,[5] bank records released to banks,[6] and telephone numbers disclosed to phone providers.[7] The public disclosure doctrine, on the other hand, focuses on a suspect making voluntary public movements that are susceptible to visual surveillance. The Court has applied this doctrine to police surveillance of suspects using beeper technology[8] or a GPS device.[9]

Courts seem to pick and choose a doctrine when analyzing cell phone location data, with little to no analysis on why one or the other applies (or doesn't apply).[10] These inconsistent choices are primarily due to the unique nature of this technology and the different ways one can conceptualize how the government collects it. The data can be viewed as nonpublic information disclosed to a cell phone provider, suggesting a potential application of the third-party doctrine, or as public movements susceptible to visual surveillance, suggesting a potential application of the public disclosure doctrine. But the key to applying the right doctrine is recognizing in which of these two contexts the government activity is taking place. It matters, for example, whether the government is seeking historical cell phone location data or acquiring real-time data. This Essay provides the first workable topology for these various scenarios and, in the process, offers some much overdue clarification on the operative elements of the respective doctrines.

Part I introduces how cell phone location data is created and collected. Part II details the contours of the third-party and public disclosure doctrines. Part III highlights the split among federal courts regarding whether the Fourth Amendment protects against the collection of cell phone location data, particularly in light of the varying applications of the third-party and public disclosure doctrines. Part IV outlines an approach for determining which of the two doctrines should apply. Finally, the Essay concludes by noting the implications of the cell phone location data Fourth Amendment conundrum for future technological developments.

A Primer on Cell Phone Location Data

Cell phones use radio waves to connect to their service providers to facilitate a host of functions, including making and receiving phone calls, sending and receiving text messages, and using the Internet.[11] Cell phone providers, in turn, maintain thousands of cell phone towers that receive these radio signals.[12] Cell phones emit these signals anytime they are turned on, after which

---

5 *Hoffa v. United States*, 385 U.S. 293 (1966).
6 *United States v. Miller*, 425 U.S. 435 (1976).
7 *Smith v. Maryland*, 442 U.S. 735 (1979).
8 *United States v. Knotts*, 460 U.S. 276 (1983).
9 *United States v. Jones*, 132 S. Ct. 945 (2012).
10 *See, e.g.*, *In re* Application of the United States for an Order Directing a Provider of Elec. Commc'n Serv. to Disclose Records to the Gov't, 620 F.3d 304, 312–13, 317–18 (3d Cir. 2010); *infra* Part III.
11 *See, e.g.*, *State v. Earls*, 70 A.3d 630, 637 (N.J. 2013) (discussing the basics of how cell phone location data works).
12 *Id.*

the nearest cell phone tower acquires a signal.[13] This process is automatic, without any notice to the user, and a user does nothing to facilitate the transmission except turning on the phone.[14] The signal moves from tower to tower as a cell phone user changes location and the location of the nearest tower is transmitted to the provider.[15] Cell phone company privacy policies typically include language that a user's location is collected in the foregoing way.[16]

It is useful to recognize three different scenarios under which the government tracks movements through the acquisition of cell phone location data: (1) historical cell phone location data, (2) real-time cell phone location data, and (3) actively "pinging" a cell phone for location data.

Cell phone providers store location data as the normal part of their business of providing service.[17] Police, in turn, can request that cell phone providers hand over this location data for a suspect over a set period of time.[18] This information is classified as historical cell phone location data.

This data stands in contrast to real-time location data. Whereas the former focuses on past locations, real-time data provides locations as they actually occur.[19] Here, cell phone providers, upon request, give police contemporaneous data on the location of the nearest cell tower for tracking purposes.[20]

Pinging a cell phone is a variation on the collection of contemporaneous cell phone location data. This time, however, the government does not wait for the phone itself to send its routine signal to the cell tower. Rather, the police request that cell phone providers send an affirmative signal to the suspect's phone to monitor her location via cell towers.[21]

---

13 *Id.*

14 *United States v. Graham*, 796 F.3d 332, 354–55 (4th Cir. 2015); *Earls*, 70 A.3d at 637.

15 Susan Freiwald, *Cell Phone Location Data and the Fourth Amendment: A Question of Law, Not Fact*, 70 MD. L. REV. 681, 702 (2011); *see also Earls*, 70 A.3d at 637 ("Network-based location tracking relies on the network of cell sites and antennas. …"). Depending on the provider and particular cell phone, the actual location of the cell phone may also be transmitted. Freiwald, *supra* at 713 (discussing how certain smart phones are equipped with GPS capability and that the phone's specific location may also be transmitted to a provider). Because this additional transmission may reveal otherwise private information, the Fourth Amendment analysis under the public disclosure doctrine could potentially come out differently. *See infra* note 40 and accompanying text.

16 *Graham*, 796 F.3d at 345.

17 *Earls*, 70 A.3d at 637.

18 *See, e.g., In re* Application of the U.S. for Historical Cell Site Data, 724 F.3d 600 (5th Cir. 2013); *Graham*, 796 F.3d at 340–41, 343 (stating "[t]he precision of this location data depends on the size of the identified cell sites' geographical coverage ranges").

19 *See* Patrick E. Corbett, *The Fourth Amendment and Cell Site Location Information: What Should We Do While We Wait for the Supremes?*, 8 FED. CTS. L. REV. 215, 217 (2015).

20 *See, e.g., In re* Smartphone Geolocation Data Application, 977 F. Supp. 2d 129, 132–33 (E.D.N.Y. 2013). If available, police may also request the historical location data of the actual cell phone. Freiwald, *supra* note 15, at 713–14 (noting that certain police departments request the actual cell phone location whereas others only request the nearest cell tower).

21 *United States v. Caraballo*, 963 F. Supp. 2d 341, 350–51, 360 (D. Vt. 2013). Users are not aware that this pinging is taking place. *Id.* at 350, 360.

Fourth Amendment Disclosure Doctrines

The Contours of the Third-Party Doctrine

The basic premise of the third-party doctrine is readily known: an individual loses all reasonable expectation of privacy to information she discloses to another person or entity.[22] The roots of the doctrine trace back to the use of government informants. The government has always had the unfettered ability to elicit incriminating statements from unwary suspects.[23] As the Court has explained, it is of no consequence that a defendant revealed the information "on the assumption that it will be used only for a limited purpose and the confidence placed in the third party will not be betrayed."[24] This misplaced belief does not change the fact that the defendant voluntarily disclosed the information and thus took the risk that the government might obtain it without a warrant and use it against her at trial.[25] The Court has expanded the application of the doctrine to include voluntary disclosures made to entities such as banks and telephone companies.[26]

A central feature of the doctrine is whether the disclosure was voluntary or otherwise not coerced. As one simple example, eliciting incriminating statements by putting a gun to a suspect's head would, in all likelihood, not satisfy the voluntariness requirement. This seems like an easy case. More recently, courts and scholars have questioned this requirement of voluntariness—and in turn, the application of the third-party doctrine—in today's technology-dominated world where we routinely (and almost necessarily) make many disclosures to many entities.[27] Whether it is disclosures to banks or e-mails sent via Internet service providers, we are constantly making disclosures to third parties. Should these actions appropriately be considered voluntary? There may not be an easy answer here.[28] Indeed, part of the disagreement on whether the third-party doctrine applies to cell phone location data stems from this issue of voluntariness.[29]

So ends the typical discussion of the doctrine. But this summary neglects some important considerations that bear on its application. The first relates to when the government can acquire

---

22 Monu Bedi, *Social Networks, Government Surveillance, and the Fourth Amendment Mosaic Theory*, 94 B.U. L. Rev. 1809, 1820–26 (2014) (discussing evolution of third-party doctrine before and after *United States v. Katz*).

23 *See Hoffa v. United States*, 385 U.S. 293, 302–03 (1966); Lopez v. United States, 373 U.S. 427, 437–39 (1963).

24 *United States v. Miller*, 425 U.S. 435, 443 (1976); *see also Hoffa*, 385 U.S. at 302 ("Neither this Court nor any member of it has ever expressed the view that the Fourth Amendment protects a wrongdoer's misplaced belief that a person to whom he voluntarily confides his wrongdoing will not reveal it.").

25 *Miller*, 425 U.S. at 443. For this reason, some scholars talk about the principle as a waiver or consent principle. *See* Orin S. Kerr, *The Case for the Third-Party Doctrine*, 107 MICH. L. Rev. 561, 588–90 (2009); Sonia K. McNeil, Note, *Privacy and the Modern Grid*, 25 HARV. J.L. & TECH. 199, 216–18 (2011).

26 *Smith v. Maryland*, 442 U.S. 735, 745–46 (1979); *Miller*, 425 U.S. at 443.

27 *See United States v. Jones*, 132 S. Ct. 945, 957 (2012) (Sotomayor, J., concurring) (questioning the viability of the third-party doctrine in today's technology-dominated society); Monu Bedi, *Facebook and Interpersonal Privacy: Why the Third Party Doctrine Should Not Apply*, 54 B.C. L. Rev. 1, 25–28 (2013) (discussing scholars' reactions to technological advancements when it comes to the application of the third-party doctrine).

28 Bedi, *supra* note 27, at 27.

29 *See infra* Part III.

the information. Is the government free to acquire the information at any point before it is conveyed to the third party, or must the information come from the third party itself?

Take the facts of *Smith v. Maryland*.[30] There, the government collected a dialed telephone number after it was conveyed to a telephone company in the normal course of making a call. But if the number is not protected due to its disclosure to the phone company, can the government acquire it before it reaches the company? On the one hand, the police could not, without first getting a warrant, enter a suspect's home and observe the suspect dial the number.[31] But what about tapping into public lines and acquiring the number before it reaches the company? This action would not otherwise seem to implicate the suspect's individual Fourth Amendment rights.[32]

The analysis in *Smith* suggests that the government must retrieve information from and with the knowledge of the third party. Otherwise, the assumption of risk analysis loses its meaning. The whole point of the expectation that a government informant or telephone company might disclose information assumes in the first instance that they have received some information.[33]

It also seems that the disclosed information must be nonpublic. It is no accident that the Court talks about misplaced trust when discussing the effect of the doctrine.[34] The premise here is that the information is not public and that the person assumes the risk that the third party will nonetheless hand it over to the government. If the information were otherwise publicly available, the individual wouldn't really be taking on any additional risk by disclosing it to the third party. The above cases bear this out.[35] Whether it is statements to a confidential informant, bank statements to a bank, or telephone numbers to a phone company, each of these types of information are private or not otherwise publicly available.

The Contours of the Public Disclosure Doctrine

Courts and scholars alike often associate the public disclosure doctrine and third-party doctrine as expressing a singular principle.[36] In some ways, this makes sense, as both doctrines involve voluntary actions by suspects that, in turn, vitiate Fourth Amendment protection. With the public disclosure doctrine, however, the focus is not on disclosing information but rather on making public movements or those movements that are susceptible to visual observation. In

---

30 442 U.S. 735.

31 *See United States v. Karo*, 468 U.S. 705, 717 (1984).

32 *See Rakas v. Illinois*, 439 U.S. 128, 133–34 (1978) (reaffirming that Fourth Amendment protection only applies where individual has a *personal* expectation of privacy).

33 This doesn't mean that the government would need a warrant to tap into the public phone lines, but rather simply that the third-party doctrine would not seem to play a role here in assessing Fourth Amendment protection (or the lack of it).

34 *See, e.g., Hoffa v. United States*, 385 U.S. 293, 302–03 (1966).

35 *See Smith*, 442 U.S. 735; *United States v. Miller*, 425 U.S. 435 (1976); *Hoffa*, 385 U.S. 293.

36 *See United States v. Jones*, 132 S. Ct. 945, 956–57 (2012) (Sotomayor, J., concurring) (discussing the general viability of the third-party doctrine when assessing the permissibility of long-term GPS surveillance); United States v. Knotts, 460 U.S. 276, 283 (1983) (referencing *Smith v. Maryland* as the "factual counterpart" to beeper monitoring); Miriam H. Baer, *Secrecy, Intimacy, and Workable Rules: Justice Sotomayor Stakes Out the Middle Ground in United States v. Jones*, 123 YALE L.J. F. 393 (2014); Bedi, *supra* note 22, at 1820–26; Kerr, *supra* note 25, at 588–90.

short, a suspect does not have a reasonable expectation of privacy in her voluntarily disclosed public movements.[37] In *United States v. Knotts*, for example, the police surreptitiously placed a beeper in the defendant's belongings and used it to follow the defendant for a few hours to his ultimate destination.[38] The Court found no problem with this type of surveillance, reasoning that:

> A person traveling in an automobile on public thoroughfares has no reasonable expectation of privacy in his movements from one place to another. When [the defendant] traveled over the public streets he voluntarily conveyed to anyone who wanted to look the fact that he was traveling over particular roads in a particular direction. ...[39]

The key here is that the police only monitored public movements, not movements within a person's home where the Fourth Amendment would clearly apply.[40] Moreover, it didn't matter that the suspect was unaware of the beeper transmission or that the police were not in constant visual contact with the car as long as the movements were susceptible to visual surveillance.[41] The analysis of *Knotts* under the third-party doctrine, on the other hand, would have come out differently. Since the suspect was not aware of the beeper and its emanating signal, the suspect could not have voluntarily disclosed his movements to the police.

The public disclosure doctrine thus does not implicate the same issues of *how* or *when* the government obtains information. The reason for this is the public nature of the movements (e.g., the car's location) serves as the sole trigger. Because this information is susceptible to visual observation, it is *per se* not protected under the Fourth Amendment.

One can still use the assumption of risk calculus with the public disclosure doctrine but it looks different than the third-party doctrine analysis. The risk here relates to the government's surveillance of a person's public movements rather than its acquisition of private information from an entity or person.[42]

---

37 Bedi, *supra* note 22, at 1820–26 (discussing evolution of public disclosure doctrine before and after *United States v. Katz*).

38 *Knotts*, 460 U.S. at 277.

39 *Id.* at 281–82.

40 *Compare Knotts*, 460 U.S. 276, *with United States v. Karo*, 468 U.S. 705, 714–15 (1984) (finding that monitoring movements within the home triggered Fourth Amendment protection). The concern over nonpublic information may potentially impact how one analyzes location data of an actual cell phone as opposed to a public cell tower under the Fourth Amendment. If the former location data reveals a person's movements in her home or a place where she has a reasonable expectation of privacy, the public disclosure doctrine would not apply. *See, e.g., In re* Application of the United States for an Order Directing a Provider of Elec. Commc'n Serv. to Disclose Records to the Gov't, 620 F.3d 304, 312–13 (3d Cir. 2010) (citing the *Knotts–Karo* distinction when discussing the potential of historical location data revealing nonpublic locations but concluding the distinction not relevant on instant facts because the government only acquired cell tower or public location data).

41 *Knotts*, 460 U.S. at 285.

42 In turn, the debate over the voluntariness of disclosing location data under the third-party doctrine isn't an issue in the public disclosure context. The cell phone user quite obviously has voluntarily exposed her public movements to potential visual observation.

The public disclosure doctrine is not without potential limits. *Knotts* itself suggested that a different conclusion may be necessary if the monitoring lasted a day or longer.[43] It is telling that the Court made explicit that "different constitutional principles" would be needed to analyze this long-term surveillance, and in doing so, cited to a First Amendment-related case.[44] This analysis implies that the public disclosure doctrine on its own would treat long-term surveillance no differently than short-term surveillance—neither would receive Fourth Amendment protection.

This concern over the potentially harsh implications of long-term electronic surveillance under the public disclosure doctrine leads to the most recent case on the doctrine, *United States v. Jones*.[45] Here, the government—without the consent of the defendant or under the terms of a warrant—installed a Global Positioning System (GPS) device under his car and tracked his public movements with the device for nearly thirty days.[46] The Court (both the majority and concurrences) wrestled with how this government activity could fall under the scrutiny of the Fourth Amendment when the public disclosure doctrine mandated that none of this surveillance would garner constitutional protection.[47] The majority focused on the initial act of placing the GPS device as constituting an unlawful physical trespass, whereas the concurrences focused on the revelation of private information (e.g., political affiliations) as a byproduct of long-term GPS surveillance.[48] Analysis of these limiting principles is beyond the scope of this Essay.[49] What matters for my purposes is that the majority decision bypassed the chance to alter the contours of the public disclosure doctrine, which for now does not hinge on the length of surveillance.[50]

---

43 The concern here was dragnet activity by the government. *Knotts*, 460 U.S. at 283–84.

44 *Id.* The Court cited to *Zurcher v. Stanford Daily*, 436 U.S. 547, 565 (1978), which found that the Fourth Amendment warrant requirement adequately protects First Amendment interests. *Knotts*, 460 U.S. at 283; *see also* Bedi, *supra* note 22, at 1848–57 (discussing First Amendment values in Fourth Amendment reasonable expectation analysis).

45 132 S. Ct. 945 (2012).

46 *Id.* at 948.

47 *Id.* at 951–52 (explaining that while there is no reasonable expectation of privacy in public movements, this did not overturn the common law trespass doctrine); *id.* at 956 (Sotomayor, J., concurring) ("I do not regard as dispositive the fact that the Government might obtain the fruits of GPS monitoring through lawful conventional surveillance techniques."); *id.* at 964 (Alito, J., concurring) (citing *Knotts* for the proposition that short-term surveillance does not trigger Fourth Amendment protection).

48 *Id.* at 950–54 (majority opinion); *id.* at 955–57 (Sotomayor, J., concurring); *id.* at 961–64 (Alito, J., concurring). The theory put forth by the concurrences has been dubbed the "mosaic theory." *See* Bedi, *supra* note 22, at 1834–38.

49 For a discussion on the physical trespass doctrine and the mosaic theory, see generally Andrew Guthrie Ferguson, *Personal Curtilage: Fourth Amendment Security in Public*, 55 Wm. & Mary L. Rev. 1283 (2014); Christopher Slobogin, *Making the Most of* United States v. Jones *in a Surveillance Society: A Statutory Implementation of Mosaic Theory*, 8 Duke J. Const. L. & Pub. POL'Y (Special Issue) 1, 17–32 (2012).

50 *Jones*, 132 S. Ct. at 954 (majority opinion) ("It may be that achieving [four-week surveillance] through electronic means, without an accompanying trespass, is an unconstitutional invasion of privacy, but the present case does not require us to answer that question."). In fact, drawing a defensible line as to when surveillance becomes *too* long to fall under the public disclosure doctrine seems untenable. *See* Bedi, *supra* note 22, at 1839–48 (discussing various problems with the mosaic theory).

Disagreement Among Federal Courts Analyzing Fourth Amendment Protection for Cell Phone Location Data

No Reasonable Expectation of Privacy

A number of federal circuits have found that cell phone location data does not garner Fourth Amendment protection. Both the Fifth and Eleventh Circuits, in their assessments of the collection of historical location data, relied on a straightforward application of the third-party doctrine and suspects making a voluntary disclosure.[51] The Fifth Circuit, for example, analogizing to *Smith v. Maryland*, reasoned, "A cell service subscriber, like a telephone user, understands that his cell phone must send a signal to a nearby cell tower in order to wirelessly connect his call."[52]

The Third Circuit, in reaching a similar conclusion, focused instead on the public disclosure doctrine.[53] Citing *Knotts*, the court explained:

> We cannot reject the hypothesis that [historical cell phone location data] may, under certain circumstances, be used to approximate the past location of a person. ... [Prior opinions] make clear that the privacy interests at issue are confined to the interior of the home. There is no evidence in this record that historical [cell phone location data] ... extends to that realm. We therefore cannot accept the ... conclusion that [this data] ... requires probable cause for its production.[54]

The Third Circuit's point here seems to be that historical cell phone location data is no different from the location data documented by other tracking device technology that simply catalogs public locations. Interestingly, however, and in contrast with the Fifth Circuit, the Third Circuit went on to explain that the third-party doctrine would not necessarily support the same conclusion because a cell phone user does not voluntarily share location data with her cell phone provider.[55]

Real-time location data would appear to stand or fall with historical location data. This information is also initially disclosed to a cell phone provider, albeit quickly transmitted to the government thereafter. For this reason, some courts have treated historical and real-time data the same way, finding no protection based on an application of the third-party doctrine.[56]

The Sixth Circuit has gone one step further by finding that pinging a cell phone user's phone to ascertain her real-time location also does not trigger Fourth Amendment protection.[57] In

---

51 *United States v. Davis*, 785 F.3d 498 (11th Cir. 2015); *In re* Application of the United States for Historical Cell Site Data, 724 F.3d 600 (5th Cir. 2013).

52 *In re* Application of the United States for Historical Cell Site Data, 724 F.3d at 613; *see also Davis*, 785 F.3d at 512.

53 *In re* Application of the United States for an Order Directing a Provider of Elec. Commc'n Serv. to Disclose Records to the Gov't, 620 F.3d 304 (3d Cir. 2010).

54 *Id.* at 312–13.

55 *Id.* at 317.

56 *See, e.g., In re* Smartphone Geolocation Data Application, 977 F. Supp. 2d 129, 145–47 (E.D.N.Y. 2013); *United States v. Booker*, No. 1:11-CR-255-1-TWT, 2013 WL 2903562, at *9 (N.D. Ga. June 13, 2013).

57 The Sixth Circuit has ruled in two cases on this matter. *United States v. Skinner*, 690 F.3d 772 (6th Cir. 2012); *United States v. Forest*, 355 F.3d 942 (6th Cir. 2004), *cert. granted, judgment vacated on other grounds sub nom., Garner v. United States*, 543 U.S. 1100 (2005).

reaching its conclusion, the court distinguished between the effects of the public disclosure doctrine and the third-party doctrine in this context.[58] The court analogized to *Knotts* and reasoned that the police could have acquired "that same information ... through visual surveillance."[59] However, in an earlier case, the court also seemed to recognize that the third-party doctrine may suggest a different outcome.[60] It was the government's act of pinging the cell phone that triggered the location, not a voluntary act by the cell phone user.[61] However, because the real-time data was simply a proxy for a suspect's public location, there was no Fourth Amendment protection.[62]

Finding Reasonable Expectation of Privacy

Other courts have found that this data should, at least in some circumstances, garner Fourth Amendment protection. These decisions often emphasize the voluntariness element (or lack of it) in the application of the third-party doctrine. The most recent decision on the issue comes from the Fourth Circuit, which found that, unlike the telephone user in *Smith v. Maryland* who knowingly conveyed the number dialed, the cell phone user did not voluntarily share her location in any meaningful way.[63] The court reasoned, "A cell phone user cannot be said to 'voluntarily convey' to her service provider information that she never held but was instead generated by the service provider itself without the user's involvement."[64] The court also found that the fact that the company's privacy policy mentioned this collection did not suggest a different conclusion since most users are not familiar with or otherwise understand their providers' policies.[65]

The Third Circuit reached a similar conclusion on the issue of voluntariness.[66] But what makes its decision so interesting is that the court simultaneously acknowledged that the public disclosure doctrine would suggest that this same data is not protected.[67] This tension between the two disclosure doctrines underscores the different foundational triggers underlying each. More on this later.

Some courts have also used the voluntariness element to distinguish *Smith v. Maryland* from real-time location data.[68] As one district court explained, "Unlike dialed telephone numbers,

---

58 *Forest*, 355 F.3d at 951–52.

59 *Skinner*, 690 F.3 at 778. Similar to *Knotts*, the court found that it was not crucial that the government may not have had visual contact throughout the full-length surveillance. The key fact was that the movements *could* be observed by visual observation. *Id.* at 779.

60 *Forest*, 355 F.3d at 951.

61 *Id.*

62 *Id.*

63 *United States v. Graham*, 796 F.3d 332, 354 (4th Cir. 2015).

64 *Id.* at 356.

65 *Id.* at 345 & n.3.

66 *In re* Application of the United States for an Order Directing a Provider of Elec. Commc'n Serv. to Disclose Records to the Gov't, 620 F.3d 304, 317–18 (3d Cir. 2010).

67 *See supra* notes 53–55 and accompanying text.

68 *In re* Application for Pen Register and Trap/Trace Device with Cell Site Location Auth., 396 F. Supp. 2d 747, 756–57 (S.D. Tex. 2005).

cell site data is not 'voluntarily conveyed' by the user to the phone company. [Rather,] it is transmitted automatically during the registration process, entirely independent of the user's input, control, or knowledge."[69]

It is interesting how these cases appear to discount the public disclosure doctrine. To the extent it applies, the doctrine does not depend on whether a court classifies the transmission of the location data as voluntary. Nor does it matter how the government acquired the data. All that matters is that the movements are vulnerable to visual observation.

The Fourth Circuit discussed the public disclosure doctrine but concluded it did not ultimately apply to the facts at hand. The court seemed to make a two-fold argument. First, it denied the basic premise that historical location data reveals otherwise public information. "[U]nlike GPS monitoring of a vehicle, examination of historical [cell phone data] can permit the government to track a person's movements between public and private spaces, impacting at once her interests in both the privacy of her movements and the privacy of her home."[70] The court cited to the risk of cell phone tower location data revealing private information such as outpatient medical treatment or regular church visits.[71]

It is not clear whether this line of reasoning is ultimately persuasive. The same objection can also apply to public car movements such as those in *Knotts*. Police can surveil a suspect's car entering a church parking lot or medical complex. These acts would also seemingly reveal personal information but none are currently protected because of the public disclosure doctrine. Both cell phone tower data and a car's movements through streets are public information and thus stand or fall together.[72]

The Fourth Circuit also relied on the *Jones* concurrences in finding that the sheer amount of data revealed (in this case, it was movements over 220 days) militated against a straightforward application of the public disclosure doctrine.[73] These discussions on the privacy implications of long-term surveillance—while interesting and worthy of consideration—are ultimately beyond the scope of this Essay because current precedent dictates that all public monitoring—regardless of length—carries no Fourth Amendment protection.[74]

---

69 *Id.*

70 *Graham*, 796 F.3d at 348.

71 *Id.* (citing United States v. Maynard, 615 F.3d 544, 562 (D.C. Cir. 2010)).

72 A different constitutional conclusion under the public disclosure doctrine could result if the location data revealed the cell phone location rather than the public tower location. *See supra* note 40. However, only cell phone tower locations were at issue in *United States v. Graham*, 796 F.3d at 343.

73 *Id.* at 349–51; *see also In re* Application of the United States for an Order Authorizing the Release of Historical Cell-Site Info., 809 F. Supp. 2d 113, 118–19 (E.D.N.Y. 2011) (considering the public disclosure doctrine when tracking occurs for 113 days). *But see United States v. Wilson*, No. 1:11-CR-53-TCB-ECS-3, 2013 WL 1129199, at *5–7 (N.D. Ga. Feb. 20, 2013) (finding no Fourth Amendment violations in a request limited to cell phone tower data over a twenty-one day period).

74 *See supra* notes 43–50 and accompanying text.

Picking and Choosing Between the Doctrines: A Road to Harmony

As the previous Part illustrates, courts seem to be all over the map when it comes to analyzing cell phone location data under the Fourth Amendment and whether this data merits protection. This disagreement largely centers on which doctrine a court uses and how it uses that doctrine.

Take, for example, the application of the third-party doctrine. A major point of contention is whether a cell phone user actually *voluntarily* discloses her location when making or receiving calls. This seems like a legitimate issue on which reasonable people can disagree. Because a user's location—unlike a dialed number—is automatically transmitted after the phone turns on, this action may not qualify as a voluntary disclosure. Scholars too disagree on this point.[75] Perhaps the question of voluntariness should influence how we analyze the doctrine in this context, particularly given how prevalent cell phone use has become.

The more troubling area of disagreement, however, and the focus of this Essay, is how we should pick between the third-party and public disclosure doctrines. The analysis is not as cut-and-dried, as evidenced by the different way courts have handled this choice. And the decision seems rather consequential when one considers that the public disclosure doctrine suggests none of this data is protected. To see the problem, one needs only to look at the Third Circuit and its explicit recognition that the two doctrines lead to different conclusions on the privacy question of historical location data.[76] Things get even more complicated when considering the other kinds of cell phone location data—real-time location data and pinged data—and the different ways courts have handled them. Are we simply left with ad hoc judgments on which doctrine to use in what context, or is there some principled way for courts to make this choice?[77]

The problem centers on the unique nature of cell phone location data. On the one hand, the government can treat it like the collection of nonpublic information, no different than dialed telephone numbers (think historical location data). On the other hand, this data can also be seen as publicly available data that facilitates surveillance, no different than GPS monitoring (think real-time location data).

Historically, the collection of nonpublic information and surveillance of public movements were neatly separated. Collection of bank records, telephone numbers, and incriminating statements

---

75 *Compare* Freiwald, *supra* note 15, at 733–34 (finding voluntariness lacking), *with* Orin Kerr, *Fourth Amendment Stunner: Judge Rules that Cell-Site Data Protected by Fourth Amendment Warrant Requirement*, VOLOKH CONSPIRACY (Aug. 31, 2010, 2:46 AM), http://volokh.com/2010/08/31/fourth-amendment-stunner-judge-rules-that-cell-site-data-protected-by-fourth-amendment-warrantrequirement [http://perma.cc/X23K-PCJA] (finding sufficient voluntariness). *See also* Monu Bedi, *Texting the Government Your Location: The Case of Historical Cell Phone Location Data and Fourth Amendment Protection*, CASETEXT (Aug. 26, 2015), https://casetext.com/posts/texting-the-governmentyour-location [http://perma.cc/Q6UR-JPNR] (discussing the issue of whether users voluntarily disclose their location data).

76 *See supra* notes 53–55, 66 and accompanying text.

77 Scholarship on the subject is not much help here because those discussions are more general in nature. *See, e.g.*, Freiwald, *supra* note 15, at 733; Recent Case, *State v. Earls, 70 A.3d 630 (N.J. 2013)*, 127 HARV. L. REV. 2164 (2014).

are all information-gathering activities of nonpublic data that have nothing to do with surveillance of the suspect's physical location. On the other hand, use of beeper technology and GPS are surveillance methods of a suspect's public movements that do nothing more than relay her physical location.[78]

Police use of cell phone location data has blurred the line between these two types of activities. The first step to harmonizing the doctrines, then, is ascertaining in which context the government activity occurs with the recognition that the application of two doctrines is not mutually exclusive. I take the three scenarios in turn.

Historical Location Data

The government seeking historical location data from the cell provider stands on the same footing as the government acquiring a history of telephone numbers from the telephone company over a period of time. Both scenarios only potentially trigger an application of the third-party doctrine. The government is collecting nonpublic information from a third party. Whether the doctrine actually applies of course still depends on whether the disclosure of data to the provider is considered a voluntary one.

One may take issue with my conclusion that the public disclosure doctrine is inapplicable here. Were these movements not public at one time, thus triggering this doctrine? To be sure, the Third and Fourth Circuits discussed this doctrine at length in the context of historical location data, albeit reaching different conclusions as to its applicability.[79] But the problem here is we're talking about public data in the past tense. These *were* public movements and *at that time* the government could have surveilled the person's location using this data without first seeking a warrant. But these data points—at the point the government is now seeking them from the provider—are no longer public (i.e., susceptible to visual surveillance) and, as such, the risk of the government observing them has now passed, along with the application of the public disclosure doctrine. In fact, it seems odd to say that the government, in collecting *historical* data, is nonetheless surveilling the suspect's public movements when those movements are no longer taking place. This is not to say that the police cannot gather this historical data to conduct prospective surveillance of the suspect, but the suspect's potential *future* public movements are conceptually different from prior public movements and the collection of her historical location data. The latter are now no different than any other nonpublic information—whether it is telephone numbers, bank statements, etc.—the government acquires from a third party.[80]

---

78 I recognize that location data (whether by GPS, beeper, or cell phone use) is also a type of information, and so even in the second scenario, the government is technically "collecting information." But the key difference here is that this information (unlike telephone data) is susceptible to visual observation and facilitates surveillance of the suspect.

79 *See supra* notes 53–54, 70–73 and accompany text.

80 A potential—though ultimately unpersuasive—counterargument would be that under the public disclosure doctrine, once something has been made public, it is public for good. This line of reasoning would conclude that historical location data—because it was at one point public—is forever considered public information. This is a strained reading of the doctrine as the Court has applied it. These cases and their operative facts, *see supra* Section II.B, clearly contemplate contemporaneous visual observation. To

In some ways, this is a better outcome for those who think historical location data deserves constitutional protection. If the public disclosure doctrine does not reach this data, there is no need to argue against its application. This conclusion renders moot much of the aforementioned Fourth Circuit discussion on the more private nature of cell phone versus automobile location data, as well as the concern over large amounts of surveillance records.

That said, the privacy implications of the latter could also work as a limiting principle for the third-party doctrine. While the operative facts of *Jones* dealt with contemporaneous surveillance, a historical map of an individual's movements over a lengthy period of time may also trigger privacy concerns for the same reason (e.g., revelation of a person's political affiliation or medical treatment).[81] Whether the effects of long-term historical data collection should be part of the third-party doctrine analysis is, again, beyond the scope of this Essay.

Real-Time Location Data

Categorizing real-time location data is a bit trickier. This kind of data can potentially be analyzed under both doctrines. In one sense, the government is acquiring information from the cell phone provider, very similar to historical data or telephone numbers. Whether the third-party doctrine is triggered, however, depends in large part on how one conceptualizes the risk of exposure. Certainly, as previously explained, the main thrust of the doctrine contemplates nonpublic information. Still, one could argue that this doctrine does not require only *one* risk. In other words, an individual could be taking on both the risk that the user's location may be disclosed by the particular third party as well as the risk that it is currently susceptible to public view.[82]

This is an interesting discussion but ultimately turns out to be irrelevant when assessing Fourth Amendment protection. Whichever way one answers the question of the *potential* reach of the third-party doctrine to real-time location data, there is no privacy protection because the public disclosure doctrine obviously applies. The government is using public location data—i.e., movements susceptible to visual surveillance—to contemporaneously track a suspect.[83] This is no different than the government using a beeper or GPS device to surveil an individual.

While the applicability of the public disclosure doctrine is straightforward, the operative facts for the third-party doctrine may not be present. This is not problematic. These doctrines were never designed to both be necessary conditions for vitiating privacy protection. Take the *Knotts* case. There, *a fortiori*, the third-party doctrine does not apply because the suspect—lacking knowledge of the beeper—could not possibly have voluntarily conveyed his location

---

hold otherwise would make meaningless the surveillance activity being conducted by the police in all these cases. Moreover, this line of reasoning would also mean that once information is made public, albeit even briefly, it could never garner Fourth Amendment protection. This seems like a drastic conclusion that would have severe, unwanted implications for privacy protection.

81 *See supra* notes 45–50, 73 and accompanying text.

82 Of course, there remains the question of whether the disclosure to the cell phone provider is voluntary.

83 I assume here that the location data only reveals public locations such as the cell tower location.

to the government. This fact was not relevant to the lack of privacy protection because the suspect's public movements fell directly under the public disclosure doctrine.

The difference in Fourth Amendment protection between real-time data (*automatically not* protected under public disclosure doctrine) and historical data (*may not* be protected under the third-party doctrine) makes sense when assessing the relative privacy concerns in each scenario. With stored data, the police can have easy access to significant amounts of location history. There is no practical limitation to the timeframe they may acquire. This concern may militate in favor of having a robust requirement of voluntariness under the third-party doctrine so it is harder to acquire this information without Fourth Amendment protection. On the other hand, use of real-time data has some built-in practical limitations. It requires at least some sort contemporaneous police surveillance (even if alleviated by the relevant technology), which naturally limits how much data is collected. Here then, a straightforward application of the public disclosure doctrine may not be as detrimental to privacy concerns.

Location Data from Pinging

Analysis of the third scenario involving pinging a cell phone would work in a similar way to real-time data. Here, the third-party doctrine is clearly not applicable because there has been no disclosure by the cell phone user. It is the cell phone company—in concert with the government—that is actively sending signals to the cell phone. Once again, though, the public disclosure doctrine squarely applies because the government is tracking the public movements of the cell phone user via the provider's cell towers.[84] Those who feel that real-time location data should garner Fourth Amendment protection must argue for the Court to adopt some limiting principle—e.g., length of surveillance—to curtail the impact of the public disclosure doctrine.

---

84 This conclusion, again, assumes that the government is only receiving the cell phone tower location and not the actual location of the cell phone. Acquiring the latter through pinging the phone may sweep in nonpublic information and thus change the analysis. *See supra* note 40. A similar conclusion would potentially apply to "stingray" devices, assuming that they also only reveal public locations. These devices mimic cell phone towers and have the ability to gather location data without permission of the cell phone provider and before it reaches the cell tower. *See, e.g.*, Brian L. Owsley, *Spies in the Skies: Dirtboxes and Airplane Electronic Surveillance*, 113 MICH. L. REV. FIRST IMPRESSIONS 75, 76 (2015). While scholars and courts seem to find that these devices constitute a search under the Fourth Amendment, *In re Application of the United States for an Order Authorizing the Installation and Use of a Pen Register and Trap and Trace Device*, 890 F. Supp. 2d 747, 752 (S.D. Tex. 2012); Owsley, *supra*; Stephanie K. Pell & Christopher Soghoian, *Your Secret StingRay's No Secret Anymore: The Vanishing Government Monopoly over Cell Phone Surveillance and Its Impact on National Security and Consumer Privacy*, 28 HARV. J.L. & TECH. 1, 32 (2014), a straightforward application of the public disclosure doctrine would suggest otherwise because these movements would be susceptible to visual observation.

Conclusion

The lessons here go beyond cell phone location data. If there is anything to be certain of, it is that technology will continue to advance. This inevitably will lead police to having better information-gathering capacity and surveillance ability. Unless the Court acts, the third-party and public disclosure doctrines will continue to stand as two central hurdles to Fourth Amendment protection in these situations. It is important we understand the historical context and unique contours of each doctrine. Only then can we intelligently discuss whether and how they should, or should not, apply to future technologies.

CHAPTER 3

Conclusion

Security and privacy do not need to be two competing forces. Sometimes privacy is ensured through security. For example, your bank's ability to keep your information secure will determine whether your private financial information will be stolen. In the context of criminal justice, however, they oftentimes serve as tradeoffs of one another. If we allow a criminal, or even a terrorist, to maintain privacy, it will be a great threat to our safety and security. On the other hand, if we expose everyone's private life under the spotlight, it will be hard for the bad guys to plan bad things, but it will also be hard for the good guys to maintain dignity. Some people like to say if you have nothing to hide, then you should not worry about the government's surveillance on you. There is truth in this statement. Nonetheless, most people probably prefer to keep certain things private even if they are not illegal. Would you like to share your phone with strangers even if you are not committing crime through your phone? If it is guaranteed that there is no real harm as long as you are not a criminal, would you be willing to make your private life visible to some unknown party without knowing when and where they are watching? Perhaps you do not care, but it does not mean those who care are wrong. As a democratic society that values civil rights, we should discuss the balance between security and privacy in the context of criminal justice. The dilemma is that we must invade a person's privacy to prove the person is a criminal, but most of the time the person whose privacy is being invaded is not a criminal. Unless we accept it is okay to treat everyone like a criminal before proven guilty, some legal and moral safeguard should be in place to avoid privacy invasion becoming abusive.

Discussion Questions

1. How does the Fourth Amendment protect privacy?
2. How has the PATRIOT Act made Fourth Amendment rights flexible?
3. Should the police be allowed to collect cell phone data without a warrant?
4. Hypothetically, the government is scanning all emails and text messages you send in an effort to identify terrorists. Should they be allowed to do so? Why?
5. Imagine someone told the authorities you are communicating with terrorists over the phone and the Internet. You have been suspected to be planning an attack. In this case, what should the police do to verify this allegation and start an investigation?

CHAPTER 4

Mental Illness and Crime

Introduction

Mental illness has become one of the most serious threats to society in terms of public safety as well as public health. It induces tremendous social costs that involve not only money but also disrupted interpersonal relationships that serve as the foundation of our social structure. Certainly, mental illness is essentially a health issue, and patients suffering from such illness need care rather than judgment. However, it would be too naïve to dismiss the potential link between mental illness and crime. This is not to say all criminals are mentally ill or all mentally ill people are bound to become a criminal. Nonetheless, in the context of criminal justice, we can no longer afford to overlook the impact that mental illness has on society and the criminal justice system.

The link between mental illness and crime has long been portrayed in movies and TV shows. Despite the dramatic effect used in those entertaining productions, one cannot help but notice some similarities in a few real-life crimes. For example, a cult leader who seemingly has mental issues and urges his followers to kill innocent strangers exists in real life too. A mentally unstable person who decided to go on a killing spree for self-righteous reasons also has been reported in some recent tragic events. It is easy to link their criminal behavior to their pre-existing mental issues in hindsight, but it is not easy to label someone as a threat before they actually do harm. Even if we know who is a threat, a more pertinent question is what we can do to help people before they engage in harmful action. Help is a concept easy to understand, but it is a task very difficult to achieve when it comes to mental illness because most of us do not possess the skills or knowledge required to be helpful. Moreover, people with mental illness may not believe they need help, or they may be aware of the problem but still refuse to seek help. Since it is a complex situation, we need a system that recognizes the problem and implements effective solutions to decrease the threat posed by mental illness. Unfortunately, our current criminal justice system is not very effective in dealing with mental illness issues. Many police officers do not know how to interact with mentally ill people without engaging in violence, and our prisons certainly are not doing much to alleviate the problem, either.

In this chapter, there are two articles to read. The first one, "Mental Disorder and Crime," addresses the link between mental illness and crime. As stressed, this is not an accusation that aims to stigmatize mental illness. Rather, it is a realistic review on how mental illness could be associated with crime, which is a valuable view because without addressing the root cause, punishment alone will be useless in preventing or deterring crime. The second article, "Mental Illness and Prisoners," addresses a different aspect of the issue. Although most people know that prisons should not be used as mental institutions, the reality is most prisons are currently housing a very high percentage of mentally ill inmates. Some of them had pre-existing mental conditions before they went to prison and some of them developed mental issues while living inside a prison. Either way, life in prison does not exactly provide an environment that helps improve mental conditions. Most patients see their conditions deteriorating inside and continue to worsen even after they leave prison because these people are the least likely to receive the adequate medical care or mental care they need, no matter where they are.

When reading these articles, students should think about how this vicious cycle can be ended. More than 95 percent of prisoners will come back to society someday, and when they come back with severe mental illness it will be a burden on the society, even if they do not commit crime again. Further, what should we do with criminals with obvious mental problems? Is it more important to punish them or to cure them? Students may think about these questions not just from a justice point of view but also from a social cost standpoint. It is noteworthy that mentally ill people are also more likely to be victimized, and victimization is another type of social cost.

READING 6

Mental Disorder and Crime

Clive R. Hollin

[... A] crime has two elements: *actus reus*, the criminal act, and *mens rea*, the intent to commit the act or 'guilty mind'. It was also noted that there are instances where some individuals, such as children below the age of criminal responsibility, are judged not to have the capacity for criminal intent and therefore do not face criminal proceedings. Another class of people who may not have the capacity for criminal intent are those people with a mental disorder.

The Law and the Mentally Disordered Offender

The notion of a mentally disordered offender has a reasonably long history in English law, with the case of Daniel M'Naghten (1813–65) generally taken to be the beginning of mental health legislation with regard to criminal acts (Quen, 1968). The name M'Naghten is spelt differently in various sources where it appears as McNaughton, M'Naghten, M'Naughton (in the original trial report), McNaughton, and McNaughten (in the records from Bethlem and Broadmoor Hospitals): the family spelling was McNaughtan and the extant example of M'Naghten's signature is spelt McNaughtun.

An overview of the M'Naghten case is given in Box 6.1.

The verdict in the M'Naghten trial of not guilty on the ground of insanity caused a public outcry and even an expression of concern from the reigning monarch, Queen Victoria. In response to these pressures, the House of Lords ordered the Lords of Justice of the Queen's Bench to produce a definition of criminal insanity. The Lords of Justice concluded that, in order to establish a defence on the ground of insanity, it must be clearly proved that at the time of committing the act the accused was

Clive R. Hollin, "Mental Disorder and Crime," *Psychology and Crime: An Introduction to Criminological Psychology*, pp. 206-237.

BOX 6.1 DANIEL M'NAGHTEN

A great deal of the detail about Daniel M'Naghten has been gathered from records of the evidence given at his trial and the various newspaper reports of the time.

M'Naghten was born in 1813 in Scotland, probably Glasgow, the illegitimate son of a Glasgow woodturner and landlord, also called Daniel M'Naghten. When his mother, Ada, died M'Naghten went to live with his father's family and worked at his father's workshop in Glasgow: he eventually left his father's employ and, after a 3-year sojourn as an actor he set up his own woodturning workshop in Glasgow in 1835. The business ran successfully for 5 years until in 1840 he sold it and spent the following 2 years in London, Glasgow, and France.

It appears that M'Naghten was hardworking and careful with his money. He attended classes and became educated, taught himself French, and is recorded as holding somewhat radical political opinions. His sympathies lay with the Chartists, a working-class organisation advocating profound social and political reform in Great Britain and Ireland and who were involved in the General Strike of 1842.

In 1841, while resident in Glasgow, he variously complained to his father, to the Glasgow commissioner of police, and to an MP that he was being persecuted and spied upon by the Tories. His claims were not believed and was seen to be deluded.

M'Naghten's place in legal history was sealed on the afternoon of 20 January 1843. On that date the Prime Minister's private secretary, a civil servant called Edward Drummond, was walking from Charing Cross towards Downing Street. M'Naghten approached him from behind, drew a pistol and fired into Drummond's back from close range; before he could fire a second pistol he was overcome by a police constable. It is assumed that M'Naghten thought that he had shot the Prime Minister, Robert Peel. At first it appeared that Drummond's wounds were not fatal but there were complications and he died 5 days later.

M'Naghten appeared at Bow Street Magistrates' Court the morning after the shooting. In a brief statement he told the court how his persecution by the Tories had driven him to the violent act. His trial for 'wilful murder' took place in 1843 at the Old Bailey in London. When asked in court to plead, M'Naghten said 'I was driven to desperation by persecution' and 'I am guilty of firing'.

At his trial the prosecution and the defence agreed that M'Naghten suffered from delusions of persecution. They therefore both advanced their case on the basis of what constituted a legal defence of insanity. The prosecution took the position that, regardless of his delusions, M'Naghten was able to distinguish right from wrong and it therefore followed that was responsible for the crime. The defence argued, supported by the testimony of medical experts, that M'Naghten's delusions had led to a breakdown of his moral sense and his loss of self-control and so that he could not be held as reasonable and responsible for his actions.

The prosecution elected not to produce any medical witnesses to testify against the defence and the trial was stopped. The judge, Chief Justice Tindal, informed the jury that that if they returned a verdict of not guilty on the ground of insanity, then M'Naghten would receive proper care. The jury duly returned a verdict of not guilty on the ground of insanity.

M'Naghten was taken from the Old Bailey to the State Criminal Lunatic Asylum at Bethlem Hospital under the 1800 Act for the Safe Custody of Insane Persons Charged with Offences. It is recoded that his hospital admission documents stated 'Imagines the Tories are his enemies, shy and retiring in his manner'. M'Naghten spent 21 years at Bethlem and in his later years developed diabetes and a heart condition. An ill man, he was moved in 1864 to the newly opened Broadmoor Asylum where he died on 3 May 1865.

labouring under such a defect of reason from disease of the mind that they did not to know the nature and quality of the act their actions; or, if they did know of their actions, then they did not know that what they were doing was wrong. This conclusion has become enshrined in law and is known as the *M'Naghten Rules*.

The M'Naghten case is significant in legal history because it gave rise to the first serious attempt to modify criminal law with respect to mentally incompetent defendants. It is now held that the M'Naghten Rules embody two tests: first, it is the responsibility of the defence to show that at the time of the offence the accused did not know the nature and quality of their actions; second, that the accused did not know that their actions were wrong. In those cases where these tests are satisfied, then the accused may be judged to be 'not guilty by reason of insanity' and the sentence of the court may be a period of treatment, sometimes indeterminate, in a secure hospital rather than a punitive disposal such as a fine or imprisonment.

The M'Naghten Rules continue to hold sway in England and Wales and there are similar legal conventions in other parts of the world. In the USA, the trial in 1881 of Charles Guiteau, who assassinated President James A. Garfield (who actually died several months after the shooting), raised similar issues. It can be surmised from the historical records that Guiteau was mentally disordered and today would probably have been diagnosed with paranoia. Guiteau was executed by hanging, but his high-profile case raised awareness of how best in law to deal with the mentally disordered offender. In the USA, rules similar to the M'Naghten Rules were as adopted in most jurisdictions (Kelly, 2009), but legislatures and courts eventually modified the rules so that there is now some variation across the USA.

In the time since the formation of the M'Naghten Rules, the law in England and Wales with regard to individuals with a mental disorder who commit a criminal act is contained in the Mental Health Act. As with most other legislation, the Mental Health Act has moved through several revisions since it was first introduced, as seen with the 1959 and 1983 Mental Health Acts. The 1957 Homicide Act also introduced the notion of *diminished responsibility*, allowing a defence for homicide to be made on the basis of proof of substantially impaired mental responsibility.

The 1983 Mental Health Act made the distinction between four types of mental disorder, namely mental illness, mental impairment, severe mental impairment, and psychopathic disorder. The most recent Mental Health Act of 2007 has, as summarised in Table 6.1, made a number of changes to the 1983 Act.

While the legislation may change both over time and from jurisdiction to jurisdiction, the legal systems of many counties—including England and Wales (Bradley, 2009; James, 2010), Ireland (Duffy, Linehan, & Kennedy, 2006), Germany (Konrad & Lau, 2010), Sweden (Svennerlind et al., 2010), the European Community generally (Salize, Dreßing, & Kief, 2007), Australia (Richardson & McSherry, 2010), Japan (Yoshikawa et al., 2007)—continue to grapple with the issues posed by the mentally disordered offender.

TABLE 6.1 Some of the changes introduced by the 2007 Mental Health Act

The 2007 Act abolished the four categories of mental disorder used in the 1983 Act—mental illness, mental impairment, severe mental impairment and psychopathic disorder—and replaced them with 'any disorder or disability of the mind'.

The types of mental disorders included in the 2007 Act are specifically noted as mental illnesses such as schizophrenia, bipolar disorder, anxiety or depression, personality disorders, eating disorders, autistic spectrum disorders and learning disabilities. A brain disorder or disability is not taken to be a mental disorder unless it also gives rise to a disability or disorder of the mind.

The Association Between Mental Disorder and Crime

There is no doubt that there is a section of population who have a diagnosable mental disorder and who also commit criminal acts (Hodgins, 1993; Markowitz, 2011). The evidence in support of this statement comes both from surveys of mental disorder in offender populations and from surveys of criminal behaviour in mentally disordered populations.

Gunn, Robertson, Dell, and Way (1978) used a combination of questionnaire and interview to assess the psychiatric morbidity of more than 600 prisoners in two English prisons. They found that between 20 and 30 per cent of the prisoners had a marked or severe psychiatric condition: depression was prevalent in almost half of the diagnosed cases; anxiety states were evident in a further one-third; drug and alcohol problems were widespread; and schizophrenia was less common. This type of survey is important in giving a snapshot of the penal population at a given time (see also Brugha et al., 2005; Singleton, Meltzer, Gatward, Coid, & Deasy, 1998; Sirdifield, Gojkovica, Brooker, & Ferriter, 2009). The pattern of a high prevalence of mental disorder, widespread alcohol and drug addiction, and physical health problems has been recorded in several studies of prison populations, both male and female, in several European countries (Dressing, Kief, & Salize, 2009; Eytan et al., 2011; Fotiadou, Livaditis, Manou, Kaniotou, & Xenitidis, 2006).

However, as shown by Prins (1980) in his overview of studies of the prevalence of mental disorder in offender populations, there can be wide variations in findings. This variation may be a function of the year when the study took place, the population included in the study, and the country in which the study took place. These variations serve as a reminder that the generalisation of research findings over time may be problematic given changes in the law regarding the definition and disposal of mentally disordered offenders. Further, the process of diagnosis may vary across studies according to both the date of the study and the country in which it was conducted. Nonetheless, the levels of psychiatric problems among imprisoned offenders are above the levels evident in the general population.

An American study of a prison population reported by Silver, Felson, and Vaneseltine (2008) looked at the relationship between mental health problems and violence. It was found that mental illness was likely to be associated with violent offences and sexual offences (violent and non-violent). The offences of mentally ill prisoners were also likely to be more deviant in that they were perpetrated against younger victims or the offender's own child. Silver et al. (2008: 423) conclude: 'Our evidence, therefore, suggests that mental illness is a causal factor in deviant behavior, some of which involves violence, and that the more deviant the behavior, the greater the effect of mental illness'. Another American study found that those prisoners with mental health problems are also likely to return to prison sooner than those without such problems (Cloyes, Wong, Latimer, & Abarca, 2010).

Surveys have also considered the prevalence of intellectual disability and psychopathy in prison populations. Fazel, Xenitidis, and Powell (2008) conducted a systematic review of the literature on the prevalence of intellectual disabilities among prisoners. This review included the findings from 10 surveys—variously conducted between 1988 and 1997 in Australia, Dubai, England and Wales, New Zealand, and the USA—with an overall sample size of 11,969 male and female prisoners. Fazel et al. reported that their findings indicated that between 0.5 per cent and 1.5 per cent of prisoners had a clinical diagnosis of an intellectual disability. This level of intellectual disability is comparable with levels found among the general population.

Finally, a number of surveys have been concerned with the prevalence of personality disorder and psychopathy (see below for a discussion of psychopathy) in prison populations. The estimates of psychopathy vary considerably from country to county: Coid et al. (2009a: 134) commented that '[t]here are remarkable differences in reported prevalence rates of psychopathy among samples of prisoners in different countries within a range of 3% to 73%'. Coid et al. (2009a) conducted a survey of the prevalence of psychopathy in a sample of 496 male and female prisoners in England and Wales. They found that the prevalence of psychopathy was 7.7 per cent in the male prisoners and 1.9 per cent in the female prisoners. This rate is much higher than would be expected in the general population, which is approximately 0.6 per cent (Coid et al., 2009b). However, given that the standard measure of psychopathy, the Psychopathy Checklist-Revised (PCL-R; Hare, 2003), includes items relating to anti-social behaviour and traits such as lying and impulsivity, it is not surprising that elevated prevalence rates are found in prison populations.

As several commentators have noted, a high prevalence of mental disorder in offender populations may be a function of disproportionate rates of arrest (Constantine et al., 2010), or the mentally disordered person being more likely to be charged or to plead guilty in court, if only for their own protection (Feldman, 1977). Further, the presence of a mental disorder when an offender is in prison does not necessarily mean that the disorder was present at the time of the crime. It is possible that the highly aversive conditions in many prisons may lead to the onset of or exacerbate a mental disorder (Yang, Kadouri, Révah-Lévy, Mulvey, & Falissard, 2009; Wormith, 1984).

As well as offenders within the criminal justice system, there are also patients resident within the psychiatric health care system who have committed criminal acts: these patients, including female patients (Long, Hall, Craig, Mochty, & Hollin, 2011), are evident within low security and community psychiatric services as well as high security services (Logan & Blackburn, 2009). In the same way as national statistics are gathered about offenders within the criminal justice system, so the same is true of mentally disordered offender. The Ministry of Justice publishes an annual bulletin that gives details of offenders subject to restriction orders or detained in secure psychiatric hospitals. The Ministry of Justice Bulletin for 2008 states that the total number of mentally disordered offenders detained in hospital at the end of 2008 in England and Wakes was 3,937: this population was composed of 3,460 males and 477 females (Ministry of Justice, 2010).

In England and Wales there are three high security hospitals: Ashworth Hospital in Liverpool, which has beds for about 500 patients; Broadmoor Hospital in Surry, which has about 250 patients; and Rampton Hospital in Nottinghamshire with about 400 patients. Scotland has a high security hospital for about 140 patients at Carstairs, South Lanarkshire, which also receives patients from Northern Ireland. These high security hospitals, previously known as *special hospitals*, are for those people with a mental disorder who are judged to be too great a risk to the community to be at liberty. There are several infamous people, including Beverley Allitt, Ian Brady, and Peter Sutcliffe, who are currently residing in the secure hospital system.

The high security hospitals are the tip of a large iceberg when considering the numbers of people detained in conditions of varying levels of security. A Ministry of Justice Report (2010: 3) notes that at the end of 2008 there were 3,937 people detained in hospital: the report comments that this figure 'represents a one per cent increase on the 2007 figure and the highest figure for the last decade. There has been a general increase in the number of restricted patients detained over the last ten years'. The relative percentage of male and female patients has, however, remained reasonably consistent at 11–13 per cent for females and 87–89 per cent for males.

There are people with a mental disorder who commit acts that, through due process of law, lead to their detention in secure hospital conditions for the safety of the wider community. However, the association between mental disorder and criminal behaviour requires an explanation: is it simply the case that mental disorder and criminal behaviour may occasionally coincide, in which case their relationship is correlational; or can mental disorder be the cause of the criminal behaviour?

The Relationship Between Mental Disorder and Crime

The relationship between mental disorder and criminal behaviour is one that is likely to unfold over the individual's lifespan. The aetiology of the relationship may be complex involving an interplay between disorders of childhood and adolescence such as attention-deficit/hyperactivity disorder (ADHD), anti-social behaviour, educational difficulties, social dysfunction and emerging major psychiatric disorders (Hofvander et al., 2011; Schilling, Walsh, & Yun, 2010). In addition, traumatic events such as childhood abuse may be associated with the development of both mental disorder and anti-social and criminal behaviour (Silberman, 2010). As well as adults, there are juveniles, both male and female, who commit crimes and who also have a psychiatric disorder (McReynolds, Schwalbe, & Wasserman, 2010). It is also the case that conduct disorders in childhood and adolescence may be antecedent to the development of schizophrenia (see Hodgins, 2008).

The causality game is a difficult one to play in the social sciences generally and, given the complexity of the issues, especially so in relation to mental disorder and crime. Thus, there are discussions to be had about the separation of mind (with the familiar debate about the concept of mind) and body in accounting for human behaviour; about the role of environmental, social, cultural, and biological variables; and about satisfying the conditions of research designs that may help to infer causality between two factors (Anckarsäter, Radovic, Svennerlind, Höglund, & Radovic, 2009; Buchanan & Zonana, 2009; Dahlin, Gumpert, Torstensson-Levander, Svensson, & Rodovic, 2009). The philosophical and other concerns regarding the origin, nature, and limits of human knowledge are not without practical implications. Buchanan and Zonana (2009) make the point that legal support for mental disorder as a cause of crime and as a criterion for culpability have been erratic. They provide the example of the inconsistencies by which different jurisdictions within the USA vary in the way they treat the nature of the relationship between mental disorder and criminal behaviour in formulation of a defence on the grounds of insanity.

The evidence that informs our understanding of criminal behaviour by individuals with a mental disorder should be seen against the backdrop of the shifting debate regarding the nature of the relationship between mental disorder and criminal behaviour. This shift, as shown in Table 6.1, is exemplified by the abolition in the Mental Health Act 2007 of the various categories of mental disorder contained in the 1983 Act and their replacement by the generic 'any disorder or disability of the mind'. Nonetheless, with this legal change in mind, the old categories of *mental illness*, *mental impairment*, and *psychopathic disorder* provide a useful way of ordering the literature. In practice, an individual may be diagnosed with two concurrent or *comorbid* mental disorders: for example, it is not uncommon for psychosis to be comorbid with alcohol or drug addiction.

Mental Illness and Crime

The term *mental illness* encompasses a wide range of conditions including psychosis, depression, and anxiety states. The criminological literature, however, is dominated by research concerned with the relationship between psychosis and criminal behaviour, particularly violent behaviour.

Psychosis

The term 'psychosis' does not refer to a specific mental disorder, rather to a cluster of disturbances of psychological functioning. Douglas, Guy, and Hart (2009: 681) offer a succinct explanation: 'Psychosis is a syndrome found in mental disorders such as schizophrenia, delusional disorders, bipolar mood disorder, and some forms of severe depression. The syndrome comprises symptoms reflecting profound disturbances in thought, perception, and behaviour'.

Disturbances in thought include delusions and disruption in the process of making associations between thoughts. The nature of the perceptual disturbances can be seen in hallucinations, which may be visual or tactile but are most commonly auditory and typically experienced as hearing voices. The behavioural disturbances may be bizarre facial grimaces, repeated gesturing, excited physical agitation, or holding an unusual posture for a long period. In addition, affect can be flat and expressionless or inappropriate to the situation.

These disturbances cluster to form three domains: (1) a *positive* domain characterised by the presence of disturbances such as delusions; (2) a *negative* domain as seen in the absence of affect; (3) a disorganised domain as with disordered communication and displays of inappropriate affect.

The criminological research in this area is not uniform, with some studies concentrating on a specific disorder, as for example with the substantial literature given to schizophrenia, while some studies prefer the broader term psychosis and others use the generic mental illness. In the following section, the exact nature of the condition is specified where possible.

Hodgins (2008: 2505) opens her overview of violent behaviour among people with schizophrenia with the following statement: 'There is now robust evidence demonstrating that both men and women with schizophrenia are at elevated risk when compared to the general population to be convicted of non-violent criminal offences, at higher risk to be convicted of violent criminal offences, and at even higher risk to be convicted of homicide'. There is a substantial body of research evidence that Hodgins draws upon in support of this position, including large-scale cohort studies focussed on a specific type of crime, systematic reviews, and meta-analyses.

Exemplars of these types of study are discussed below. While most studies are concerned with violence in the community, it is also the case that violence, sometimes serious violence, occurs within in-patient settings (Hodgins, Alderton, Cree, Aboud, & Mak, 2007; Hodgins, Cree, Alderton, & Mak, 2008).

Cohort Studies

An Australian study by Wallace, Mullen, and Burgess (2004) compared the criminal records, over a 25-year period, of a cohort of 2,861 male and female patients who had contact with psychiatric services for schizophrenia with a matched sample drawn from the same community. It was found that the patients with schizophrenia were more likely to have received a criminal conviction than the comparison group (21.6 per cent and 7.8 per cent): this pattern was evident for both the male and female patients. With regard to type of crime, the frequency of violent offending was higher in the schizophrenic patients than the comparison group (8.2 per cent and 1.8 per cent), with the majority of the violent offences in both groups committed by men. There were four schizophrenic patients convicted of murder and none in the comparison group. The same basic pattern as with violent offences was found with property-related offences and substance-related offences. The male schizophrenia patients were more likely to be convicted of a sexual offence than the comparison group (1.8 per cent and 0.7 percent), with only nine women convicted of this type of offence.

Wallace et al. also noted that 327 patients with schizophrenia had a comorbid diagnosis of substance use disorder. The rates of offending were higher among patients with a known substance abuse problem. Wallace et al. made the observation that while the patients' rates of crime rose over the 25 years spanned by the study, the same was also true of the comparison group.

A German study reported by Soyka, Graz, Bottlender, Dirschedl, and Schoech (2007) reviewed the criminal records of a cohort of 1,662 patients with schizophrenia up to 12 years after their discharge from psychiatric hospital. It was found that just over 1 in 10 patients committed one or more crimes after discharge. The majority of the crimes were non-violent, such as theft and fraud, with a smaller number of violent crimes, mainly physical assault, and one case of murder. There were a substantial number of drug offences which, as Soyka et al. suggest, most probably reflects the frequent comorbidity of schizophrenia and substance misuse. There were only two cases involving sex offences, one sexual assault and one rape. However, a study of psychotic disorders and sex offending in a Danish cohort of 358,180 people born between 1944 and 1947 reported higher levels of sex offending among those with a psychotic disorder (Alden, Brennan, Hodgins, & Mednick, 2007). Specifically, Alden et al. found that, across the cohort, 2.2 per cent of the men were admitted to psychiatric hospital with a psychotic disorder. When compared with the other, non-psychotic, men in the cohort, an interesting pattern emerged: the psychotic men were three times more likely than the non-psychotic men to have been arrested for non-physically aggressive sexual offences such as exhibitionism and voyeurism. When the psychosis was comorbid with personality disorder or substance use disorder, the risk of non-physically aggressive sexual offending, again compared with the non-psychotic men, was three to five times greater, while the risk of physically aggressive offences, such as rape, was six times greater. Alden et al. also reported that 2.6 per cent of the women in the cohort were admitted to hospital with a psychotic disorder: there were 3 women (0.07 per cent) with a psychotic disorder arrested for a sexual offences compared with 19 non-psychotic women (0.01 per cent). Thus, as found in mainstream offender populations, sexual offending among those with a psychotic disorder is primarily committed by men.

A Swedish cohort study reported by Fazel, Grann, Carlström, Lichtenstein, and Långström (2009a) looked at patients with two or more periods of hospitalisation for schizophrenia: the cohort consisted of 8,891 men and 4,951 women who were followed up over an average period of 12 years. It was found that just over 17 per cent of the men and 5.6 per cent of the women were convicted of a violent offence after their discharge from hospital. Physical assault was the most common type of crime followed by threats and harassment, with very few sexual offences: there were 109 homicides committed by men and 16 by women. The strongest risk factors for violent convictions were previous violent crime, comorbid drug, and alcohol abuse—which increased the risk by a factor of two for women and by a factor of four in men—and parental violent crime.

Systematic Reviews and Meta-Analyses

Bonta, Law, and Hanson (1998) conducted a meta-analytic review to investigate whether the predictors of recidivism are different in mainstream and mentally disordered offender populations. The meta-analysis was conducted on 58 studies, incorporating 64 unique samples. The findings indicated that the strongest predictors of recidivism, for both general offending and violent offending, were the same for mentally disordered offenders as for mainstream offenders. The strong predictors were *criminal history* variables such as a juvenile delinquency, previous violent and non-violent offences, and the seriousness of previous offences; and *deviant lifestyle* variables such as family problems, low levels of employment, and substandard accommodation. In the personal domain, the strong predictors were age, male, antisocial personality, and a history of substance misuse. Bonta et al. (1998: 139) conclude: 'The results support the theoretical perspective that the major correlates of crime are the same, regardless of race, gender, class, and the presence or absence of a mental illness'. It follows that understanding the criminal behaviour of mentally disordered offenders requires engagement with criminology and social psychology as much, if not more, than psychopathology.

A British study reported by Phillips et al. (2005) used the findings of the Bonta et al. (1998) meta-analysis to investigate the prediction of reoffending among mentally disordered offenders. They found that it was predominately the criminogenic variables, such as age at first offence and number of previous offences, which were the most powerful predictors of all types of further offending. Clinical diagnosis alone lacked any predictive power.

Douglas et al. (2009) carried out a meta-analysis involving 204 studies concerned with psychosis as a risk factor for interpersonal violence. They found that 'psychosis was reliably associated with a 49%–68% increased likelihood of violence' (Douglas et al., 2009: 692). However, there were several moderators to take into account when looking at the overall finding: in particular, the association was significant when the psychosis was schizophrenia but it was not significant for affective psychoses. Douglas et al. make the point that it may well not be good research practice to aggregate different disorders under the generic heading of psychosis.

Large, Smith, and Nielssen (2009) conducted a meta-analysis of 25 studies concerned with the relationship between schizophrenia and homicide. They reported that approximately one in 20 homicide offenders had a diagnosis of schizophrenia, which is higher than would be anticipated from the overall prevalence of schizophrenia in the community. Large et al. suggest that this pattern of findings provides confirmatory evidence for the association between schizophrenia and homicide. However, an association does not demonstrate causality: there may be factors common to both the rate of homicide and to variations in the incidence of schizophrenia. Large et al. suggest that these factors may include the availability of weapons, social deprivation, and substance use.

Fazel, Gulati et al. (2009) conducted a systematic review and meta-analysis, incorporating 20 individual studies and involving a total of 18,423 cases, of research investigating the association between violence and schizophrenia (and other psychoses). Fazel et al. recorded four principal findings: (1) there is an increased risk of violence in those people with schizophrenia compared with the general population; (2) comorbid substance use substantially increases the risk of violence; (3) there were a cluster of variables, including whether the diagnosis was schizophrenia or other psychosis and the country in which the study took place, which did *not* influence the outcome; (4) the increased risk of violence with comorbid substance use was no different to the risk of violence for people with a primary diagnosis of substance use disorder.

The evidence concerning psychosis and criminal behaviour highlights two related areas: first, the association between schizophrenia and acts of violence; second, the high levels of co-morbidity with schizophrenia and alcohol abuse in relation to violence.

As discussed above, there are several clusters of clinical symptoms that define schizophrenia. Is there any evidence that there are any particular symptoms of schizophrenia that are related to criminal behaviour? There is some indication that certain symptoms, collectively known as 'control/threat override'—delusions such as someone is trying inflict personal harm, or control your mind, or command you to act in certain ways—are related to violence (Link, Stueve, & Phelen, 1998). However, it is debatable whether there is a direct link between these symptoms and acts of violence and the association is probably mediated by other psychological factors such as personality, the acuity of the symptoms, and previous experience of violence (Appelbaum, Robbins, & Monahan, 2000; Braham, Trower, & Birchwood, 2004; Spidel, Lecomte, Greaves, Sahlstrom, & Yuille, 2010). Skeem et al. (2006) found that it was elevated levels of anger, rather than clusters of symptoms, in the week before the violent episode that best predicted serious violence. In this respect, the acts of violence by high-risk patients are not substantially different to those found in mainstream violent populations [...].

Large and Nielssen (2010) reported a review and meta-analysis of nine studies concerned with violence in first episode psychosis. They found that on average one-third of those people presenting for treatment of first episode psychosis had committed an act of violence. The majority of the acts of violence were relatively minor but there were some serious incidents. The specific association between schizophrenia and homicide has been examined in several studies.

A Swedish study by Fazel, Buxrud, Ruchkin, and Grann (2010) compared 47 individuals who committed homicide within 6 months of discharge from a psychiatric hospital with 105 people who did not commit any violent offence after discharge. The diagnoses on admission were schizophrenia, bipolar disorder, and other psychoses. In comparing the two groups, the factors on admission associated with homicide included poor self-care (including not taking prescribed medication), substance misuse, previous hospitalisation for a violent episode, and having a severe mental illness for 1 year prior to admission. There was no relationship between homicide and depression or the presence of delusions or hallucinations.

In a survey of perpetrators of homicide in England and Wales, Meehan et al. (2006) reviewed the cases, including psychiatric reports, of 1,594 people who had been convicted of homicide in England and Wales between 1996 and 1999. They reported that of these 1,594 individuals there were 85 (5 per cent) with schizophrenia. Where data were available for these 85 people, just over half had been ill for less than a year, and just over one-quarter had had no previous contact with psychiatric services. In terms of the pertinent clinical features, Meehan et al. pointed the role of delusions and particularly the intensity of the individual's emotional response to their delusions in the days leading up to the offence.

There may also be gender differences in the quality of the violent acts committed by people with psychosis (Taylor & Bragado-Jimenez, 2009). Flynn, Abel, Menta, and Shaw (2011) gathered data on 4,126 men and 446 women who had been convicted of homicide in England and Wales between 1997 and 2004. They reported that significantly more of the women had a lifetime history of mental illness (which included schizophrenia, depression, and personality disorder) than the men, and that at the time the offence took place the women were more likely than the men to be to be mentally ill. There were also gender differences with regard to the victim: women were more likely to kill family members, including their own children; men were more likely to kill acquaintances or strangers.

A study of filicide by mentally ill mothers in New Zealand, reported by Stanton, Simpson, and Wouldes (2000), found that the women were experiencing their mental state as extremely distressing at the time they killed their child. The women said that they committed the offence for altruistic reasons, such as saving the child from a stressful life, or as part of their own attempted suicide.

Walsh et al. (2010) looked another form of violence, intimate partner violence, among 225 male and 111 female psychiatric patients (psychotic disorders and depression were among a range of diagnoses). They found higher rates of intimate partner violence for women but more violence towards people other than their partner among men. The men were characterised by higher levels of psychopathic traits and anti-social personality disorder as well as substance use disorders, while the women showed higher rates of borderline personality disorder and anxiety.

Alcohol Abuse

Substance use, particularly alcohol and cannabis, is known to be prevalent among people with schizophrenia (Eriksson, Tengström, & Hodgins, 2006). Indeed, Volkow (2009) estimates that almost half of those with schizophrenia will have a lifetime substance use disorder.

Fazel et al. (2009a), continuing the series of studies from Sweden, considered the relationship between schizophrenia, substance abuse, and violent crime using longitudinal data gathered between 1973 and 2006. They compared the rates of conviction for a violent crime—including homicide, assault, robbery, arson, and sexual offences—of a group of 8,003 individuals after their diagnosis of schizophrenia with a non-schizophrenic control group drawn from the general population. For those people with schizophrenia, 13.2 per cent had one or more violent offences compared with 5.3 per cent of the control group. However, when the schizophrenia was comorbid with substance abuse, the rate of violent offending was three times greater than when the schizophrenia was not comorbid with substance abuse. Fazel, Gulati, Linsell, Geddes, and Grann (2009b: 12) suggest: 'Individuals with substance use disorders may be more dangerous than individuals with schizophrenia and other psychoses, and that the psychoses comorbid with substance abuse may confer no additional risk over and above the risk associated with the substance abuse'.

As Hodgins and Janson (2002) note, there are three broad types of explanation for criminality within mentally disordered populations. The first is increased likelihood of arrest and conviction, the second is a dearth of effective treatment, and the third concerns the role of psychotic symptoms. The third of these explanations, particularly within schizophrenia research, has expanded to include neurobiological and neuropsychological correlates of mental disorder and criminal behaviour.

Neurological Factors

In their overview of the literature, Naudts and Hodgins (2006a,b) point to two groups of people with schizophrenia who commit crimes. The first are adults with schizophrenia who have a stable lifetime pattern of anti-social and aggressive behaviour; the second are adults with schizophrenia but with no history of anti-social or aggressive behaviour. Naudts and Hodgins (2006b) concluded their overview by pointing to variations in functioning between these two groups: those people with schizophrenia and a lifetime history of anti-social and aggressive behaviour when compared with those with schizophrenia but no such history, perform less well on assessments of orbitofrontal functions, have fewer neurological soft signs, more abnormalities of the orbitofrontal system and of white matter in the amygdala-orbitofrontal system, and smaller reductions in hippocampal volume. Yang et al. (2010) also pointed to reduced hippocampal volumes as a characteristic of murderers with schizophrenia.

Schug and Raine (2009) conducted meta-analyses of neuropsychological functioning in anti-social schizophrenic people. They found that anti-social schizophrenic people were characterised by lower levels of intellectual functioning when compared both with people with schizophrenia who were not anti-social and with people who were not schizophrenic. The anti-social schizophrenic group were also characterised by deficits across a range of areas of functioning, including full-scale IQ, verbal and performance IQ, attention, executive function and memory. However, it was memory dysfunction that was the principal distinction between the anti-social schizophrenic and the non-anti-social schizophrenic groups. Schug and Raine (2009:

239) suggest that their analyses support the view that there may be 'an antisocial subtype of schizophrenia with a neurobiological basis'.

It is evident that a great deal remains to be understood at a biological level about the interactions between psychosis, including schizophrenia, and antisocial and violent behaviour. As Schug and Raine suggest, the enrichment of this level of understanding will play an important part in the development of effective treatment regimes.

Intellectual Disability

As seen in Table 6.1, the 2007 Mental Health Act uses the broad terminology of 'any disorder or disability of the mind'. The phrase used in the Act includes a group of people who have traditionally been characterised by low levels of intellectual functioning. The name given to this group has varied over time and between countries: the following are to be found in the various diagnostic systems and in the research literature, *mentally defective*, *mental handicap*, *mental retardation*, and *learning disability*. The current terminology speaks to *developmental intellectual impairment* (learning or developmental disabilities). Holland (2004: 26) notes that the term 'developmental disability' refers to 'a highly heterogeneous group of people who have in common evidence of some delay in reaching, or a failure to reach developmental milestones, a delay in or failure to acquire living, educational and social skills as expected for their age, and evidence, on standard psychological assessment, of a significant intellectual impairment'.

As Holland explains, the emergence of the notion of development disability brings together two groups previously considered in the literature to be distinct. For one group there is a genetic or environmental explanation for their impaired functioning, such as people with diagnosable chromosomal abnormalities, head injury, or identifiable pregnancy and birth complications such as infection *in utero* as, for example, with rubella, birth complications such as anoxia, or a childhood disease such as meningitis. For the second group, a combination of adverse biological and environmental factors is involved in the learning disability.

Given the a range of terms in use across the literature, to maintain a thread within the research which focuses on intelligence, the term intellectual disability (ID) is used here, acknowledging the arguments in favour of the term developmental disability.

ID is not the same as mental illness, although the two can be co-morbid, and involves both intellectual and social ability. There is no legal level of IQ score by which to define intellectual disability. However, on standard IQ tests that give a mean score of 100, such as the Wechsler Adult Intelligence Scales (WAIS), an IQ in the region of 70 is taken as 'borderline'. An IQ of 70 or below together with a low level of social functioning may be indicative of learning disability (having eliminated other explanations such as memory loss or trauma).

There are two main approaches to considering the relationship between intellectual disability and criminal behaviour: first, to look at the intellectual functioning of offender populations; second, to examine the criminal behaviour of those with an intellectual disability. An innovative departure from these two approaches was reported in an American study that showed a correlation between IQ estimates at a state level and state-level crime rates (Beaver & Wright, 2011).

Intelligence in Offender Populations

As long ago as 1913, Charles Goring concluded from his study of 3,000 English convicts that criminals were generally of low intelligence. Goring's work has been replicated over the following decades, with various studies from different countries reporting an association between low IQ and criminal behaviour (e.g., Bartels, Ryan, Urban, & Glass, 2010; Beaver & Wright, 2011; Craft, 1984; Hirschi, 1969; Moffitt, Gabrielli, Mednick, & Schulsinger, 1981; West & Farrington, 1973; Woodward, 1955).

However, low intelligence, as indicated by IQ scores between 70 and 80, is not the same as intellectual disability: this point is illustrated by an American study reported by Denkowski and Denkowski (1985). Denkowski and Denkowski estimated that approximately 2.5 per cent of prisoners, across 20 states, have an IQ below 70. The importance of adaptive social functioning in intellectual disability is evident from the figures presented: in states that rely on IQ testing alone, 2.25 percent of prisoners are classified as 'retarded'; in the five states where IQ and adaptive behaviour were assessed (using a standard psychometric test) the figure fell to 1.28 per cent of the prisoners.

In a study carried out in an English Young Offender Institution, Herrington (2009) investigated the prevalence of ID among 185 young male prisoners aged between 18 and 21 years. The prisoners completed an intelligence test and a measure of social adaptation (the Vineland Adaptive Behaviour Scales). The assessments indicated that about 1 in 10 of the prisoners had an IQ of 69, which indicates an impairment in functioning. When scores on a measure of adaptive behaviour were taken into consideration, Herrington notes that none of the offenders met the diagnostic criteria for ID but that 11 per cent were borderline ID. Herrington also makes the point that the prisoners with borderline ID were housed within the main part of the institution and that it was unlikely that their level of functioning had been recognised.

Offending in ID Populations

Barron, Hassiotis, and Banes (2002) conducted a study, based in north-east London and west Essex, of 61 adults with an IQ below 80 who had offended within the previous 5 years. Alongside low IQ, the sample was marked by high levels of comorbid psychosis and lower levels of autistic symptomatology. Barron et al. reported that just over half of the sample had their first contact with the criminal justice system before the age of 16 years. The sample was characterised by high levels of family criminality, experience of abuse, conduct disorder, problems at school, and a long history of offending—all of which could be found in any mainstream offender group, low IQ or not. The type of offences most frequently found were violent offences, sex offences, and firesetting, for which more than one-quarter of the sample had served a custodial sentence. Indeed, reinforcing the point regarding similarities between ID and mainstream offenders, Gray, Fitzgerald, Taylor, MacCulloch, and Snowden (2007) found that risk assessments developed with general offenders groups functioned accurately with ID offenders.

A Scottish study of court reports completed by the Tayside learning disability service since 1986 was reported by Smith, White, and Walker (2008). There were 64 people with a learning disability who faced charges for a range of offences, most commonly public order offences with a relatively high level of arson and sexual offending. Schizophrenia was the most common comorbid diagnosis.

A Finnish study reported by Männynsalo, Putkonen, Lindberg, and Kotilainen (2009) reviewed the pre-trial forensic psychiatric reports of 44 people (36 male, 8 female) with ID over the period 1996–2006. They found that about half of the offenders had committed previous crimes, with arson the most frequent offence. There were very high levels of alcohol and drug abuse and dependency, and about half of those assessed were intoxicated when committing their crime. In addition to the comorbid substance use, about one-quarter of the sample also met the diagnostic criteria for anti-social personality disorder. The comorbidity of ID and personality disorder is one that is beginning to come to prominence (Morrissey & Hollin, 2011).

Hobson and Rose (2008) conducted a review of 14 studies concerned with the mental health of people with ID who commit offences. They concluded that a substantial proportion of people with ID had comorbid mental health problems, particularly schizophrenia and other psychotic disorders. Hobson and Rose noted that the offences committed by people with ID ranges across the full spectrum of types of crime, from property offences to acts of serious violence. However, as noted by Lindsay and Taylor (2005), it is aggression, firesetting, and inappropriate sexual behaviour that attracts the main body of attention.

When looking at offending in mentally disordered offenders, including offenders with ID, the source of the sample used in the research is important. Some mentally disordered offenders are deemed to be such a risk to the public that they are detained in conditions of high security, while others of much lower risk are accommodated in lower security or within the community. Lindsay et al. (2010) reviewed the case files of 477 people in England and Scotland with ID who were referred to offender services—including community and low, medium, and maximum security—over a 12-month period. They found that violence, both verbal and physical, was the most frequently seen behaviour: however, for those in maximum security, who were the younger members of the sample, sexual offenses were much more evident. A similar survey in the north of England found that among 60 people with ID, the most frequent offences were violence against the person, sexual offences, and arson (Crossland, Burns, Leach, & Quinn, 2005).

Sex Offending

There is a longstanding history of research concerned with the high prevalence of improper sexual behaviour among low IQ groups (Day, 1993; Robertson, 1981; Walker & McCabe, 1973). In a review of the research concerned with sex offenders with intellectual and developmental disabilities, Lindsay (2002) pointed to methodological variations across studies, such differences in inclusion criteria, the source of the sample and in the way that IQ was measured, which could affect prevalence rates of sex offenders. Lindsay concludes that, overall, the research does indicate that sex offenders with ID are less discriminating in their victims, committing offences against children both male and female. Lindsay makes the point that assessment methods for sex offenders with ID, which could be used to inform the court with respect to decisions regarding sentencing and treatment, are not well developed.

Rice, Harris, Lang, and Chaplin (2008) addressed the issue of offenders with an ID who offend against children. The question they specifically addressed was do these offenders sexually assault children because of their own sexual immaturity and lack of social skills, or is it because they have a sexual preference for children? In order to answer this question, Rice et al. compared the personal characteristics, offence records, and phallometric assessment of 69 male sex offenders with an ID (IQ below 80) and a control group of 69 sex offenders (IQ average or above). In terms of offending history, the sex offenders with ID were more likely to have previous victims who were prepubescent or very young and male. However, they were no more likely than the comparison group to show a preference for highly coercive sex with children, nor were the offenders with ID any more likely to commit further violent sexual offences.

In conclusion, an explanation for the relationship between ID and anti-social and criminal behaviour may be due to a combination of various factors. The person with ID may not learn the difference between socially acceptable and unacceptable behaviour. In addition, poor social skills may mean that behaviour intended to be friendly is perceived as aggressive or hostile and so results in altercations. It is possible the person with ID is easily influenced by more able offenders and so becomes involved in crime. Finally, the person with ID may carry out the crime clumsily so that detection and arrest is made easier.

The point regarding a failure to learn to distinguish socially acceptable and unacceptable behaviour may be particularly applicable to sexual offending. The term 'counterfeit deviance' has been used to refer to behaviour that is clearly anti-social but is explicable by the individual's lack of sexual knowledge and by limitations in their social skills and opportunities to establish sexual relationships in a socially acceptable fashion. Thus, any sexually inappropriate behaviour is a consequence of sexual naïveté rather than sexual deviance (Luiselli, 2000). Nonetheless, social naïve behaviour may be seen by other people as assault, reported to the police and criminal proceedings may follow.

Personality Disorder

The generic term 'personality disorder' masks a myriad of diagnostic categories. The two major diagnostic systems, the International Statistical Classification of Diseases and Related Health Problems (ICD) and Diagnostic and Statistical Manual of Mental Disorders (DSM), have both traditionally included substantial numbers of types of personality disorder. As shown in Box 6.2, following DSM conventions, it is now usual to think of clusters of personality disorders rather than a multitude of individually named disorders.

Personality disorders are relatively common across the both general population and among mentally disordered populations, where they are often comorbid with alcohol and drug problems. As might be predicted, anti-social personality disorder (APD) is highly prevalent among offender populations and is predictive of high rates of recidivism, particularly when comorbid with substance use disorders (Walter, Wiesbeck, Dittmann, & Graf, 2010). A survey of psychiatric morbidity among prisoners in England and Wales found that:

BOX 6.2 PERSONALITY DISORDERS CLASSIFIED

ICD-10 Classification

Specific personality disorders

- Paranoid personality disorder
- Schizoid personality disorder
- Dissocial personality disorder
- Emotionally unstable personality disorder (impulsive type and borderline type)
- Histrionic personality disorder
- Anankastic personality disorder
- Anxious [avoidant] personality disorder
- Dependent personality disorder
- Other specific personality disorders
- Personality disorder, unspecified

Mixed and other personality disorders
- Mixed personality disorders
- Troublesome personality changes

DSM IV-TR

- Paranoid personality disorder
- Schizoid personality disorder
- Schizotypal personality disorder
- Anti-social personality disorder
- Borderline personality disorder
- Histrionic personality disorder
- Narcissistic personality disorder
- Avoidant personality disorder
- Dependent personality disorder
- Obsessive-compulsive personality disorder

DSM Clusters

Cluster A: 'odd or eccentric' types: paranoid, schizoid, and schizotypal personality disorders

Cluster B: 'dramatic, emotional, or erratic' types: histrionic, narcissistic, anti-social, and borderline personality disorders

Cluster C: 'anxious and fearful' types: obsessive-compulsive, avoidant, and dependent personality disorders

> Antisocial personality disorder had the highest prevalence of any category of personality disorder. This would be expected, since the category of antisocial personality disorder requires the presence of antisocial behaviour before the age of 15 years which persists into adulthood. Among the sub-sample who had a clinical interview, 63% of male remand prisoners, 49% of male sentenced prisoners and 31% of female prisoners were assessed as having antisocial personality disorder. These prevalence rates for antisocial personality disorder are broadly in line with the results of studies carried out within the United States penal system.
>
> (Singleton et al., 1998: 10)

Roberts and Coid (2010) reported that among a sample of male prisoners in England and Wales a range of personality disorders was evident. In terms of criminal behaviour, APD was associated with a range of crimes including robbery, blackmail, and burglary.

The *DSM-IV-TR* diagnostic criteria for APD are summarised in Table 6.2.

TABLE 6.2 *DSM IV-TR* criteria for APD

A) There is a longstanding pattern of a disregard for the rights of other people. This pattern may have been evident from childhood onwards and is indicated by three or more of the following criteria:

i) a failure to conform to social norms with as seen by repeated behaviours that are grounds for arrest;
ii) deceitfulness as seen with repeated lying or cheating others for profit or pleasure;
iii) impulsivity;
iv) irritability and aggressiveness leading to repeated involvement in fights or assaults;
v) a reckless disregard for the safety of self or others;
vi) consistent irresponsibility in failing to hold employment respect financial obligations;
vii) a lack of remorse for their victims.

B) The individual is at least 18 years of age.
C) There is evidence of conduct disorder with onset before the age of 15 years.
D) The occurrence of anti-social behaviour is not evident only during an episode of schizophrenia or mania.

As may be predicted, those with APD cause a great deal of harm as given their involvement in a range of anti-social, including violent, behaviours. In addition, APD is likely to be comorbid with other psychiatric disorders, meaning that anti-social behaviour is often evident within psychiatric hospitals, alongside high rates of educational failure, family breakdown, unemployment, and other social problems.

It is established that the first signs of APD are to be found in childhood conduct disorder, followed by high levels of anti-social behaviour during adolescence (Robins, 1978). As is the case with many childhood disturbances, it is likely that an explanation for ASP lies in combination of impoverished environment, genetic constitution and biological functioning, and harsh parenting (De Brito & Hodgins, 2009).

The way in which offenders with personality disorders, including ASP, are managed and treated within the metal health and criminal justice systems is a longstanding issue. Those people diagnosed as personality disordered are difficult to manage within institutions and there is only a very small evidence-base to inform the design of effective treatments with such a complex group (see De Brito & Hodgins, 2009). In England in the late 1990s and early 2000s, concerns were being voiced that there was a reluctance to offer treatment to people, including offenders, with a personality disorder. This reluctance may have been based on the fact that some personality disordered offenders are dangerous to work with alongside the view that others were untreatable by mainstream psychiatric services. This concern lead the National Institute for Mental Health in England in 2003 to issue the best practice guide *Personality Disorder: No Longer a Diagnosis of Exclusion*. This guide addressed issues such as the assessment and treatment of personality disorder within psychiatric and forensic services. The overarching aim of the guidelines was to emphasise that people with personality disorder should be perceived as legitimate users of mental health services.

As this initiative to draw personality disorder into mainstream psychiatric services unfolded there was, paradoxically, a different agenda coming into force. This new focus was aimed at a group of people whose violence (including sexual violence) led to their being a significant danger to the community. Feeney (2003) traces the name given to this group to a statement in 1999 by the then Home Secretary, Jack Straw (1999): 'There is, however, a group of dangerous and severely personality disordered individuals from whom the public at present are not properly protected'. The notion of dangerous and severe personality disorder (DSPD) was at large even if, as Mullen (2007: s3) states, it was '[b]orn out of a populist law and order reaction, based on false premises', or as Maden (2007: s8) puts it: 'Politicians and civil servants invented dangerous and severe personality disorder in 1999'. One of the main reservations about the DSPD programme was expressed by Buchanan and Leese (2001: 1955): 'The proposals have provoked debate on the morality of preventatively detaining people who have not been convicted of an offence'.

Dangerous and Severe Personality Disorder

As Feeney (2003) makes clear in his comprehensive review, the machinery of government churned into action with £126 million funding for a 3-year programme for the development of specialist services for DSPD. These specialist services were eventually established in both high security hospitals (Broadmoor and Rampton) and prisons (Frankland and Whitemoor). It was planned that there would be 312 beds for those male offenders who fulfilled the criteria for DSPD. Those individuals who fulfilled the criteria for DSPD could be detained in conditions of security at one of the specialist centres. All three diagnostic criteria for DSPD, as specified by the Home Office and the Department of Health (2001), should be satisfied in each individual case: (1) they are more likely than not to commit an offence within 5 years that might be expected to lead to serious physical or psychological harm from which the victim would find it difficult or impossible to recover; (2) they have a significant disorder of personality; (3) the risk presented appears to be functionally linked to the significant personality disorder. As Tyrer et al. (2010) point out, these criteria present a challenge to those who work in the field: the prediction of future offending is fraught with multiple difficulties, the assessment of dangerousness is less than straightforward, and how precisely to establish a functional relationship between personality disorder and risk posed remains uncertain.

In spite of this daunting range of conceptual and practical problems, the DSPD initiative was translated into action as the funding was made available: innovative assessments were developed, new treatment centres were built, and new treatment regimes appeared (Howells & Tennant, 2010), and screening of large numbers of prisoners was undertaken to identify those individuals with DSPD (Ullrich, Yang, & Coid, 2010).

The provision of these new services was an expensive task: Barrett et al. (2009) estimated that it cost the public purse £25,150 per patient over a 6-month period to house and treat those people contained within DSPD Units. This cost is £3,500 more expensive than keeping a prisoner in conditions of similar security.

BOX 6.3 CHARACTERISTICS OF THE 203 MALES IN THE FIRST DSPD COHORT (FROM KIRKPATRICK ET AL., 2010)

Mean age 35.7 years (SD = 8.6)

Common offences

Rape/attempted rape	31.0%
Indecent assault	26.5%
Murder	19.4%
Assault	16.9%

Personality disorder diagnoses

93.8% had a diagnosed personality disorder
75.3% had more than one personality disorder
The most common combination was anti-social personality disorder with borderline personality disorder (28.8%), followed by paranoid personality disorder with borderline (41.5%)

Most frequently assessed treatment needs

Violent lifestyle	97.9%
Criminal personality	96.5%
Criminal attitudes	95.1%
Work ethic	76.9%
Criminal peers	52.4%

The clinical profile of the first 203 male patients admitted to the new high security DSPD units was described by Kirkpatrick et al. (2010). A summary of the characteristics of this cohort is given in Box 6.3.

Of course, the figures about the cost of the new services are meaningless unless set against outcomes: if the DSPD initiative demonstrably and significantly reduced offending and facilitated community rehabilitation then the benefits may well outweigh the costs. However, the evaluation of the DSPD programme has proved to be a far from straightforward task. Tyrer et al. (2009) have pointed to the organisational issues that, despite the protestations from the government department charged with delivering the DSPD programme (Ramsay, Saradjian, Murphy, & Freestone, 2009), seriously compromised the evaluation that relied upon the use of a randomised control trial (RCT). Tyrer et al. (2009: 140) noted that their negative findings 'should be tempered by the observations that there were smaller numbers than expected, protocol violations meant that only a minority completed the study as planned, and certain outcomes such as retention in the treatment programme might have been more relevant outcomes for the assessment'. Indeed, the history of evaluations of forensic mental health services is blighted by the problems inherent in running RCTs (Hollin, 2008).

Psychopathic Disorder

The 1983 Act defined psychopathic disorder as a 'persistent disorder or disability of mind (whether or not including significant impairment of intelligence) which results in abnormally aggressive

BOX 6.4 CLECKLEY'S DESCRIPTION OF THE PSYCHOPATH

1. Superficial charm and good intelligence.
2. Absence of delusions and other signs of irrational thinking.
3. Absence of nervousness or psychoneurotic manifestations.
4. Unreliability.
5. Untruthfulness and insincerity.
6. Lack of remorse and shame.
7. Inadequately motivated anti-social behaviour.
8. Poor judgement and failure to learn by experience.
9. Pathologic egocentricity and incapacity for love.
10. General poverty in major affective reactions.
11. Specific loss of insight.
12. Unresponsiveness in general interpersonal relations.
13. Fantastic and uninviting behaviour with drink and sometimes without.
14. Suicide threats rarely carried out.
15. Sex life impersonal, trivial and poorly integrated.
16. Failure to follow any life plan.

or seriously irresponsible conduct' (section 1(2)). This definition is no longer prevalent as the 2007 Act uses the more general 'any disorder or disability of the mind'.

What is a psychopath? The modern-day formulation of the notion of a person who can be identified as a psychopath (the notion has been around since the 19th century) are often credited to the American psychiatrist Hervey Milton Cleckley (1903–84). Cleckley's 1941 book, *The Mask of Sanity*, took its title from Cleckley's clinical observations that, unlike people with mental disorders such as schizophrenia or depression, the psychopath presents as sociable and personally engaging but this 'mask' of normality conceals a personality characterised by coldness and a ruthless disregard for the feelings of other people. Cleckley continued to refine the notion of the psychopath in later editions of *The Mask of Sanity*, finally producing a fifth and final edition in 1976.

The psychopath was not Cleckley's only well-known work: he seems to have had the ability to corner the market in usual psychological conditions and snappy book titles. Alongside *The Mask of Sanity*, in 1956 he was a co-author, with Corbett H. Thigpen, of *The Three Faces of Eve*, a case study about a woman with multiple personality disorder that was later made into a film.

As shown in Box 6.4, Cleckley described psychopaths as having a range of readily identifiable characteristics that typify their emotional and social emptiness.

Robert Hare and the PCL

Cleckley gave a clinically informed description of the psychopath but it was the Canadian psychologist Robert Hare who brought the formal assessment of psychopathy to the fore. Some of the terms used by Cleckley are vague and imprecise, causing difficulties for clinicians and researchers alike, so the development of a psychometrically sound scale by which to assess psychopathy has many obvious applications.

BOX 6.5 CHARACTERISTICS OF THE PSYCHOPATH (HARE, 1980)

1. Glibness/superficial charm.
2. Previous diagnosis as a psychopath (or similar).
3. Egocentricity/grandiose sense of self-worth.
4. Proneness to boredom/low frustration tolerance.
5. Pathological lying and deception.
6. Conning/lack of sincerity.
7. Lack of remorse or guilt.
8. Lack of affect and emotional depth.
9. Callous/lack of empathy.
10. Parasitic lifestyle.
11. Short-tempered/poor behavioural controls.
12. Promiscuous sexual behaviour.
13. Early behaviour problems.
14. Lack of realistic long-term plans.
15. Impulsivity.
16. Irresponsible behaviour as a parent.
17. Frequent marital relationships.
18. Juvenile delinquency.
19. Poor probation or parole risk.
20. Failure to accept responsibility for own actions.
21. Many types of offence.
22. Drug or alcohol abuse not direct cause of anti-social behaviour.

Hare (1980) conducted a factor analysis of data derived from the Cleckley criteria and found five factors. These factors offer a succinct description of the psychopath: (1) an inability to develop warm, empathic relationships; (2) an unstable lifestyle; (3) an inability to accept responsibility for anti-social behaviour; (4) an absence of intellectual and psychiatric problems; (5) weak behavioural control. From this analysis, Hare (1980) constructed a scale for the assessment of psychopathy in criminal populations. This scale, shown in Box 6.5, was subsequently amended and became the 20-item Psychopathy Checklist (PCL; Hare 1991), subsequently revised (PCL-R; Hare 2003). The items on the PCL-R are informed by file review and interview with the individual being assessed. Each of the 20 items is scored by the assessor on a three-point scale, with 0 indicating not present, 1 indicating possibly present, and 2 definitely present. Thus, the scale has a maximum score of 40, with a cut-off point of 30 taken to indicate psychopathy. This cut-off point of 30 may vary across countries and according to the gender of the person being assessed (Cooke & Michie, 1999; Cooke, Michie, Hart, & Clark, 2005a,b; Dolan & Völlm, 2009), although the need for adjustment by country has been called in question (Bolt, Hare, & Neumann, 2007).

The PCL-R has become a widely used assessment in clinical forensic practice (Archer, Buffington-Vollum, Stredny, & Handel, 2006; Flores-Mendoza, Alvarenga, Herrero, & Abad, 2008), used either alone or in conjunction with other measures, and particularly with regard to the assessment of risk of future violent conduct (Lestico, Salekin, DeCoster, & Rogers, 2008; Mokros, Osterheider, Hucker, & Nitschke, 2010). This widespread use of the PCL-R includes not just the assessment of women (Warren et al., 2003; Weizmann-Henelius et al., 2010) as well as men, but also children and adolescents (Salekin, Lee, Schrum Dillard, & Kubak, 2010; Stockdale, Olver, & Wong, 2010)—for whom a Youth Version has been developed (PCL: YV; Forth, Kosson, & Hare, 2003)—and mentally disordered and ID offenders (Morrissey et al., 2007; Vitacco, Rogers, Neumann, Harrison, & Vincent, 2005). These assessments are often undertaken in the context of violent and sexually violent crimes (e.g., Blackburn & Coid, 1998; Mokros et al., 2010; Vincent, Odgers, McCormick, & Corrado, 2008).

Given the predictive utility of the PCL-R a body of research, primarily with males, has investigated the factor structure of the scale.

The Structure of the PCL-R

The longstanding position, based on factor analysis of PCL-R scores, was that the scale consisted of two correlated factors: factor 1 relates to interpersonal and affective functioning such as superficial charm, cheating, and lack of empathy; factor 2 concerns anti-social behaviour, impulsiveness, and irresponsibility (Harpur, Hakistan, & Hare, 1991). However, this two-factor model was called into question by Cooke and Michie (2001) who used confirmatory factor analysis with a combination of 10 Canadian and American data sets (n = 2067) to re-examine the factor structure of the PCL-R. Cooke and Michie reported a a three-factor structure underpinning the PCL-R: these three factors are (1) arrogant and deceitful interpersonal style, (2) deficient affective experience, and (3) impulsive and irresponsible behavioural style. This three-factor structure did not include PCL-R items that were concerned with anti-social and criminal behaviour. Cooke and Michie suggest that their model moves to the heart of the psychological construct of psychopathy, of which anti-social and criminal behaviour is a consequence not a core component. With the benefit of hindsight it is at about this point in the research that the debate started that would eventually lead to threats of legal proceedings.

In response to Cooke and Michie, Hare (2003) proposed a four-facet model: factor 1 was affective/interpersonal and consisted of two facets (affective and interpersonal), factor 2 (lifestyle/anti-social) also with two facets (lifestyle and anti-social). In later publications, Hare and Neumann (2008, 2009) have expounded upon this four-facet model and its implications for understanding the nature of psychopathy and how it is measured. While both sides questioned the statistical models used by their adversary, the debate, as Blackburn (2007a) has made clear, ran much deeper than statistics. Indeed, Blackburn notes his own position, remaining consistent with his own research [...], that the core of psychopathy reflects narcissistic and histrionic personality disorders rather more than antisocial personality disorder. However, the development of the four facet model failed to impress Cooke and Michie who, joined by Skeem, maintained their position that the PCL-R confounded personality and antisocial behaviour, two quite separate and distinct constructs, with potentially misleading consequences both theoretically and practically (Andrade, 2008; Cooke, Michie, & Skeem, 2007).

These types of exchange and polarisation of opinions are not uncommon in academic journals. However, the Cook et al. versus Hare debate about the role of criminal behaviour in psychopathy was about to take an unusual twist, as discussed in Box 6.6, with a paper by Skeem and Cooke (2010a).

Psychopathy and Personality Disorder

What is the relationship between psychopathy and personality disorder? Is psychopathy a type of personality disorder or is it something quite separate, a taxon i.e., a distinct grouping of individuals different in kind to other people?

> Blackburn (1988) proved to be remarkably prescient with regard to the debate captured in Box 6.5 in his discussion of the 'myth of psychopathic personality'. Blackburn argues that a cluster of personality traits, including egocentricity, hostility, and impulsivity, all associated with socially deviant behaviour, have attracted the label 'psychopathy'. This confluence of personality traits, Blackburn argues, suggests a *dimension* of personality which is not the same as a discrete *type*. Blackburn (1988: 510) takes the argument a stage further: 'Extremes on one dimension may characterise several personality types that differ significantly on other dimensions. The traits claimed by Cleckley and others to identify a 'distinct entity' may therefore represent a personality dimension that is common to more than one class of personality disorder'.

This question of classification continues to vex researchers (e.g., Blackburn, 2007b; Blackburn, Logan, Renwick, & Donnelly, 2005; Coid & Ullrich, 2010; Ogloff, 2006; Skeem, Poythress, Edens, Lilienfeldd, & Cale, 2003) with the consequence that the concept of psychopathy remains a

BOX 6.6 WHEN RESEARCHERS DISAGREE

It is an integral part of the scientific process that research findings challenge accepted theory and that theory evolves as the evidence accumulates. In the case of the PCL-R, Hare and his colleagues have rightly defended their position in the journals when they have been challenged (as documented by Poythress and Petrila, 2010). However, when Jennifer Skeem and David Cooke submitted a paper that, following peer review, was accepted for publication in the academic journal *Psychological Assessment*, a very different train of events ensued:

> Prior to publication, Professor Hare's counsel issued a letter to the authors and the editor of *Psychological Assessment* in which he stated that the paper 'was fraught with misrepresentations and other problems and a completely inaccurate summary of what amounts to his life's work.' [14] The letter charged that the authors of the paper 'deliberately fabricated or altered quotes of Dr. Hare, and substantially altered the sense of what Dr. Hare said in his previous publications.' The letter asserted that publication of the article 'will constitute defamation on the part of the authors, and also *Psychological Assessment*,' and issued a 'demand' that the paper be pulled from publication in its current state.
>
> The summary of events in this section is taken from a letter dated November 8, 2007, from Hare's attorney to Professors Cooke and Skeem, and to Dr. Milton E. Strauss, the editor of *Psychological Assessment*.
>
> (Poythress & Petrila, 2010: 4)

The threat of litigation against both the journal and the authors significantly changes the nature of academic debate and the freedom to publish scholarly work without fear of reprisal.

The errant paper was eventually published (Skeem and Cooke, 2010a) with comments (Hare and Neumann, 2010) and replies (Skeem and Cooke, 2010b). However, as Hart (2010) suggests, this situation leaves journal editors with much to ponder.

matter of debate. Now, given that the concept is uncertain and therefore measurement is unsure, the development of a cogent explanation for psychopathy is a daunting task! In spite of these problems in terminology, definition, and measurement, a literature has nonetheless accumulated that examines a range of correlates of psychopathy. The familiar variables of biological influences, childhood behaviour, and family functioning have all been considered with respect to psychopathy and its development (Lynam & Gudonis, 2005). The biological research has progressed from studies of autonomic and central nervous system functioning (e.g., Blackburn, 1979) to consider genetic influences (Forsman, Lichtenstein, Andershed, & Larsson, 2008; Tikkanen et al., 2010), brain abnormalities (Weber, Habel, Amunts, & Schneider, 2008), neurological functioning (Dolan, 2010; Harenski, Harenski, Kiehl, & Shane, 2010; Nilsson et al., 2010). It seems likely that research, including biological research, has some way to go before solving the puzzle that is psychopathy.

Conclusion

The mentally disordered offender sets several challenges: there are the legal issues concerning *mens rea* and the definition of what exactly constitutes a mental disorder; there are empirical questions around the nature of the relationship between symptomatology and criminal behaviour; and there are practical issues regarding the treatment of the mentally disordered offender. The research concerned with all these aspects of the mentally disordered offender, as is evident from the range of professions with a direct interest in the area, continues to gather with some momentum. One of the priorities for the future is to use this knowledge to design effective treatment regimes.

Chapter Summary

- Where there is an overlap between mental disorder and criminal behaviour, the principle of *mens rea* is not seen to be applicable. Thus, alongside criminal law, there is mental health law for those cases where the offender is mentally disordered.
- The legal definition of mental disorder has shifted and changed over time but can be seen as broadly including mental illnesses such as schizophrenia, personality disorders, and learning disabilities.
- The proportion of people with a mental disorder who commit crimes is very small. People with a mental disorder are, however, overrepresented in prison populations.
- Anti-social personality disorder (APD) is highly prevalent among offender populations and is predictive of high rates of recidivism, particularly when comorbid with substance use disorders.
- The introduction of the classification of dangerous and severe personality disorder (DSPD) and the development of associated services brought about a good deal of debate within the literature. The same is true of the topic of the psychopathic individual.

Points for Discussion

- As we have mental health laws, why are so many people with a mental disorder prevalent in the prison population?
- Why is alcohol abuse often comorbid with the main psychiatric diagnosis in mentally disordered offenders?
- What was the thinking behind the introduction of the category of dangerous and severe personality disorder (DSPD)?

Essential Reading

Anckarsäter, H., Radovic, S., Svennerlind, C., Höglund, P., & Radovic, F. (2009). Mental disorder is a cause of crime: The cornerstone of forensic psychiatry. *International Journal of Law and Psychiatry, 32*, 342–347.

This paper offers an excellent discussion of the issues surrounding the debate between the association between mental disorder and criminal behaviour.

Lindsay, W. R., Hastings, R. P., & Beech, A. R. (Eds.) (2011). Special issue: Forensic research in offenders with intellectual and developmental disabilities (parts 1 and 2). *Psychology, Crime, & Law, 17* (1 & 2).

These two volumes of the journal *Psychology, Crime, and Law* are given to the topic of offenders with intellectual and developmental disabilities.

De Brito, S. A. & Hodgins, S. (2009). Antisocial personality disorder. In M. McMurran & R. Howard (Eds.), *Personality, Personality Disorder and Violence* (pp. 133–153). Chichester, Sussex: John Wiley & Sons.

This chapter presents an excellent overview of anti-social personality disorder.

A. R. Felthous & H. Sa (2007). *International Handbook on Psychopathic Disorders and the Law: Two Volume Set.* Chichester, Sussex: John Wiley & Sons.

More than anyone could ever want to know about psychopathy is contained in these two volumes—perhaps rather wide-ranging in scope and American in flavour, they are nonetheless a wealth of information.

Lynam, D. R. & Gudonis, L. (2005). The development of psychopathy. *Annual Review of Clinical Psychology, 1*, 381–407.

A comprehensive overview of the factors involved in the aetiology of psychopathy.

The Lighter Side

The Three Faces of Eve, starring Joanne Woodward, is a film about a woman with multiple personality disorder.

Useful Websites

Mental Health Act (2007). www.legislation.gov.uk/ukpga/2007/12/contents. Mentally Disordered Offenders, www.justice.gov.uk/publications/mentally-disordered-offenders.htm.

References

Alden, A., Brennan, P., Hodgins, S., & Mednick, S. (2007). Psychotic disorders and sex offending in a Danish birth cohort. *Archives of General Psychiatry, 64*, 1251–1258.

Anckarsäter, H., Radovic, S., Svennerlind, C., Höglund, P., & Radovic, F. (2009). Mental disorder is a cause of crime: The cornerstone of forensic psychiatry. *International Journal of Law and Psychiatry, 32*, 342–347.

Andrade, J. T. (2008). The inclusion of antisocial behaviour in the construct of psychopathy: A review of the research. *Aggression and Violent Behavior, 13*, 328–335.

Appelbaum, P., Robbins, P. C., & Monahan, J. (2000). Violence and delusions: Data from the MacArthur Risk Assessment Study. *American Journal of Psychiatry, 157*, 566–572.

Archer, R. P., Buffington-Vollum, J. K., Stredny, R. V., Handel, R. W. (2006). A survey of psychological test use patterns among forensic psychologists. *Journal of Personality Assessment, 87*, 84–94.

Barrett, B., Byford, S., Seivewright, H., Cooper, S., Duggan, C., & Tyrer, P. (2009). The assessment of dangerous and severe personality disorder: Service use, cost, and consequences. *Journal of Forensic Psychiatry & Psychology, 20*, 120–131.

Barron P., Hassiotis A., & Banes, J. (2002). Offenders with intellectual disability: The size of the problem and therapeutic outcomes. *Journal of Intellectual Disability Research, 46*, 454–463.

Bartels, J. M., Ryan, J. J., Urban, L. S., & Glass, L. A. (2010). Correlations between estimates of state IQ and FBI crime statistics. *Personality and Individual Differences, 48*, 579–583.

Beaver, K. M. & Wright, J. P. (2011). The association between county-level IQ and county-level crime rates. *Intelligence, 39*, 22–26.

Blackburn, R. (1979). Cortical and autonomic arousal in primary and secondary psychopaths. *Psychophysiology, 16*, 143–150.

—— (1988). On moral judgements and personality disorders: The myth of psychopathic personality revisited. *British Journal of Psychiatry, 153*, 505–512.

—— (2007a). Personality disorder and antisocial deviance: Comments on the debate on the structure of the Psychopathy Checklist-Revised. *Journal of Personality Disorders, 21*, 142–159.

—— (2007b). Personality disorder and psychopathy: Conceptual and empirical integration. *Psychology, Crime & Law, 13*, 7–18.

Blackburn, R. & Coid, J. W. (1998). Psychopathy and the dimensions of personality disorder in violent offenders. *Personality and Individual Differences, 25*, 129–145.

Blackburn, R., Logan, C., Renwick, S. J. D., & Donnelly, J. P. (2005). Higher-order dimensions of personality disorder: Hierarchical structure and relationships with the five-factor model, the interpersonal circle, and psychopathy. *Journal of Personality Disorders, 19*, 597–623.

Bolt, D. M., Hare, R. D., & Neumann, C. S. (2007). Score metric equivalence of the Psychopathy Checklist-Revised (PCL-R) across criminal offenders in North America and the United Kingdom: A critique of Cook, Michie, Hart, and Clarke (2005) and new analyses. *Assessment, 14*, 44–56.

Bonta, J., Law, M., & Hanson, K. (1998). The prediction of criminal and violent recidivism among mentally disordered offenders: A meta-analysis. *Psychological Bulletin, 123*, 123–142.

Bradley, K. (2009). *The Bradley Report: Lord Bradley's Review of People with Mental Health Problems or Learning Disabilities in the Criminal Justice System*. London: DH Publications.

Braham, L. G., Trower, P., & Birchwood, M. (2004). Acting on command hallucinations and dangerous behavior: A critique of the major findings in the last decade. *Clinical Psychology Review, 24*, 513–528.

Brugha, T., Singleton, N., Meltzer, H., Bebbington, P., Farrell, M., Jenkins, R., & Lewis, G. (2005). Psychosis in the community and in prisons: A report from the British National Survey of Psychiatric Morbidity. *American Journal of Psychiatry, 162*, 774–780.

Buchanan, A. & Leese, M. (2001). Detention of people with dangerous severe personality disorders: A systematic review. *The Lancet, 358*, 1955–1959.

Buchanan, A. & Zonana, H. (2009). Mental disorder as the cause of crime. *International Journal of Law and Psychiatry, 32*, 142–146.

Cleckley, H. (1941). *The Mask of Sanity*. St. Louis, MO: Mosby.

—— (1976). *The Mask of Sanity* (5th ed.). St. Louis, MO: Mosby.

Cloyes, K. G., Wong, B., Latimer, S., & Abarca, J. (2010). Time to prison return for offenders with serious mental illness released from prison: A survival analysis. *Criminal Justice and Behavior, 37*, 175–187.

Coid, J. & Ullrich, S. (2010). Antisocial personality disorder is on a continuum with psychopathy. *Comprehensive Psychiatry, 51*, 426–433.

Coid, J., Yang, M., Ullrich, S., Roberts, A., Moran, P., Bebbington, P., & Hare, R. (2009a). Psychopathy among prisoners in England and Wales. *International Journal of Law and Psychiatry, 32*, 134–141.

—— (2009b). Prevalence and correlates of psychopathic traits in the household population of Great Britain. *International Journal of Law and Psychiatry, 32*, 65–73.

Constantine, R. J., Petrila, J., Andel, R., Givens, E. M., Becker, M., Robst, J., & Howe, A. (2010). Arrest trajectories of adult offenders with a serious mental illness. *Psychology, Public Policy, and Law, 16*, 319–339.

Cooke, D. J. & Michie, C. (1999). Psychopathy across cultures: North America and Scotland compared. *Journal of Abnormal Psychology, 108*, 55–68.

—— (2001). Refining the construct of psychopathy: Towards a hierarchical model. *Psychological Assessment, 13*, 171–188.

Cooke, D. J., Michie, C., Hart, S. D., & Clark, D. (2005a). Searching for the pan-cultural core of psychopathic personality disorder. *Personality and Individual Differences, 39*, 283–295.

—— (2005b). Assessing psychopathy in the UK: Concerns about cross-cultural generalisability. *British Journal of Psychiatry, 186*, 335–341.

Cooke, D. J., Michie, C., & Skeem, J. L. (2007). Understanding the structure of the Psychopathy Checklist-Revised: An exploration of methodological confusion. *British Journal of Psychiatry, 190* (Suppl. 49), s39–s50.

Craft, M. (1984). Low intelligence, mental handicap and criminality. In M. Craft & A. Craft (Eds.), *Mentally Abnormal Offenders* (pp. 177–185). London: Baillière Tindall.

Crossland, S., Burns, M., Leach, C., & Quinn, P. (2005). Needs assessment in forensic learning disability. *Medicine, Science, and Law, 45*, 147–153.

Dahlin, M. K., Gumpert, C. H., Torstensson-Levander, M., Svensson, L., & Rodovic, S. (2009). Mentally disordered criminal offenders: Legal and criminological perspectives. *International Journal of Law and Psychiatry, 32*, 398–405.

Day, K. (1993). Crime and mental retardation: A review. In K. Howells & C. R. Hollin (Eds.), *Clinical Approaches to the Mentally Disordered Offender* (pp. 111–144). Chichester, Sussex: John Wiley & Sons.

De Brito, S. A. & Hodgins, S. (2009). Antisocial personality disorder. In M. McMurran & R. Howard (Eds.), *Personality, Personality Disorder and Violence* (pp. 133–153). Chichester, Sussex: John Wiley & Sons.

Denkowski, G. C. & Denkowski, K. M. (1985). The mentally retarded offender in the state prison system: Identification, prevalence, adjustment, and rehabilitation. *Criminal Justice and Behavior, 12*, 55–70.

Dolan, M. C. (2010). What imaging tells us about violence in anti-social men. *Criminal Behaviour and Mental Health, 20*, 199–214.

Dolan, M. & Völlm, B. (2009). Antisocial personality disorder and psychopathy in women: A literature review on the reliability and validity of assessment instruments. *International Journal of Law and Psychiatry, 32*, 2–9.

Douglas, K. S., Guy, L. S., & Hart, S. D. (2009). Psychosis as a risk factor for violence to others: A meta-analysis. *Psychological Bulletin, 135*, 679–706.

Dressing, H., Kief, C., & Salize, H. J. (2009). Prisoners with mental disorders in Europe. *British Journal of Psychiatry, 194*, 88.

Duffy, D., Linehan, S., & Kennedy, H. G. (2006). Psychiatric morbidity in the male sentenced Irish prisons population. *Irish Journal of Psychological Medicine, 23*, 54–62.

Eriksson, Å., Tengström, A., & Hodgins, S. (2006). Typologies of alcohol use disorders among men with schizophrenic disorders. *Addictive Behaviors, 32*, 1146–1163.

Eytan, A., Haller, D. M., Wolff, H., Cerutti B., Sebo, P., Bertrand, D., & Niveau, G. (2011). Psychiatric symptoms, psychological distress and somatic comorbidity among remand prisoners in Switzerland. *International Journal of Law and Psychiatry, 34*, 13–19.

Fazel, S., Buxrud, P., Ruchkin, V., & Grann, M. (2010). Homicide in discharged patients with schizophrenia and other psychoses: A national case-control study. *Schizophrenia Research, 123*, 263–269.

Fazel, S., Grann, M., Carlström, E., Lichtenstein, P., & Långström, N. (2009a). Risk factors for violent crime in schizophrenia: A national cohort study of 13,806 patients. *Journal of Clinical Psychiatry, 70*, 362–369.

Fazel, S., Gulati, G., Linsell, L., Geddes, J. R., & Grann, M. (2009b). Schizophrenia and violence: Systematic review and meta-analysis. *PLOS Medicine, 6*, 1–15.

Fazel, S., Långström, N., Hjern, A., Grann, M., & Lichtenstein, P. (2009c). Schizophrenia, substance abuse, and violent crime. *Journal of the American Medical Association, 301*, 2016–2023.

Fazel, S., Xenitidis, K., & Powell, J. (2008). The prevalence of intellectual disabilities among 12000 prisoners: A systemic review. *International Journal of Law and Psychiatry, 31*, 369–373.

Feeney, A. (2003). Dangerous severe personality disorder. *Advances in Psychiatric Treatment, 9*, 349–358.

Feldman, M. P. (1977). *Criminal Behaviour: A Psychological Analysis*. Chichester, Sussex: John Wiley & Sons.

Flores-Mendoza, C. E., Alvarenga, M. A. S., Herrero, Ó., & Abad, F. J. (2008). Factor structure and behavioural correlates of the Psychopathy Checklist-Revised [PCL-R] in a Brazilian prisoner sample. *Personality and Individual Differences, 45*, 584–590.

Forsman, M., Lichtenstein, P., Andershed, H., & Larsson, H. (2008). Genetic effects explain the stability of psychopathic personality from mid- to late adolescence. *Journal of Abnormal Psychology, 117*, 606–617.

Forth, A. E., Kosson, D. S., & Hare, R. D. (2003). *Psychopathy Checklist: Youth Version (PCL: YV)*. Toronto, Ontario: Multi-Health Systems.

Fotiadou, M., Livaditis, M., Manou, I., Kaniotou, E., & Xenitidis, K. (2006). Prevalence of mental disorders and deliberate self-harm in Greek male prisoners. *International Journal of Law and Psychiatry, 29*, 68–73.

Flynn, S., Abel, K. M., Menta, H., & Shaw, J. (2011). Mental illness, gender and homicide: A population-based descriptive study. *Psychiatry Research, 185*, 368–375.

Goring, C. (1913/1972). *The English Convict: A Statistical Study*. Montclair, NJ: Patterson Smith.

Gray, N. S., Fitzgerald, S., Taylor, J., MacCulloch, M. J., & Snowden, R. J. (2007). Predicting future reconviction in offenders with intellectual disabilities: The predictive efficacy of VRAG, PCL-SV, and the HCR-20. *Psychological Assessment, 19*, 474–479.

Gunn, J., Robertson, G., Dell, S., & Way, C. (1978). *Psychiatric Aspects of Imprisonment*. London: Academic Press.

Hare, R. D. (1980). A research scale for the assessment of psychopathy in criminal populations. *Personality and Individual Differences, 1*, 111–119.

—— (1991). *The Hare Psychopathy Checklist-Revised*. Toronto, Ontario: Multi-Health Systems.

—— (2003). *The Hare Psychopathy Checklist-Revised* (2nd ed.). Toronto, Ontario: Multi-Health Systems.

Hare, R. D. & Neumann, C. S. (2008). Psychopathy as a clinical and empirical construct. *Annual Review of Clinical Psychology, 4,* 217–246.

—— (2009). Psychopathy and its measurement. In P. J. Corr & G. Matthews (Eds.), *The Cambridge Handbook of Personality Psychology* (pp. 660–686). Cambridge: Cambridge University Press.

—— (2010). The role of antisociality in the psychopathy construct: Comment on Skeem and Cooke (2010). *Psychological Assessment, 22,* 446–454.

Harenski, C. L., Harenski, K. A., Kiehl, K. A., & Shane, M. W. (2010). Aberrant neural processing of moral violations in criminal psychopaths. *Journal of Abnormal Psychology, 119,* 863–874.

Harpur, T. J., Hakistan, A. R., & Hare, R. D. (1991). Factor structure of the Psychopathy Checklist. *Journal of Consulting and Clinical Psychology, 56,* 227–232.

Hart, S. D. (2010). The dark side of peer review. *International Journal of Forensic Mental Health, 9,* 1–2.

Herrington, V. (2009). Assessing the prevalence of intellectual disability among young male prisoners. *Journal of Intellectual Disability Research, 53,* 397–410.

Hirschi, T. (1969). *Causes of Delinquency.* Berkeley and Los Angeles, CA: University of California Press.

Hobson, B. & Rose, J. L. (2008). The mental health of people with intellectual disabilities who offend. *The Open Criminology Journal, 1,* 12–18.

Hodgins, S. (Ed.) (1993). *Mental Disorder and Crime.* Newbury Park, CA: Sage.

—— (2008). Violent behaviour among people with schizophrenia: A framework for investigations of causes, and effective treatment, and prevention. *Philosophical Transactions of the Royal Society B, 363,* 2505–2518.

Hodgins, S., Alderton, J., Cree, A., Aboud, A., & Mak, T. (2007). Aggressive behaviour, victimization and crime among severely mentally ill patients requiring hospitalisation. *British Journal of Psychiatry, 191,* 343–350.

Hodgins, S., Cree, A., Alderton, J., & Mak, T. (2008). From conduct disorder to severe mental illness: Associations with aggressive behaviour, crime and victimization. *Psychological Medicine, 38,* 975–987.

Hodgins, S. & Janson, C. G. (2002). *Criminality and Violence Among the Mentally Disordered: The Stockholm Metropolitan Project.* Cambridge: Cambridge University Press.

Hofvander, B., Ståhlberg, O., Nydén, A., Wentz, E., degl'Innocenti, A., Billstedt, E., & Anckarsäter, H. (2011). Life history of aggression scores are predicted by childhood hyperactivity, conduct disorder, adult substance abuse, and low cooperativeness in adult psychiatric patients. *Psychiatry Research, 185,* 280–285.

Holland, A. J. (2004). Criminal behaviour and developmental disability: An epidemiological perspective. In W. R. Lindsay, J. L. Taylor, & P. Sturmey (Eds.), *Offenders with Developmental Disabilities* (pp. 23–34). Chichester, Sussex: John Wiley & Sons.

Hollin, C. R. (2008). Evaluating offending behaviour programmes: Does only randomisation glister? *Criminology and Criminal Justice, 8,* 89–106.

Home Office & Department of Health (2001). *DSPD Programme: Dangerous People with Severe Personality Disorder Initiative. Progress report.* London: Home Office.

Howells, K. & Tennant, A. (2010). Ready or not, they are coming: Dangerous and severe personality disorder and treatment engagement. In A. Tennant & K. Howells (Eds.), *Using Time Not Doing Time: Practitioner Perspectives on Personality Disorder and Risk* (pp. 33–44). Chichester, Sussex: John Wiley & Sons.

James, D. V. (2010). Diversion of mentally disordered people from the criminal justice system in England and Wales: An overview. *International Journal of Law and Psychiatry, 33*, 241–248.

Kelly, B. D. (2009). Criminal insanity in 19th-century Ireland, Europe and the United States: Cases, contexts and controversies. *International Journal of Law and Psychiatry, 32*, 362–368.

Kirkpatrick, T., Draycott, S., Freestone, M., Cooper, S., Twiselton, K., & Maden, T. (2010). A descriptive evaluation of patients and prisoners assessed for dangerous and severe personality disorder. *Journal of Forensic Psychiatry and Psychology, 21*, 264–282.

Konrad, N. & Lau, S. (2010). Dealing with the mentally ill in the criminal justice system in Germany. *International Journal of Law and Psychiatry, 33*, 236–240.

Large, M. M. & Nielssen, O. (2011). Violence in first-episode psychosis: A systematic review and meta-analysis. *Schizophrenia Research, 125*, 209–220.

Large, M. M., Smith, G., & Nielssen, O. (2009). The relationship between the rate of homicide by those with schizophrenia and the overall homicide rate: A systematic review and meta-analysis. *Schizophrenia Research, 112*, 123–129.

Lestico, A. R., Salekin, R. S., DeCoster, J., & Rogers, R. (2008). A large scale meta-analysis relating Hare measures of psychopathy to antisocial conduct. *Law and Human Behavior, 32*, 28–45.

Lindsay, W. R. (2002). Research and literature on sex offenders with intellectual and developmental disabilities. *Journal of Intellectual Disability Research, 46*, 74–85.

Lindsay, W. R., O'Brien, G., Carson, D., Holland, A. J., Taylor, J. L., & Johnston, S. (2010). Pathways into services for offenders with intellectual disabilities: Childhood experiences, diagnostic information, and offense variables. *Criminal Justice and Behavior, 37*, 678–694.

Lindsay, W. R. & Taylor, J. L. (2005). A selective review of research on offenders with developmental disabilities: Assessment and treatment. *Clinical Psychology and Psychotherapy, 12*, 201–214.

Link, B., Stueve, A., & Phelen, J. (1998). Psychotic symptoms and violent behaviors: Probing the components of "threat/control override" symptoms. *Social Psychiatry and Psychiatric Epidemiology, 33*, S55–S60.

Logan, C. & Blackburn, R. (2009). Mental disorder in violent women in secure settings: Potential relevance to risk for future violence. *International Journal of Law and Psychiatry, 32*, 31–38.

Long, C. G., Hall, L., Craig, L., Mochty, U., & Hollin, C. R. (2011). Women referred for medium-secure inpatient care: A population study over a six-year period. *Journal of Psychiatric Intensive Care, 7*, 17–26.

Luiselli, J. K. (2000). Presentation of paraphilias and paraphilia related disorders in young adults with mental retardation: Two case profiles. *Mental Health Aspects of Developmental Disabilities, 3*: 42–46.

Lynam, D. R. & Gudonis, L. (2005). The development of psychopathy. *Annual Review of Clinical Psychology, 1*, 381–407.

Maden, A. (2007). Dangerous and severe personality disorder: Antecedents and origins. *British Journal of Psychiatry, 190* (Suppl. 49), s8–s11.

Markowitz, F. E. (2011). Mental illness, crime, and violence: Risk, context, and social control. *Aggression and Violent Behavior, 16*, 36–44.

Männynsalo, L., Putkonen, H., Lindberg, N., & Kotilainen, I. (2009). Forensic psychiatric perspective on criminality associated with intellectual disability: A nationwide register-based study. *Journal of Intellectual Disability Research, 5*, 279–288.

McReynolds, L. S., Schwalbe, C. S., & Wasserman, G. A. (2010). The contribution of psychiatric disorder to juvenile recidivism. *Criminal Justice and Behavior, 37*, 204–216.

Meehan, J., Flynn, S., Hunt, I. M., Robinson, J., Bickley, H., Parsons, R., & Shaw, J. (2006). Perpetrators of homicide with schizophrenia: A national clinical survey in England and Wales. *Psychiatric Services, 57*, 1648–1651.

Ministry of Justice (2010). *Statistics of Mentally Disordered Offenders 2008 England and Wales.* Ministry of Justice Statistics Bulletin. London: Ministry of Justice.

Moffitt, T., Gabrielli, W., Mednick, S., & Schulsinger, F. (1981). Socioeconomic status, IQ, and delinquency. *Journal of Abnormal Psychology, 90*, 152–156.

Mokros, A., Osterheider, M., Hucker, S. J., & Nitschke, J. (2010). Psychopathy and sexual sadism. *Law and Human Behavior, 35*, 188–199.

Morrissey, C., Hogue, T., Mooney, P., Allen, C., Johnston, S., & Taylor, J. L. (2007). Predictive validity of the PCL-R in offenders with intellectual disability in a high secure hospital setting: Institutional aggression. *Journal of Forensic Psychiatry and Psychology, 18*, 1–15.

Morrissey, C. & Hollin, C. (2011). Antisocial and psychopathic personality disorders in forensic intellectual disability: What do we know so far? *Psychology, Crime, & Law, 17*, 133–149.

Mullen, P. E. (2007). Dangerous and severe personality disorder and in need of treatment. *British Journal of Psychiatry, 190* (Suppl. 49), s3–s7.

National Institute for Mental Health in England (2003). *Personality Disorder: No Longer a Diagnosis of Exclusion. Policy Implementation Guidance for the Development of Services for People with Personality Disorder.* London: Department of Health.

Naudts, K. & Hodgins, S. (2006a). Schizophrenia and violence: A search for neurobiological correlates. *Current Opinion in Psychiatry, 19*, 533–538.

——(2006b). Neurobiological correlates of violent behavior among persons with schizophrenia. *Schizophrenia Bulletin, 32*, 562–572.

Nilsson, T., Bromander, S., Anckarsäter, R., Kristiansson M., Forsman, A., Blennow, K., & Wass, C. (2010). Neurochemical measures co-vary with personality traits: Forensic psychiatric findings replicated in a general population sample. *Psychiatry Research, 178*, 525–530.

Ogloff, J. P. (2006). Psychopathy/antisocial personality disorder conundrum. *Australian and New Zealand Journal of Psychiatry, 40*, 519–528.

Quen, J. M. (1968). An historical view of the M'Naghten trial. *Bulletin of the History of Medicine, 42*, 43–51.

Phillips, H. K., Gray, N. S., MacCulloch, S. I., Taylor, J., Moore, S. C., Huckle, P., & MacCulloch, M. J. (2005). Risk assessment in offenders with mental disorders: Relative efficacy of personal demographic, criminal history, and clinical variables. *Journal of Interpersonal Violence, 20*, 833–847.

Poythress, N. & Petrila, J. P. (2010). PCL-R Psychopathy: Threats to sue, peer review, and potential implications for science and law. A commentary. *International Journal of Forensic Mental Health, 9*, 3–10.

Prins, H. (1980). *Offenders, Deviants, or Patients? An Introduction to the Study of Socio-Forensic Problems*. London: Tavistock Publications.

Ramsay, M., Saradjian, J., Murphy, N., & Freestone, M. (2009). Commentary on the article by Peter Tyrer and others about the assessment phase of the Dangerous and Severe Personality Disorder Programme. *Journal of Forensic Psychiatry & Psychology, 20*, 147–150.

Rice, M. E., Harris, G. T., Lang, C., & Chaplin, T. C. (2008). Sexual preferences and recidivism of sex offenders with mental retardation. *Sexual Abuse: A Journal of Research and Treatment, 20*, 409–425.

Richardson, E. & McSherry, B. (2010). Diversion down under—programs for offenders with mental illnesses in Australia. *International Journal of Law and Psychiatry, 34*, 249–257.

Roberts, A. D. L. & Coid, J. W. (2010). Personality disorder and offending behaviour: Findings from the national survey of male prisoners in England and Wales. *Journal of Forensic Psychiatry and Psychology, 21*, 221–237.

Robertson, G. (1981). The extent and pattern of crime amongst mentally handicapped offenders. *Apex: Journal of The British Institute of Mental Handicap, 9*, 100–103.

Robins, L. N. (1978). Sturdy childhood predictors of adult antisocial behavior: Replication from longitudinal studies. *Psychological Medicine, 8*, 611–622.

Salekin, R. T., Lee, Z., Schrum Dillard, C. L., & Kubak, F. A. (2010). Child psychopathy and protective factors: IQ and motivation to change. *Psychology, Public Policy, and Law, 16*, 158–176.

Salize, H. J., Dreßing, H. & Kief, C. (2007). *Mentally Disordered Persons in European Prison Systems—Needs, Programmes and Outcome (EUPRIS)*. Health & Consumer Protection Directorate General, European Commission.

Schilling, C. M., Walsh, A., & Yun, I. (2010). ADHD and criminality: A primer on the genetic, neurobiological, evolutionary, and treatment literature for criminologists. *Journal of Criminal Justice, 39*, 3–11.

Schug, R. & Raine, A. (2009). Comparative meta-analyses of neuropsychological functioning in antisocial schizophrenic persons. *Clinical Psychology Review, 29*, 230–242.

Silberman, M. (2010). Sexual abuse in childhood and the mentally disordered female offender. *International Journal of Offender Therapy and Comparative Criminology, 54*, 783–802.

Silver, E., Felson, R. B., & Vaneseltine, M. (2008). The relationship between mental health problems and violence among criminal offenders. *Criminal Justice and Behavior, 35*, 405–426.

Singleton, N., Meltzer, H., Gatward, R., Coid, J., & Deasy, D. (1998). *Psychiatric Morbidity Among Prisoners in England and Wales*. London: The Stationary Office.

Sirdifield, C., Gojkovica, D., Brooker, C., & Ferriter, M. (2009). A systematic review of research on the epidemiology of mental health disorders in prison populations: A summary of findings. *Journal of Forensic Psychiatry & Psychology, 20* (S1), S78–S101.

Skeem, J. L., Schubert, C., Odgers, C., Mulvey, E. P., Gardner, W., & Lidz, C. (2006). Symptoms and community violence among high-risk patients: A test of the relationship at the weekly level. *Journal of Consulting and Clinical Psychology, 74*, 967–979.

Skeem, J. L. & Cooke, D. J. (2010a). Is criminal behavior a central component of psychopathy? Conceptual directions for resolving the debate. *Psychological Assessment, 22*, 433–445.

—— (2010b). One measure does not a construct make: Directions toward reinvigorating psychopathy research—reply to Hare and Neumann (2010). *Psychological Assessment, 22*, 455–459.

Skeem, J. L., Poythress, N., Edens, J. F., Lilienfeldd, S. O., & Cale, E. M. (2003). Psychopathic personality or personalities? Exploring potential variants of psychopathy and their implications for risk assessment. *Aggression and Violent Behavior, 8*, 513–546.

Smith, H., White, T., & Walker, P. (2008). Offending in the learning disabled population: A retrospective audit of Tayside learning disability service court reports. *Medicine, Science, and the Law, 48*, 31–36.

Soyka, M., Graz, C., Bottlender, R., Dirschedl, P., & Schoech, H. (2007). Clinical correlates of later violence and criminal offences in schizophrenia. *Schizophrenia Research, 94*, 89–98.

Spidel, A., Lecomte, T., Greaves, C., Sahlstrom, K., & Yuille, J. C. (2010). Early psychosis and aggression: Predictors and prevalence of violent behaviour amongst individuals with early onset psychosis. *International Journal of Law and Psychiatry, 33*, 171–176.

Stanton, J., Simpson, A., & Wouldes, T. (2000). A qualitative study of filicide by mentally ill mothers. *Child Abuse & Neglect, 24*, 1451–1460.

Stockdale, K. C., Olver, M. E., & Wong, S. C. P. (2010). The Psychopathy Checklist: Youth Version and adolescent and adult recidivism: Considerations with respect to gender, ethnicity, and age. *Psychological Assessment, 22*, 768–781.

Straw, J. (1999). Severe personality disorders. *Hansard (UK Parliamentary Reports, House of Commons)*, 15 February, pp. 601–613.

Svennerlind, C., Nilsson, T., Kerekes, N., Andiné, P., Lagerkvist, M., Forsman, A., & Malmgre, H. (2010). Mentally disordered criminal offenders in the Swedish criminal system. *International Journal of Law and Psychiatry, 33*, 220–226.

Taylor, P. J. & Bragado-Jimenez, M. D. (2009). Women, psychosis and violence. *International Journal of Law and Psychiatry, 32*, 56–64.

Tikkanen, R., Auvinen-Lintunen, L., Ducci, F., Sjöberg, R. L., Goldman, D., Tiihonen, J., Ojansuu, I., & Virkkunen, M. (2010). Psychopathy, PCL-R, and MAOA genotype as predictors of violent reconvictions. *Psychiatry Research, 185*, 382–386.

Thigpen, C. H. & Cleckley, H. M. (1957). *The Three Faces of Eve.* New York, NY: McGraw-Hill.

Tyrer, P., Cooper, S., Rutter, D., Seivewright, D., Duggan, C., & Byford, S. (2009). The assessment of dangerous and severe personality disorder: Lessons from a randomised controlled trial linked to qualitative analysis. *Journal of Forensic Psychiatry & Psychology, 20*, 120–131.

Tyrer, P., Duggan, C., Cooper, S., Crawford, M., Seivewright, H., Rutter, D., & Barrett, B. (2010). The successes and failures of the DSPD experiment: The assessment and management of severe personality disorder. *Medicine, Science and Law, 50*, 95–99.

Ullrich, S., Yang, M., & Coid, J. (2010). Dangerous and severe personality disorder: An investigation of the construct. *International Journal of Law and Psychiatry, 33*, 84–88.

Vincent, G. M., Odgers, C. L., McCormick, A. V., & Corrado, R. R. (2008). The PCL: YV and recidivism in male and female juveniles: A follow-up into young adulthood. *International Journal of Law and Psychiatry, 31*, 287–296.

Vitacco, M. J., Rogers, R., Neumann, C. S., Harrison, K. S., & Vincent, G. (2005). A comparison of factor models on the PCL-R with mentally disordered offenders: The development of a four-factor model. *Criminal Justice and Behavior, 32*, 526–545.

Volkow, N. D. (2009). Substance use disorders in schizophrenia—clinical implications of comorbidity. *Schizophrenia Bulletin, 35*, 469–472.

Walker, N. & McCabe, S. (1973). *Crime and Insanity in England.* Edinburgh: Edinburgh University Press.

Wallace, C., Mullen, P. E., & Burgess, P. (2004). Criminal offending in schizophrenia over a 25-year period marked by deinstitutionalization and increasing prevalence of comorbid substance use disorders. *American Journal of Psychiatry, 161*, 716–727.

Walsh, Z., Swogger, M. T., O'Connor, B. P., Schonbrun, Y. C., Shea, M. T., & Stuart, G. L. (2010). Subtypes of partner violence perpetrators among male and female psychiatric patients. *Journal of Abnormal Psychology, 119*, 563–574.

Walter, M., Wiesbeck, G. A., Dittmann, V., & Graf, M. (2010). Criminal recidivism in offenders with personality disorders and substance use disorders over 8 years of time at risk. *Psychiatry Research, 186*, 443–445.

Warren, J. I., Burnettea, M. L., Southa, S. C., Chauhana, P., Balec, R. Friend, R., & Van Patten, I. (2003). Psychopathy in women: Structural modeling and comorbidity. *International Journal of Law and Psychiatry, 26*, 223–242.

Weber, S., Habel, U., Amunts, K., & Schneider, F. (2008). Structural brain abnormalities in psychopaths: A review. *Behavioral Sciences and the Law, 26*, 7–28.

Weizmann-Henelius, G., Putkonen, H., Grönroos, M., Lindberg, N., Eronen, M., & Häkkänen-Nyholm, H. (2010). Examination of psychopathy in female homicide offenders—confirmatory factor analysis of the PCL-R. *International Journal of Law and Psychiatry, 33*, 177–183.

West, D. J. & Farrington, D. P. (1973). *Who Becomes Delinquent?* London: Heinemann Educational.

Woodward, M. (1955). The role of low intelligence in delinquency. *British Journal of Delinquency, 6*, 281–303.

Wormith, J. S. (1984). The controversy over the effects of long-term incarceration. *Canadian Journal of Criminology, 26*, 423–437.

Yang, S., Kadouri, A., Révah-Lévy, A., Mulvey, E. P., & Falissard, B. (2009). Doing time: A qualitative study of long-term incarceration and the impact of mental illness. *International Journal of Law and Psychiatry, 32*, 294–303.

Yang, Y., Raine, A., Han, C. B., Schug, R. A., Toga, A. W., & Narr, K. L. (2010). Reduced hippocampal and parahippocampal volumes in murderers with schizophrenia. *Psychiatry Research: Neuroimaging, 182*, 9–13.

Yoshikawa, K., Taylor, P. J., Yamagami, A., Okada, T., Ando, K., Taruya, T., Matsumoto, T., & Kikuchi, A. (2007). Violent recidivism among mentally disordered offenders in Japan. *Criminal Behaviour and Mental Health, 17*, 137–151.

Mental Illness and Prisoners

Concerns for Communities and Healthcare Providers

Samantha Hoke

Inmate X is a 49-year-old Caucasian male who was first seen for mental health concerns at age 26 while incarcerated; he was diagnosed with schizoaffective disorder and antisocial personality disorder. Inmate X was born to working class parents and grew up with two younger brothers, a twin sister and an older sister. He was never married, but has a 15-year-old daughter.

Records indicate there is no family history of drug/alcohol abuse or mental illness. However, inmate X has an extensive substance abuse history beginning at the age of 11; he has admitted to abusing alcohol, marijuana, cocaine and hallucinogens. Inmate X graduated high school, worked several jobs, and also served briefly in the United States Navy until his less than honorable discharge. Inmate X's original offense was rape and burglary, but he sustained many additional probation violation charges for drug use, violation of restraining orders, and shoplifting. While incarcerated, inmate X picked up an additional charge for mailing threatening letters to the United States President. All of his time on these sentences has been served.

Since his incarceration, inmate X has been stabilized on Olanzapine, Fluphenazine Deconate, Cogentin and Clonazepam. Inmate X was transferred to an open mental health unit and has been a stellar resident indicated by job performance, medication compliance, group attendance and cooperation with other peers. Upon inmate X's risk panel assessment he was deemed to no longer be a risk to society and was released from prison. A short 5 months after release, inmate X reoffended while under the influence and was brought back into custody on violation of parole. Shortly thereafter, inmate X has again been stabilized on medications and according to his reviewing treatment team, inmate X appears to be upholding qualities deeming him appropriate for society.

Samantha Hoke, "Mental Illness and Prisoners: Concerns for Communities and Healthcare Providers," *Online Journal of Issues in Nursing*, vol. 20, no. 1, pp. 36-45.

This case study presents one story that illustrates the fate of thousands of inmates. Prison inmates represent a very vulnerable population exposed to many stressors. These stressors can lead to outcomes such as substance use, suicide, and recidivism. This article will explore the issue of recidivism in corrections; discussion will include characteristics of corrections, reasons for recidivism, and the limitations presented to corrections in the treatment of mental health. The article will also describe current efforts to reduce recidivism and offer alternative, literature based strategies to reduce recidivism that are compliant with jail/prison protocols in the United States.

Facts About Imprisonment

The above inmate's story is one reflection of the inundated prison system. There are approximately 2.2 million pretrial and 1.6 million posttrial inmates in county, state, and federal prisons; this equates to approximately 756 per 100,000 people incarcerated in the United States (Carson & Golinelli, 2013; Exworthy, Samele, Urquia & Forrester, 2012). The United States has only 5% of the world's population, but 25% of the world's prisoners (Liptak, 2008). China, with a population four times the United States, has an average of 1.6 million prisoners (Liptak, 2008). Russia may be the only industrialized country that is close to the U.S. incarceration rate with an average of 627 per 100,000 (Liptak, 2008). The United Kingdom (U.K.) has an average of 152 per 100,000 people incarcerated, higher than other European countries that have an average of 120 (Exworthy et al., 2012). The U.S. prison system is thus the largest in the world.

In America, imprisonment was considered unusual in the beginning of the 18th century. Today the prison system is viewed as both a necessity to keep the public safe and as a mode of punishment for crimes. Imprisonment comes at an average cost per inmate of $31,286 per year (Henrichsen & Delaney, 2012). Medical care alone accounts for an estimated 12% of prison budgets, second only to security costs, which include employee salaries, insurance, and retirement costs (Stephan, 2004). Cost concerns are a pressing issue as accommodating the expanding inmate population results in increased individual taxes to fund the necessary budget.

Recidivism and Mental Health Concerns

Recidivism, or repeat offenders, further strains the prison budget. Recidivism is defined as a repeated arrest or incarceration (Baillargeon, Binswanger, Penn, Williams & Murray, 2009). In a 15 state study, over 2/3 of released prisoners reoffended or were rearrested within 3 years; this equates to 4 out of every 10 people released from prison are re-incarcerated (Bureau of Justice, 2013; Stephan, 2004). However, evidence shows the largest impact on prison budgets is from altering sentences and release policies, rather than altering per-inmate costs (Stephan, 2004). Operating a safe, humane, and well programmed institution is not cheap and low per-inmate cost is not necessarily a priority (Stephan, 2004).

Mental healthcare for this population is both expensive and crucial (Stephan, 2004). A 2006 Department of Justice study found more than half of all inmates have a mental health problem compared to 11% of the general population (James & Glaze, 2006). Mentally ill inmates are often inappropriately treated due to lack of knowledge about the rising mental health population (FRONTLINE, 2005). With recognition that prisons are not well equipped for the mentally ill, community programs have arisen to decrease sentencing of nonviolent offenders and the mentally ill. These community efforts have helped to educate the general public and debunk myths about mental illness.

Brief Overview of Healthcare in Corrections

Many people assert that the "right to health" is a fundamental human right, in which any person, regardless of legal status, is entitled to receive adequate healthcare. This right is the driving force behind establishing standards and protocols in the treatment of inmates (Burns, 2011). The World Health Organization (WHO) used this basic right to establish a guide detailing conditions that governments must generate to promote optimum health for their peoples, specifically stating that healthcare in prisons must be improved to better serve inmates. The integration of structured programs to serve populations endemic to corrections, such as persons with substance abuse issues and/or mental illness, is one bridge to provide quality healthcare (Eytan et al., 2010). The goal of these programs is for healthcare providers to ultimately contribute to the rehabilitation of inmates and thus reduce recidivism.

The U.S. prison system often falls short of meeting acceptable standards of care. Reasons may range from lack of resources to conflicts of interest between healthcare providers and security protocols (Exworthy et al., 2012). The U.K., considered more advanced in prison healthcare, strives to improve prison healthcare based on the concept of equivalence. Improvements in prison mental health care are driven by the idea that, whenever possible, healthcare should be equivalent to care available in the community. This concept of equivalence has underpinned

BRIEF OVERVIEW OF PRISON NURSING: ONE NURSE'S PERSPECTIVE

All inmate patients arrive at the prison in Receiving & Discharge (R & D). Here they are screened by several different disciplines including nursing (for a medical history and nursing intake), psychology, and a unit counselor. During this intake screening with the nurse, an inmate's medications are initially ordered. The nurse reviews the medications and receives a verbal/telephone physician order to continue any medication(s) for the inmate during the period of incarceration. The inmate will then receive that medication during the next designated pill line time, when oral medications are distributed. Most medications are continued; however, like other facilities, there are medications that require nonformulary requests. For these medications, an alternative medication may be prescribed as an equivalent or the medication will be continued through a pharmacy nonformulary request process.

Following the initial intake, a patient designated to be on an inpatient unit must have a physical completed within 24 hours by a midlevel practitioner/provider (MLP). Inmate patients are also required to be seen by psychiatry services within 24 hours. Inpatient inmates, as well as inmates designated to a general population housing unit, must be followed up by a physician for a physical within 14 days.

A prison lifestyle includes a rigorous routine. There are predetermined times for meals as well as medications, including "insulin lines." Inmates prescribed insulin and other medications arrive at three separate, predetermined, designated times for pill line and insulin line to receive these medications. Medications are typically given on time. Exceptions to this may include: staff otherwise occupied handling medical emergencies; responding to body alarms for staff who need assistance during an altercation; or other institutional level emergencies. These exceptions typically cause a delay of less than 15 minutes.

Similar processes are in place for nursing treatments. There are designated times for procedures such as dressing changes and intravenous (IV) and other injections. Challenges are not typically a matter of lacking supplies, as one might imagine, but rather more about every day nursing supplies being locked up or a need for additional prudence when accounting for items (e.g., medications, supplies). All items (e.g., IV flush, epinephrine (EPI) pens) have to be counted and withdrawn from a medication dispensing machine. Other items that are locked and must be inventoried daily are: scissors required for a dressing changes, oxygen tanks, suture removal kits, catheter kits, and insulin pump supplies.

efforts in the U.K. to improve prison healthcare (Exworthy et al., 2012).

Both the U.S. and U.K. face limitations in prison settings. The supply of resources and treatment facilities is continuously challenged with the high demand and overcrowding of prison systems. Rates of mental illness and the lack of a clear legal framework for treating inmates with severe mental illness are other challenges to implementing the equivalence model. Identical services provided in the community may not be acceptable levels of care for the complexity of psychiatric cases present within the prison system. Healthcare providers are often restricted by policies and security protocols that limit interventions they may prescribe. These limitations and restrictions suggest a great need for improvement in prison mental healthcare. The next section will explore several factors that affect mental healthcare in prison settings, such as characteristics of the prison population and the impact of politics.

Factors Affecting Mental Healthcare in Prisons

Characteristics of the Prison Population

Rates of mental illness within prison systems across western countries are very high. A systematic review of 62 studies of mental health disorders within western countries found the following diagnoses among male prisoners: 3 to 7% psychotic disorder, 10% major depression, 47% antisocial personality disorder, and 65% personality disorder, including antisocial personality disorder (Fazel & Danesh, 2002). The same review yielded higher results for women. Among the female prisoners, diagnoses included: 4% psychotic disorder, 12% major depression, 21% antisocial personality disorder, and 42% personality/antisocial disorder (Fazel & Danesh, 2002). In addition to these diagnoses, a significant number had anxiety disorders, organic disorders, traumatic brain injuries (TBI), suicidal behaviors, distress associated with all forms of abuse, attentiondeficit hyperactivity disorder (ADHD) and other developmental disorders, including mental retardation and Asperger's syndrome (Daniel, 2007).

Rates of mental illness in the U.S. alone are burdensome. The U.S. Department of Justice (USDOJ) found that more than half of all inmates, or over than 1 million individuals, have a mental illness compared to 11% of the general population; and yet only 1 of 3 prison inmates and 1 of 6 jail inmates receive any form of mental health treatment (Daniel, 2007; James & Glaze, 2006). Thus 56% of state, 46% of federal, and 64% of jail prisoners have either a current or recent history of mental health problems (James & Glaze, 2006). The USDOJ also studied the distribution of mental health problems and found that 43% of state prisoners and 54% of jail inmates reported symptoms that met criteria for mania; 23% of state and 30% of jail inmates reported symptoms of major depression; and 15% of state and 24% of jail inmates reported symptoms that met criteria for a psychotic disorder (James & Glaze, 2006). Furthermore, approximately 70% had a primary or comorbid substance abuse disorder (James & Glaze, 2006). The high amount of mental health disorders alone constitutes but one of the many limitations to appropriate healthcare presented in correctional settings.

Social Policy and Increased Incarceration Rates

Many question why rates of mental illness are so high among incarcerated individuals. The answer is complex as several synergistic factors related to social policy have contributed to high rates of persons with mental illness behind bars. The first factor was the mass closing of public mental health hospitals in the 1960s. This national movement followed the availability of new antipsychotic medications, such as Olanzapine®. Movement leaders believed moving patients into a community based setting was a humane alternative to overcrowded and understaffed institutions (Baillargeon et al., 2009). Unfortunately, resources fell short, coordination lacked, and promised clinics and halfway houses were not provided to care for released hospital patients (Baillargeon et al., 2009; FRONTLINE, 2005). Following this movement, health insurers restricted mental health coverage; private hospitals restricted enrollment of psychotic patients; and civil commitment laws became more restrictive (Baillargeon et al., 2009).

As these changes occurred, another policy change ensued that resulted in dramatic increases in rates of incarcerations of persons with mental illness(es). The 1980s "war on drugs" led to an increase in drug related arrests and mandatory sentencing laws (Baillargeon et al., 2009). These arrests resulted in an increase in the proportion of inmates with psychiatric disorders and substance abuse problems (Baillargeon et al., 2009). Prison sentences and substance abuse remain significant contributing factors to the increased population of prisoners with mental health concerns.

Mentally Ill and Prison Sentences

Policy changes have increased the length of time served for mentally ill inmates. State prisoners who had a mental health problem served an average sentence of four months longer than those without a mental health problem (James & Glaze, 2006). In general, studies have found that individuals with a mental health problem serve an average sentence of 15 months longer than those without (Baillargeon et al., 2009; FRONTLINE, 2005). There was little variation noted in expected time served for jail inmates (approximately 55% with a mental health problem and 54% without one both expecting to serve 6 months or less) (James & Glaze, 2006).

Often the reason individuals with mental illness serve longer sentences is related to the inability to follow the strict rules of prison life. Individuals with a mental health problem tend to obtain conduct violations. Statistics estimate that among state prisoners, 58% with a mental health problem (compared to 43% without) had been charged with rule violations (James & Glaze, 2006). Depending on the violation level, this may result in revoked privileges and changed security level and/or release date. For example, the resulting disciplinary record may lead to more difficulty achieving parole. Parole boards are also reluctant to release individuals with a mental health disorder back into the community due to inadequate community services available for them to obtain treatment (Rossman, 2001; FRONTLINE, 2005).

Mentally Ill and Substance Use

It is a common misperception that people with mental illness are dangerous. Two recent studies revealed illegal drugs as the primary contributor to violence, not mental illness (Dolan, Castle, & McGregor, 2012; Fazel, Gulati, Linsell, Geddes & Grann, 2009). The studies examined the potential link between mental illness and risk of violence and found violence risk was not significantly increased when compared to the general public. The studies also indicated that the risk of violence in persons with mental illness combined with substance use was not different than the risk of violence for individuals with a diagnosis of solely substance use.

There is a high rate of substance abuse among prisoners, but especially among those also diagnosed with mental illness. At the time of arrest, over a third of inmates who had a mental health diagnosis were under the influence of substances compared to a quarter of inmates without mental illness (James & Glaze, 2006). An assessment of nonviolent crimes found persons with schizophrenia or nonschizophrenia psychotic disorders had lower rates of driving under the influence, but higher rates of drug possession (Baillargeon et al., 2009). Dual diagnosis was common; 74% of prisoners who had a mental health problem met criteria for substance dependence or abuse, compared to 56% without a mental health problem (James & Glaze, 2006).

An individual who has both an alcohol or drug problem and an emotional/psychiatric problem has a dual diagnosis (Mental Health America, 2013). Dual diagnoses are common, but this concept has not always been accepted. However, research has demonstrated that simultaneous treatment of mental illness and substance abuse supports better outcomes, which has furthered the acceptance of dual diagnoses. Approximately 50% of the mentally ill population also has a substance abuse problem (National Alliance on Mental Illness, 2013a). Additionally, 6 of 10 people with a substance use disorder also suffer from another mental illness (National Institute on Drug Abuse, 2007). Of those individuals who are incarcerated, the number increases to almost 70%, or nearly 3 of 4 persons (Daniel, 2007; Skeem, Manchak & Peterson, 2010).

These statistics beg the question: why are individuals with mental illness more prone to substance abuse over those without a mental health problem? Self-medicating and social factors are viewed as common contributors to substance abuse amongst mentally ill individuals. Like their healthy counterparts, individuals with mental illness may begin to use drugs or alcohol for recreational use. Continued use has often been attributed to a misguided attempt to treat symptoms of their mental illness. In the short term, individuals may find they can reduce their level of anxiety or depression by self-medicating. Genetic vulnerabilities are hypothesized as a reason for continued use as well. Genetic factors predispose individuals to both mental disorders and addictions, or to having a greater risk of the second disorder once the first appears. (National Alliance on Mental Illness, 2013a; National Institute on Drug Abuse, 2007; McKean & Ransford, 2004).

Other factors contribute to substance abuse in this population. Mentally ill persons are often socially disenfranchised. Poverty situates them to live in neighborhoods endemic with illicit substances, unemployment, and other marginalized citizens. Research has also demonstrated that mentally ill individuals are more likely to have a history of victimization. Individuals who have difficulty developing social relationships, often as a consequence of mental illness, find themselves more easily accepted by groups whose social activities is based on drug use. Some believe that an identity based on drug addictions is more acceptable than one based on mental illness. (National Alliance on Mental Illness, 2013a). Together, social stresses and traumas and early exposure to drugs are common factors that can lead to addiction and mental illness (James & Glaze, 2006; National Alliance on Mental Illness, 2013a; Skeem et al., 2010).

Finally, some areas of the brain are affected by both drug abuse and mental disorders. For example, brain circuits linked to reward processing, as well as those implicated in the stress response, are affected by substance abuse and also abnormalities in specific mental disorders. With the commonality of dual diagnoses, it is naïve to discount the evidence and fail to address both issues of substance use and mental illness when addressing mental health concerns and care for prisoners. (National Institute on Drug Abuse, 2007).

Mentally Ill Persons and Incarceration

A prison lifestyle is rigorous and routine with specific times for eating, sleeping, taking medications, standing for institutional counts, attending work, recreation or other structured programs and even moving from one place in the prison to the next. Prison rules are strict and inflexible and violation of rules is often addressed with segregation or revoked privileges. Most importantly, prison is a drug-free setting. Federal prisons have even banned tobacco products since 2004. Mental health treatment can help prisoners to make appropriate lifestyle adjustments, but is not available in every setting. Even when mental health treatment is in place, there are barriers for providers to consider.

Access to Mental Health Treatment

When necessary, psychiatric treatment is also mandated for those incarcerated. Many inmates with mental illness and access to treatment typically have psychiatric symptoms controlled and can function well while incarcerated. How can we best transition appropriately functioning inmates in the prison environment to continue stable behaviors upon release into the community, and thus decrease the chance of recidivism? Supporters of the legislation to close state hospitals urged funding for halfway houses and clinics. Those supporters, along with community mental health supporters, share the belief that offering the least restrictive environment to citizens is most beneficial. It seems prudent to suggest increased funding for public works, to ensure housing, employment, and structured community programs upon release for prisoners with mental illness to mirror the social circumstances found in prisons where inmates performed well. However, access to mental health services is not the case in all prison settings. The next section will discuss several barriers to mental health treatment for inmates.

Barriers to Mental Health Treatment

The main duty of prisons is to keep society safe; therefore security of the institution is the primary concern. Perhaps the most obvious hurdle to providing mental health treatment is the mission of corrections: to maintain security within the institution, providing a safe environment for both staff and inmates (Federal Bureau of Prisons, n.d. b). For instance, a core value of the Federal Bureau of Prisons is correctional excellence. This means all employees, even healthcare providers, are correctional workers first (Federal Bureau of Prisons, n.d. b). It is unquestionable this is an appropriate value in a correctional setting as it is the most economical way of ensuring the security of institutions. However, healthcare providers within corrections also have their own mission of providing the best possible care to their patients. Balancing this dual mission is often a challenge for healthcare providers. Three important areas of consideration for healthcare providers are segregation, suicide, and drug abuse.

Segregation

Segregation is the housing of inmates in special units separate from the general population (Federal Bureau of Prisons, n.d. a). Within federal prisons there are two types of segregation, disciplinary and administrative. Disciplinary segregation is a form of separation from the general population for a specified period of time as a mode of punishment for violating rules. There is a specified hearing process directed by the Disciplinary Hearing Officer (DHO) to which each inmate charged with a violation is entitled. A Segregation Review Official (SRO) reviews these inmates every seven days and can release an inmate from disciplinary segregation if he or she finds segregation is no longer necessary or has fulfilled its purpose. (Federal Bureau of Prisons, n.d. a).

Administrative detention is a form of separation from general population used when the presence of an individual poses a serious threat to the security of the institution. This housing status includes inmates who, a) require protective custody, b) cannot be placed in general population because they are pending travel to another institution (holdovers), or c) those awaiting a hearing for a disciplinary violation. (Federal Bureau of Prisons, n.d. a).

Being confined to a single area for 23 hours a day for a prolonged period of time has proven to be psychologically harmful. Psychological effects can include anxiety, depression, anger, cognitive disturbances, perceptual disturbances, obsessive thoughts, paranoia, and psychosis

(Smith, 2006). The nature and severity of the effects is dependent on the individual, length of stay, and conditions (e.g. access to natural light, books, radio). These effects are especially significant for individuals with mental illness. Individuals with mental illness often have an impaired ability to cope with stress as a result of their illness. The lack of social contact, unstructured days, and stress can exacerbate psychiatric symptoms or provoke recurrence (Metzner & Fellner, 2010). This may translate to bizarre, annoying, or dangerous behaviors.

Correctional workers generally respond to these behaviors as they would for other individuals who violate rules by issuing a conduct violation resulting in disciplinary segregation. Once the inmate is placed in segregation they can continue to receive conduct violations and be housed there indefinitely for continued misconduct, often as a result of psychiatric symptoms. This housing status of mentally ill inmates often proves challenging to mental health providers, who have an already burdensome caseload and, due to lack of time and resources, are unable to provide therapeutic interventions. Class action cases have ruled the segregation of mentally ill inmates to be cruel because of the psychological harm it can inflict. Yet, despite these rulings, in some prisons mentally ill inmates continue to be segregated. Segregation of mentally ill inmates is an ongoing issue and will continue to be a hurdle to mental health providers (Metzner & Fellner, 2010).

Suicide

The World Health Organization (WHO, 2007b) estimates one suicide attempt occurs approximately every three seconds and one completed suicide occurs approximately every minute. The causes of suicide are multifaceted. One indisputable fact is that individuals are especially vulnerable when faced with a combination of stressors (WHO, 2007b). Not surprisingly, inmates are an especially vulnerable group who face stressors such as separation from family, legal battles, and dealing with a new culture and environment.

Suicide rates within corrections illuminate the harsh reality of prison life. Suicide is the third leading cause of death in U.S. prisons, exceeded only by natural causes and AIDS (Daniel, 2007; WHO, 2007b). Pretrial inmates have a suicide attempt rate of about 7.5 times greater, and sentenced inmates have a rate of almost six times greater, than the general suicide rate of males in the community (WHO, 2007b).

Within corrections, suicide profiles, based on research studies, are used to target highrisk individuals. Pretrial inmates are generally male, young (20 25 years), unmarried, and arrested for minor, often substance related, crimes. This profiled group is at high risk during their first few hours of incarceration and near the time of a court hearing, especially when a guilty verdict and harsh sentencing is anticipated (WHO, 2007b). Another high profile group is sentenced individuals who are violent offenders, aged 30 35 who have served a good amount of time of their sentence (5 or more years); these suicides are often precipitated by a conflict, either within the prison, marital, or denial of parole. Extended length of incarceration presents a new set of stressors, such as victimization, loss of family support, fear of the unknown, embarrassment, and internal conflicts (WHO, 2007b). Accordingly, individuals with life sentences are particularly vulnerable to suicide attempt.

Inmates with mental illnesses are an especially vulnerable population as they have an impaired ability to cope with stress, further heightening mounting stressors. Depressive disorders are the most often linked psychiatric illness to suicide, yet hopelessness is the most common psychological state preceding suicide (Daniel, 2006). Furthermore, anxiety heightens the risk factor of suicide as well as situational factors, such as segregation (Daniel, 2006). The accumulations of risk factors reiterate the increased risk of suicide amongst inmates with mental illness. Mounting stressors, such as those inevitable with incarceration, are inescapable for mental health providers in corrections. These stressors, coupled with subsequent worsening psychiatric illness, present a significant hurdle in correctional mental health treatment.

Drug Abuse

An estimated 20% of people in the U.S. take prescription medications for nonmedical reasons (National Institute on Drug Abuse, 2013). This is considered prescription drug abuse, a growing problem in the United States. This increase is attributed to prescription drugs being easier to obtain and the medications being perceived as "safe" because a licensed professional prescribed it. Providers often have good intentions when prescribing medications, yet substance abuse and drug seeking is a harsh reality.

Given the high rates of substance abusers among the incarcerated population, misuse of prescription medications is a consideration amongst correctional providers. As in the community, medications may be used recreationally to achieve an altered mental state or high, instead of the intended therapeutic effect. A significant proportion of inmates seek prescribed medications for their psychotropic effect, rather than the intended use.

Misuse of anticholinergic agents (e.g. benztropine, trihexyphenidal) is well documented in the literature. However, abuse of other psychotropic medications is a growing concern in corrections. Gabapentin (Neurontin®) is known to create an altered mental state or high from snorting the gabapentin powder. This is often preferred by inmates with a prior history of cocaine dependence due to the similar effects it creates. Quetiapine (Seroquel®) has become increasingly popular amongst incarcerated individuals. Quetiapine, referred to as "quell," "susie Q," or "baby heroin" is used in its powder form for its potent sedative and anxiolytic properties. Wellbutrin, nicknamed "welbys," is used intranasally to achieve a "rush." Other psychotropics such as Olanzapine (Zyprexa®) and tricyclic antidepressants (TCA) (amitriptyline, nortriptlyine, desipramine) are abused for sedative properties, mind altering effects, or the potential to get a high. In addition to sedation, TCAs are lethal when hoarded and taken as an overdose. (Paggio, 2012).

Psychotropic drugs that can create an altered mental state or high are valuable among a dense population of substance abusers. Even inmates who may actually need a medication may be tempted to barter, sell, or trade. Inmates may trade for commissary items, cash, or contraband items such as alcohol or illicit substances. Of greater concern, prescription drugs may be used as a currency to purchase services such as protection, assaults, and sexual favors (Burns, 2009).

Trading prescribed medications (and associated transactions and debts) could compromise patient security, staff security, and the overall security of the institution. Furthermore, it could worsen and inmate's mental and physical health (Royal College of General Practitioners, 2011).

Abuse of some medications (e.g., quetiapine) has led to a nonformulary medication list. When a medication is considered nonformulary, it necessitates additional paperwork for providers to support its use. Providers may limit prescribing a medication that otherwise seems suitable in the community, based on the prison environment alone. Providers are presented with the challenge of finding alternative medications that closely equate the same results as nonformulary medications (Paggio, 2012).

The above issues are not an encompassing list of the difficulties presented to correctional mental health, but they do provide reasons to encourage action to provide funding to support the root of the problems. As a society, many want to offer the "right to health" to all citizens, regardless of legal status, to our citizens. In addition, appropriate treatment for mental health disorders within the prison system combined with a strong transition with appropriate supports, upon release may be able to impact the significant concern of recidivism. The Table summarizes common mental health treatments barriers encountered in prison settings and select nursing interventions.

TABLE 7.1 Treatment Barriers and Potential Nursing Interventions

Mental Health Treatment Barriers in Prisons	Nursing Interventions
Segregation Confined in a single living area for 23 hours/day Psychological effects: Anxiety, depression, anger, cognitive disturbances, perceptual disturbances, obsessive thoughts, paranoia & psychosis	1) Provide 1:1 social interaction 2) Encourage inmates to attend recreation 3) Provide routine structure to days 4) Reorient daily/discuss current events 5) Offer structured recreation programs to encourage socialization and interaction; ie. Music therapy, psychology worksheets, activity worksheets, books, magazines, activities
Suicide People are especially vulnerable when faced with a combination of stressors	1) Be vigilant of high risk suicide groups: • Pre-Trial inmates • Inmates with extended sentences; "lifers" • Sexual offender inmates • Mentally ill inmates • Inmates in locked units/single cells 2) Provide structure and activities to decrease stress, provide distraction and encourage hope
Drug Abuse Taking a prescription medication for nonmedical reasons	1) Be aware of highly abused prescription medications: • Anticholinergics • Psychotropic medications 2) Complete appropriate "mouth checks" to ensure inmates are not "cheeking" or diverting the medications 3) Crush highly abused medications 4) Be cognizant of intoxication and withdrawal symptoms

Research and Recidivism

Four of 10 inmates released from prison are reincarcerated within three years (Bureau of Justice, 2013; Stephan, 2004). Recidivism rates amongst general population inmates are well studied. Only a few studies have examined the association between psychiatric disorders and the risk of having a single repeat incarceration. State prisoners with a mental health problem (61%) were more likely than state prisoners without a mental health problem (56%) to have a current or past violent offense (James & Glaze, 2006). Among those who were repeat offenders, 47% were violent recidivists (compared to 39% without a mental problem) (James & Glaze, 2006). More recent statistics have indicated that 81% of mentally ill inmates currently in state prisons, 76% in federal prisons, and 79% in jails have prior convictions (FRONTLINE, 2013). There are several hypotheses related to recidivism.

Criminalization of Mental Illness

When the above statistics are considered in context, we see that individuals with mental illness are disproportionately represented in corrections and more likely to fail under correctional supervision (evidenced by rule violation records, longer sentences, and higher recidivism rates). These facts suggest that the mental health community has failed these individuals or that the perceived root of the problem is "criminalization" of mental illness. Criminalization of mental illness refers to the belief that if the mentally ill that are incarcerated had received the psychiatric services they needed, they would not be in trouble with the law (Skeem, Manchak & Peterson, 2010).

The perception of this criminalization as the sole problem has guided the corrections industry to the most logical solution: provide psychiatric treatment as a way of decreasing recidivism. In support of the criminalization hypothesis, one study of 113 jail arrestees with a dual diagnosis of a psychiatric disorder and substance abuse disorder concluded that approximately 8% of their study population had been arrested as a direct or indirect result of their psychiatric symptoms (Junginger, Claypoole, Laygo & Christiani, 2006). These results suggest that the criminalization hypothesis should not be completely discarded (Skeem et al., 2010). However, the hypothesis does not fully account for the link between mental illness and crime. The fact that the strongest predictors of violence and crime are the same for offenders with and without mental illness (substance use), and there being a common third variable of increased social risk factor leading to crime, suggests an alternate hypothesis. Additional study of these predictors may yield a more successful solution.

Social Hypothesis

The social hypothesis is related to lifestyle factors. Supporters of this hypothesis assert that people with mental illness engage in deviant behavior not because of a mental disorder, but because they are poor. Offenders with mental illness are more likely to live in disadvantaged neighborhoods (or are homeless); be under or unemployed; have a history of victimization; and/or abuse substances (James & Glaze, 2006). Poverty situates them socially to live in settings that are rife with illicit substances, unemployment, health burdens, and many similarly marginalized citizens (Skeem et al., 2010). Although each of these variables has been linked with criminal behavior, the extent to which they play a role in this behavior has not been established with research (Skeem et al., 2010).

In support of this social hypothesis, as already mentioned previously, results showed that major predictors of recidivism were the same for mentally disordered and for nondisordered individuals. Yet, mentally ill prisoners had higher recidivism rates or were more likely to reoffend. The social hypothesis suggests this is because, statistically, these prisoners have more risk factors than their healthy counterparts. Further supporting the potential impact of lifestyle choices on recidivism was the finding that psychiatric symptoms have not demonstrated strong correlations with repeat arrests (Callahan & Silver, 1998; Monson, Gunnin, Fogel & Kyle, 2001; Phillips et al., 2005). The strongest predictors of recidivism were prior history, employment problems, and antisocial personality (Skeem et al., 2010). Moreover, studies found that illicit substance abuse was the strongest risk factor for violence; mental illness was not an indicator of violence.

Conclusion: Implications for Practice

Current Efforts to Reduce Recidivism

Although it is hard to compare, the most common programs that have led to recidivism reduction have been substance abuse treatment, education, and employment services. However, there are an abundance of programs in action.

The Bureau of Prisons philosophy is that preparation for release begins the first day of imprisonment. It is a responsibility of the Bureau to provide inmates with skills needed to lead crime-free lives after release. Structured programs such as education, vocational training, institutional jobs, substance abuse treatment, parenting, anger management, counseling, recreation, faith-based offerings, and other programs teach inmates essential skills necessary for successful community reintegration.

The goal of inmate programs is to assist in rehabilitating convicted felons into lawabiding citizens in order to decrease rising costs associated with recidivism. Research has demonstrated that these programs play a major role to improve public safety. Of note, inmates enrolled in the Bureau's Federal Prison Industries (FPI) program, where inmates are employed in factories and are compensated, has 1) significantly reduced recidivism in comparison to study control group members, 2) demonstrated that inmates are more likely to be employed during their first year after release, and 3) demonstrated that the inmates earn higher per average wages than counterparts not enrolled in the program. Inmates enrolled in education programs demonstrated a significant decline in recidivism rates. Those enrolled in the residential drug abuse treatment programs (RDAPs) (an intense half-day treatment program 5 days a week, for 9 months followed by enrollment and another inmate program for the remainder of the day) were significantly less likely to recidivate or relapse to drug use for at least three years as compared to similar non-participating inmates. These programs do not typically enroll a high population of mentally ill inmates. However, it is likely that these programs would be beneficial as research has demonstrated that reasons for recidivism were similar among general population and mentally ill inmates. (Federal Bureau of Prisons, 2011).

Other community efforts aim to reduce recidivism by diverting nonviolent mentally ill individuals away from correctional institutions and towards community based mental health services. There are two major types of diversion programs, prebooking and postbooking. Prebooking programs are based on formal liaisons between law enforcement and mental health personnel that are designed to resolve psychiatric emergencies without resorting to arrest. One example of prebooking is crisis intervention teams. These teams include specially trained officers who redirect individuals to treatment rather than through the justice system.

Postbooking programs, on the other hand, aim to divert mentally ill offenders to community resources after they have been arrested. One promising postbooking program is the mental health court. The mental health court is utilized to transition nonviolent mentally ill individuals from prison to supervised treatment programs. Evidence reveals participation in a mental health court is correlated with longer periods without criminal recidivism (Baillaregeon et al., 2009).

Additional Implications for Mental Healthcare

To address mental health concerns for prisoners, health providers need to educate the public about mental illness in general, and in this population. National movements, such as the National Alliance on Mental Illness, that encourage mental health public awareness should also provide information pertinent to the inmate population and their challenges.

Parole officers should receive specified training about mental illness to support their efforts as a resource to avoid recidivism in released prisoners. Parole officers are often inundated with inmate caseloads beyond what they can handle. For inmates with mental health concerns, parole officers assume a role similar to that of a hospital case manager. These officers would likely benefit from smaller caseloads with time assist parolees to access appropriate services, such as day programs and home services.

National level emphasis on mental health concerns remains a necessity and should include specific directives that address the inmate population. Community programs that provide housing and employment opportunities could supplement national initiatives. Healthcare providers can advocate for funding and emphasize the financial relief correctional facilities would likely gain by providing a stable environment to support inmate mental health needs and decrease costs associated with decreased recidivism.

Despite correctional challenges (segregation, suicide, drug abuse), inmates are provided housing, employment, psychiatric treatment, and a controlled environment inhibiting substance use while behind bars, thus eliminating social risk factors that may contribute to both the primary incarceration and recidivism. Healthcare providers can and should continue to educate the public to reduce the stigma of mental illness. Mental health concerns and high recidivism is a self-made public health crisis that can be transformed. Use of current evidence to support community level mental healthcare can lead to initiatives to avoid incarceration and decrease recidivism.

Author

Samantha Hoke, MSN, PMHNPBC, RN

Email: SHoke@bop.gov Samantha Hoke completed her Bachelor of Science in Nursing from Worcester State College in Worcester, MA in spring 2009. Samantha became a commissioned corps nurse officer in the United States Public Health Service where she was and currently is stationed with the U.S. Department of Justice Federal Bureau of Prisons in Devens, MA. It was here that Samantha worked as a lead nurse on the mental health units. This professional experience and interaction with the mentally ill inspired Samantha to achieve her Master of Science in Nursing in Psychiatric/Mental Health. Samantha completed her MSN in Spring 2014 and became board certified and licensed as a PMHNP. She is currently awaiting new orders from the USPHS to continue her work serving the underserved, incarcerated, mentally ill population as a PMHNP BC within the Bureau.

References

Bailargeon, J., Binswanger, I.A., Penn, J.V., Williams, B.A., & Murray, O.J. (2009). Psychiatric disorder and repeat incarcerations: The revolving prison door. *American Journal of Psychiatry,* 166(1), 103–109.

Bureau of Justice. (2013). *Reentry trends in the U.S.* Retrieved from www.bjs.gov/content/reentry/recidivism.cfm

Burns, K. (2009). Commentary: The top ten reasons to limit prescription of controlled substances in prisons. *Journal of the American Academy of Psychiatry and the Law Online, 37*(1), 50–52.

Burns, K. (2011). Psychiatry behind bars: Practicing in jails and prisons. *Current Psychiatry,* 10(2), 15–20.

Callahan, L. & Silver, E. (1998). Revocation of conditional release: A comparison of individual program characteristics across four U.S. states. *International Journal of Law and Psychiatry, 21,* 177–186. DOI:10.1016/S0160-2527(98)00011-9.

Carson, E. & Golinelli, D. (2013). Prisoners in 2012: Trends in Admissions and Releases, 1991–2012 (Rev. ed.). Bureau of Justice Statistics, December 2013, NCJ 243920. Retrieved from, www.bjs.gov/content/pub/pdf/p12tar9112.pdf

Daniel, A. (2006). Preventing suicide in prisons: A collaborative responsibility of administrative, custodial, and clinical staff. *Journal of American Academy of Psychiatry Law, 34,* 165–75.

Daniel, A. (2007). Care of the mentally ill in prisons: Challenges and solutions. *Journal of American Academy of Psychiatry Law, 35,* 406–10.

Dolan, M., Castle, D., & McGregor, K. (2012). Criminally violent victimization in schizophrenia spectrum disorders: The relationship to symptoms and substance abuse. *BMC Public Health, 12,* 445. doi:10.1186/1471-2458-12-445.

Eytan, A., Haller, D.M., Wolff, H., Cerutti, B., Sebo, P., Bertrand, D., & Niveau, G. (2010). Psychiatric symptoms, psychological distress and somatic comorbidity among remand prisoners in Switzerland. *International Journal of Law and Psychiatry. 34*, 139. doi:10.1016/j.ijlp.2010.11.003

Exworthy, T., Samele, C., Urquia, N., & Forrester, A. (2012). Asserting prisoners' right to health: Progressing beyond equivalence. *Psychiatric Services, 63*(3), 270–275.

Fazel, S. & Danesh, J. (2002). Serious mental disorder in 23,000 prisoners: A systematic review of 62 surveys. *Lancet, 359*: 545–50.

Fazel S., Gulati G., Linsell L., Geddes J.R., & Grann M. (2009). Schizophrenia and violence: Systematic review and meta analysis. *PLoS Medicine, 6*(8): e1000120. doi:10.1371/journal.pmed.1000120

Federal Bureau of Prisons. (n.d. a). *Guide to segregation in federal prisons*. Retrieved from www.washlaw.org/pdf/Guide_to_Segregation_in_Federal_Prisons.pdf

Federal Bureau of Prisons. (2011). *About the Federal Bureau of Prisons*. Retrieved from www.bop.gov/news/PDFs/ipaabout.pdf

Federal Bureau of Prisons. (n.d. b). *Agency pillars*. Retrieved from www.bop.gov/about/agency/agency_pillars.jsp

FRONTLINE. (2005). *The new asylums*. Retrieved from www.pbs.org/wgbh/pages/frontline/shows/asylums/etc/faqs.html

Henrichson, C. & Delaney, R. (2012). The price of Prisons: What Incarceration Costs Taxpayers. New York: Vera Institute of Justice, 2012.

James, D. & Glaze, L. (2006). *Mental health problems of prison and jail inmates*. United States Department of Justice, September 2006, NCJ 213600. Retrieved from www.bjs.gov/content/pub/pdf/mhppji.pdf

Junginger, J., Claypoole, K., Laygo, R., & Crisanti, A. (2006). Effects of serious mental illness and substance abuse on criminal offenders. *Psychiatric Services*, 57, 879–882.

Liptak, A. (2008, April 23). Inmate count in U.S. dwarfs other nations' *The New York Times*. Retrieved from www.nytimes.com/2008/04/23/us/23prison.html?pagewanted=all

McKean, L. & Ransford, C. (2004). *Current strategies for reducing recidivism*. Retrieved from www.impactresearch.org/documents/recidivismexecutivesummary.pdf

Mental Health America. (2013). *Co-occurring disorders*. Retrieved from www.nmha.org/go/information/get-info/co-occurring-disorders/dual-diagnosis

Metzner, J. & Fellner, J. (2010). Solitary confinement and mental illness in U.S. prisons: A challenge for medical ethics. *Journal of the American Academy of Psychiatry and the Law, 38*(1), 104–108.

Monson, C., Gunnin, D., Fogel, M., & Kyle, L. (2001). Stopping the revolving door: Factors related to NGRI acquitees' maintenance of a conditional release. *Law and Human Behavior*, 25, 257–267. doi: 10.1023/A:1010745927735.

National Alliance on Mental Illness (NAMI). (2013a). *Dual diagnosis: Substance abuse and mental illness*. Retrieved from www.nami.org/Template.cfm?Section=By_Illness&Template=/TaggedPage/TaggedPageDisplay.cfm&TPLID=54&ContentID=23049

National Alliance on Mental Illness (NAMI). (2013b). *The criminalization of people with mental illness.* Retrieved from www.nami.org/Content/ContentGroups/Policy/WhereWeStand/The_Criminalization_of_People_with_Mental_Illness WHERE_WE_STAND.htm

National Institute on Drug Abuse. (2007). Comorbidity: Addition and other mental disorders. Retrieved from www.drugabuse.gov/publications/topics-in-brief/comorbid-drug-abuse-mental-illness

National Institute on Drug Abuse. (2013). *Prescription drug abuse.* Retrieved from www.nlm.nih.gov/medlineplus/prescriptiondrugabuse.html

Paggio, D.D. (2012). Psychotropic medication abuse by inmates in correctional facilities. *Mental Health Clinician, 1*(8):13.

Phillips, H., Gray, N., MacCulloch, S., Taylor, J., Moore, S., Huckle, P. & MacCulloch, M. (2005). Risk assessment in offenders with mental disorders: Relative efficacy of personal demographic, criminal history, and criminal variables. *Journal of Interpersonal Violence*, 20, 833–847. doi: 10.1177/088626050427898.

Rossman, S. (2001). *Services integration: Strengthening offenders and families while promoting community health and safety.* Retrieved from http://aspe.hhs.gov/hsp/prison2home02/rossman.htm

Royal College of General Practitioners. (2011). *Safer prescribing in prisons: Guidance for clinicians.* Retrieved from www.emcdda.europa.eu/attachements.cfm/att_146300_EN_UK51_Safer_Prescribing_in_Prison%20(2011).pdf

Skeem, J., Manchak, S., & Peterson, J. (2010). Correctional policy for offenders with mental illness: Creating a new paradigm for recidivism reduction. *Law Human Behavior, 35,* 110–126. doi:10.1007/s10979-010-9223-7.

Smith, P.S. (2006). The effects of solitary confinement on prison inmates: A brief history and review of the literature. *Criminal Justice,* 34, 441–568.

Stephen, J. (2004). State Prison Expenditures, 2001. Bureau of Justice Statistics, June 2004, NCJ 202949. Retrieved from, www.bjs.gov/content/pub/pdf/spe01.pdf

Torrey, E.F., Kennard, A.D., Enslinger, D., Lamb, R., & Pavle, J. (2010). *More mentally ill persons are in jails and prisons than hospitals: A survey of the states.* Retrieved from www.nami.org/Template.cfm?Section=CIT2&template=/ContentManagement/ContentDisplay.cfm&ContentID=101344

World Health Organization. (2007a). Health in prisons. Retrieved from www.euro.who.int/data/assets/pdf_file/0009/99018/E90174.pdf

World Health Organization. (2007b). Preventing Suicide in Jails and Prisons. Retrieved from www.who.int/mental_health/prevention/suicide/resource_jails_prisons.pdf

CHAPTER 4

Conclusion

Mental illness is primarily a health problem, but its impact on the society also concerns criminal justice. Since most criminal justice practitioners are not trained or equipped to deal with mental illness, the criminal justice system ought to work with social workers and healthcare providers to construct a protocol that can prevent mental illness from turning into criminal behavior and that can offer needed assistance to criminals suffering from mental issues, even if such issues are not necessarily the main cause of their criminal behavior. The "warehousing" approach is not solving any problems. At best, we separate the patients from society for a while, but most of them will come back with the same problem or possibly more severe. To be fair, many people in the criminal justice domain are already eager to do something about this growing issue, but they often cannot acquire the resources they need. Before more resources will be allocated to address mental illness issues, better public awareness needs to be raised to understand why this is necessary.

Discussion Questions

1. Research the connection between mental illness and crime. List five myths and five facts.
2. If you were in charge, what would you do with prisoners who have severe mental illness?

3. A doctor has confirmed that Dante suffers from a mental illness that causes him to turn violent from time to time, even without provocation. Now, Dante has been convicted of smashing his neighbor's car for no apparent reason. If you were the judge, how would you sentence him? Explain your reasoning.
4. Should taxpayers pay for the treatment needed for mentally ill prisoners? If not, who should?
5. As a society, is there anything we can do to reduce mental illness?

CHAPTER 5

Hate Crime

Introduction

Hate and discrimination are a centuries-old phenomenon in all human societies. People always seem to be able to find a cause to form division by promoting the "us vs. them" mentality. There is no shortage of reasons for us to hate someone who does not look like us, who does not have the same lifestyle, who does not share the same belief, who does not speak our language, or who is simply too old, too young, too slow, too small, too fat, too sick, too poor, too rich, or just too different from whatever our self-righteous judgement prefers.

It is normal to dislike what we do not find appealing, and it is natural to become hateful when we encounter those who we find annoying. There is no need to deny human nature, and it is futile trying to suppress it as if such a feeling does not exist. Hate, make no mistake, is part of human nature, and therefore, it is part of what we are. However, civilization requires humans to control their human nature and act in a way that does not infringe on other people's rights. There are many rights protected by the law, but to say the least, people have the right to safely exist in the society no matter how annoying you think they are. When we cross the line and allow hate to motivate us to attack people, it becomes hate crime. When a crime is considered a hate crime, the punishment can usually be increased or even doubled. It means the criminal would be punished not only for the criminal act but also for the hateful motive. Some would argue all crimes are hate crimes, as you do not kill or steal out of love. It is a valid point, but in most crimes the motive is either practical or personal. If you commit crime for money, the criminal act is a practical way to get what you want. If you kill someone who has wronged you, the criminal act is for personal revenge. On the other hand, in a hate crime the motive is based on prejudice against a certain group of people, not just the victim. It is about what the victim represents rather than who the victim is. Of course, the definition is not clear cut, and that is why it is always debatable as to which crimes should be considered hate crime. We have lawyers to do that. Students reading this chapter do not have to make that decision right now. Instead, in this chapter the two articles are meant to help students understand how hate, as a natural human feeling, escalates into criminal acts.

READING 8

The Internet and Racial Hate Crime

Offline Spillovers from Online Access

Jason Chan, Anindya Ghose, and Robert Seamans

Introduction

Widespread Internet penetration is associated with several benefits, but it has also introduced unique societal challenges as documented by other research.[1] One such challenge is online hate content. The Internet provides an accessible, affordable, unscreened, and anonymous channel for posting and sharing hate ideologies. Anecdotally, this has led to an increase in hate-related websites.[2] In 2011, close to 14,000 sites were reported to contain hate-related content, representing a six-fold increase from that in 2000.[3] In particular, over 65 percent of the active hate sites tracked by the anti-bigotry NGO, Southern Poverty Law Center, is found to contain racial and ethnicity related hate ideologies (SPLC 2009). More recently, a multitude of hate activity has appeared on social media and networking sites such as Facebook, Twitter,

1 For example, Ayyagari et al. (2011) draw a connection between online enabled technologies and stress, Bhuller et al. (2013) uncover a positive relationship between sex crimes and Internet availability, Chan and Ghose (2014) and Greenwood and Agarwal (2015) find a link between online classified ads and HIV incidence, and White and Horvitz (2009) show how online medical searches can lead to unfounded escalations of concerns about common illnesses (i.e., cyberchondria).

2 In fact, extremists were among the earliest to adopt Internet technologies. For instance, hate groups were utilizing Internet Relay Chat channels (e.g., #Nazi and #Klan), online newsgroups (e.g., alt.politics.white-power and alt.revisionism), and listservs to spread hate agendas even before the first hate site, Stormfront, was launched in 1995.

3 Figures for online hate activity for various years come from the Digital Terror and Hate Report issued by the Simon Wiesenthal Center.

and YouTube (Gerstenfeld 2013) and extremist social media sites such as *NewSaxon*, all of which further facilitates the ease with which racial extremists link to one another.[4]

It is not clear, however, whether or how the increase in online hate content affects offline racial hate crimes.[5] There are a number of channels through which greater Internet availability may increase the number of hate crimes committed. For example, increased Internet access may increase the efficiency with which extremists can spread hate ideology and connect with like-minded members. Anecdotally, there is evidence that hate related material found on the Internet has led to hate crimes (Wolf 2004). For example, Benjamin Nathaniel Smith, who went on a shooting spree in 1999 that targeted racial and ethnic minorities, told a documentary film maker: "It wasn't really 'til I got on the Internet, read some literature of these groups that ... it really all came together" (Wolf 2004). Another way in which greater Internet availability may increase the number of hate crimes committed is by facilitating the training of individuals to commit hate crimes. For example, the Tsarnaev brothers reportedly relied on online instructions to build the pressure cooker bombs used in the 2013 Boston marathon bombing.[6] To the best of our knowledge there has been no systematic study about whether increased access to online hate content would increase offline hate crimes. In addition, it would be useful to get a better understanding of conditions under which offline hate crimes increase so as to motivate proper policy responses.

To empirically examine these issues, we use geographic and temporal variation in county-level broadband availability to study the effect of Internet penetration on hate crime in the United States between 2001 and 2008. We find evidence that increases in the number of broadband providers leads to increases in racial hate crimes, on average. The relationship between Internet access and these hate crimes further holds after using an instrumental variable (IV) approach to address endogeneity and is robust to a number of auxiliary checks and falsification tests. The positive relationship does not appear to be due to increased crime reporting or reclassification of crimes over time. The positive relationship between Internet penetration and offline racial hate crime is most evident in areas with higher levels of racism, as indicated by higher levels of segregation and higher propensity to search for racially charged words. On the other hand, we observe that Internet access does not have an impact on racial hate crimes in areas with lower levels of racism. We do not find any evidence that an increase in Internet access leads to an increase in local hate group formation, and the presence of a local hate group does not seem to strengthen the link between Internet penetration and hate crimes. However, Internet access appears to increase the incidence of racial hate crimes committed by "lone wolf" actors.

---

4 Available at http://www.civilrights.org/publications/hatecrimes/exploiting-internet.html, accessed on May 27, 2015.

5 For ease of readability, the term *hate crimes* is used henceforth to refer to racial hate crimes. These crimes are traditional offenses that are committed against individuals or groups based on real or perceived social and physical traits including race.

6 Todd Wallack and Beth Healy, "Tsarnaev brothers appeared to have scant finances," *The Boston Globe*, April 24, 2013. Available at: http://www.bostonglobe.com/metro/2013/04/23/tsarnaev-brothers-appeared-have-scant-finances/ZbNBuN2Gcz8lOFddKDlU0N/story.html

This paper aims to make the following contributions: First, we believe our study is the first to document the relationship between the Internet and hate crime using a large-scale dataset and econometric techniques. This finding should be of interest to an ongoing academic effort to document some of the downsides to increased online access (e.g., Ayyagari et al. 2011; Bhuller et al. 2013; Chan and Ghose 2014; Greenwood and Agarwal 2015; White and Horvitz 2009) that has been enabled by the platform nature of the Internet in connecting disparate groups of users (Bailey and Bakos 1997; Bennett, Seamans and Zhu 2015; Parker and Van Alstyne 2005). Second, we document conditions under which the positive relationship is present, which we believe can help motivate policy responses. Specifically, we focus on two salient factors—entropy scores (Massey and Denton 1988) and racially charged search terms (Stephens-Davidowitz 2014)—that show interesting moderating effects of the Internet on hate crime. We therefore believe that our findings should be of interest to policy-makers, interest groups, NGOs, and academics. Third, we provide insights into some plausible mechanisms driving the relationship between the Internet and hate crimes. In particular, our results appear to challenge the general notion that the Internet has played a role in the increase in hate group formation. Additionally, the analyses found some support that Internet-induced hate crimes arise mainly from lone-wolf perpetrators.

Data

To examine the link between Internet penetration and hate crime, we combine detailed data from various official sources including the Federal Bureau of Investigation (FBI), the Federal Communications Commission (FCC), the U.S. Census Bureau, and the U.S. Bureau of Labor Statistics. Hate crime data come from the FBI's annual report, *Hate Crime Statistics*. We restrict our empirical focus to the years 2001–2008 because the population coverage in the hate crime data is relatively stable for this time period.[7] Table 8.1 provides the descriptive statistics of our data.

Our main dependent variable is *hate crime*$_{it}$, which is the number of hate crimes in county *i* in year *t*. In the study sample, close to two-thirds of reported hate crimes arise from racial-bias motivations (60.4%), making it by far the most typical form of bias-motivated crime in the United States. The distinct divide in prevalence between racially motivated crimes and other categories of hate crimes drives our main focus on racially motivated hate crimes. Moreover, the nature of hate crime varies as a function of the target group, and the prevalence of each type of hate crime is affected by a different set of predictor variables (Glaser et al. 2002).[8]

7 The coverage is over 80% for this time period, with a high of 88.6% in 2008 and a low of 82.8% in 2003.The high coverage of *Hate Crime Statistics* is an effort due in part to local agencies consistently furnishing hate crime reports to the FBI, voluntarily. In states that do not impose data collection statutes (e.g., Alabama, Georgia, and Mississippi), some agencies have nevertheless chosen to submit their reports.

8 Though the FBI data on hate crime is unlikely to suffer from documentation issues and ambiguous classification, it may still face the problem of changing levels in reporting behavior (DiIulio 1996). We address the potential effects of crime reporting trends through a separate test described in Section 6.

Our main independent variable is the average number of broadband providers in county *i* in year *t*, $Internet_{it}$, which we use to measure broadband availability.[9] We choose to focus on broadband access to the Internet over other forms of access such as dial-up, as extant research shows that broadband adoption significantly increases the overall usage of the Internet, heightens the consumption of online content in quantity and diversity, and affects a range of online and offline activities (Hitt and Tambe 2007; Kolko 2010a). Specifically, the reduction in waiting times for loading images, sounds, and videos via broadband availability facilitates the likelihood and willingness to consume hate content online.

Data on broadband availability comes from FCC Form 477, which reports the number of broadband providers offering broadband services at 200 kilobits per second or faster in a ZIP code.[10] The FCC data is the only comprehensive indicator of U.S. broadband availability that has been recorded annually since 1999 (Kolko 2010b), and is extensively used by policy makers and academics to assess broadband availability (California Public Utilities Commission 2006; Grubesic 2008; Kolko 2012; Seamans and Zhu 2014; Xiao and Orazem 2011). Using data on the number of broadband providers from the FCC and proprietary data on broadband use from Forrester Research, Kolko (2010b) shows that the extent of broadband availability increases monotonically with the number of broadband providers.[11] Given that broadband policies often work by adding providers to an area via public provision, subsidization, and regulation, it is meaningful in a policy context to employ the number of broadband providers as a proxy for Internet penetration.

As noted in past literature, the use of the FCC data to measure broadband availability may introduce measurement error for certain study contexts (Greenstein and Mazzeo 2006; GAO 2006, 2009; Kolko 2010b; Xiao and Orazem 2011).[12] For example, there may be business but not residential subscribers in a given ZIP code, so the FCC's count will overstate residential broadband availability. In addition, the FCC does not report the actual number of providers for locations with one to three providers, instead grouping them into a single category. Following Kolko (2012), we assign a value of two to ZIP codes reported as having one to three providers, which introduces measurement error in our estimations. Below we describe an IV approach to help account for endogeneity, which also helps address the measurement error inherent in our measure of broadband availability.

We combine hate crime and broadband availability measures with demographic, socioeconomic, and crime-related variables from a variety of official sources which allow us to control for the underlying propensity of hate crimes across locations. The U.S. Census and the U.S. Bureau of Labor Statistics provide county-level information on population density, age proportions, race

9 Counts of ZIP code level providers are averaged across each county to derive this measure.

10 Broadband providers include telephone-line DSL, cable modems, wireless, satellite, and power-line technologies.

11 To assess the integrity of the broadband provider data, we correlate it with household Internet adoption data at the state level. Results show a strong positive correlation between broadband providers and the Internet measures from two other official data sources (see Table A1 of the Online Appendix).

12 The FCC does not report whether providers serve consumers or businesses, how much they charge for service, the speed of their service, and whether they provide service to the whole or only part of a ZIP code.

proportions, international migration rates, number of persons below the poverty line, employment level, and size of various industry sectors. These demographic and socioeconomic factors are important for controlling for characteristics which are known to influence crime rates (Bell et al. 2013; Dollard et al. 1939; Glaser and Sacerdote 1999; Hansmann and Quigley 1982; Kelly 2000; Sampson et al. 1997), although there is some debate about the relative importance of some of the characteristics as they pertain to hate crime in particular. For example, Dollard et al. (1939) argue that economic factors are important determinants of hate crime, and others, including Green and Rich (1998), find evidence of a positive relationship between unemployment and hate crime. On the other hand, Krueger and Pischke (1997) find no relationship between unemployment and hate crime. While not the focus of our research, we discuss the impact of our control variables on hate crime in our setting, thereby shedding additional light on a topic that has been subject to much debate in prior literature. We also account for crime-related prevalence by controlling for the number of police employees and prevailing crime levels. The FBI database *Law Enforcement Officers Killed and Assaulted* provides information on the annual count of police employees by county, and the FBI's *Uniform Crime Report* provides counts of general crime levels by county. All log transformed variables are constructed using log(X+1) to account for zero values.

Empirical Methodology

We first motivate our approach with graphical evidence of the positive relationship between broadband availability and hate crime. Figure 8.1 provides scatter plots of number of broadband providers (x-axis) and number of racial hate crimes (y-axis) for each of the years 2001 to 2008. The plots include a linear trend, which indicates a positive relationship between the number of broadband providers and racial hate crimes. OLS results (provided in Online Appendix Table B1) include the full set of controls and confirm the statistical relationship apparent in the raw data. The OLS results may be biased due to endogeneity or measurement error, so we next describe our econometric approach to address these issues and more rigorously investigate the relationship between Internet providers/availability and hate crime.

Cross Sectional IV Specification

Our baseline cross-sectional regression is of the following specification:

$$\ln(1 + y_{it}) = \alpha + \beta \ln(1 + Internet_{it-1}) + \lambda X_{it-1} + \varepsilon_i \qquad (1)$$

for each year 2001–2008, where y_{it} is the number of racial hate crimes in county *i* for year *t*, $Internet_{it-1}$ is the number of broadband providers in county *i* for year *t-1*, and X_{it-1} includes various demographic, socioeconomic, and crime-related characteristics of county *i* in year *t-1*. In these specifications, all covariates are lagged by one period to avoid simultaneity biases. In all regressions, we report robust standard errors, clustered at county *i*.

To address potential endogeneity issues such as omitted variable biases and measurement error in broadband availability, we apply an IV identification strategy on our cross-sectional specification. Specifically, we run IV regressions on Equation (1) by instrumenting for *Internet* using the *Slope* of the local terrain. This is the same instrument used by Kolko (2012). To be a valid instrument, slope should directly affect broadband availability and not directly affect hate crime. The slope instrument identifies cross-sectional variance in the costs to broadband providers in extending Internet service to an area. As noted by the Government Accounting Office (GAO 2006) and Prieger (2003), terrain features such as slope affect the cost to extend broadband service in an area. Since much of the cost in providing broadband service comes from the fixed costs in setting up telecommunications infrastructure, providers would face high cost barriers to deploy broadband services in areas with steep terrain. This negative relationship is empirically confirmed in Kolko (2012). In Figure 8.2, we provide scatter plots of terrain slope (x-axis) and the number of broadband providers (y-axis), as well as a trend line. Across the years, we observe a consistent negative relationship between the two variables. Note, however, that the negative relationship appears weaker in early years and stronger in later years. This suggests that the relationship between terrain slope and number of broadband providers may vary by year, which we will exploit in our panel IV approach described in [the IV Fixed Effects Specifications section].

The exclusion restriction holds if slope does not have a direct effect on the incidence of racial hate crime, independent of its relationship with Internet availability. Terrain characteristics such as slope are unlikely to bear direct effects on hate crime, as these criminal acts are largely induced by human ideologies, prejudices, and influences. Although there may not be direct effects on hate crime, the slope of a location may be linked to crime incidence indirectly. Locations with flat terrains are likely to be urbanized areas that may possess demographic and economic features associated with higher incidence of crime levels (Glaeser and Sacerdote 1999). To account for these effects, demographic, socioeconomic, and crime-related variables mentioned earlier are included in the first stage regressions as controls.[13] In later sections, we describe additional checks that are performed to test the exclusion restriction.

IV Fixed Effects Specifications

An additional issue we face is that the relationship between hate crimes and broadband providers may be heterogeneous across locations (Cornwell and Trumbull 1994). Unobserved local conditions such as the level of racial intolerance, discriminatory cultures and practices may cause some counties to experience a greater effect from broadband availability on its incidence of hate crimes. In order to address this issue, we specifically pool racial hate crime data across the years 2001–2008 and use county-level fixed effects models of the following type:

$$\ln(1 + y_{it}) = \quad + \quad \ln(1 + Internet_{it-1}) + \quad X_{it-1} + C_i + Y_t + \quad _{it} \qquad (2)$$

13 A correlation table consisting of the correlations of slope and covariates is provided in Online Appendix Table B2.

where y_{it} is the number of racial hate crimes in county *i* in year *t*, $Internet_{it-1}$ is the number of broadband providers in county *i* in year *t–1*, and X_{it-1} includes various time-varying demographic, socioeconomic, and crime characteristics of county *i* in year *t–1*. The county-level fixed effects C_i help address the unobserved heterogeneity across counties that may explain the observed relationship between number of broadband providers and racial hate crime. We include year dummies Y_t to account for temporal shocks such as the occurrence of terrorism that may produce shifts in racial attitudes (e.g., the September 11, 2001 terrorism incident).

To simultaneously address endogeneity and measurement error issues, we rely on panel IV regressions in which we instrument for broadband providers using a variant of terrain slope. Specifically, we interact the slope values with year dummies to construct instruments that allow for heterogeneous time impacts on broadband growth. We then include these instruments in IV regressions that follow Equation (2). The approach of utilizing cross-sectional instruments interacted with time dummies has been used in past research (e.g., Forman and van Zeebroeck 2013, Stevenson 2008), and, we believe, is valid in our setting. Notably, the slope of terrain not only affects the number of broadband providers in the cross-section, but also influences the *growth rate* of broadband providers over time. That is, the number of broadband providers at locations with steep terrain will increase at a slower rate, compared to areas with flat terrain. Reports have noted a similar trend in favor of this argument, in that broadband growth has been unevenly focused on areas that already have broadband capabilities, namely the urban areas, but proceeds sluggishly in rural and remote areas over the years (OCED 2008). We verify graphically that the broadband growth patterns within our dataset are similar (see Online Appendix Figure A1).

Alternative Model Specifications

Alternative specifications are used to assess the IV assumptions and stability of the results. First, we follow Kolko (2012) and use a first-difference IV model of the following form:

$$\ln\left(\frac{1+y_{it+1}}{1+y_{it}}\right) = \alpha + \beta \ln(1 + Internet_{it+1} - Internet_{it}) + \lambda X_{it} \qquad (3)$$

$$+ \delta X_{it} \times \ln(1 + Internet_{it+1} - Internet_{it}) + \wedge Z_{it} + {}_{it}$$

where the dependent variable is the log change in racial hate crime, the independent variable is the log change in broadband providers, accompanied by covariates (X_{it}), interactions of these covariates with the log change in broadband providers, and additional controls (Z_{it}) to account for local economic growth and crime trends.[14] Whereas the fixed effects specification detailed in Equation (2) requires us to use slope-year interacted instruments, the first-differences specification

14 The choice of variables to be interacted with change in broadband providers follows closely those proposed by Kolko (2012), including population density, population size, median household income, and college attainment percentage. Road density is also included as a covariate as per the specification in Kolko (2012).

detailed in Equation (3) allows us to use slope alone as an instrument. County-level effects are controlled for in either case, either by differencing out or by including a county-specific intercept. Thus, the results from Equation (3) will serve to cross-validate the directionality of the results from the panel IV model.

Second, we collapse the data set into pre- and post-intervention periods to check whether our results are sensitive to measurement issues that arise from serially correlated outcomes (Bertrand et al. 2004). To do this, we supplement the current set of racial hate crime data with that from 1992 to 1998. We then create a pre-broadband period and a post-broadband period and use average values of racial hate crimes and broadband providers for each county in each of these two periods. We also check that the results using this approach are robust to alternate cut-offs for the definition of pre and post. Finally, we run a large number of robustness tests with additional controls, alternative functional forms, and outlier removal. Various falsification checks are also employed to assess whether the main results arise spuriously and to test for the possibility of alternative explanations.

Results

Cross-Sectional IV Regression

Table 8.2 reports our IV regression results linking broadband availability to racial hate crime. We report both the first stage and second stage coefficients in the same table. Across all years, we see that the slope coefficient is consistently negative and significant in the first stage results, satisfying the correlation requirement that instruments should have with the endogenous regressor, conditional on other covariates. This result supports the claims in Kolko (2012) and the negative trend observed in Figure 8.2. To assess whether slope suffers from problems of being a weak instrument, we check the significance of the first-stage F-statistics and find that they are all significant above the 1% level. We further contrast the F-statistics with the Stock and Yogo (2005) critical thresholds for weak instruments. Across all years, the F-statistics surpass the critical value, suggesting that the slope variable does not suffer from weak instrument biases.

Next, we turn to the second stage regression results. We observe that the coefficients for broadband providers are positive and significant in all years, except in 2001.[15] We also note that the magnitude of the relationship differs across the years. Contrasting the year with the smallest significant coefficient (2006) to the year with the largest significant coefficient (2002), we see that a one-unit increase in broadband providers produces a 66.8 and 271.4 percent, respectively, increase in racial hate crimes, mapping out to 1,176 to 4,779 annual cases of racial hate crime across all counties.[16]

15 We note that cross-sectional OLS results across the years also produce a similar result (Online Appendix Table B1).

16 A one-unit increase in broadband providers corresponds to an approximately 65% increase in the average number of providers (1.56). We estimate the annual increase in racial hate crimes by multiplying

The regression results also reveal other relationships that are of interest. Poverty, police staffing, and crime levels appear to be positively correlated with the incidence of racially motivated crimes, although we find little effect from the rate of unemployment on racially motivated hate crime, in line with findings in Krueger and Pischke (1997). Locations with higher mean ages appear to experience more racial hate crimes in general. This trend agrees with the findings of von Hippel et al. (2000), which reasoned that older individuals are less likely to inhibit innate prejudices. In addition, employment levels hold a negative but not significant relationship with racial hate crimes. Finally, the negative relationships between racial hate crimes and proportion of African Americans and foreign nationals seem to suggest that a larger presence of racial/national minorities in a community may reduce racial tensions, possibly by introducing greater familiarity and acceptance.

As a robustness check, we repeat the above analysis for ethnicity hate crimes.[17] Given that a significant proportion of the online hate content contains racial and ethnicity ideologies (SPLC 2009), we expect to see a similar positive relationship between online access and ethnicity hate crimes. Results for ethnicity hate crimes are provided in Table B3 of the Online Appendix. The Internet appears to also have a positive effect for ethnicity hate crimes, although the magnitude of this effect is not as large as that for racial hate crimes. Contrasting the smallest and largest coefficients, we see that a one-unit increase in broadband provider brings about 15.6 to 188.6 percent increase in ethnicity hate crimes.

Panel IV Regression Results

Table 8.3 gives the results of our fixed effects IV regressions. Model 1 is the IV regression based on the pooled sample in which we use slope as the instrument along with year fixed effects. In Models 2 and 3, we include slope-year dummies as instruments and add county-fixed effects, respectively. We further estimate a model that includes additional covariates to reflect the sizes of common industries in urbanized locations in Model 4. As expected, the instrument is negatively associated with broadband availability and this relationship is significant under various model specifications. Of greater importance, we observe that the magnitudes of the interaction terms are generally increasing over the years; interaction terms for early years (i.e., 2004 and earlier) tend to hold smaller coefficient values, while those for later years tend to hold larger coefficient sizes. This set of estimates supports our argument that the slope of terrain affects the rate at which broadband providers enter into locations over time. The first stage F-statistics are all significant above the 1% level and they surpass the critical values indicated by the threshold given by Stock and Yogo (2005), indicating that the slope-year instrument is quite strong.

In the second stage results, the estimates for broadband providers are all positive and significant, suggesting that racial hate crimes increase as broadband availability increases. Results

---

the percentage increases (66.8 and 271.4) by the average annual number of racial hate crimes across the study period (1,761).

17 Victims of ethnicity hate crimes are targeted as a result of their nationality and cultural heritage. The FBI identifies ethnicity hate crimes as separate from racial hate crimes.

significant, suggesting that racial hate crimes increase as broadband availability increases. Results from Model 3 suggest that a one-unit increase in broadband providers leads to a 21.39 percent increase in racial hate crimes, which equates to 865 additional annual incidents of racially driven crimes in the United States. We further find that the estimates for broadband providers in Model 4 remain qualitatively similar after including additional urbanization factors that may correlate with terrain slope. However, goodness-of-fit for Model 4 performed worse in terms of root mean square error. Taken jointly, this indicates that the existing framework of covariates and fixed effects in Model 3 are sufficiently robust in capturing extraneous effects that may affect the exclusion restriction, without undermining model fit. The over-identification statistics in the full models indicate that the exclusion restriction of our instruments cannot be rejected at conventional levels, indicating that the slope-time instrument does not correlate with the error term in the explanatory equation. We also performed an auxiliary check on the exclusion restriction by regressing racial hate crimes on the instrument and the abovementioned covariates and find that the instrument is not correlated with racial hate crimes after controlling for these demographic, socioeconomic, and crime-related factors (see Online Appendix Table B4).

We next provide analyses that further explore the nature of the relationship between broadband providers and racial hate crimes in Table 8.4. In particular, we consider situations in which there are indicators that racial and ethnic differences are salient. In line with the Dollard et al. (1939) frustration-aggression hypothesis, we expect the effects to be heightened in these situations. We use two state-level variables to identify these situations, and we then split the sample using the median values of these measures. The level of racism at a location is likely indicated by the intensity of its racial segregation (Cell 1982). A common racial segregation measure used in sociology is *entropy*, which indicates the level of integration or segregation exhibited in a subarea's population composition (Massey and Denton 1988).[18] Lower levels of entropy reflect lower levels of racism and vice versa. In fact, Glaeser (2005) writes: "Hatred declines when there is private incentive to learn the truth. Increased economic interactions with a minority group may provide that incentive (p. 45)." In addition, we use on an online measure of racial animus, using the volume of Google search queries that include racially charged language (Stephens-Davidowitz 2014).[19]

Models 1 and 2 of Table 8.4 examine the impact of broadband availability split by entropy scores, and Models 3 and 4 examine the impact of broadband availability split by racially charged online searches. The results show an interesting pattern. The coefficient on broadband providers is positive and significant for the areas with above-median segregation and racially charged search, but not significant for the areas with below-median segregation and racially charged search. Thus, while increased Internet access leads to an *increase* in hate crime, on average, there are situations in which Internet access does not affect hate crime incidence. These findings

18 Gentzkow and Shapiro (2011) use similar indices of segregation to construct measures of ideological segregation.

19 Stephens-Davidowitz creates the index by averaging the counts of searches for racial epithets in each market from 2004–2007. He notes that the racial epithet is typically preceded or followed by search terms including "hate" or "joke(s)."

suggest that the Internet's impact on hate crime is not uniform and is predominantly present in areas with higher racism tendencies.[20]

Robustness Checks

In this section, we investigate the robustness of the main results to a variety of alternative specifications, models, and other tests. By performing these checks, we hope to rule out as many alternative explanations as possible. We proceed in several steps. First, as discussed in [the Alternative Model Specifications section], we show that our findings are robust to alternate model specifications. These robustness tests help to rule out the possibility that our findings arise because of model misspecification. Second, we show that our findings are robust to a large number of robustness tests with additional time-varying and time-invariant covariates, as well as to the removal of outliers. These tests help to rule out the possibility that our findings are biased by omitted variables. Finally, we conduct several tests to rule out our findings being driven by changes in crime reporting behavior over time or by changes in hate crime classification over time. Collectively, these tests help to rule out our findings having arisen spuriously because of other factors that are changing at the same time as broadband penetration.

Results Using Alternate Models

As described in [the Alternative Model Specifications section], we utilize two approaches to address concerns with potential model misspecification. First, we cross-validate the coefficient signs and significance using a first difference model specification that relies on a different identification strategy as described in Equation (3). The results in Online Appendix Table B6 show that the broadband provider coefficient in the first difference specification holds a positive and significant relationship with racial hate crime trends.[21] First stage results also suggest that the slope does not suffer from weak instrument issues. For the second approach, we adopt the pre- and post-intervention specification in Bertrand et al. (2004) to assess the stability of the results with respect to serial correlations issues that may be present in multiple-period panels. Analyses using the collapsed dataset (Online Appendix Table B7) indicate a positive and significant relationship between Internet availability and racial hate crime, which provides further confidence in the validity of the baseline results.

We also perform a falsification check using lagged values of racial hate crime to rule out that the relationship is arising spuriously. A significant coefficient in this check would suggest that there

20 In additional checks included in the Online Appendix Table B5, we break out locations by high and low proportion of poverty and employment. These characteristics are chosen for additional focus given prior literature and our results from the cross-sectional panel. Poverty in particular appears to be a strong moderator of the relationship between the Internet and hate crime.

21 The magnitude of the broadband provider estimate in Model 1 of Table B6 is comparable to its equivalent counterpart (Model 3) of Table 8.3, lending weight to the validity of the results under the panel IV framework.

is some omitted variable that drives the trends in racial hate crimes and broadband expansion simultaneously, as values of the predictor variable should not be related to past values of the outcome variable. Under a stricter test, we look for a relationship between racial hate crimes in the period 1992–1998 and broadband availability in the period 1999–2006. Given limited availability and accessibility to online hate content in the pre-broadband period, coefficients on broadband availability are expected to be smaller and nonsignificant. Significant estimates would suggest that the IV is correlated with underlying location-specific trends in racial hate crimes, which undermines its exclusion restriction. In addition, these two falsification checks could jointly reveal potential inflation of estimates that the slope-time instrument creates.[22] We find no evidence of significant correlations between the broadband availability and racial hate crime in both falsification checks (see Online Appendix Table B8).

Results Using Additional Covariates and Removal of Outliers

Next, we explore the robustness of the results to the inclusion of additional or alternate control variables in order to assuage potential concern about omitted variables bias. Broadband availability may increase more rapidly in locations that have large population sizes and rapid income growth—factors that are also known to correlate with crime levels (Glaeser and Sacerdote 1999; Levitt 1999).[23] In addition to these two factors, racial hate crimes may be driven by the racial composition of the location, which may be associated with broadband growth due to differences in the socioeconomic status of these racial groups. To assess the potential impact of this endogeneity bias on our baseline estimates, we examine the coefficient magnitudes and significance of broadband providers with respect to the inclusion of population size, median household income, proportion of Whites, and proportion of Asians as additional covariates. We also run these additional models using non-log model specifications to assess result stability with respect to non-logarithm transformation. The coefficients on our broadband measure in logged models are of comparable magnitudes to the baseline estimate in Table 8.3 (see Online Appendix Table B9). Improvements in model fit from including these covariates are marginal, suggesting that the estimation framework of Equation (2) performs well. Moreover, our results do not appear to be affected by the log-transformation process which smoothens out skewed data points.

We also check the robustness of our cross-section results after adding additional nontime-varying covariates such as college attainment proportion, entropy scores, racially charged searches, and road density, as these variables may correlate with unobserved factors that are related with slope and crime levels. College attainment levels may affect the intensity of Internet usage and is also indicative of the population size of young adults, the largest population group who

---

22 In the case where slope-time instrument artificially inflates estimates, we would expect to see significant estimates.

23 For instance, the probability of incarceration for committing crimes is lower in places with large populations as the pool of potential suspects is larger, thereby giving rise to a positive link between population size and crime rates. Also, families with high household incomes tend to cluster in better neighborhoods with lower crime rates.

constitute the group committing hate crimes. Entropy and racially charged search are indicators of racism that are likely to be correlated to neighborhood segregation patterns. These are added to control for residential segregation that might result from steep slope features. Road density is a proxy for transportation costs of a location, which in turn is correlated with the slope of the terrain and the ease of accessing target victims in the area. Results remain qualitatively similar even after including these variables (see Online Appendix Table B10).

Next we remove potential outlier years, which might upwardly bias our main results. The prevalence of racial hate crimes may reach abnormally high levels in periods experiencing external shocks. Our dataset includes the period in which the major terrorist attack on September 11, 2001, took place. Anger, frustration, and fear after a terrorist attack can result in indiscriminate, racially based attacks on innocent individuals who appear to be of Muslim, Middle Eastern, or South Asian descent (Kaplan and Moss 2003). We rerun the baseline regression models after removing observations from 2001 and 2002, and obtain similar result to those in Table 8.3 (see Online Appendix Table B11).

Checks on Crime Reporting and Classification

Finally, we consider the possibility that the positive link between racial hate crime and broadband availability may be an artifact of heightened levels of crime reporting that coincided with the period of broadband expansion, or may be due to changes in classification of what constitutes a hate crime. To this end, we first assess the effect of broadband providers on the likelihood of crime reporting via a separate dataset constructed through the combination of the National Crime Victimization Survey (NCVS) and the FCC.[24] These results are provided in Table 8.5. The coefficients on broadband providers are not statistically significant, suggesting that broadband availability does not shift crime reporting behaviors. Thus, it is unlikely that the relationship between Internet access and racial hate crime is driven by an increase in crime reporting behavior facilitated by better broadband availability.

We also examine the regression coefficients for additional types of crime (see Online Appendix Table B12). Aggravated and simple assault are commonly committed forms of hate crime. A reclassification of these crimes as hate crime via the increased ability to recognize their inherent bias motivations may result in an artificial spike in hate crime statistics, which may coincide with the broadband growth trends. However, the coefficient on broadband providers is not significant, suggesting that crime reclassification is unlikely. We also assess the impact of broadband providers on alternative crimes that are unlikely to be affected by the growth in broadband usage. For this, we focus on murder, robbery, and burglary as alternative crimes.[25] The presence of a

---

24 Details of the NCVS dataset and the regression specifics are provided in Online Appendix C.

25 According to FBI statistics, most hate crimes manifest through assault, intimidation, and vandalism/property damage, with very few (if not any) manifesting via murder, robbery, and burglary. Less than 2% of hate crimes fall under murder, robbery or burglary. Also, the latent risk factors for murder, robbery, and burglary are not known to have any relationships with Internet availability, unlike other crimes such as rape and other sexual offenses, which are found to be exacerbated by increased access to online pornography (Bhuller et al. 2013).

statistical relationship between the incidence of these crimes and broadband providers would suggest that the observed relationships in the main results arise spuriously. However, we find the coefficients on broadband providers are not significant across these alternative crimes, providing additional confidence that the main results are not spurious.

Post Hoc Analyses

In [the Results section] we provide evidence that increased Internet access leads to an *increase* in hate crime, on average, but that there are situations in which Internet access does not affect hate crime prevalence. The results from Table 8.4 suggest that the positive relationship between Internet penetration and racial hate crimes increases in areas with more segregation (higher entropy scores) and more racially charged search behavior, but that the relationship is not affected by Internet access in areas with less segregation (lower entropy scores) and less racially charged search behavior. In this section we conduct additional *post hoc* analyses to uncover the potential mechanism underlying these results.

There are several pathways through which the Internet might increase offline hate crime. We focus our discussion on two potential pathways. First, online hate sites can be used to recruit individuals to offline hate groups and coordinate group efforts. In fact, both hate group membership and the number of hate groups increased dramatically during the 2000s (Potok 2010). Given that Internet usage is highly prevalent among youths, hate groups have utilized specific strategies for recruiting youths including the use of online membership forms, subscription-based mailing lists, hate-related music, video games, and other activities on hate sites (Gerstenfeld et al. 2003; Schafer 2002). Internet communications can also help hate groups in the coordination of their activities by facilitating the interactions between committed group members to discuss strategies and tactics (Anti-Defamation League 2001). Content analyses of hate websites suggest a fair amount of grass-roots mobilization (Bostdorff 2004). For instance, the Imperial Klans of America posted an invitation on the White Camelia Knights' website to a "Unity Gathering" in Kentucky. Thus, a potential mechanism through which access to/use of the Internet increases hate crimes is the enhancement of offline hate group operations through more efficient recruitment and coordination.

Another major pathway through which access to/use of the Internet might increase offline hate crime is by advocating for racial based ideologies online and compelling individuals to act on the hate agenda by carrying out hate crimes on their own, as was apparently the case for Benjamin Nathaniel Smith. Adams and Roscigno (2005), using text-based analysis of material from six supremacist websites, find that in addition to recruitment, the texts of these websites advise on courses of action that one could take. They specifically write that a "relatively new strategy that makes these organizations a legitimate threat is the 'lone wolf' approach to social action" (p. 771). In fact, survey responses in our NCVS data revealed that over sixty-four percent of hate crimes in the United States during the period 2004–2008 were committed by single perpetrators, lending plausibility to the idea that the mechanism through which the Internet induces more hate crime is by motivating more individual-based hate crimes (Appendix C). Below, we elaborate potential ways to further investigate the role of hate group recruitment and lone-wolf attacks in the link between Internet and increased hate crimes.

To examine whether use of/access to the Internet increases hate crimes via the enhancement of offline hate group operations through more efficient recruitment and coordination, we perform several analyses using hate group data obtained from the Southern Poverty Law Center (SPLC).[26] We use a specification similar to Equation (2) to estimate the relationship between broadband providers and number of offline hate groups. If the Internet enables hate groups to recruit members more effectively, we would expect the coefficient on broadband providers to be positive and significant. Note that this rests on the assumption that the number of hate groups is positively correlated with the number of members. There is some anecdotal evidence in support of this assumption (Mulholland 2010), but it is possible that the number of hate groups is uncorrelated with total hate group membership. Models 1 and 2 of Table 8.6 analyze the relationship between the Internet and number of hate groups. The coefficients on broadband providers are negative but statistically insignificant in both of these models.[27] Thus there is little support for the notion that the Internet has led to an increase in offline hate group formation (although it is possible that hate group membership has increased without the number of hate groups increasing).

Second, we explore the impact of broadband providers on racial hate crimes in areas with varying levels of hate group presence. Specifically, we contrast the effect of broadband providers in counties with at least one hate group during the study period to that of counties with no hate groups in all years of the same period. If the underlying mechanism is that the Internet facilitates the coordination of attacks by offline hate groups, then we would expect counties with one or more hate groups to experience a larger effect than counties with no hate groups. Models 3 and 4 of Table 8.6 provide results from our baseline specification (Table 8.3, Column 3) after splitting the sample into those counties with no hate groups and those with one or more hate groups. The coefficient on broadband providers is positive and significant in Model 3 (counties with no hate groups) and negative but insignificant in Model 4 (counties with one or more hate groups). Thus, it does not appear that hate crime increases more in counties with hate groups.

In order to examine whether hate content motivates lone wolves to engage in hate crimes, we perform several analyses using additional hate crime perpetrator information obtained from the FBI. In order to perform this analysis, we obtained the hate crime yearly master records directly

---

26 Founded in the 1970s, the SPLC is the leading center in tracking and exposing activities of hate groups. SPLC provides data on city and state location of hate groups on its website http://www.splcenter.org/get-informed/hate-map.We obtained historical data on hate group locations using the Internet Archive https://archive.org/.

27 The SPLC has noted an increase in the number of hate groups between 2000 and 2008 (see http://www.splcenter.org/home/2013/spring/the-year-in-hate-and-extremism). The insignificant result here suggests that the Internet is unlikely to be responsible for the increase in hate group formation.

from the FBI. These records contains perpetrator information about the hate crimes committed.[28] We proceeded by identifying racial hate crimes that were committed by a single perpetrator versus those that were committed by more than one perpetrator. The number of perpetrators in the dataset is recorded by the police officer(s) in charge of the hate crime incident and it denotes the number of known offenders who are involved in executing the crime. This information is largely derived from the accounts of the victims and the efforts of police investigations. We sum the number of racial hate crimes committed by single and multiple perpetrators separately by county and year. We then use each of these counts as dependent variables and replicate the regression specification in Table 8.3, Column 3. These results are presented in Columns 5 and 6 of Table 8.6. When the dependent variable is the log count of racial hate crimes committed by single perpetrators, the coefficient on the number of broadband providers is positive and significant, and similar in magnitude to the main results. When the dependent variable is the log count of racial hate crimes committed by multiple perpetrators, the coefficient on the number of broadband providers is positive but not significant. To better understand the lone-wolf mechanism, we did a further investigation via a split-sample analysis to explore the impact of Internet access on the incidence of racial hate crimes committed by single and multiple perpetrators for locations with high and low levels of racism. Similar to our previous analysis in Table 8.4, racism levels are measured by entropy scores and incidence of racially charged searches. Based on this analysis, we find that the impact of Internet access largely induces lone-wolf attacks in areas with a high level of racism. In contrast, racial hate crimes committed by multiple perpetrators do not exhibit any meaningful patterns by racism levels. These results are reported in Table B14 of the Online Appendix.

In summary, the results in Table 8.6 provide suggestive evidence that the main result is driven by the number of single perpetrator acts of hate crime, which is consistent with the explanation that our results are driven by lone-wolf actors. In contrast, the results of our analyses on the role of hate groups does not lend much support to the idea that the primary mechanism through which the Internet increases hate crimes is through the enhancement of offline hate group operations through more efficient recruitment and coordination. However, additional work is needed in order to fully understand what role, if any, hate groups play in mediating the link between the Internet and hate crime.

Discussion and Implications

The Internet, like other information and communications technologies (ICTs), has had both positive and negative spillovers to society (Kling 1996). In this paper, we study the link between broadband availability and racial hate crimes. We use slope of terrain as an instrument for the number of broadband providers and a fixed effects framework to address potential endogeneity

28 An email request was made to the FBI to access the master records. Requests can be made via crimestatsinfo@ic.fbi.gov.

issues. Our results provide evidence consistent with the idea that an increase in Internet access leads to an increase in racial hate crimes, on average. This increase is most evident in areas with higher levels of racism, as indicated by more segregation and higher propensity to search for racially charged words. On the other hand, we observe that Internet access does not have an impact on racial hate crimes in areas with lower levels of racism. We do not find any evidence that an increase in Internet access leads to an increase in local hate group formation, and the presence of a local hate group does not seem to strengthen the link between Internet access and hate crime. However, Internet access appears to increase the incidence of racial hate crimes committed by lone-wolf perpetrators. Our findings provide several key insights for academics, policy makers, and law enforcement officials on the societal challenges related to Internet growth.

First, our study is the first to use a large-scale dataset to empirically quantify the impact of Internet access on hate crimes—in particular, racially motivated hate crimes. We further show that this positive relationship is unlikely to be driven by an increase in crime reporting or reclassification schemes over time. Translating the coefficient estimates from our cross sectional IV regression to raw counts, the results suggest that a one unit increase in broadband providers could lead to between 1,200 and 4,800 additional cases of hate crime per year. We also note that hate crime has tangible and intangible costs. Tangible costs to victims include property damage, medical expenses, lost earnings due to injuries, and to society through police protection costs, legal and adjudication costs, and correction costs (McCollister et al. 2010). Intangible costs of these crimes involve pain and suffering for the victims, and emotions of fear and anger directed toward members of the same racial community (Anderson 2012).[29]

Second, the findings on the moderating impact of racism indirectly support the notion that Internet facilitates the specialization of individual interests (Van Alstyne and Brynjolfsson 2005). A heightened effect of online access on racial hate crimes in areas with higher levels of racism suggests that individuals go online to engage in the construction and affirmation of individual racial identities (Byrne 2007; Daniels 2009). This finding contributes to the literature on how users interact with the online medium and the resulting consequences of increased Internet usage (e.g., Kraut et al. 1998; Teo et al. 1999; Wellman et al. 2003). In particular, the specialization of interests allows the Internet medium to amplify the messages, values, and ideas that are posted on it (Earl and Schussman 2003), which have the opposite effect of promoting the more inclusive, democratic society that was envisioned by early thought leaders regarding usage of the Internet (Jenkins and Thorburn 2003).

29 These costs can be quite large. The 2011 Norway massacre and 2013 Boston marathon bombing are instances of bias-motivated crimes linked to online hate materials (Beirich 2014; Bergen and Rowland 2014), that have dire consequences including multiple deaths, injuries, business disruptions, subsequent copycat terror acts, and social instability, which can in turn fuel retaliatiatory responses as evidenced in the post-September 11 spike in hate crimes. NBC reports the financial loss of the Boston bombing to be over $330M (see http://usnews.nbcnews.com/_news/2013/04/29/17975443-adding-up-the-financial-costs-of-the-boston-bombings).

Third, we find little evidence that increased Internet access facilitates offline hate group operations (e.g., member recruitment and organizing planned attacks).[30] This result is perhaps not surprising given the mixed evidence linking hate groups to hate crimes. For example, Daniels (2009) found in her interview studies that while online hate content holds the danger of eroding ideas and values of racial equality, it is ineffective at recruiting teenagers into hate groups. A qualitative study on the major white extremist sites reveal that their recruitment efforts are more reactive than proactive, and are far less aggressive than suggested by the media (Ray and Marsh 2001). Ryan and Leeson (2011) find no relationship between hate groups and hate crime, and suggest that "hate groups, though populated by hateful people, may be a lot of hateful bluster" (p. 260). As their quote suggests, it is possible that hate groups provide an outlet that serves to ultimately *reduce* the number of hate crimes by allowing racists to express their frustrations in less physical ways (Glaser et al. 2002). Mulholland (2010) finds support for the idea that hate groups are more likely to form in areas with fewer government services. In these situations, hate groups serve as a social and/or economic net. On the other hand, there may be reasons to believe that hate groups do lead to greater hate crime. For example, Dharmapala and McAdams (2005) use a formal economic model to argue that a desire for fame or esteem may in part drive individuals to commit hate crimes, and Adamczyk et al. (2014) find a positive relationship between hate groups per capita and ideologically motivated homicide attacks.

Fourth, we find some evidence that much of the increase in racially motivated hate crime is due to an increase in crimes committed by single perpetrators. While further work is needed in order to fully understand the mechanisms, we believe a fruitful avenue to consider is the role played by lone wolf, single perpetrators and how Internet communication facilitates the grooming of these individuals. Spaaij (2010) notes an increasing threat from lone-wolf extremists who carry out attacks individually and independently from established organizations. The increase in lone-wolf attacks may arise partly due to a change in hate group strategy that involves adopting a leaderless resistance operating model. In this process, racial extremists are employing the Internet to provide ideological motivation, encouragement, and justification through online propaganda and instructions to spur like-minded individuals in carrying out lone-wolf attacks.[31] In particular, Ray and Marsh (2001) found evidence that all major white-extremist sites have promoted the lone-wolf mentality to varying degrees. Moreover, an online "Lone Wolf Point System" was instituted by the racial extremist, Alex Curtis, on his website to encourage and reward individuals who engage in lone-wolf attacks on victims.[32] In addition to these findings, the split sample results suggest that the impact of

30 As seen in Table B13 of the Online Appendix, the number of hate groups does not hold a significant relationship with racial hate crimes at the county-level analysis. Similar results are found when the analysis is conducted at the state level. This suggests that the null result holds even when accounting for the possibility of individuals travelling out of local vicinities for organized hate group activities.

31 For instance, the White American Resistance has listed lone wolf tactics on its hate site: http://www.resist.com/Articles/literature/LawsForTheLoneWolfByTomMetzger.htm.

32 Available on http://archive.adl.org/learn/ext_us/curtis.html?LEARN_Cat=Extremism, accessed on June 2, 2015.

online access on lone-wolf attacks tends to be stronger in locations where there are preexisting levels of racism. In line with the notion of specialization of personalized interests, it is likely that racially biased individuals tend to self select into the personal consumption of online content that supports their racial ideologies, which in turn motivate and incite them toward being lone-wolf extremists. The lack of a distinct pattern for racial hate crimes executed by multiple perpetrators further suggests that the selective viewing of online hate content is largely an individual process.

This paper has several limitations. First, given that experimental variation of broadband availability across counties does not exist, we have to rely on variation generated by instrumental variables for identification. While the diagnostic checks provide statistical validation of our IV, future research may wish to explore alternative IVs and verify our findings. Second, while we have examined two potential mechanisms through which Internet access might affect hate crime, additional research is needed to study each of these mechanisms in greater depth. In addition to these two mechanisms, future research may wish to explore alternative mechanisms that are beyond the scope of this study. For instance, our work did not examine micro-level online interactions that hate crime perpetrators had prior to committing the crimes. Future work may wish to examine the various online communication patterns involved in the grooming process of racial extremists. In particular, are offline communications used in conjunction with online media at some point in time, and do "to-be perpetrators" communicate with the other extremists using more intimate forms of online communication (e.g., email, site messaging) as opposed to broadcast types of communication (e.g., forum thread discussions, public poll responses)? Knowledge of the communication patterns of perpetrators can allow for a better understanding of the online process of inciting and motivating perpetrators to action. In addition, another alternative mechanism could be that enhanced Internet access may provide a faster and more voluminous inflow of information related to the attacks on U.S. troops in foreign countries, which may in turn incite extremists to perpetrate hate crimes locally. It is important to test such alternative mechanisms as the pertinent policy implications can be very different from that of increased hate crimes induced by a growth in online hate propaganda. Finally, forward-looking questions on this topic remain unanswered due to the nascent nature of technological events. For instance, with the increased use of video and social networking sites in the last six years,[33] will Internet access promote even more hate crimes, and will this lead to new and sophisticated forms of bias-driven activity?

Our findings also suggest some possible policy implications. By assessing the impact of Internet access on racial hate crimes over the years, the study results serve to evaluate the early policies that were erected to keep the effects of online hate content at bay. First, given that online access continues to exert a positive influence on racial hate crimes despite existing

33 Reuters report that the use of sites like YouTube, Facebook and Twitter by militant and hate groups grew by almost 20% from 2009 to 2010. See http://www.reuters.com/article/2010/03/15/us-internet-hate-idUSTRE62E40O20100315.

efforts in monitoring and screening online hate content,[34] it is reasonable to infer that these technologically driven solutions fall short in addressing an issue that is inherently social in nature (Daniels 2009). In particular, extremists' use of sophisticated techniques in presenting racial ideologies online (e.g., cloaked websites and implicit messages) could undermine the effectiveness of these technological solutions.[35] Instead of engaging in a technological rat race with extremists, it may be more worthwhile to incorporate critical multiple literacies of digital media, anti-racism, and social justice in the education curriculum for youths, so that individual users can be skillful in analyzing online content, criticizing stereotypes, values, and ideologies, and be competent in interpreting the multiple meanings and messages found in online media (Kahn and Keller 2005). Second, the fact that most of the increase in hate crimes is concentrated in areas with a history of racism, and that there appears to be no impact on hate crimes in areas with lower levels of racism, implies that policies drawn to combat online hate content would need to consider the peculiar pattern users take in traversing the Internet. Empowered by online search engines and automatic filters, Internet users are able to play an active role in choosing information sources to interact with, making them more likely to seek out content that is aligned with their personal preferences (Van Alstyne and Brynjolfsson 2005). Given that users are unlikely to seek out online content that is counter to their viewpoints, strategies aimed at shining light on hate and exposing the lies underlying online hate propaganda may have limited applicability.[36] As such, findings from this study suggest a need to consider alternative strategies apart from counter-speech tactics, which cannot be effectively deployed on the same online medium as hate propaganda. Third, our findings suggest that efforts directed at identifying and stopping lone wolves might be an effective means to mitigate the proliferation of hate crimes induced by the Internet. Given that lone wolves can come from various backgrounds and have widely varying motives for their actions (Spaaij 2010), a major challenge is to distinguish individuals who intend to commit actual hate crimes from those who have radical beliefs but stay within the law. The use of big data techniques to search for digital traces on online hate sites and communities may be an appropriate solution. Going forward, this motivates the need to develop additional data-driven approaches within the MIS field in order to harvest and analyze large volumes of texts (e.g., Brynielsson et al. 2013; Cohen et al. 2014), with specific goals of identifying potential lone-wolf attackers.

---

34 The FBI has been monitoring websites of hate groups since the early 2000s. See http://www.firstamendmentcenter.org/fbi-steps-up-monitoring-of-hate-groups-web-sites. Most public libraries and schools frequented by children use filtering software to screen out hate content from search results (Daniels 2009).

35 Since the monitoring and filtering software can only respond to certain predetermined words or themes, new websites and social media sites devoted to hate propaganda may not even be identified as such.

36 Christopher Wolf, chair of the Anti-Defamation League's Internet Task Force, listed such a strategy to combat online hate content, available at http://www.firstamendmentcenter.org/hate-speech-online.

References

Adamczyk, A., Gruenewald, J., Chermak, S. M., & Freilich, J. D. (2014). The Relationship Between Hate Groups and Far-Right Ideological Violence. *Journal of Contemporary Criminal Justice.*

Adams, J., & Roscigno, V. J. (2005). White Supremacists, Oppositional Culture and the World Wide Web. *Social Forces, 84*(2), 759–778.

Anderson, D. A. (2011). The Cost of Crime. *Foundations and Trends in Microeconomics, 7*(3), 209–265.

Anti-DefamationLeague. (2001). The consequences of right-wing extremism on the Internet. Retrieved Oct 25, 2013, from http://www.adl.org/internet/extremism_rw/cord.asp

Ayyagari, R., Grover, V., & Purvis, R. (2011). Technostress: technological antecedents and implications. *MIS Quarterly, 35*(4), 831–858.

Bailey, J. P., & Bakos, Y. (1997). An exploratory study of the emerging role of electronic intermediaries. *International Journal of Electronic Commerce, 1*(3), 7–20.

Beirich, H. (2014). White Homicide Worldwide. Retrieved Oct 28, 2014, from http://www.splcenter.org/sites/default/files/downloads/publication/white-homicide-worldwide.pdf

Bell, B., Fasani, F., & Machin, S. (2013). Crime and Immigration: Evidence from Large Immigrant Waves. *Review of Economics and Statistics, 95*(4), 1278–1290.

Bennett, V., Seamans, R. & Zhu, F. (2015). Cannibalization and Option Value Effects of Secondary Markets: Evidence from the US Concert Industry. *Strategic Management Journal*. Forthcoming.

Bergen, P., & Rowland, J. (2014). Four things we learned about the Boston bombing. Retrieved Oct 24, 2014, from http://www.cnn.com/2014/04/08/opinion/bergen-boston-bombing-five-things/

Bertrand, M., Duflo, E., & Mullainathan, S. (2004). How Much Should We Trust Differences-In-Differences Estimates? *Quarterly Journal of Economics, 119*(1), 249–275.

Bhuller, M., Havnes, T., Leuven, E., & Mogstad, M. (2013). Broadband Internet: An Information Superhighway to Sex Crime? *Review of Economic Studies, forthcoming.*

Bostdorff, D. M. (2004). The internet rhetoric of the Ku Klux Klan: A case study in web site community building run amok. *Communication Studies, 55*(2), 340–361.

Brynielsson, J., Horndahl, A., Johansson, F., Kaati, L., Mårtenson, C., & Svenson, P. (2014). Harvesting and analysis of weak signals for detecting lone wolf terrorists. *Security Informatics C7–11, 2*(1), 1–15.

Byrne, D. N. (2007). The Future of (the) "Race": Identity, Discourse, and the Rise of Computer-Mediated Public Spheres. In A. Everett (Ed.), *Learning Race and Ethnicity: Youth and Digital Medi.* Cambridge, Mass: MIT Press.

California Public Utilities Commission. (2006). Connecting California: Broadband Report Update. ftp://ftp.cpuc.ca.gov/PUC/Telco/Reports/california+broadband+report+for+sept+2006+cetf+-meeting.pdf.

Cell, J. (1982). *The Highest Stage of White Supremacy: The Origin of Segregation in South Africa and the American South.* New York: Cambridge University Press.

Chan, J., & Ghose, A. (2014). Internet's Dirty Secret: Accessing the Impact of Online Intermediaries on HIV Transmission. *MIS Quarterly, 38*(4), 955–976.

Cohen, K., Johansson, F., Kaati, L., & Mork, J. C. (2013). Detecting Linguistic Markers for Radical Violence in Social Media. *Terrorism and Political Violence, 26*(1), 246–256.

Cornwell, C., & Trumbull, W. N. (1994). Estimating the Economic Model of Crime with Panel Data. *The Review of Economics and Statistics, 76*(2), 360–366.

Daniels, J. (2009). *Cyber Racism: White Supremacy Online and the New Attack on Civil Rights*. Lanham: Rowman & Littlefield Publishers Inc.

Dharmapala, D., & McAdams, R. H. (2005). Words that Kill? An Economic Model of the Influence of Speech on Behavior (with Particular Reference to Hate Speech). *The Journal of Legal Studies, 34*(1), 93–136.

Dilulio, J. (1996). Help Wanted: Economists, Crime and Public Policy. *The Journal of Economic Perspectives, 10*(1), 3–24.

Dollard, J., Doob, L. W., Miller, N. E., Doob, L. W., Mowrer, O. H., & Sears, R. R. (1936). *Frustration and Aggression*. New Haven: Yale Press.

Earl, J., & Schussman, A. (2003). The New Site of Activism: Online Organizations, Movement Entrepreneurs, and the Changing Location of Social Movement Decision Making. In P. G. Coy (Ed.), *Consensus Decision Making, Northern Ireland and Indigenous Movements* (Vol. 24). Boston: JAI Press.

Forman, C., & van Zeebroeck, N. (2013). From Wires to Partners: How the Internet Has Fostered R&D Collaborations Within Firms. *Management Science, 58*(8), 1549–1568.

GAO. (2006). Broadband Deployment is Extensive throughout the United States, but it is Difficult to Assess the Extent of Deployment Gaps in Rural Areas. *GAO-06-426 Report to Congressional Committees*, Government Accountability Office, Washington, DC.

GAO. (2009). Current Broadband Measures Have Limitations, and New Measures Are Promising but Need Improvement. *GAO-10-49 Report to Congressional Committees*, Government Accountability Office, Washington, DC.Gentzkow, M., & Shapiro, J. M. (2011). Ideological Segregation Online and Offline. *Quarterly Journal of Economics, 126*(4).

Gerstenfeld, P. B. (2013). *Hate crimes: Causes, controls, and controversies*: Sage.

Gerstenfeld, P. B., Grant, D. R., & Chiang, C.-P. (2003). Hate Online: A Content Analysis of Extremist Internet Sites. *Analyses of Social Issues and Public Policy, 3*(1), 29–44.

Glaeser, E. L. (2005). The Political Economy of Hatred. *The Quarterly Journal of Economics, 120*(1), 45–86.

Glaeser, E. L., & Sacerdote, B. (1999). Why Is There More Crime in Cities? *Journal of Political Economy, 107*(S6), S225–S258.

Glaser, J., Dixit, J., & Green, D. P. (2002). Studying Hate Crime with the Internet: What Makes Racists Advocate Racial Violence? *Journal of Social Issues, 58*(1), 177–193.

Green, D. P., & Rich, A. (1998). White Supremacist Activity and Cross Burnings in North Carolina. *Journal of Quantitative Criminology, 14*(3), 263–282.

Greenstein, S., & Mazzeo, M. (2006). The Role of Differentiation Strategy in Local Telecommunication Entry and Market Evolution: 1999–2002. *The Journal of Industrial Economics, 54*(3), 323–350.

Greenwood, B., & Agarwal, R. (2015). Two Sided Platforms and HIV Incidence among the Digitally Disadvantaged. *Management Science,* Forthcoming.

Grubesic, T. H. (2008). The spatial distribution of broadband providers in the United States: 1999–2004. *Telecommunications Policy, 32*(3–4), 212–233.

Hansmann, H. B., & Quigley, J. M. (1982). Population Heterogeneity and the Sociogenesis of Homicide. *Social Forces, 61*(1), 206–224.

Hitt, L., & Tambe, P. (2007). Broadband adoption and content consumption. *Information Economics and Policy, 19*(3–4), 362–378.

Jenkins, H., & Thorburn, D. (2003). *Democracy and New Media.* Cambridge, Mass: MIT Press.

Kahn, R., & Kellner, D. (2005). Reconstructing technoliteracy: A multiple literacies approach. *E-Learning, 2*(3), 238–251.

Kaplan, J. E., & Moss, M. P. (2003). *Investigating Hate Crimes on the Internet.* Partners Against Hate, US Dept of Justice.

Kelly, M. (2000). Inequality and Crime. *Review of Economics and Statistics, 82*(4), 530–539.

Kling, R. (1996). *Computerization and Controversy: Value Conflicts and Social Choices.* San Diego: Academic Press.

Kolko, J. (2010a). How broadband changes online and offline behaviors. *Information Economics and Policy, 22*(2), 144–152.

Kolko, J. (2010b). A new measure of US residential broadband availability. *Telecommunications Policy, 34*(3), 132–143.

Kolko, J. (2012). Broadband and local growth. *Journal of Urban Economics, 71*(1), 100–113.

Kraut, R., Patterson, M., Lundmark, V., Kiesler, S., Mukopadhyay, T., & Scherlis, W. (1998). Internet paradox. A social technology that reduces social involvement and psychological well-being? *The American Psychologist, 53*(9), 1017–1031.

Krueger, A. B., & Pischke, J.-S. (1997). A Statistical Analysis of Crime against Foreigners in Unified Germany. *The Journal of Human Resources, 32*(1), 182–209.

Levitt, S. (1999). The Changing Relationship between Income and Crime Victimization. *Economic Policy Review, 5*(3), 87–98.

Massey, D. S., & Denton, N. A. (1993). *American Apartheid: Segregation and the Making of the Underclass.* Harvard University Press.

Massey, D. S., & Denton, N. A. (1988). The Dimensions of Residential Segregation. *Social Forces, 67*(2), 281–315.

McCollister, K. E., French, M. T., & Fang, H. (2010). The cost of crime to society: New crime-specific estimates for policy and program evaluation. *Drug and Alcohol Dependence, 108*, 98–109.

Mulholland, S. E. (2010). Hate Fuel: On the Relationship Between Local Government Policy and Hate Group Activity. *Eastern Economic Journal, 36*(4), 480–499.

OECD. (2008). *Broadband Growth and Policies in OECD Countries.* Organisation for Economic Co-operation and Development, Seoul, Korea.

Parker, G. G., & Alstyne, M. W. V. (2005). Two-Sided Network Effects: A Theory of Information Product Design. *Management Science, 51*(10), 1494–1504.

Potok, M. (2010). Rage on the Right: The Year in Hate and Extremism. *Southern Poverty Law Center Intelligence Report, Issue 37,* http://www.splcenter.org/get-informed/intelligence-report/browse-all-issues/2010/spring/rage-on-the-right.

Prieger, J. E. (2003). The Supply Side of the Digital Divide: Is There Equal Availability in the Broadband Internet Access Market? *Economic Inquiry, 41*(2), 346–363.

Ray, B., & Marsh, G. E. (2001). Recruitment by extremist groups on the Internet. *First Monday,* Available at: <http://ojphi.org/ojs/index.php/fm/article/view/834/743>.

Ryan, M. E., & Leeson, P. T. (2011). Hate groups and hate crime. *International Review of Law and Economics, 31*(4), 256–262.

Sampson, R. J., Raudenbush, S. W., & Earls, F. (1997). Neighborhoods and Violent Crime: A Multilevel Study of Collective Efficacy. *Science, 277*(5328), 918–924.

Schafer, J. A. (2002). Spinning the Web of Hate: Web-based Hate Propaganda by Extremist Organizations. *Journal of Criminal Justice and Popular Culture, 9*(2), 69–88.

Seamans, R. & Zhu, F. (2014). Responses to Entry in Multi-Sided Markets: The Impact of Craigslist on Local Newspapers. *Management Science, 60*(2), 476–493.

Spaaij, R. (2010). The Enigma of Lone Wolf Terrorism: An Assessment. *Studies in Conflict & Terrorism, 33*(9), 854–870.

SPLC. (2009). Hate Websites Active in 2008. *Intelligence Report, Spring 2009,* Southern Poverty Law Center, 59–65.

Stephens-Davidowitz, S. (2014). The Cost of Racial Animus on a Black Candidate: Evidence Using Google Search Data. *Journal of Public Economics, 118,* 26–40.

Stevenson, B. (2008). The Internet and Job Search. *NBER Chapters.*

Stock, J. H., Wright, J. H., & Yogo, M. (2002). A Survey of Weak Instruments and Weak Identification in Generalized Method of Moments. *Journal of Business and Economic Statistics, 20*(4), 518–529.

Stock, J. H., & Yogo, M. (2005). Testing for Weak Instruments in Linear IV Regression. In D. W. K. Andrews & J. H. Stock (Eds.), *Identification and Inference for Econometric Models: A Festschrift in Honor of Thomas J. Rothenberg.* Cambridge, UK: Cambridge University Press.

Teo, T. S. H., Lim, V. K. G., & Lai, R. Y. C. (1999). Intrinsic and extrinsic motivation in Internet usage. *Omega, 27*(1), 25–37.

Van Alstyne, M., & Brynjolfsson, E. (2005). Global Village or Cyber-Balkans? Modeling and Measuring the Integration of Electronic Communities. *Management Science, 51*(6), 851–868.

Von Hippel, W., Silver, L. A., & Lynch, M. E. (2000). Stereotyping Against Your Will: The Role of Inhibitory Ability in Stereotyping and Prejudice among the Elderly. *Personality and Social Psychology Bulletin, 26*(5), 523–532.

Wellman, B., Quan-Haase, A., Boase, J., Chen, W., Hampton, K., Díaz, I., et al. (2003). The Social Affordances of the Internet for Networked Individualism. *Journal of Computer-Mediated Communication, 8*(3).

White, R. W., & Horvitz, E. (2009). Cyberchondria: Studies of the escalation of medical concerns in Web search. *ACM Transactions of Information Systems, 27*(4), 1–37.

Wolf, C. (2004). Regulating hate speech qua speech is not the solution to the epidemic of hate on the Internet. *Paris: OSCE Meeting, 16*, Available at http://www.inach.net/content/wolf2.pdf.

Xiao, M., & Orazem, P. F. (2011). Does the fourth entrant make any difference?: Entry and competition in the early U.S. broadband market. *International Journal of Industrial Organization, 29*(5), 547–561.

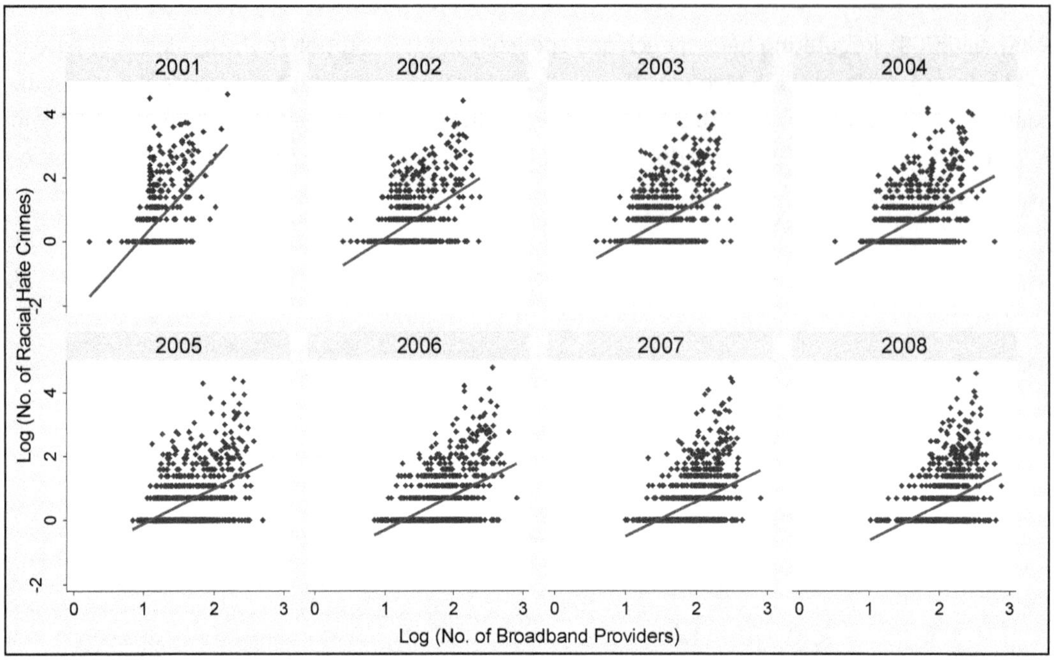

FIGURE 8.1 Relationship between racial hate crimes and the number of broadband providers

Notes: One-year lagged values of number of broadband providers are matched to racial hate crime observations from the study period (2001 to 2008) to derive this graph. As seen, the positive slope is particularly steep for 2001, the year when the September 11 terrorism incident took place.

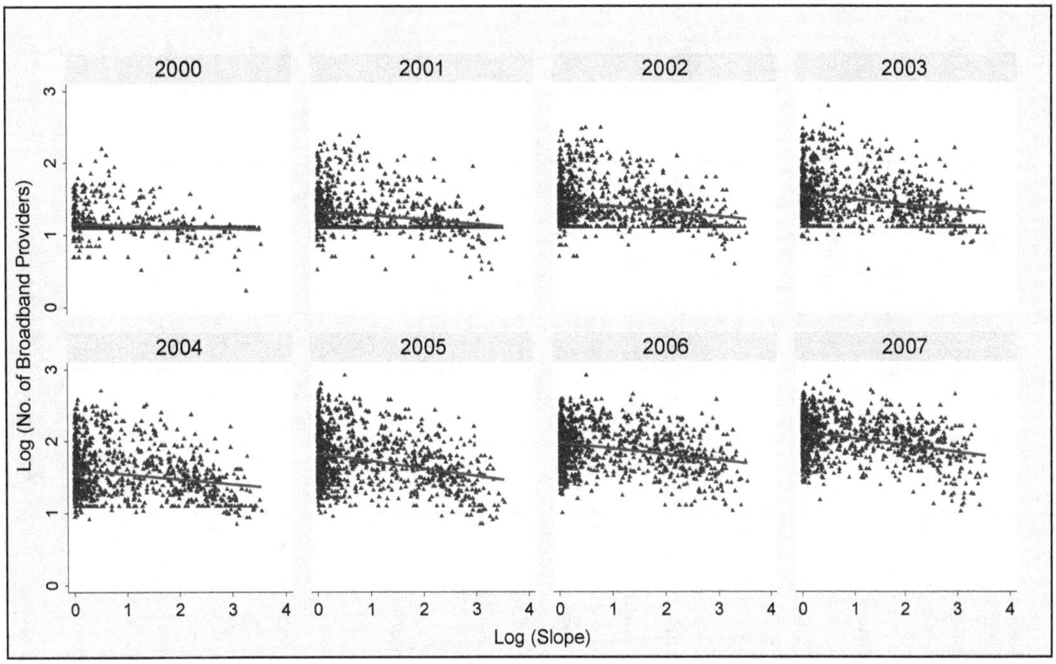

FIGURE 8.2 Relationship between the number of broadband providers and slope

Notes: Since one-year lagged values of broadband providers are used in our analyses, we show the graphical correlation between broadband providers and slope for 2000 to 2007. A trend is apparent in this graph: counties with low slope values (situated on the left side of each cell) are gaining more broadband providers than counties with high slope values (situated on the right side of each cell) over time. The trend leads to a stronger negative relationship over the years (i.e., steeper downward-sloping red line), which motivates the use of the slope-year interaction term as an instrument variable.

TABLE 8.1 Descriptive Statistics (N = 8200)

Variables	Mean	Std. Dev.	Min.	Max.	Description	Source
Dependent Variables:						
No. of Racial Hate Crimes	1.718	5.65	0	118.00	Count of crimes with anti-Black, anti-White, anti-American Indian, anti-Asian and anti-Multiple races biases	FBI
Log (No. of Racial Hate Crimes)	0.477	0.80	0	4.78		
No. of Religion Hate Crimes	0.656	3.39	0	79.00	Count of crime with anti-Jewish, anti-Catholic, anti-Protestant, anti-Islamic, anti-other religion anti-Atheism and anti-multiple religion biases	FBI
Log (No. of Religion Hate Crimes)	0.190	0.54	0	4.38		
No. of Sexual Orientation Hate Crimes	0.398	1.69	0	51.00	Count of crimes with anti-male homosexuals, anti-female homosexuals, anti-homosexuals, anti-heterosexuals, and anti-bisexuals biases	FBI
Log (No. of Sex. Orientation Hate Crimes)	0.172	0.44	0	3.95		
No. of Ethnicity Hate Crimes	0.378	1.85	0	62.00	Count of crimes with anti-Hispanic, and anti-other national origin biases	FBI
Log (No. of Ethnicity Hate Crimes)	0.152	0.43	0	4.14		
No. of Disability Hate Crimes	0.036	0.38	0	16.00	Count of crimes with anti-physical disability and anti-mental disability biases	FBI
Log (No. of Disability Hate Crimes)	0.018	0.14	0	2.83		
Broadband Availability and Instrument:						
Avg. No. Broadband Providers	4.268	2.41	1.33	17.38	Average number of broadband providers across county	FCC
Log (Avg. No. of Broadband Providers)	1.562	0.42	0.22	2.91		
Slope	3.607	5.85	0	33.43	Steepness of the terrain	Arc GIS
Log (Slope)	0.937	1.01	0	3.54		
Demographic Factors:						
Population Density	261.86	768.47	0	11999	Population per square mile	US Census
Log (Population Density)	4.553	1.33	0	9.39		
Population Size	0.124M	0.214M	2068	2.057M	Annual population estimates for counties	US Census
Log (Population Size)	10.922	1.21	7.63	14.54		
Mean Age	38.189	2.51	29.34	52.80	Average age of population, calculated across different age groups	US Census
Log (Mean Age)	3.666	0.06	3.41	3.99		
No. of International Migrants	286.85	1002.05	0	15827	Annual inflow of foreign migrants to county	US Census
Log (No. of International Migrants)	3.324	2.15	0	9.67		
Proportion of African American	0.093	0.13	0	0.80	Ratio of African American to total population	US Census
Proportion of Whites	0.879	0.14	0.17	0.99	Ratio of Whites to total population	US Census
Proportion of Asians	0.011	0.02	0	0.20	Ratio of Asians to total population	US Census

Variables	Mean	Std. Dev.	Min.	Max.	Description	Source
Socioeconomic Indicators:						
Median Household Income	41239	10916	17345	107200	Median household income in each county	US Census
Log (Median Household Income)	10.596	0.24	9.76	11.58		
No. of People in Poverty	13041	23734	203	407333	Count of people below the poverty level	US Census
Log (No. of People in Poverty)	8.732	1.15	5.32	12.92		
Employment Percentage	0.948	0.02	0.86	0.99	Percentage of employed individuals out of the employable population	BLS
Crime-related factors:						
No. of Police Employees	279.22	604.24	0	8342	Annual number of staff including police officers in police agencies	FBI
Log (No. of Police Employees)	4.653	1.34	0	9.03		
No. of Crimes	723.44	1455.75	0	21075	Annual number of crimes reported	FBI
Log (No. of Crimes)	5.186	2.01	0	9.96		
Industry sector size:						
Utilities Industry Payroll	10764	39261	0	0.692M	Total annual payroll of employees in industry with NAICS code 22 (in $1000)	US Census
Log (Utilities Industry Payroll)	2.943	4.44	0	13.45		
Information Industry Payroll	79703	278490	0	6.00M	Total annual payroll of employees in industry with NAICS code 51 (in $1000)	US Census
Log (Information Industry Payroll)	8.099	3.70	0	15.61		
Finance & Insurance Industry Payroll	181874	677938	0	13.7M	Total annual payroll of employees in industry with NAICS code 52 (in $1000)	US Census
Log (Finance & Insurance Ind. Payroll)	9.831	2.28	0	16.44		
Professional, Sci. & Tech. Industry Payroll	189627	703088	0	15.3M	Total annual payroll of employees in industry with NAICS code 54 (in $1000)	US Census
Log (Professional, Sci. & Tech. Ind. Payroll)	9.481	2.72	0	16.55		
Administrative and Support Industry Payroll	95713	262142	0	2.69M	Total annual payroll of employees in industry with NAICS code 56 (in $1000)	US Census
Log (Admin. & Support Industry Payroll)	8.720	3.52	0	14.81		

Notes. Hate crime data are from the years 2001 to 2008, while the regressors are from 2000 to 2007. Statistics are tabulated at the county-year level for all variables. All log transformed variables are constructed using log (X + 1). Payroll information for each industry sector is used as a proxy to denote the size of each industry for each county.

TABLE 8.2 Cross Sectional IV Regressions for Racial Hate Crimes

	Year 2001 (1)	Year 2002 (2)	Year 2003 (3)	Year 2004 (4)	Year 2005 (5)	Year 2006 (6)	Year 2007 (7)	Year 2008 (8)
1st stage DV: Log (No. of BB Providers)								
Log (Slope)	−0.012***	−0.012***	−0.032***	−0.051***	−0.057***	−0.042***	−0.080***	−0.042***
	(0.00)	(0.00)	(0.01)	(0.01)	(0.01)	(0.01)	(0.01)	(0.01)
Log (Population Density)	0.028***	0.028***	0.058***	0.075***	0.084***	0.073***	0.089***	0.071***
	(0.01)	(0.01)	(0.01)	(0.01)	(0.01)	(0.01)	(0.02)	(0.01)
Log (Mean Age)	0.101	0.101	0.173	−0.311**	−0.114	−0.100	−0.075	−0.327***
	(0.08)	(0.08)	(0.12)	(0.13)	(0.14)	(0.15)	(0.15)	(0.12)
Log (No. International Migrants)	0.031***	0.031***	0.047***	0.040***	0.027***	0.058***	0.055***	0.047***
	(0.00)	(0.00)	(0.01)	(0.01)	(0.00)	(0.01)	(0.01)	(0.01)
Proportion of African Americans	−0.015	−0.015	0.143**	−0.082	−0.060	−0.176***	−0.158**	0.183***
	(0.04)	(0.04)	(0.06)	(0.06)	(0.07)	(0.06)	(0.07)	(0.05)
Log (No. of People in Poverty)	0.035***	0.035***	0.067***	0.094***	0.141***	0.101***	0.095***	0.027*
	(0.01)	(0.01)	(0.01)	(0.01)	(0.01)	(0.02)	(0.02)	(0.01)
Employment Percentage	1.236***	1.236***	3.930***	2.424***	3.489***	2.471***	2.137***	1.285***
	(0.42)	(0.42)	(0.50)	(0.48)	(0.49)	(0.56)	(0.58)	(0.47)
Log (No. of Employees in Police Force)	−0.032***	−0.032***	−0.034**	−0.038**	−0.044***	−0.031*	−0.018	0.002
	(0.01)	(0.01)	(0.02)	(0.02)	(0.02)	(0.02)	(0.02)	(0.01)
Log (No. of Crimes)	0.004	0.004	−0.001	−0.001	−0.003	−0.004	−0.013***	−0.007*
	(0.00)	(0.00)	(0.00)	(0.00)	(0.00)	(0.00)	(0.00)	(0.00)
2nd stage DV: Log (No. of Racial Hate Crimes)								
Log (No. of BB Providers)	2.322	2.322	2.620***	1.582***	1.254***	1.224**	1.022***	1.573***
	(1.86)	(1.86)	(0.74)	(0.43)	(0.39)	(0.53)	(0.27)	(0.55)
Log (Population Density)	−0.034	−0.034	−0.131***	−0.063*	−0.035	−0.051	−0.052	−0.078*
	(0.05)	(0.05)	(0.05)	(0.04)	(0.04)	(0.04)	(0.03)	(0.04)
Log (Mean Age)	0.230	0.230	−0.239	0.928*	0.787*	0.821*	0.261	0.833*
	(0.40)	(0.40)	(0.45)	(0.47)	(0.44)	(0.42)	(0.40)	(0.47)
Log (No. International Migrants)	−0.005	−0.005	−0.096**	−0.048*	0.009	0.021	−0.013	−0.002
	(0.07)	(0.07)	(0.04)	(0.03)	(0.02)	(0.04)	(0.03)	(0.04)
Proportion of African Americans	−0.024	−0.024	−0.561**	−0.309*	−0.178	−0.166	0.169	−0.537**
	(0.16)	(0.16)	(0.25)	(0.16)	(0.16)	(0.16)	(0.17)	(0.23)
Log (No. of People in Poverty)	0.119*	0.119*	0.041	0.121**	0.038	0.003	0.064*	0.090**
	(0.07)	(0.07)	(0.06)	(0.05)	(0.05)	(0.05)	(0.04)	(0.04)
Employment Percentage	2.487	2.487	−5.798*	1.448	−1.127	−2.225	−1.239	−3.607**
	(3.16)	(3.16)	(3.51)	(1.91)	(2.03)	(1.98)	(1.53)	(1.67)
Log (No. of Employees in Police Force)	0.145**	0.145**	0.174***	0.104***	0.112***	0.125***	0.131***	0.098***
	(0.06)	(0.06)	(0.05)	(0.04)	(0.03)	(0.04)	(0.04)	(0.04)
Log (No. of Crimes)	0.024*	0.024*	0.037***	0.043***	0.030*	0.051***	0.060***	0.055***
	(0.01)	(0.01)	(0.01)	(0.01)	(0.02)	(0.01)	(0.02)	(0.02)
Observations	1025	1025	1025	1025	1025	1025	1025	1025
First stage F–statistics	49.319	49.319	34.781	37.519	37.338	37.99	38.898	31.285
Stock Yogo Critical Value	8.96	8.96	8.96	8.96	8.96	8.96	8.96	8.96
Root MSE	0.6424	0.6424	0.7075	0.6706	0.6609	0.6682	0.6452	0.6963

*Notes. All models are 2SLS regressions. Robust clustered standard errors are reported in parentheses. All regressors in the second stage are lagged by one period to avoid simultaneity biases. Following Stock et al. (2002), we report Stock and Yogo (2005) critical values for maximal IV size > 15%. * Significant at 10%; ** Significant at 5%; *** Significant at 1%.*

TABLE 8.3 Panel IV Regressions, Baseline Specifications

	(1)	(2)	(3)	(4)
1st Stage DV: Log (No. of BB Providers)				
Log (Slope)	−0.049*** (0.00)			
Log (Slope) * Year = 2001		−0.038*** (0.01)	−0.039*** (0.01)	−0.043*** (0.01)
Log (Slope) * Year = 2002		−0.048*** (0.01)	−0.041*** (0.01)	−0.047*** (0.01)
Log (Slope) * Year = 2003		−0.052*** (0.01)	−0.042*** (0.01)	−0.051*** (0.01)
Log (Slope) * Year = 2004		−0.043*** (0.01)	−0.036*** (0.01)	−0.041*** (0.01)
Log (Slope) * Year = 2005		−0.085*** (0.01)	−0.079*** (0.01)	−0.085*** (0.01)
Log (Slope) * Year = 2006		−0.060*** (0.01)	−0.053*** (0.01)	−0.062*** (0.01)
Log (Slope) * Year = 2007		−0.074*** (0.01)	−0.064*** (0.01)	−0.072*** (0.01)
2nd stage DV: Racial Hate Crimes				
Log (No. of BB Providers)	1.448*** (0.16)	1.208*** (0.16)	0.387** (0.19)	0.332* (0.19)
Log (Population Density)	−0.058*** (0.01)	−0.044*** (0.01)	0.066* (0.04)	0.063 (0.04)
Log (Mean Age)	0.544*** (0.15)	0.478*** (0.15)	3.052*** (0.97)	3.434*** (1.08)
Proportion of African Americans	−0.011 (0.01)	−0.000 (0.01)	0.007 (0.01)	0.009 (0.01)
Log (No. of People in Poverty)	−0.208*** (0.06)	−0.181*** (0.06)	−0.010 (1.78)	−0.033 (2.05)
Employment Percentage	0.067*** (0.02)	0.082*** (0.02)	0.092 (0.10)	0.093 (0.10)
Log (No. of employees in Police Force)	0.125*** (0.01)	0.124*** (0.01)	0.026 (0.04)	0.055 (0.04)
Log (No. of Crimes)	0.049*** (0.01)	0.047*** (0.00)	−0.012 (0.01)	−0.005 (0.01)
Year Fixed Effects	✓	✓	✓	✓
County Fixed Effects			✓	✓
Industry Size Controls				✓
Observations	8200	8200	8200	7530
First Stage F-statistics	323.152	45.943	25.687	28.228
Stock–Yogo Critical Value	8.96	11.29	11.29	11.29
Hansen J Statistics	–	17.471	6.692	6.755
P-value of Hansen J Statistics	–	0.008	0.35	0.344
Root MSE	0.6724	0.6551	0.4199	0.4282

Notes. All models are 2SLS IV regressions. We estimate the baseline specification by incrementally adding slope-year instruments and county fixed effects in Models 1 to 3. In Model 4, we estimate the basic specification with the addition of industry size covariates, which are captured by the annual aggregate payrolls of various industries common in urbanized locations. Robust clustered standard errors are reported in parentheses. All covariates are lagged by one period to avoid simultaneity biases. Following Stock et al. (2002), we report the Stock and Yogo (2005) critical values for maximal IV size > 15% (for just-identified models) and for relative bias > 10% (for over-identified models). Demographic controls include population density, mean age, no. of international migrants and proportion of African Americans; socioeconomic controls include no. of people in poverty and employment percentage; crime-related controls include no. of police employees and no. of crimes at the county level. Significant at 10%; ** Significant at 5%; *** Significant at 1%.*

TABLE 8.4 Panel IV Regressions, Split Sample Specifications

Subsample Description:	Low Entropy	High Entropy	Low Racially Charged Search	High Racially Charged Search
	(1)	(2)	(3)	(4)
2nd Stage DV: Racial Hate Crimes				
Log (No. of BB Providers)	−0.242	0.945***	−0.770	0.507**
	(0.21)	(0.33)	(0.82)	(0.20)
Log (Population Density)	0.272**	0.098**	0.033	0.108*
	(0.13)	(0.05)	(0.04)	(0.06)
Log (Mean Age)	2.784**	3.387*	1.276	5.527***
	(1.14)	(1.77)	(1.30)	(1.49)
Proportion of African Americans	0.016	−0.008	0.015	−0.001
	(0.01)	(0.02)	(0.01)	(0.02)
Log (No. of People in Poverty)	0.512	0.075	−0.493	1.776
	(1.51)	(3.72)	(2.55)	(2.04)
Employment Percentage	0.254**	−0.049	0.550*	0.033
	(0.12)	(0.16)	(0.32)	(0.12)
Log (No. of employees in Police Force)	−1.770**	−0.992	2.425	−1.337
	(0.90)	(1.26)	(2.27)	(0.92)
Log (No. of Crimes)	0.078	−0.045	0.026	0.062
	(0.06)	(0.05)	(0.06)	(0.06)
Year Fixed Effects	✓	✓	✓	✓
County Fixed Effects	✓	✓	✓	✓
Observations	4144	4056	3952	4024
First Stage F-statistics	19.412	11.522	2.242	28.105
Stock-Yogo Critical Value	11.29	11.29	11.29	11.29
Hansen J Statistics	5.933	9.091	7.788	4.531
P-value of Hansen J Statistics	0.431	0.169	0.254	0.605
Root MSE	0.403	0.45	0.431	0.416

Notes. All models are 2SLS IV regressions. Models 1–4 replicate Model 3 from Table 3A and split the sample into below (low) and above (high) median value for entropy score (Models 1–2) and racially charged search score (Models (3–4). Robust clustered standard errors are reported in parentheses. All covariates are lagged by one period to avoid simultaneity biases. Following Stock et al. (2002), we report the Stock and Yogo (2005) critical values for maximal IV size > 15% (for just-identified models) and for relative bias > 10% (for over-identified models). Demographic controls include population density, mean age, no. of international migrants and proportion of African Americans; socioeconomic controls include no. of people in poverty and employment percentage; crime-related controls include no. of police employees and no. of crimes at the county level. Significant at 10%; ** Significant at 5%; *** Significant at 1%.*

TABLE 8.5 Effect of Broadband on Crime Reporting Behavior

	Logistic Regression			
	Zero for 1995 and earlier		Zero for 1990 and earlier	
	(1)	(2)	(3)	(4)
Log (No. of BB Providers)	−0.007	−0.004	0.000	0.003
	(0.01)	(0.01)	(0.01)	(0.01)
MSA and Year-quarter Dummies	✓	✓	✓	✓
Demographic Controls		✓		✓
Crime-related Controls		✓		✓
Observations	131237	131232	88343	88338
Log Pseudo-Likelihood	−86140.36	−78290.00	−58047.85	−52885.21

*Notes. The dependent variable is a binary variable denoting whether the respondent reported the crime. In Models 1 and 2, the broadband providers are imputed with zeros for the years 1995 and earlier. In Models 3 and 4, the broadband providers are imputed with zeros for the years 1990 and earlier. All regressions include MSA dummies and year-quarter dummies. Robust clustered standard errors are reported in parentheses. Demographic controls include race, gender, household income, marital status, and educational attainment of the respondent. Crime-related controls include the crime location and crime type. Five observations were dropped in Models 2 and 4, as the covariates predicted the outcomes perfectly. * Significant at 10%; ** Significant at 5%; *** Significant at 1%.*

TABLE 8.6 Hate Groups and Single vs. Multiple Perpetrator Effects

2nd Stage DV: Listed at the Top of Each Column	No. of Hate Groups		Log (No. Racial Hate Crimes)		Log (No. Racial Hate Crimes)	
	Log Specification	Non-log Specification	Counties with No Hate Groups	Counties with Hate Groups	Single Perpetrator	Multiple Perpetrators
	(1)	(2)	(3)	(4)	(5)	(6)
BB Providers Measure	−0.200	−0.042	0.440*	−0.070	0.229**	0.043
	(0.15)	(0.03)	(0.26)	(0.26)	(0.12)	(0.06)
Log (Population Density)	−0.002	0.040	0.065**	0.047	−0.004	0.013
	(0.02)	(0.07)	(0.03)	(0.05)	(0.01)	(0.01)
Log (Mean Age)	−1.694***	−3.848***	1.572*	4.212**	1.596***	−0.156
	(0.54)	(1.07)	(0.95)	(1.82)	(0.49)	(0.31)
Log (No. International Migrants)	−0.003	−0.007	−0.001	0.013	−0.003	0.000
	(0.01)	(0.01)	(0.01)	(0.01)	(0.01)	(0.00)
Proportion of African Americans	−1.476**	−1.734	−0.001	−0.541	1.125*	0.257
	(0.73)	(1.28)	(1.49)	(3.12)	(0.66)	(0.42)
Log (No. of People in Poverty)	0.117	0.187	−0.034	0.390**	−0.027	0.042
	(0.07)	(0.12)	(0.10)	(0.15)	(0.06)	(0.03)
Employment Percentage	0.106	−0.212	0.066	−2.242*	−0.787*	0.404
	(0.40)	(0.73)	(0.85)	(1.33)	(0.41)	(0.26)
Log (No. of Employees in Police Force)	0.000	−0.011	0.002	0.074	−0.004	−0.000
	(0.02)	(0.03)	(0.04)	(0.08)	(0.02)	(0.01)
Log (No. of Crimes)	0.004	−0.000	−0.010	−0.014	0.003	−0.002
	(0.01)	(0.01)	(0.01)	(0.03)	(0.01)	(0.00)
Year Fixed Effects	✓	✓	✓	✓	✓	✓
County Fixed Effects	✓	✓	✓	✓	✓	✓
Observations	7175	7175	4976	3224	8200	8200
First Stage F–statistics	17.497	42.377	12.244	19.201	18.737	18.737
Stock-Yogo Critical Value	11.12	11.12	11.29	11.29	11.29	11.29
Hansen J Statistics	3.907	1.418	6.226	12.486	2.159	8.865
P-value of Hansen J Statistics	0.563	0.922	0.398	0.052	0.905	0.181
Root MSE	0.2108	0.4192	0.3646	0.4900	0.233	0.1393

*Notes. All models are 2SLS IV regressions. Models 1 and 2 are examining the impact of broadband providers on hate group incidence. Model 1 is a log specification where both the dependent and independent variables are logged; Model 2 is a non-log specification which regresses number of hate groups on number of broadband providers. Models 3 and 4 examine the effect of broadband providers on racial hate crime across locations without and with hate group presence, respectively. Models 5 and 6 examine the impact of broadband providers on the incidence of racial hate crimes committed by single perpetrator and multiple perpetrators, respectively. Covariates used are similar to that in Table 3. * Significant at 10%; ** Significant at 5%; *** Significant at 1%.*

A General *Theories* of Hate Crime?

Strain, Doing Difference and Self Control

Mark Austin Walters

Introduction

Criminological research on the causes of hate crime remains scant. This is partly due to the fact that hate motivated offences are a relatively new form of criminalisation.[1] The paucity of empirical research is, however, more likely the result of conceptual difficulties found when deciphering what actions and motivations fall within the 'hate crime' label (Jacobs and Potter 1998; Lawrence 1999). The failure of academics, legislatures and state agencies to find a common definition of hate crime means that criminologists continue to struggle to identify which offenders are 'hate offenders' (Perry 2009a).

Despite the complexities found in conceptualising hate crime two dominant criminological theories of causation have emerged. Most common, has been to link elements of Robert Merton's (1968) strain theory with various forms of hate crime (Kelly 1993; Levin and McDevitt 1993, 2002; Ray and Smith 2002), while Barbara Perry's structured action theory of 'doing difference' has also become influential (Perry 2001). These macro level explanations continue to be of significant importance to the aetiology of hate crime. In particular, the theories have illuminated several socio-structural and socio-economic factors that help to explain why hate crimes continue to be a pervasive form of offending.

However, while the extant literature on causation is of great epistemological value, several shortcomings can be identified. Firstly, there has been little which attempts to examine the intersections between the various theories espoused within criminology

1 Most hate crime laws were introduced during the 1990s and early 2000s both in the US and the UK.

Mark Walters, "A General Theories of Hate Crime? Strain, Doing Difference and Self Control," *Critical Criminology*, vol. 19, no. 4, pp. 313-330.

and other disciplines. The tendency to focus on disparate disciplinary analyses of hate crime has meant that the aetiology of 'hate' and more specifically hate motivated behaviour has been shaped within this or that field of study. Even within individual fields of study, researchers have failed to get to grips with linking macro level theory to individual agency. For example, within the criminological body neither strain theory nor 'doing difference' have been used to adequately explain why only some individuals commit hate crimes while others, equally affected by socio-economic strains and social constructions of 'difference', do not.[2]

This article therefore begins by re-examining the theories of strain and 'doing difference' in order to form a nexus between the two. In doing so the article attempts to show how that, far from diverging as theories of hate crime, they are intrinsically intertwined in ways which help to cultivate 'cultures of prejudice', within which various minority identity groups become the targets of hate abuse. Building from this analysis, the article then attempts to bridge the gap between macro theory and micro level offending by drawing upon Gottfredson and Hirschi's (1990) *A General Theory of Crime*. Using various typology studies that provide persuasive empirical evidence as to the motivations and behaviours of offenders, tentative assumptions are made about the levels of self control that the *majority* of hate offenders are *likely* to possess. This analysis not only provides for a new dynamic within the 'hate debate' but it is hoped will help to open up new avenues of empirical investigation into the causes of hate crime.

The theoretical model presented in this article does not deny that diverging causal variables exist between different forms of hate offending. Nor does the analysis contend that combining the three theories is exhaustive in explaining *all* types of hate crime. There are a multitude of psychological, social psychological, political, geographical and/or economic explanations of hate motivated crime which will continue to remain relevant (see Green et al. 2001; Perry 2009a). Rather, this article attempts to create a more comprehensive criminological framework of hate crime causation, essentially arguing that sociocultural and socio-economic conditions combine to create environments of hate that act to trigger the hate motivated behaviour of individuals with low self control.

What is Hate Crime?

The proliferation of hate crime laws across the Western world has resulted in an expanse of mainly legal scholarship exploring what is meant by the term (see Jacobs and Potter 1998; Lawrence 1999). The resulting academic debate on hate crime has been complex as those who have attempted to define the term 'hate' have struggled to reach agreement on its meaning (Perry 2009a). It has generally been accepted, however, that an offender need not actually 'hate' his or her victim in order to have committed a 'hate crime'. 'Hate' has instead been conceptualised by most to mean 'prejudice' (Jacobs and Potter 1998; Lawrence 1999). Conceptualising hate in this way has ignited further debate as to how prejudice should be defined and whether such

2 Perhaps a criticism which can be made about strain theory in general.

a phenomenon can be attached to the mens rea element of a criminal act (Jacobs and Potter 1998; Lawrence 1999).

For Jacobs and Potter (1998), there are two important questions to be asked when defining hate crime. Firstly, how do we define prejudice in the criminal context, and secondly what prejudices are deserving of criminal attention? Defining prejudice can be extraordinarily difficult. Some prejudices may be viewed as positive, such as anti-fascist or anti-racist. Other prejudices are innocuous such as a dislike of the colour green (Jacobs and Potter 1998: 12). However, certain prejudices are deemed to be wholly unacceptable and damaging to the social cohesiveness of society. These may include, amongst various other forms of prejudice, racism, homophobia, and anti-religious views.

Gordon Allport in his seminal book *The Nature of Prejudice* (1954:10) has been instrumental in the conceptualisation of prejudice. He defined 'ethnic prejudice' as, 'an antipathy based upon a faulty and inflexible generalisation. It may be felt or expressed. It may be directed towards a group as a whole, or towards an individual because he is a member of that group'. Clearly under this definition of prejudice a person must feel or express animosity toward a whole group based on generalisations made about its members. Such generalisations are often the result of stereotyping (discussed in more detail below). Negative stereotypes attached to certain identity groups are perpetuated through communication networks most notably between family and friends (Byers et al. 1999) but also via news and television mediums (see Green et al. 2001).

Some have argued that Allport's definition of prejudice may, however, be restrictive in defining hate crime. As Green et al. (2001) point out hate crime can be influenced by economic competition and resentment rather than a faulty generalisation about a group of individuals. Nonetheless, as this article will explore, the economic strain and the ensuing resentment felt towards some minority groups may well be based on false generalisations about the perceived economic prosperity and access to state welfare that certain minority groups supposedly receive (Ray and Smith 2002).

The conceptual complexities involved in defining hate crime act to remind us of the intractable nature of the phenomenon. However, such difficulties do not prevent us from exploring the causes of hate crime, instead they simply make the task that little bit more difficult. For the purposes of exploring causation in this article, hate crime is therefore defined as any type of crime or anti-social act aimed at intimidating and harming the victim which has been motivated (or partly motivated) by a prejudice, based on a generalisation about the victim's actual or perceived membership of an identity group[3] (which is different, at least in part, to that of the perpetrator's), and which is typically based on a fear or belief that the victim (and others like him or her) will encroach upon the offender's group identity, cultural norms and/or socio-economic security.

---

3 In general, the victim's identity group will be minority. In granting certain identity groups hate victim status there should be a history of marginalisation and discrimination against that group (Lawrence 1999).

Part I: Strain Theory and Socio-Economic Insecurity

Perhaps the most common criminological theory that has been used, at least in part, to explain hate crime is Merton's (1968) strain theory (see Kelly 1993; Levin and McDevitt 1993, 2002). Simply explained, Merton (1968) argued that deviant behaviour results from a 'disequilibrium' borne out of the gap between culturally prescribed goals and the means and opportunities of attaining these legitimately (Merton 1968). Due to inequalities in income, education and individual capacities, many citizens will simply be unable to obtain the goals that have been established within capitalist societies. The result is a strain placed upon those persons who desire material possessions essential to individual success. In responding to the pressures of capitalism some will turn to illegitimate avenues, including violence, in order to gain the materials and respect that allow them to acquire the social status society encourages (Merton 1968).

Agnew (1992: 48) has expanded upon this theory formulating three specific types of strain that can affect an individual's inclination towards crime. These relate closely to negative relationships with others who may impinge upon an individual's ability to obtain socially valued goals. Firstly, Agnew argued that others may prevent individuals from 'achieving their positively valued goals, including monetary, status, and autonomy goals'. Secondly, they may 'remove or threaten to remove positively valued stimuli that individuals possess (e.g., the death of friends or family members, the loss of romantic partners)' and thirdly, they could 'present or threaten to present individuals with noxious or negatively valued stimuli (e.g., verbal insults, physical assaults)' (Agnew et al. 2002: 44). If an individual who attempts to realise his or her expected goals is limited by someone else, he or she may react by feeling angry and frustrated and as such may be persuaded to adopt illegitimate means to attain these goals.

From both a Mertonian conception of strain and Agnew's use of negative relationships, we can begin to see violence committed against black minority ethnic (BME) groups, or other identity groups, as possibly rooted to the perceived socio-economic instability in a perpetrator's own life, which he or she believes is the fault of such groups. As minority identity groups move into new locales they will often be seen as invaders of indigenous (or dominant) group territory (Green et al. 1998; Perry 2009b: 67). Those already residing in the community can become fearful that incoming groups will impose upon their already unstable social and economic security and therefore to the positively valued goals that they hold (Green et al. 1998; Levin and McDevitt 2002: 57; Ray and Smith 2002). Some individuals become resentful towards 'foreigners' for obtaining what are primarily *perceived* as being 'British' (for example) homes and social benefits (Bowling and Phillips 2003; Ray and Smith 2002; Gadd et al. 2005).[4] Rumours that certain minority groups receive extra benefits from the government fuel the disgruntled sentiments towards their perceived economic advantage (see Sibbitt 1997; Ray and Smith 2002; Ray et al. 2004; Gadd et al. 2005: Levin and McDevitt 2002). Levin and McDevitt (2002: 33) state that in some cases certain

4 This can also be related to 'realistic conflict theory' which suggests that prejudice stems from competition between social groups for goods and services. However this does not necessarily take into account socioeconomic structures and social expectations which are better explained using strain theory.

groups are perceived to be 'the undeserving recipients of extraordinary treatment', to such an extent that many people become convinced that society has changed for the worse (Gadd et al. 2005; Levin and McDevitt 2002: 52).

As a result, various minority identity groups become the scapegoats for the woes felt by indigenous (or dominant) members of society (Young 1999). Blaming others for frustrations relating to unemployment, housing and jobs is amplified as certain media outlets portray immigrants (and other identity groups) as the root cause of society's problems (Gordon 1994; Sibbitt 1997: 13–14; see further below under 'Feeling the strain in a culture of prejudice: the importance of fear'). At the heart of these feelings of animosity towards immigrants and other 'foreigners' is a sense of unfairness, frustration, anger and even a sense of victimisation against white British folk (see Agnew 1992).

Unsurprisingly, hate crime studies have uncovered these negative sentiments amongst offenders. For example, Ray and Smith's (2002) research into racist hate crime in Greater Manchester found that many offenders felt a sense of being victimised by the Asian community who were seen to be getting preferential treatment by state authorities while at the same time encroaching upon British values and customs by introducing their own traditions and ways of life into the area. Research carried out by Gadd et al. (2005), also into racist hate crime, similarly demonstrates the pervasiveness of animosity held against certain identity groups, exacerbated by socio-economic (dis)advantage. Using discussion groups with 86 people from the Stoke on Trent area they found that both young and old people associated industrial decline and social change with the incoming foreigners into the area (Gadd et al. 2005: 5). Foreigners were seen to be both the symptom and the cause of social problems. The decline of community in what was seen as once a homogenous white area was blamed on the presence of people that were seen as 'outsiders'. Participants in the focus groups spoke of 'them', those who were perceived as outsiders or 'foreigners', and 'us' those who belonged to Britain (Gadd et al. 2005: 5). Foreigners were seen to be overrunning the local area and were not adapting to 'our' ways of life.

Conversely, rather than *hating* minority individuals because of their minority identity, hate offenders may in fact be more concerned with their own socio-economic inadequacies (Ray and Smith 2002; Sibbitt 1997). Ray and Smith argue that socio-economic disadvantage can frustrate individuals who see their general lack of social status, framed by their lack of obtaining of material goods and property, as a personal failing. Adding to this analysis Gadd and Dixon (2009: 85), reflecting on their earlier research in Stoke on Trent, state:

> It was if people we spoke to were aware that others perceived them as cultural and economic failures—as losers—and that, try as they might, there was little they could do [to] counter this evaluation.

Frustrations can weigh heavy on the minds of many individuals. For some their frustration is internalised as negative feelings about the 'self' but quickly resurfaces as a feeling of anger which is then directed towards 'outsiders'; seen as the source of an offender's own problems (see Gadd et al. 2005; Ray and Smith 2002; Ray et al. 2004; Sibbitt 1997). In this sense, some types of hate violence (especially racist or anti-immigrant) have been characterised as the culmination of unacknowledged shame rooted to a perpetrator's own social and economic disadvantage which is inevitably projected onto those perceived to be restricting the attainment of socially constructed goals (Ray and Smith 2002).

Part II: 'Doing Difference'

While linking hate crime to experiences of strain has improved upon the paucity of hate crime theorisation, it is difficult to explain all hate crime in terms of socio-economic disadvantage and/or feelings of unacknowledged shame. In her influential book, *In the Name of Hate: Understanding Hate Crime* (2001), Barbara Perry argues that strain theory cannot account for all hate crime as it does not explain why the most atrocious hate crimes are carried out by the most economically and politically powerful people in society. Indeed, while it is accepted that many hate offenders will be socio-economically disadvantaged, others will inevitably come from a wide-range of socio-economic backgrounds (Sibbitt 1997). Hate offenders can be employers, neighbours, state agency workers and even leaders of political parties (Garland and Chakraborti 2006; McGhee 2005; Perry 2001).

Perry argues that hate crime is better understood as the extreme form of discrimination which emulates from a culture of segregation, discrimination and marginalisation of people who are somehow 'different'. It is therefore important to consider the power dynamics that demarcate modern society when explaining hate crime (Perry 2001). Perry (2001) states that within modern society power hierarchies are now constituted by dominance over 'difference'. Difference has been used to construct intersecting social hierarchies pertaining to gender, race, sexuality and class, amongst others (Perry 2001: 46: see also Spalek 2008). Paradoxically, the notion of 'difference' results from people 'belonging' to groups whose members they see as having the same or similar identity characteristics as them. People become bound to their cultural and ethnic identity through common interest or, as Green and Seher (2003: 520) state, through a 'natural—some might say spiritual—affinity'. Identity groups may coalesce around ethnicity, religion, sexual orientation, or other such characteristics (forming 'in-groups'). Categories of identity often assume binary classifications. One is either white or black, white or Asian, gay or straight, Christian or Muslim (Perry 2001: 47). In creating an 'ingroup' we seek out the Other; the person who is most definitely not like 'us'.

Positioning our own identity entails the creation of a hegemonic form, 'what Audre Lorde refers to as a "mythical norm" '(Perry 2001: 47). Inevitably those who fall outside society's construction of identity are seen as 'different' (Perry 2001). Those who are deemed to be different are resisted because they are feared. Feelings of fear are based on the assumption that Others will encroach upon the 'ingroup's' identity and cultural norms. For some individuals this creates a feeling of helplessness and insecurity about their place in society. In response to these negative emotions, individuals frequently attempt to transpose their feelings of helplessness into animosity, an emotive reaction which is used to gain a sense of control over those who they see as causing their insecurity, thus temporarily relinquishing the original negative feeling of fear.

Ultimately, Others who continue to transcend the identity ideal threaten dominant normality and will be forced to take a subordinate position within society whereby individual members receive unequal distributions of wealth and access to housing and education (Perry 2001; see also Home Office 2005a, b). Subordination is also played out through private and state agencies (including the criminal justice system) that systematically discriminate against Others via the practices and policies that they implement (see Macpherson 1999; Phillips and Bowling 2007). The various forms of discrimination endured by marginalised identity groups—a product of what Perry terms 'doing difference'—can be taken a step further to include more severe acts of prejudice, such as hate violence (Perry 2001). For instance, if gay people make public their sexual orientation through visible displays of affection or by opening establishments patronised predominantly by gay people, they threaten the heteronormativity of civilised society (Bibbings 2004). In response to this blatant deviation from society's sexual norm, many people will wish to suppress gay people for fear that they will increasingly encroach upon society's sexual identity. In some cases people will believe that 'gayness' will pervert their children and lead to the degradation of society. Violence and other forms of intimidation are therefore used to vanquish gay people and various Others for having over stepped social and cultural boundaries (Perry 2001: 59).

Part III: Feeling the Strain in a Culture of Prejudice: The Importance of Fear

Perry's analysis of 'doing difference' encompasses many types of hate crime. The theory, although somewhat deterministic, is useful in that it is able to explain most attempts to suppress 'difference' as resulting from the threat posed by Others to dominant norms. However, Perry's theory fails to explain, *by itself*, why so many hate crimes (particularly racist and anti-immigrant motivated incidents) are committed by those most affected by socio-economic strain (Gadd et al. 2005; Ray and Smith 2002). Therefore in an effort to better explain the aetiological determinants of hate crime this article suggests that the theories of strain and 'doing difference' are better understood when they are synthesised.

Ray and Smith (2002), Gadd et al. (2005) and Sibbitt (1997) all refer in their empirical studies to a general culture of racism within society that, generally speaking, must be understood within a context of socio-economic disadvantage (see further Bowling 1998; Chahal and Julienne 1999). Cultures of prejudice are nurtured within families, friendship circles and by neighbours. Their views on race, religion and sexual orientation (and other identities) have been normalised by media (mis)representations and political discourse on race, immigration, and sexuality etc. (Sibbitt 1997: 14). Negative labels are frequently attached to whole identity groups who are seen as posing a threat to the status quo of dominant cultural normality *and* to socio-economic security (a form of 'doing difference' and strain). Labels give rise to beliefs about a group's worthiness as respectable citizens (Levin and McDevitt 2002; Levin and Rabrenovic 2009). Certain identity groups become labelled as deviants and/or are classified as inferior. Some labels can be particularly insidious, demonising the very essence of a group of individuals. By stigmatising whole identity groups, dominant groups begin to dehumanise swathes of individuals (Levin and Rabrenovic 2009). Over time prejudices can become entrenched and are difficult to change, leaving certain identity groups in a perpetual state of marginalisation (Craig 2002; Levin and McDevitt 2002).

Gordon (1994, cited in Sibbitt 1997: 13) highlights how the British media have frequently skewed the reality of certain identity groups' lives, stating:

> The Sun newspaper carried a story claiming Camden Council was housing 'penniless immigrant families' in 'dream homes'. Not only did the Council receive a hundred threatening phone calls following this story, but two Asian children living in the street named by the paper were attacked as they played.

That coverage from the early 1990s is illustrative of the power that media outlets have in stirring up negative sentiments against certain sections of society. It appears little has changed since that decade. In 2008, for example, the Sun carried the headline 'We must be mugs' (October 11th) stating that 'SUN readers struggling to cope with the credit crunch are outraged that a migrant Afghan mum gets £170,000 a year in handouts so she can live in a £1.2 million mansion.' Such headlines help to fuel the disgruntled sentiments held against immigrants and other 'outsiders' who are targeted by sections of the national media.

Feelings of animosity directed towards certain identity groups can therefore be fuelled by two separate sources: socio-economic instability and internalised frustrations about economic security, while at the same time social constructions of difference and distrust of the Other act to further exacerbate feelings of hatred and prejudice. Both sociological factors are systematically propelled by the emotion of *fear* inevitably creating a culture of prejudice—sustained by various communication networks—through which hate crime then emerges.

Part IV: The Risk of Strain Posed By Those Deemed to be 'Different'

We begin to see here that rather than diverging as explanatory models of hate crime the theories of strain and 'doing difference' are interconnected through the emotion of fear. It is the fear that Others will encroach upon dominant group identity *and* socio-economic security, that fuels the climate of prejudice against them. Fear affects some people more than others. However, as it sweeps through a community it can affect almost everyone—including those who are socio-economically privileged. While socio-economically powerful people may not directly feel 'the strain', they will equally be, if not more, susceptible to the pressures of conforming to a hegemonic form of identity. After all, in many ways they are beacons of the dominant identity ideal. Dominant group members will undoubtedly act to protect the social norms through which they live their lives and from which they have come to wield socio-economic power. In this sense, the powerful may act to suppress identity groups that fail to fit within identity expectations because they fear that they may potentially lose socio-economic prosperity to the 'outgroup' at some point in the future. The intersection between 'doing difference' and strain (for socio-economically powerful people) can accordingly be seen in two possible ways:

1. Strain may be experienced as a fear rather than as a reality. It may be viewed as a dystopic vision of what is to come if we fail to suppress 'difference'.
2. The strain may be felt vicariously by people who see other 'ingroup' citizens experiencing actual economic and material strain because of Others.

As a result, dominant groups in society use hate crime in two ways. First, hate crime is used as a mechanism to suppress Others preventing them from climbing socio-economic ladders, taking with them a larger bite of capitalist resources and with that political power, potentially changing the way that dominant groups live their lives (a direct reaction to points 1 and 2). Second, the incitement of hate crime by powerful citizens maybe a means of placing blame onto Others (i.e. scapegoating) for causing the strain and disenfranchisement of certain sections of society (the under classes—classic Marxist theory) (Young 1999). By doing this, the powerful displace their own blame for perpetuating socioeconomic divisions between social classes onto Others (i.e. a means of protecting the socio-economic status quo, particularly relevant to point 1). For example, many socioeconomically powerful people engage in discourse which focuses on the unfairness of Others taking British jobs, resources and housing while at the same time they accuse minority groups of causing crime and anti-social problems ('BNP Exposed: The Secret Agent' *BBC documentary* 2008; Gadd et al. 2005; McGhee 2005). They act to incite those who are socio-economically unstable into blaming Others for their disadvantaged situation.

The actions of the powerful can therefore be seen as just as much about protecting socio-economic security as is the case with those who are socio-economically disadvantaged. Their hate motivated behaviours occur at different ends of the socio-economic scale, but it is the fact that they act on the *same* scale which is of importance. Therefore, unlike Perry's contention that strain cannot explain why the socio-economically secure commit hate crime, using a broader interpretation of strain theory we might see strain, not simply as a direct experience of deprivation, but as a *risk* of it. The risk of strain not only affects the most disenfranchised into acting against difference but the most powerful too.

Part V: Macro to Micro?

The use of strain theory and further exploration of the affects of socio-economic insecurity, along with Perry's 'doing difference', are fundamental to our understanding of hate crime. Yet, the theories suffer from a single explanatory problem. Neither theory, even when they are connected, explains why only certain individuals commit hate crimes while others, equally open to the same strains and hegemonic constructions of identity, choose not to. There is little within the hate crime literature which tackles this quandary. Within the psychological literature some attempts have been made to explain the individual actions of offenders by linking hate crime with the theory of 'authoritarian personality'. In essence, it is argued that some parents tend to treat their children in an overtly critical, rejecting or dismissive manner. Children learn that power and authority are integral to human relations. As these children grow up any frustrations felt towards their parents are redirected onto other people seen as most vulnerable (see Green et al. 2001: 485). The theory is most compelling in explaining the actions of those who develop extremist views against certain identity groups (Gerstenfeld 2004: 84). They are individuals likely to join groups whose sole aim is to target others who are deemed as 'different'. However, Gerstenfeld (2004) states that there is scant evidence to show the link between authoritarian personality and hate crime. Moreover, as we have already seen in Parts I–III, for many offenders their primary motivation relates to frustrations about their own socio-economic security. They are also compelled to act in order to defend 'their' geographical territory. We will also see below how many other young offenders use their bigotry as a means of seeking out a 'thrill' (Levin and McDevitt 1993). In other words, while authoritarian personality theory may have some relevance to extremist forms of hate crime it is less relevant to most hate crimes which are only *partly* motivated by prejudice.

Self Control and Hate Crime: The Missing Link?

In connecting macro level influences of hate crime with individual agency the article now turns to an analysis of Gottfredson and Hirschi's theory of self control (Gottfredson and Hirschi 1990).[5] Though the theory has been one of the most scrutinised since its inception in 1990, it has remained completely absent from the 'hate debate'. In their book *A General Theory of Crime,* (1990) argued that most individuals will have control over their actions which prevents them from succumbing to the temptation of criminal opportunity. The ability to exert self control over one's behaviour is a trait instilled in us from an early age. We are taught to defer gratification that comes from acting upon our natural impulses. Failure to instil upon children and young adults the need to withhold our temptations results in some people forming low levels of self control. Gottfredson and Hirschi (1990: 90) argue that such people are impulsive, insensitive and short sighted. They are people who often take physical risks and lack consideration for others around them. They further expound that people with low self control are often 'gregarious' and social individuals who have a 'low tolerance' threshold for others (Gottfredson and Hirschi 1990: 90). It is this lack of self control that Gottfredson and Hirschi (1990: 111) state is 'the primary individual characteristic causing criminal behaviour'. Crime provides an often easy way of obtaining

5 Agnew et al. (2002) have attempted to bridge the gap between strain theory and micro level offending by drawing upon general strain theory (GST) and personality traits. While this research may well have potential linkages to hate crime offending it does not consider the interaction between other factors such as social constructions of difference and personality traits, instead concentrating solely on strain. Moreover, the typology research which has been carried out by Levin and McDevitt (1993, 2002), amongst others, fits more neatly into Gottfredson and Hirschi's conception of self control, focusing in particular on offenders' desire to seek out thrills much in the same way that self control theory contends. It is for these reasons that the article expands upon the potential link between self control and not GST.

a thrill, excitement and, in the case of acquisitive crime, the desirable product. Linked to low self control and the desire for instant gratification is the likelihood of committing 'psychological equivalents' such as drinking too much alcohol, taking drugs and/or other anti-social behaviours (Gottfredson and Hirschi 1990: 92).

Gottfredson and Hirschi contend that low self control is the result of ineffective parenting (1990). Parents who fail to properly nurture, discipline and supervise their children will produce adults who will not have the levels of control needed for law abiding behaviour. These individuals are likely to have parents who have failed to give them adequate affection. As children they will not have been adequately monitored and/or punished for any wrong doing they committed. Because of this, it is argued that they are likely to fail academically and will ultimately struggle to find full-time skilled employment.

Individuals who display low levels of self control are consequently the product of 'poor socialisation'. Their parents are themselves likely to be involved in criminal activity and anti-social behaviour (Gottfredson and Hirschi 1990). By contrast, Gottfredson and Hirschi argue that children who have been monitored and appropriately disciplined will be able to defer their desire for instant gratification, resisting frivolous temptations before building long-term satisfaction.[6]

Typologies of Hate Offenders: A Picture of Low Self Control

This article does not test empirically whether a connection between self control and hate crime exists. Neither does it intend to critique self control theory in full here—that has been done elsewhere in the literature (see a summary in Newburn 2007: 237). Rather, the aim is to open the hate debate up to the possibility of explaining hate crime (partly) using self control theory. This endeavour begins here with an exploration of the various theoretical connections which can be made between the theory and hate crime. In particular, parallels are drawn between Gottfredson and Hirschi's theory and empirical findings about the typology of hate offenders. Connections between self control theory and typology results are then linked back to the theories of strain and difference.

Research which explores the 'type' of offenders that commit hate crimes remains relatively limited. However, several empirical studies have begun to uncover some of the background traits of perpetrators (Byers et al. 1999; Franklin 2000; Levin and McDevitt 1993, 2002; McDevitt et al. 2002; Sibbitt 1997). These studies tell us a lot about the behaviours of hate offenders and what their primary motivations are.[7] One of the most commonly referenced typology studies is that

6 Empirical research has largely supported the assertion that low self control can predict criminal behaviour (see Pratt and Cullen's (2000) meta analysis; see also Armstrong (2005).

7 It should noted that hate crimes remain massively underreported (Perry 2009a). This means that we cannot be certain about the motives and background traits of *all* hate offenders due to the fact that no simple random sample of perpetrators is obtainable. However, it does not necessarily follow that hate crimes which go unreported will be qualitatively different to those that are. The theories discussed here and elsewhere that explain the motivations and behaviours of offenders remain persuasive, and by inference should apply to offenders whether they come to the attention of state authorities or not.

reported in Levin and McDevitt's (1993) book entitled *Hate Crimes: The Rising Tide of Bigotry and Bloodshed* which was later expanded upon by McDevitt et al. (2002). Using 169 hate crime case reports from the Boston Police Department, Levin and McDevitt explain that hate offenders can be divided into the following categories: 'thrill', 'defensive', 'retaliatory' and 'mission'. Despite certain methodological limitations in Levin and McDevitt's study, in particular the medium sized sample, the use of police files, and a single location, the study remains the most comprehensive to date. However, in forming a more comprehensive picture of the types of hate offenders that exist, this article also relies on typology data provided by Byers et al. (1999) Franklin (2000) and Sibbitt (1997). While research findings from various other hate crime studies, most of which have already been highlighted above, are also used.

Thrill Seekers: Looking for Trouble in a World of 'Difference'

Levin and McDevitt (1993, 2002) found that most hate offenders (66%) were primarily motivated by the 'thrill' of offending (Levin and McDevitt 1993, 2002). Such offenders are likely to be impulsive people already prone to physical risk taking (Levin and McDevitt 1993, 2002). Levin and McDevitt found that groups of young men often venture into areas populated by those they actively seek to target. Led by one or two ring leaders, they vociferously verbalise their bigotry before physically attacking their victim/s (Levin and McDevitt 1993, 2002). Various other researchers have concurred with Levin and McDevitt's findings that offenders frequently seek out the excitement of a hate attack (Byers et al. 1999; Franklin 2000). For example, in Byers et al.'s (1999) study into hate crimes against the Amish in Fulham County, USA, the authors conclude that 'An ideology of hate is typically absent ... Rather ... offending rests largely with the thrill or excitement experienced' (1999: 84). Again, within that study young offenders typically acted in small groups. They were often fuelled by alcohol (another symptom Gottfredson and Hirschi highlight as being connected to low self control) and were seen to carry out their attacks almost like a sport or pass-time. Further evidence of thrill seeking amongst hate offenders was reported by Franklin who found that a key motivating factor behind homophobic harassment was the search for a thrill, with offenders often finding anti-gay behaviours as 'amusing' (2000: 354). Such findings, which take into account different types of hate crime from different locations, suggest that a large proportion of hate crime, committed by young men, will be at least partly motivated by an immature urge to seek out excitement.

If many offenders are motivated by the excitement of offending we must surely ask why these offenders seek out such a thrill in the first place? This remains unclear within hate crime literature. McDevitt et al. (2002: 308) simply report that according to interviews with police investigators, thrill motivated cases are 'triggered by an immature desire to display power and to experience a rush at the expense of someone else'. However, this still does not explain why only certain young men wish to experience such a rush while other similarly immature young men do not. Instead, thrill seeking might better be viewed in terms of Gottfredson and Hirschi's description of criminals as 'adventuresome, active, and physical' (Gottfredson and Hirschi 1990: 89).

The very fact that thrill seekers undertake risky physical behaviours in an order to fulfil their urge for excitement places them at the heart of the self control model of crime causation. Nonetheless, self control theory alone cannot fully explain the behaviour of these types of hate offenders. Rather, it is the forming of a nexus between self control and structured action theory that we begin to fully understand the motivations of the thrill seeker.

Let us take an example of how 'doing difference' and the theory of self control converge to create the foreground for thrill seeking behaviour. Thrill seekers often target gay men to abuse (Levin and McDevitt 1993). The reason for this is twofold. Firstly, as mentioned above, thrill seekers are typically young men who act in groups. These young offenders frequently congregate in town centres drinking alcohol. They search for ways to enjoy themselves, often at the expense of others (Levin and McDevitt 2002: 72; see also Craig 2002). Secondly, homosexuality is seen by many young men as an affront to their own masculinity. Gay men (or any male who displays what might be seen as 'effeminate attributes') have been constructed as 'different' and are thus judged to be socially unacceptable (Franklin 2000; Perry 2001). Some young men react to these social conditions by verbally or physically abusing other men/boys thought to be gay. Homophobic abuse is a means of asserting masculinity; it is a demonstration of solidarity to the perpetrator's 'ingroup' while simultaneously attempting to suppress difference (see Franklin 2000). But most importantly, for young men, it is simply a means of 'having a laugh' (see similarly Byers et al. 1999).

A clear interaction exits here between, on the one hand an offender's prejudice, formed in part by his or her fear of difference, and on the other his or her desire to seek out excitement. The climate of prejudice, as explained by Perry (2001) and others, within which the offender operates, is just part of the reason why he or she chooses to commit a hate crime. The desire to feel the rush of such a crime provides the impetus for their offending. Subsequently, the hatred underlying most thrill seekers acts mainly at a 'superficial level' (Levin and McDevitt 1993). There exists a crucial intersection here between the socio-structural influences affecting an individual's perception of 'difference' and his or her desire for instant gratification (the thrill). Hence, in acquiring the thrill, offenders use their prejudices, the result of constructions of difference, stereotyping and the perceived threats posed by certain minority individuals, as a means of justifying their *partly* hate motivated actions.

Defending Turf: Gregarious Characters with Low Tolerance Thresholds for Others

While the thrill seeking category of offending takes in elements of both 'doing difference' and self control theory, demonstrating why only some young offenders attack those who are different, thrill seekers do not account for all hate crimes. What then is to be said of other types of hate offenders and whether they are likely to have low self control? As we saw in Parts I–III many hate offenders are less concerned with excitement but instead with protecting geographical space and their socio-economic security. In line with such findings is Levin and McDevitt's second largest category of hate offenders (at 25%) labelled 'defensive'. These offenders were said to be those who acted in defence of what was perceived as a threat to their 'territory'. Part I explained how defensive offenders often deem minority individuals to be 'invaders' who have no 'rights' to the resources that have been built up by the indigenous population. Ray and Smith (2002) argue that many individuals end up feeling a sense of resentment and anger which is internalised and then projected onto Others. The demographic movement of people of difference into new locales therefore sparks a violent response from the homogenous local dominant group (Green et al. 1998). 'Defensive' hate incidents are likely to occur in the context of offenders' everyday lives (Iganski 2008). People of difference will frequently come into contact with other members of the community during their daily routine activities, such as in communal hall ways, at bus stops, in shops or even at work. A perceived grievance, for instance, someone pushing past on a bus, a failure to say thank you in a shop or speaking too loudly in a 'foreign' voice near to someone's front door can be enough to trigger a hate motivated response by those who deem the presence of such individuals as a threat to their socio-economic security.

However, like thrill seeking, the defensive category does not explain why it is that only certain individuals lash out against Others; given that large proportions of a community will feel a sense of grievance against them (Gadd et al. 2005; Iganski 2008; Sibbitt 1997). In examining who these individual offenders might be, we can consider that amongst those who experience actual or perceived strain will be those with *low tolerance* thresholds for Others. Hate crime studies have already indicated that many offenders are likely to be gregarious people, outspoken about their disdain for the 'invaders' of their territory (Gadd et al. 2005; Sibbitt 1997). They will often be heard telling racist or homophobic jokes and/or laughing at others who do the same (Levin and McDevitt 2002; Sibbitt 1997). Offenders are also likely to vent their frustrations using physical force and will regularly use violence as a means of dealing with inter-personal conflict in general (Gadd et al. 2005; Ray and Smith 2002). It is here that we again begin to see traits of low self control amongst hate offenders who are primarily concerned with defending geographical and socio-economic territory. For those who have low self control will be less able to tolerate any form of personal threat. It is likely that they will be less able to control their feelings of animosity towards those who they deem as being 'different'. It therefore follows that individuals with low self control are most likely to lash out against those who threaten their socio-economic security.

Poor Socialisation: Unemployment, Poor Academics and General Patterns of Crime

It is instructive to turn now to Gottfredson and Hirschi's reference to people with low self control as lacking academic qualifications and later in life, professional employment—a direct result they argue of poor socialisation. Connecting these attributes of low self control with hate crime is research which has shown that hate offenders frequently lack academic qualifications and ultimately end up unemployed or in low-skilled jobs (Levin and McDevitt 2002; Ray and Smith 2002; Sibbitt 1997). Ray and Smith's (2002) study, for example, found that half of their sample was unemployed while the majority of the rest were in low-skilled jobs. Other researchers such as Sibbitt (1997: 78–79) have highlighted the fact that many racist perpetrators come from families with various physical, mental and economic difficulties (see also Gadd et al. 2005). Sibbitt (1997: 78–79) explains that such families:

> ... behave abusively towards their children and towards others in general. The children, experiencing abusive and threatening behaviour from their parents, behave abusively towards others. Like their parents, they are low achievers educationally. The family is described as a single 'type' because they see themselves as rejected by society and tend to act as a unit, encouraging and reinforcing each other's behaviour. The family is constantly abusive and threatening towards neighbours in general, and engages in many forms of anti-social behaviour.

Such a finding concurs with research by Glueck and Glueck (1950), referred to by Gottfredson and Hirschi (1990: 98), which found that fathers who were less warmly disposed to their children and mothers who were hostile or indifferent towards them produced young adults with low self control. In fact, there is now a growing body of research that has examined the effect of parenting (family processes) on levels of self control (see Vazsonyi and Belliston 2007: 307 for a review of these). In general, these studies have supported Gottfredson and Hirschi's hypothesis that poor parenting will produce children (and later adults) with low self control—though some studies have produced mixed results. Sibbitt's finding therefore creates the inference that hate offenders have lacked the discipline and parental supervision required of them to form the levels of self control needed to obtain longer term goals.

Further corroborating the link between self control theory and hate crime is research findings that show how perpetrators are likely to be involved in an array of different types of crime (Ray and Smith 2002; Sibbitt 1997). In Ray and Smith's (2002: 95) study they reported that 64% of racist perpetrators had previous convictions for other offences including theft, assault and drugs. Sibbitt (1997: 101–102) similarly found that some offenders 'terrorise not only members of ethnic minorities but others in the community more generally'. While Franklin (2000: 355) states that, 'Although societal norms provide these individuals with justification for selection of homosexual targets, their anti-gay violence is likely to be part of a larger lifestyle of violence, criminality and-ultimately-incarceration' (see further Ray et al. 2004: 351).

When viewed together the correlation between research findings into hate crime and Gottfredson and Hirschi's theory is highly suggestive of the role that self control is likely to play in explaining the phenomenon, depicting perpetrators of hate, not as criminals who focus their attentions solely on prejudice motivated behaviour but as individuals who are prone to delinquency in all its guises. However, while drawing parallels between hate crime typologies with self control theory has been illuminating it does not provide unequivocal evidence of a connection. It must be noted, for example, that only mere inferences can be drawn between self control theory and research which depicts hate offenders as poorly socialised by their families. It remains empirically unclear whether the poor socialisation of hate offenders causes low self control or whether poor socialisation is simply correlated with hate crime offending. In order to form more solid assertions about the levels of self control displayed by perpetrators of hate and/or the effect that 'poor socialisation' has on offenders, further empirical research is required (see suggestion below).

Part VI: Limitations

Other 'Types'

Within this article several theoretical connections have been made between hate crime research and self control theory. However, linking *all* types of hate crime to the theory would be a step too far. This article does not purport that all hate crime can be explained using self control theory. One problem with the connection is that not all 'types' of offenders will fit neatly into the model. For example, 8% of offenders in Levin and McDevitt's study were classified as 'retaliators'. These offenders only commit a hate offence if they feel their 'ingroup' is under attack. National or international events such 9/11 or 7/7 can evoke violent reactions by those who wish to protect their identity group. As these offenders tend to *react* only to being attacked (whether actual or perceived) they cannot be said to be seeking out a thrill. Neither can they be said to be intolerant of Others simply because of their presence within the community—though their failure to restrain their violent urges may well be due to low levels of self control.

There are further difficulties in applying the theory to hard-line extremists. Levin and McDevitt's (2002) call these hate perpetrators 'mission offenders'. However, within their study these offenders were rarest, making up less than 1% of cases (one case out of 169). Such offenders purposively go out of their way to hunt down and attack victims. Again it is difficult to show whether such offenders display traits of low self control. They may instead be highly socialised individuals with high levels of self control in most areas of their life.[8] The fact that they are often members of an organised group also suggests that mission offenders hold high levels of self control enabling them to carry out organised attacks.

Powerful Actors

Finally, the article returns to Perry's (2001) assertion that some hate crimes are carried out by the most powerful people in society. It was suggested in Part IV that such people are fearful of difference and the *potential* strain that Others might place on their socio-economic security in the future. These people incite hatred or use policies to discriminate against Others in an attempt to suppress their social mobility. However, it is unlikely that powerful perpetrators of hate display traits of low self control, as defined by Gottfredson and Hirschi. For in order to gain the socio-economic power that they now wield they will have had to sustain a self controlled effort towards socio-economic success.

While most of these perpetrators are unlikely to violently assault people on the street, they cannot be denied as a type of hate offender. They are inciters of hatred operating from above in an attempt to mobilise others, possibly with low self control, into acting against difference.

8 They may display traits of 'authoritarian personality' as explained in Part V.

Some may even commit verbal acts of hate themselves, especially if provoked (whether real or perceived) (Iganski 2008). Such offenders cannot be disregarded as irrelevant to the theoretical model proffered in this article. Inciters of hatred are no less culpable for the spread of hate crimes in society; indeed they are often instrumental in the perpetuation of cultures of prejudice and therefore the hate crimes that follow. As such, both inciters of hate and the likely small amount of highly socialised actors of violence make up part of the larger hate milieu. It is in this sense that the applicability of self control theory to *all* hate offenders is simply unsustainable.

Conclusion

The theory of self control becomes a cogent explanation of why certain individuals commit hate crimes *only* once other pathways to hate are considered. With this in mind the article began by exploring the intersections between Merton's strain theory and Perry's 'doing difference', showing how both socio-cultural structures and socio-economic strains cultivate cultures of prejudice within which hate crime flourishes. Central to the analysis of both theories has been the emotion of fear. It is this emotive reaction to *difference* which encourages the proliferation of hate incidents in order to suppress the social mobility of certain identity groups. Synthesising strain theory with structured action theory provides a more illuminating macro explanation of hate motivated behaviour. However the analysis still fails to explain why only some individuals commit hate crimes while others, equally affected by socio-structural and socio-economic factors, do not; other than to say that some people may be affected by prejudice, strain and fear more than others. Hence the gap between macro and micro remained.

In drawing together macro level causational mechanisms with micro level offending patterns this article has suggested that an individual's propensity to commit hate crime may ultimately turn on his or her levels of self control. By viewing hate offending in terms of self control we begin to understand why many disgruntled racists or homophobes remain simply that and why others' prejudiced sentiments trigger a criminal response. Indeed, the current research body on hate perpetrator typology provides a persuasive account of offending suggesting that most perpetrators will display one or more of the following characteristics: thrill seeking, a tendency towards taking physical risks, defensive of territory, low tolerance levels of difference, a disposition towards violence and other antisocial behaviours, a lack of academics qualifications and/or low-skilled employment. The profile of hate offenders therefore creates a picture of offending which fits into almost all aspects of Gottfredson and Hirschi's theory of self control.

The theoretical model suggested within this article does not explain *all* types of prejudice motivated behaviour. Nuances exist between different types of hate crime that will inevitably see certain independent variables as being causal to one type of hate crime but irrelevant to others (see Craig 2002; Green et al. 2001). However, in exploring the interconnectivities between strain, difference and self control a more holistic vision of hate crime can be constructed. This may help to form a small but important epistemic movement towards better understanding the phenomenon by uncovering the highly complex aetiological determinants of many incidents of hate.

To this end it will be necessary to improve upon the paucity of hate crime research by empirically testing which macro and micro level variables lead to disproportionately high levels of hate crime. Attitudinal scales used in a variety of self control studies (many based on Grasmick et al.'s 1993 scale) can be used to test whether hate offenders have low self control as well as examining the correlation between this and other variables such as socioeconomic background. Scales can also measure other attitudes, including those relating to 'rights' over jobs, resources and welfare, while fears relating to the perceived threats posed by certain identity groups to norms, traditions and conventions can also be measured.

For now it is hoped that the vision put forward in this article will help to create a more holistic theoretical framework of hate crime from which we can continue to build upon our knowledge of causation. Perhaps in time criminology may find ways to help prevent and respond to hate crime by attending to both the cultures of prejudice found within many communities and to the low levels of self control that are likely to be found amongst many hate offenders.

Acknowledgments The author would like to that thank Carolyn Hoyle, Mary Bosworth and Jon Garland for their thoughtful comments on earlier versions of this paper and to the editor and anonymous reviewers for their helpful suggestions.

References

Agnew, R. (1992). Foundation for a general strain theory of crime and delinquency. *Criminology, 30*, 47–87.

Agnew, R., Brezina, T., Wright, J. P., & Cullen, F. T. (2002). Strain, personality traits, and delinquency: Extending general strain theory. *Criminology, 40*(1), 43–71.

Allport, G. W. (1954). *The nature of prejudice*. Cambridge, MA: Addison-Wesley.

Armstrong, T. (2005). Evaluating the competing assumptions of Gottfredson and Hirschi's (1990) a general theory of crime and psychological explanations of aggression. *Western Criminology Review, 6*(1), 12–21.

Bibbings, L. (2004). Heterosexuality as harm: Fitting in. In P. Hillyard, C. Pantazis, S. Tombs, & D. Gordon (Eds.), *Beyond criminology. Taking harm seriously*. London: Pluto.

Bowling, B. (1998). *Violent racism: Victimization, policing, and social context*. Oxford: Clarendon Press.

Bowling, B., & Phillips, C. (2003). Racist victimization in England and Wales. In D. Hawkins (Ed.), *Violent crime, assessing race & ethnic difference*. Cambridge: Cambridge University Press.

Byers, B., Crider, B. W., & Biggers, G. K. (1999). Bias crime motivation: A study of hate crime offender neutralization techniques used against the Amish. *Journal of Contemporary Criminal Justice, 15*(1), 78–96.

Chahal, K., & Julienne, L. (1999). *'We Can't All Be White!': Racist victimisation in the UK*. York: York Publishing Services.

Craig, K. M. (2002). Examining hate-motivated aggression: A review of the social psychological literature on hate crimes as a distinct form of aggression. *Aggression and Violent Behaviour, 7*, 85–101.

Franklin, K. (2000). Antigay behaviors among young adults: Prevalence, patterns, and motivators in a noncriminal population. *Journal of Interpersonal Violence, 15*(4), 339–362.

Gadd, D., & Dixon, B. (2009). Posing the "Why" question: Understanding the perpetration of racially motivated violence and harassment. In B. Perry (Ed.), *Hate crimes* (Vol. 1). London: Praeger.

Gadd, D., Dixon, B., & Jefferson, T. (2005). *Why do they do it? Racial harassment in North Staffordshire*. Keele: Centre for Criminological Research, Keele University.

Garland, J., & Chakraborti, N. (2006). Recognising and responding to victims or rural racism. *International Review of Victimology, 13*(1), 49–69.

Gerstenfeld, P. (2004). *Hate crimes causes, controls, and controversies*. London: Sage Publications.

Gordon, P. (1994). Racist harassment and violence. In E. A. Stanko (Ed.), *Perspectives on violence*. London: Howard League.

Gottfredson, M., & Hirschi, T. (1990). *A general theory of crime*. Stanford, CA: Stanford University Press.

Grasmick, H. G., Tittle, C. R., Bursik, R. J., Jr., & Arneklev, B. J. (1993). Testing the core empirical implications of Gottfredson and Hirschi's general theory of crime. *Journal of Research in Crime and Delinquency, 30*, 5–29.

Green, D. P., McFalls, L. H., & Smith, J. K. (2001). HATE CRIME: An emergent research agenda. *Annual Review of Sociology, 27*, 479–504.

Green, D. P., & Seher, R. L. (2003). What role does prejudice play in ethnic conflict? *Annual Review of Political Science, 6*, 509–531.

Green, D. P., Strolovitch, D. Z., & Wong, J. S. (1998). Defended neighbourhoods, integration, and racially motivated crime. *American Journal of Sociology, 104*(2), 372–403.

Home Office. (2005a). *Race equality in public services*. London: Home Office.

Home Office. (2005b). *Improving opportunity, strengthening society: The government strategy to increase race equality and community cohesion*. London: Home Office.

Iganski, P. (2008). *Hate crime and the city*. Bristol: The Policy Press.

Jacobs, J. B., & Potter, K. (1998). *Hate crimes*. New York: Oxford University Press.

Kelly, R. J. (Ed.). (1993). *Bias crime: American law enforcement and legal responses*. Washington, DC: Office of International Criminal Justice.

Lawrence, F. M. (1999). *Punishing hate: Bias crimes under American law*. London: Harvard University Press.

Levin, J., & McDevitt, J. (1993). *Hate crimes: The rising tide of bigotry & bloodshed*. New York: Plenum.

Levin, J., & McDevitt, J. (2002). *Hate crimes revisited: America's war on those who are different*. New York: Basic Books.

Levin, J., & Rabrenovic, G. (2009). Hate as cultural justification for violence. In B. Perry (Ed.), *Hate crimes* (Vol. 1). London: Praeger.

Macpherson, W. Sir (1999). *The Stephen Lawrence inquiry.* Cm 4262-I. London: The Stationery Office.

McDevitt, J., Levin, J., & Bennet, S. (2002). Hate crime offenders: An expanded typology. *Journal of Social Studies, 58*(2), 303–317.

McGhee, D. (2005). *Intolerant Britain?: Hate, citizenship and difference.* New York: Open University Press.

Merton, R. K. (1968). *Social theory and social structure.* New York: Free Press.

Newburn, T. (2007). *Criminology.* Cullompton: Willan Publishing.

Perry, B. (2001). *In the name of hate: Understanding hate crimes.* New York: Routledge.

Perry, B. (Ed.). (2009a). *Hate crimes* (Vol. 1). London: Praeger.

Perry, B. (2009b). The sociology of hate: Theoretical approaches. In B. Perry (Ed.), *Hate crimes* (Vol. 1). London: Praeger.

Phillips, C., & Bowling, B. (2007). Racism, ethnicity, crime and criminal justice. In R. Morgan, R. Reiner, & M. Maguire (Eds.), *Oxford handbook of criminology.* Oxford: Oxford University Press.

Pratt, T. C., & Cullen, F. T. (2000). The empirical status of Gottfredson and Hirschi's general theory of crime: A meta-analysis. *Criminology, 38*, 931–964.

Ray, L., & Smith, D. (2002). Hate crime, violence and cultures of racism. In P. Iganski (Ed.), *The hate debate.* London: Profile Books.

Ray, L., Smith, D., & Wastell, L. (2004). Shame, rage and racist violence. *British Journal of Criminology, 44*, 350–368.

Sibbitt, R. (1997). *The perpetrators of racial harassment and racial violence, Home Office Research Study 176.* London: Home Office.

Spalek, B. (2008). *Communities, identities and crime.* Bristol: The Policy Press.

Vazsonyi, T. A., & Belliston, L. M. (2007). The family–low self control–deviance: A cross-cultural and cross national test of self control theory. *Criminal Justice and Behaviour, 34*(4), 505–530.

Young, J. (1999). *The exclusive society: Social exclusion, crime and difference in late modernity.* London: Sage Publications.

CHAPTER 5

Conclusion

As our society continues to develop, one would expect people to become more tolerant and civil. Unfortunately, when a society develops, it does not always make progress. Sometimes it can actually be regressing. Despite the decades of effort and education, hate crime remains a noteworthy problem in our society. According to the US Department of Justice, the top three motives behind hate crime are racial bias, religious bias, and bias about sexual orientation. As mentioned in the introduction, hate crime is not easy to define, and therefore, only a few crimes are officially categorized as hate crime every year. The real problem, however, is the political rhetoric that attempts to justify hate and discrimination. Hiding behind the freedom of speech, many people are intentionally trying to promote biases. Some even use false information to create biases. With the help of the Internet, this can be accomplished rather efficiently. While it is not yet a crime to promote hate, we can hardly expect such a hateful environment will make the world a better place. Perhaps, we do not care for a better world because we just want a better home for ourselves. Perhaps, we deem our hate as justifiable and righteous because whatever we hate must be wrong and bad. Perhaps, it is others who hate us first, so we have every right to hate them back. Perhaps we are always in the right. Nonetheless, we should at least try not to turn our hate into crime. Let us all simply hate each other without taking any action to hurt anyone.

Discussion Questions

1. What do you hate? Discuss what you hate and how you are coping with such hateful feelings.
2. Should we label a crime as hate crime? Since we have rights to hate what we hate, is it right to punish hate in addition to the criminal act itself?
3. Go on the Internet, and find examples of hateful speeches. What are the haters saying?
4. Find an actual hate crime in the news. What happened in that incident? Do you believe it is a hate crime?
5. The FBI collects hate crime statistics every year. Find the statistics, and discuss what you learned from these numbers. What do they tell you about hate crime?

CHAPTER 6

Racial Disparity

Introduction

Very few topics have been subject to debate in criminal justice longer than racial disparity. It has always been suggested that racial minorities, especially African Americans, are being treated differently within the criminal justice system. As a result, they are overrepresented in the prison population and tend to receive longer sentences than their White counterparts who commit similar crimes. Since it is a debate, it implies that not everyone agrees. An opposing view suggests there is no racial disparity or discrimination in criminal justice. Some racial groups account for a higher percentage of crime and, therefore, make up a higher percentage of the prison population. Since they commit more crimes, they naturally receive harsher punishments given the longer criminal history. Both sides have done research and believe their view is supported by empirical data, hence the debate.

A more neutral view suggests there is racial disparity indeed but it is unlikely to be a result of racial discrimination. It is perhaps more concerned about the fact that certain racial minority groups tend to have a lower socioeconomic status and, therefore, live in a neighborhood that breeds more crime. The unfair treatment they face in the system might be real sometimes, but it is due to the stereotype associated with social class rather than race, although in many American societies race and social class are intertwined.

If racism exists in our society, it would be naïve to deny its existence in the criminal justice system. However, it would be too quick to conclude that race is always a factor in criminal justice proceedings. It is important to remember that we should not jump to a conclusion based on a few anecdotal stories or research reports. You cannot find a bad man and then claim all men are bad. In this chapter, the article selected does a good job reviewing some studies aimed at examining racial disparity and discussing what they found. It reveals the compound nature of the issue and illustrates why the answer might not be as simple as yes or no. Students are encouraged to forgo their pre-existing assumptions about race and look at research findings from a professional viewpoint. Let the evidence speak. Reading this article should help students not only gain better understanding on the complexity of racial disparity, but also learn how to objectively interpret research findings.

Racial and Ethnic Disparity and Criminal Justice

How Much is Too Much?

*Robert D. Crutchfield, April Fernandes, and Jorge Martinez**

Introduction: Why is the "How Much is Too Much" Question Important?

Race differences in criminal involvement and racial patterns in the criminal justice system have been important topics since the beginning of American criminology.[1] The question of whether there are meaningful racial disparities in the justice system has been important since the 1960s.[2] In recent decades, a considerable literature focused on racial profiling by police and racial differences in imprisonment, sentencing, and other areas of criminal and juvenile justice processing has grown. There are both studies that report no significant racial differences in criminal justice processing and studies that report substantial differences. Taken together, how meaningful are observed differences? Wilbanks concludes that they are not.[3] He maintains that even

* Robert Crutchfield is a professor in the Department of Sociology at the University of Washington. His research focuses on labor market participation and crime, and racial and ethnic disparities in the criminal justice system. April Fernandes is a Ph.D. student in the Department of Sociology at the University of Washington. Her research interests include the fear of crime, neighborhood policing, and incarceration. Jorge Martinez is a graduate student in the Department of Sociology at the University of Washington. His research focuses on immigration and crime, prison and street gangs, and deviance and social control.

1 Hans von Hentig, *Criminality of the Negro*, 30 J. AM. INST. CRIM. L. & CRIMINOLOGY 662 (1940); F. Emory Lyon, *Race Betterment and the Crime Doctors*, 5 J. AM. INST. CRIM. L. & CRIMINOLOGY 887 (1915); Booker T. Washington, *Negro Crime and Strong Drink*, 3 J. AM. INST. CRIM. L. & CRIMINOLOGY 384 (1912).

2 *See generally* Donald Black & Albert J. Reiss, Jr., *Police Control of Juveniles*, 35 AM. SOC. REV. 63 (1970); Irving Piliavin & Scott Briar, *Police Encounters with Juveniles*, 69 AM. J. SOC. 206 (1964).

3 WILLIAM WILBANKS, THE MYTH OF A RACIST CRIMINAL JUSTICE SYSTEM (1987).

Robert D. Crutchfield, April Fernandes, and Jorge Martinez, "Racial and Ethnic Disparity: How Much is Too Much?," *Journal of Criminal Law & Criminology*, vol. 100, no. 3, pp. 903-932.

in the studies that report statistically significant racial differences in criminal justice outcomes, the effect sizes are too small to really matter. In other words, Wilbanks argues that these differences are not "too much." Other criminologists have been heard to say that while the difference is statistically significant, it really isn't enough to make a real, cognizable difference in daily life. We cannot help but wonder, though, if the minority driver pulled over a few extra times by profiling officers, or the Latino sentenced to just a bit more time in prison, or the African American with just a slightly higher probability of receiving a capital sentence would agree that small effect sizes can be dismissed as inconsequential.

We began this Article by acknowledging that there is a wide range of research results, but we do not concede that only small effect sizes have been observed. Some studies find no racial or ethnic differences.[4] Others find modest differences,[5] and some report rather substantial racial disparities in criminal justice processing.[6] Clearly, if we compare American criminal justice practices in the last decades of the twentieth century and the first of the twenty-first with earlier periods, the former probably looks to be fairer and more just than the latter. That does not necessarily mean that we have reached that Promised Land that Martin Luther King spoke hopefully of in his "I Have a Dream" speech.[7]

Early American History of Disparity

There was racial disparity in the American criminal justice system during the antebellum period, but it did not look like most would expect. Crutchfield and Finke examined records of the U.S. Census in the nineteenth century for the Southern states.[8] Until the start of the Great Migration, the massive movement of African Americans out of the rural South into the cities of the South, North, and West, one could only really study race and imprisonment below the Mason-Dixon line. Elsewhere in America there were not enough people of color in the Census to study. Crutchfield and Finke found that prior to the Civil War, very few blacks were sent to Southern prisons.[9] Instead, the prison populations before 1870 were nearly all white. There are two explanations for this pattern. First, antebellum Southern states did not seem to make heavy use of penitentiaries as a form of punishment.[10] This is not surprising. The penitentiary "movement," which began in Pennsylvania and New York in the 1830s, spread slowly to other regions and nations of the

---

4 *Id.*

5 Rodney L. Engen & Sara Steen, *The Power to Punish: Discretion and Sentencing Reform in the War on Drugs*, 105 AM. J. SOC. 1357 (2000); Gary Kleck, *Racial Discrimination in Criminal Sentencing: A Critical Evaluation of the Evidence With Additional Evidence on the Death Penalty*, 46 AM. SOC. REV. 783 (1981).

6 Traci Schlesinger, *Racial and Ethnic Disparity in Pretrial Criminal Processing*, 22 JUST. Q. 170 (2005).

7 Martin Luther King, Jr., I Have a Dream (Aug. 28, 1963), *reprinted in* MARTIN LUTHER KING, JR., I HAVE A DREAM: WRITINGS AND SPEECHES THAT CHANGED THE WORLD 102 (James M. Washington ed., 1992).

8 Robert D. Crutchfield & Roger Finke, *Convict Lease Systems: The Political Economy of Post-Civil War Development* (1983), presented at the meetings of the American Society of Criminology, Denver, CO (on file with author).

9 *Id.*

10 Christopher R. Adamson, *Punishment After Slavery: Southern State Penal Systems, 1865–1890*, 30 SOC. PROBS. 555, 557–58 (1983).

world.[11] Prior to the war, it had not made as much of an in-road into the practices of the South as it would later. The second reason that few blacks, compared to whites, were imprisoned in the South was slavery. Most African Americans were not free. To lock up a slave was to "punish" his master by depriving the latter of labor. The Southern economic and social system dictated that when possible, punishment should be meted out by the owner rather than the state.[12] This practice was clearly a result of economic consideration.

Adamson studied the convict lease systems that emerged in the post-bellum South.[13] He found a system that endeavored, in part, to "replace" slavery. Convicts, disproportionately black, were leased to plantation owners to work the same fields that they had as slaves before emancipation. They were also sent to work for private industries in the particularly dangerous tasks of mining and railroad building.[14] A superficial examination of the numbers of people who were sentenced in this system suggests that it did not "replace" slavery.[15] But if seen as a system that supported the emerging racial order, which was based on share cropping and tenant farming, the convict lease system supported these new quasi-slavery arrangements. Freedmen who walked away from share cropping or tenant farmer arrangements were subject to strict loitering and Black Code laws that, in some circumstances, landed them in prison, workhouses, or convict lease systems.[16]

Much of the early criminological literature on race focused on racial differences in criminal involvement,[17] but in the 1950s, scholars began to show some interests in race and the criminal justice system. Dobbins and Bass studied the differential effects of unemployment on white and black inmates in Louisiana.[18] They found that unemployment was more related to the imprisonment of whites than of blacks.[19] Early in the 1960s, the first signs that criminologists recognized racial conflict appeared. For example, Rudwick published a paper with recommendations for how police departments might do a better and *fairer* job when policing "Negros,"[20] and he also wrote about the need to have black police officers in Southern cities to make sure that Negro neighborhoods were adequately policed.[21] In 1964, Cross published "Negro, Prejudice, and the

11 *See* MICHAEL IGNATIEFF, A JUST MEASURE OF PAIN: THE PENITENTIARY IN THE INDUSTRIAL REVOLUTION 1750–1850, at 143–173 (1978).

12 Adamson, *supra* note 10, at 555.

13 *Id.*; Christopher R. Adamson, *Hard Labor and Solitary Confinement: Effects of the Business Cycle and Labor Supply on Prison Discipline in the United States, 1790–1835*, *in* 6 RES. L., DEVIANCE & SOC. CONTROL 19, 19 (Steven Spitzer & Andrew T. Scull eds., 1984).

14 Adamson, *supra* note 10, at 562–63.

15 Crutchfield & Finke, *supra* note 8.

16 Adamson, *supra* note 10, at 558–62.

17 *See generally* Lyon, *supra* note 1; James Edward McKeown, *Poverty, Race and Crime*, 39 J. CRIM. L. & CRIMINOLOGY 480 (1948); Julian B. Roebuck, *The Negro Drug Addict as an Offender Type*, 53 J. CRIM. L., CRIMINOLOGY & POLICE SCI. 36 (1962); von Hentig, *supra* note 1; Washington, *supra* note 1.

18 D. A. Dobbins & Bernard M. Bass, *Effects of Unemployment on White and Negro Prison Admissions in Louisiana*, 48 J. CRIM. L., CRIMINOLOGY & POLICE SCI. 522, 522–25 (1958).

19 *Id.* at 523.

20 Elliott M. Rudwick, *Police Work and the Negro*, 50 J. CRIM. L., CRIMINOLOGY & POLICE SCI. 569 (1959).

21 Elliott M. Rudwick, *The Negro Policeman in the South*, 51 J. CRIM. L., CRIMINOLOGY & POLICE SCI. 273, 276 (1960).

Police" calling for police officers to recognize the social circumstances of blacks and for the fair treatment of individuals. That same year, Piliavin and Briar published their now classic paper, reporting that demeanor, which is related to race, was an important factor determining when police exercised the discretion to formally arrest.[22] Black and Reiss followed with their report that demeanor was important, but less so than the wishes of victims, and that there are racial differences in the preferences of those victims; black victims more frequently demanded arrest.[23]

Race, Crime, Justice, and Criminology

The contemporary debate on racial and ethnic differences in criminal justice processing began with Christianson's state-by-state enumeration of black and white imprisonment rates.[24] He showed that in all states, the proportion of blacks imprisoned exceeded their representation in the general population. He concluded that this disproportionate imprisonment was evidence of disparate treatment in criminal justice processing based on race.

In contrast, Kleck reviewed a number of studies of individual sentencing. In that review, he found some evidence of modest disparate sentencing in some jurisdictions, but not in others.[25] Kleck's general conclusion was that there is not substantial evidence of unfair racial differences in how defendants are sentenced.

Critics of Christianson countered his conclusions by arguing that he had not accounted for racial differences in criminal involvement, especially for the crimes most likely to lead to state prison sentences. Blumstein used racial differences in arrest for violent crimes to measure disparate criminal involvement.[26] For the most serious crimes, Blumstein reasoned that there would be less of the discretion in systemic decisionmaking that Piliavin and Briar and Black and Reiss discussed, making the disparities for serious crimes reasonable measures of actual crime differences. Blumstein concluded that 80% of the racial difference in imprisonment rates can be accounted for by African Americans' higher arrest rates for violent crimes.[27]

Langan avoided the question of whether arrest rates are themselves biased by using responses from the National Crime Survey (NCS).[28] For the surveys, respondents who had been victims of face-to-face victimization were asked, among other things, the race of the perpetrator. Langan compared racial differences in these victim reports to racial distributions in prisons and concluded that Blumstein was essentially correct: about 80% of the racial differences in American prisons can be accounted for by higher rates of black criminality.[29] Crutchfield, Bridges, and Pitchford

---

22 Piliavin & Briar, *supra* note 2, at 210.

23 Black & Reiss, *supra* note 2, at 71.

24 Scott Christianson, *Legal Implications of Racially Disproportionate Incarceration Rates*, 16 CRIM. L. BULL. 59 (1980).

25 Kleck, *supra* note 5.

26 Alfred Blumstein, *On the Racial Disproportionality of United States' Prison Populations*, 73 J. CRIM. L. & CRIMINOLOGY 1259, 1259–60 (1973).

27 *Id.* at 1267–68.

28 Patrick A. Langan, *Racism on Trial: New Evidence to Explain the Racial Composition of Prisons in the United States*, 76 J. CRIM. L. & CRIMINOLOGY 666, 671–73 (1985).

29 *Id.* at 679–80.

examined each state using the Blumstein approach.[30] They reported that the 80% estimate was correct as an average, but that it masked gross differences across the states.[31] In some states, all or nearly all of the observed racial disparities in imprisonment could be accounted for using racial differences in violent crime arrests. But in other states, a far lower proportion of the difference could be accounted for accordingly. Other analyses indicated that just as Christianson found in the post-bellum South, state variations in black/white disparities in imprisonment are related to economic, social, and political conditions, and not just to crime.[32]

These studies (other than Kleck's study and the research he reviewed) are based on aggregate data. They do not look at what happens to individuals in the criminal justice system. They do, however, capture the accumulation of individual decisions from arrest to imprisonment. Wilbanks, like Kleck, focused on individual-level studies.[33] These studies allow for a close examination of the processing of individual defendants. After reviewing these studies, Wilbanks wrote:

> [M]any studies of possible discrimination focus on the extent to which the results are statistically significant. However, statistical significance may be confused in the minds of the public (or the researchers) with practical significance. Statistical significance tells us only whether the results found in the sample are likely to have occurred by chance if the relationship in the "population" (from which the sample was drawn) was zero. Statistical significance is a function of two factors, the strength of the relationship and the sample size. If the sample size is great enough, even a very small relationship is statistically significant.[34]

What is missing that allows one to draw this conclusion is the pattern that the aggregated studies reveal: some substantial racial disparities exist that cannot be explained by purely legally relevant factors like the severity of the crime and the criminal history of the offender.[35] Because these aggregate studies are population analyses, they are not subject to Wilbanks's criticism of studies with large sample sizes. The studies of individual sentencing also do not take into account differences in juvenile justice processing, which may play a part in later decisions in some jurisdictions,[36] including arrest, bail, prosecution, and parole decisions. Perhaps the accumulation of decisions at all of the decision points in criminal justice processing produces

---

30 Robert D. Crutchfield, George S. Bridges & Susan R. Pitchford, *Analytical and Aggregation Biases in Analyses of Imprisonment: Reconciling Discrepancies in Studies of Racial Disparity*, 31 J. Res. Crime & Delinq. 166, 170 (1994). Both Blumstein, *supra* note 26, and Langan, *supra* note 28, aggregated state and federal imprisonment and crime measures for the United States rather than analyzing state-level patterns.

31 Crutchfield, Bridges & Pitchford, *supra* note 30, at 173.

32 George S. Bridges & Robert D. Crutchfield, *Law, Social Standing and Racial Disparities in Imprisonment*, 66 Soc. Forces 699, 709–11 (1988); George S. Bridges, Robert D. Crutchfield & Edith E. Simpson, *Crime, Social Structure and Criminal Punishment: White and Nonwhite Rates of Imprisonment*, 34 SOC. Probs. 345, 354–55 (1987).

33 Wilbanks, *supra* note 3; Kleck, *supra* note 5.

34 Wilbanks, *supra* note 3, at 47.

35 Blumstein, *supra* note 26; Crutchfield, Bridges & Pitchford, *supra* note 30; Langan, *supra* note 28.

36 In some states, some consideration of juvenile court records is allowed in adult criminal court prosecutions, and with increased treatment of juveniles as adults, we must consider disparity there, too. *See, e.g.*, Wash. State Sentencing Guidelines Comm'n, Adult Sentencing Manual 2009 Supplement 22 (2009), *available at* http://www.sgc.wa.gov/Pub.S/Adult_Manual/AdultSentencingManualSupplement2009.pdf.

the patterns that are observed in aggregate studies that do not show up, or only modestly so, in individual sentencing studies.

An accurate assessment of the degree of racial disparity unjustified by criminal involvement differences requires that we both consider multiple jurisdictions and examine multiple decision points in the criminal justice process. Studying multiple jurisdictions is important because, as found by Crutchfield and his colleagues,[37] there may be unwarranted disparity in some but not in others. Crutchfield et al.'s study was of state-level imprisonment rates. Clearly the processing of criminal defendants takes place in sub-state government courts, departments, and agencies. Thus, state-level comparisons may gloss over important, possible intra-state variation in how cases are processed. In some places there may be unwarranted disparity, while in others, there is not. Where problematic differences exist, it is likely that the level, amount, or effect sizes that researchers report will also vary. Kleck, in reviewing sentencing differences by race, reports some jurisdictions with no disparity, a few with a disparity, and a few multiple jurisdiction studies with "mixed" results.[38] Only by looking at multiple jurisdictions, as he did, can one make an accurate description of a sentencing or other system disparities. This does not mean that every study must include multiple jurisdictions; however, in drawing conclusions about what we learn from the research literature, we should take caution to include studies of as many different jurisdictions as possible.

Studying multiple decision points is important for two reasons. First, if unwarranted racial disparity exists in a state or a county's processing of defendants, it can occur anywhere in the process. It might be at arrest, the decision to prosecute, a bail hearing, a court decision, a finding of guilt, sentencing, or parole. In two different jurisdictions, disparity might exist, but in one it might appear in a decision that is rendered early in processing, and in the other at a later stage. Frequently, studies of the processing of individual cases have focused on sentencing. It is possible that differential decisions were made earlier in the system. If we do not consider the varying risk of getting to sentencing, the cases considered may be problematic because of selection bias.

In addition to considering multiple jurisdictions, we must examine multiple decision points in the criminal justice process in order to accurately assess the presence or absence of racial disparity in case processing. Disparity may occur at many different points between a person's first contact with law enforcement and the prison door. Ideally, studies should account for patterns of decisions that were made prior to the decision point that is being studied. Studies that do not account for selection bias may draw erroneous conclusions. For instance, courts in a county may sentence everyone who is convicted of drug offenses to similarly severe sentences, but African-American or Latino defendants may be more likely to be arrested than white drug offenders, or once arrested, they may be more likely to have charges filed against them. Simply examining differences at sentencing, without controlling for differential exposure to the chance of being convicted, will produce erroneous conclusions. Although inferior to formally controlling for selection bias, reviewers should, at a minimum, examine studies of multiple decision points in

37 Crutchfield, Bridges & Pitchford, *supra* note 30, at 173.
38 Kleck, *supra* note 5, at 789–92.

the criminal justice system. Researchers must begin studying these multiple points and formally controlling for differing risks of reaching each succeeding decision point if we are to ever fully understand patterns of racial disparity in the criminal justice process.

Another shortcoming of the extant literature is that it nearly completely focuses on disparities between blacks and whites in the criminal justice system. To the extent possible, we must begin to more fully consider the experiences of other racial and ethnic groups. African Americans are no longer the largest minority group in the United States—Latinos are, yet our research has not adequately considered them, Native Americans, or Asian Americans.

In this Article, we will be mindful of the necessity to examine multiple jurisdictions and multiple decision points in both the juvenile and criminal justice systems and the treatment of more than just blacks and whites in the justice systems. Both the juvenile and criminal justice systems are looked at because in some jurisdictions, juvenile court records can be considered when a person is processed in the adult system. Also, presumably, experiences in the juvenile justice system affect the behavior of individuals later in life.

Racial Disparity in the Juvenile Justice System

In 2005, more than thirty-one million youth were under juvenile court jurisdiction. The total delinquency case rate for black juveniles (108.4 per 1,000 juveniles) was more than double the rate for whites (44.4 per 1,000 juveniles) and for American Indians (53.3 per 1,000 juveniles).[39] African Americans aged ten to seventeen comprise about 15% of their age group in the population, yet they represent about 25% of all juvenile arrests, 30% of referrals to juvenile court, 40% of all incarcerated juveniles, and close to 60% of waivers to adult criminal court.[40] In this Part, we will discuss how each of the procedural decision points is important to the understanding of racial disparity and over-representation of minorities in the juvenile justice system.

Police Contacts, Arrests, Referrals, and Intake Decisions. Law enforcement agencies refer the majority of cases to the juvenile court, although in some jurisdictions, others—parents, schools, and social service workers—petition young people as well. As of 2005, 81% of all delinquency cases were referred by law enforcement agencies; they refer 91% of property offenses and drug law violations, 87% of person offenses, and 61% of public order offenses.[41] At the point of contact, police officers exercise a great deal of discretion over which juveniles are processed

39 CHARLES PUZZANCHERA & MELISSA SICKMUND, NAT'L CTR. FOR JUVENILE JUSTICE, JUVENILE COURT STATISTICS 2005, at 20 (2008). In OJJDP data, Hispanic ethnicity is not treated as a separate category. Individuals who identify as Hispanic are included with whites or blacks, and in some instances, there is a separate "ethnicity" item.

40 MICHAEL A. JONES & EILEEN POE-YAMAGATA, AND JUSTICE FOR SOME 28 (Nat'l Council on Crime and Delinq. ed., 2000); NAT'L RESEARCH COUNCIL & INST. OF MED., JUVENILE CRIME, JUVENILE JUSTICE 34 (Joan McCord, Cathy Spatz Widom, and Nancy A. Crowell eds., 2001).

41 PUZZANCHERA & SICKMUND, *supra* note 39, at 31.

TABLE 10.1 Racial Disparities in the Juvenile Justice System Studies

Study	Jurisdiction	Decision Point	Dependent Variable	Race Relationship Significant?
Bridges & Steen (1998)	3 Washington counties	disposition	probation reports	yes
Brown & Alarid (2004)	11 Missouri counties	referral, detention, adjudication, disposition	referred, detention adjudication, placement	mixed
DeJong & Jackson (1998)	Pennsylvania	intake, disposition	referred, residential placement	yes (blacks and Latinos more likely to be referred), no (no racial difference in residential placement)
Graham & Lowery (2004)	Urban locations	intake, probation	racial stereotypes	yes
Leiber (2009)	Black Hawk County, Iowa	intake, petition, adjudication, disposition	release, diversion, petition adjudication disposition	yes (detention, petition, and adjudication, some dispositions) no (diversion, some dispositions)
Leiber & Fox (2005)	20 Iowa counties	intake, petition, adjudication, disposition	pretrial detention, Intake 1 petition, disposition	yes (detention, diversion, and sentencing) no (refer youth at intake petition)
Leiber & Johnson (2008)	4,182 Iowa juvenile court case files	intake, disposition	intake decisions, disposition	yes

into the system. When offenses are minor, police officials exercise more discretion as to whether or not to arrest juveniles or refer them to the juvenile court.

Research on the role of police and arrests on disproportionality in the juvenile justice system is limited.[42] Crutchfield and colleagues found that racial differences in contact with police (obviously a necessary precondition for arrest) and arrest were only partially explained

42 Alex R. Piquero, *Disproportionate Minority Contact*, 18 FUTURE OF CHILD. 59, 60 (2008). Exceptions to this include George S. Bridges & Sara Steen, *Racial Disparities in Official Assessments of Juvenile Offenders: Attributional Stereotypes as Mediating Mechanisms*, 63 AM. SOC. REV. 554 (2008) and Sandra Graham & Brian S. Lowery, *Priming Unconscious Racial Stereotypes About Adolescent Offenders*, 28 LAW & HUM. BEHAV. 483 (2004).

by self-reported delinquency.[43] Variations in the social environments of children, in particular having family members who are known to the justice system, getting in trouble in school, and associating with deviant peers and adults, helps explain observed racial differences in contact and arrest. Earlier, Smith found that neighborhood context explains variations in police officers' decisions to arrest.[44] According to Smith, police are more likely to arrest suspects in racially mixed or minority neighborhoods. African-American suspects are treated more harshly, compared to others, across neighborhoods, but they are treated with more leniency when arrested in predominately white neighborhoods. White suspects, however, are treated more favorably compared to African Americans across the board regardless of which neighborhood context they are arrested in.

In a study of property crime cases in Missouri, Brown and Alarid reported that black juveniles are at a significant disadvantage compared to whites at the earlier stages of the juvenile justice process.[45] Even when controlling for legal factors, such as prior delinquency and seriousness of the current offense, blacks were more likely to be formally referred and detained.[46] Brown and Alarid found that although black youths had more contact with the justice system through a higher referral rate, whites were more likely to be adjudicated delinquent for more serious offenses.[47] Blacks were referred at higher rates initially for less serious offenses compared to whites.[48]

DeJong and Jackson included Hispanic juveniles in their analyses of a random sample of juvenile cases in all counties in Pennsylvania outside Philadelphia.[49] They found that referred black and Hispanic juveniles are marginally younger than white juveniles, more likely to be referred for drug charges, and more likely to live in single-mother households.[50] Controlling for legal characteristics, DeJong and Jackson found that juveniles with more arrests, particularly for serious and drug offenses, are more likely to be petitioned to the court. Bivariate relationships between race and various legal characteristics show that overall juvenile offenders who are

---

43 Crutchfield, et al., *Racial Disparities in Early Criminal Justice Involvement*, 1 Race & Soc. Probs. 218, 228 (2009).

44 Douglas A. Smith, *The Neighborhood Context of Police Behavior*, 8 Crime & Just. 313, 331 (1986).

45 Katherine E. Brown Ray & Leanne Fiftal Alarid, *Examining Racial Disparity of Male Property Offenders in the Missouri Juvenile Justice System*, 2 Youth Violence & Juv. Just. 107, 108 (2004). Data come from court cases in Missouri juvenile jurisdictions in 1994. Missouri is 85% white and 15% non-white. *Id.* at 111. Of the non-white population, 11.2% are black and the remaining 3.8% are American Indians, Hispanics, Asian Americans, and Pacific Islanders combined. *Id.* Non-violent property crimes included burglary, stealing, tampering, fencing, vandalism, victimless arson, fraud, and trespassing. *Id.* at 110. The analysis of non-violent offenses will not likely be affected by the violent youth trend that existed between 1986 and 1994. This provides conservative estimates that suggest the possibility of a discriminatory process. Girls and other races were omitted from analysis. *Id.*

46 *Id.* at 119.

47 *Id.* at 116.

48 *Id.* at 119.

49 Christina DeJong & Kenneth C. Jackson, *Putting Race Into Context: Race, Juvenile Justice Processing, and Urbanization*, 15 Just. Q. 487, 492 (1998).

50 *Id.* at 494.

male, black, and older are formally referred at higher rates when compared to female, white, and younger juveniles.[51]

There are also variations in referral rates across jurisdictions. Brown and Alarid report that in Missouri, race is a significant factor in referrals.[52] In one of the state's largest urban counties, race plays a significant role, but it has no significant bearing in any decision process in one small rural county.[53] This finding affirms the importance of contextual variability. In 1998, DeJong and Jackson found that after controlling for county, Latinos, but not blacks, are more likely to be referred.[54] These Latinos were more likely to come from rural counties.

However, at least one study has found that race is not a direct predictor of referral to juvenile court when controlling for pre-hearing release and diversion. In one juvenile court jurisdiction in Iowa, researchers found that African Americans overall are more likely to be referred and less likely to participate in diversion given pretrial detention.[55] Pretrial detention decreases the odds of diversion relative to court referral by 96%.[56] For whites, however, pretrial detention decreases the likelihood of court referral by 33%.[57] In fact, not one single African American that was secured in pretrial detention received diversion.[58] African Americans are 48% less likely to participate in diversion than they are to be released.[59] The decision for pretrial detention has significant impacts at different decision levels.

Pretrial Detention

Juvenile courts may decide to place a youth in pretrial detention if officials believe that doing so ensures the protection of the community or the protection of the juvenile himself, guarantees the juvenile's appearance in future court hearings, or allows for further evaluation of the juvenile.[60]

Between the years 1985 and 2005, 38% of all U.S. delinquency cases resulted in detention.[61] During that time, 29% of all delinquency cases involving black youth resulted in detention.[62] African Americans represent 31% of drug offenses and are detained 49% of time.[63] They are twice as likely as whites and Native Americans to be detained for drug offenses.[64] Similar trends are

---

51 *Id.* at 496–97.
52 Ray & Alarid, *supra* note 45, at 119.
53 *Id.* at 119.
54 DeJong & Jackson, *supra* note 49, at 497.
55 Michael J. Leiber, *Race, Pre- and Postdetention, and Juvenile Justice Decision Making*, CRIME & DELINQ. (manuscript at 12) (forthcoming 2011).
56 *Id.*
57 *Id.*
58 *Id.* at 5, 12.
59 *Id.* at 12.
60 ROBERT W. TAYLOR, ERIC J. FRITSCH & TORI J. CAETI, JUVENILE JUSTICE: POLICIES, PROGRAMS, AND PRACTICES 103 (2006).
61 PUZZANCHERA & SICKMUND, *supra* note 39, at 33.
62 *Id.*
63 *Id.*
64 *Id.* at 35.

exhibited in terms of property offenses. African Americans represent 29% of property offenses and 39% of detainment for all youth arrested for property offenses.[65]

Based on a study of cases in an Iowa county, Leiber reported that African-American juveniles are almost two times more likely to be secured in pretrial detention than their white counterparts, even after controlling for legal and extra-legal factors.[66] Coming from a single-parent household increases the probability of referral to juvenile court, especially for African Americans.[67] This effect is echoed at the decision to place a youth in pretrial detention. Being in a single-parent household increases the likelihood of pretrial detention for African Americans 2.5 times relative to whites.[68]

Leiber also found that the nature of the crime charged also has an effect on pretrial detention. For example, being charged with property offenses decreases the probability of pretrial detention for whites by 77%, while having no influence for African Americans.[69] African Americans involved in a violent or drug offense decrease their likelihood of being released at intake by 18% and 16%, respectively.[70] These offenses are related to release for whites. Whites experience an inverse but non-significant relationship with detention. However, the probability of being placed in pretrial detention increases by 10% for African Americans.[71] Although it appears to be counterintuitive, Leiber found that for African Americans, an indication of problems in school decreases the odds of pretrial detention by 55%.[72] Though not statistically significant, whites also experience a decrease in pretrial detention when there is an indication of problems at school.[73]

Petitions and Waivers

From the point of referral, prosecutors decide whether to petition for formal processing in the juvenile court or (attempt to) waive the case to the adult criminal system. Overall, the proportion of all delinquency cases petitioned to court increased for all racial groups in 2005.[74] However, cases involving black juveniles were more likely to be petitioned than any other racial group. In 2005, 53% of white, 62% of black, 56% of American Indian, and 59% of Asian-American juveniles were petitioned for adjudication.[75] In terms of offense type, racial disparity was most

---

65 *Id.* at 33.

66 Leiber, *supra* note 55, at 4, 6–7. Five-hundred and fifty juvenile court cases resulting in detention were selected in Black Hawk County, Iowa. For comparison, 449 juvenile court non-detained cases were selected randomly. The total sample size was 927. *Id.*

67 *Id.* at 10.

68 *Id.*

69 *Id.*

70 Michael J. Leiber & Kristan C. Fox, *Race and the Impact of Detention on Juvenile Justice Decision Making*, 51 CRIME & DELINQ. 470, 483 (2005).

71 *Id.* at 481.

72 Leiber, *supra* note 55, at 10.

73 *Id.*

74 PUZZANCHERA & SICKMUND, *supra* note 39, at 39.

75 *Id.*

prominent among petitioned drug offenses: 71% involved black youth and only 52% involved white juveniles.[76]

In a study of juvenile jurisdictions by county in Iowa, Leiber found that black juveniles are twice as likely as white juveniles to be petitioned as delinquent.[77] Family is an important predictor of petitioning. Black juveniles from single-parent households were 5.5 times more likely to be petitioned compared to others.[78] Furthermore, black juveniles under court authority at the time of petition are 4.75 times more likely than others to be petitioned.[79] Leiber also found that the likelihood of adjudication decreases by 83% for while females compared to African-American females.[80]

Adjudication and Disposition

After being petitioned, the case reaches the point of adjudication. According to the National Center for Juvenile Justice, between 1985 and 2005, delinquency cases involving black youth were less likely to result in delinquency adjudications than cases involving white youth.[81] The likelihood of being adjudicated delinquent decreased between 1985 and 1995 for both black and white juveniles (58% to 53% and 66% to 58%, respectively).[82] The likelihood of being adjudicated delinquent increased from 1995 to 2000 for both groups. This increasing trend was dampened for black youth by 2% by the end of 2005, when the likelihood of adjudication for black youth reached 62%.[83] By the end of 2005, white youth adjudicated delinquent increased to 68%.[84]

If a juvenile is deemed delinquent, the judge may place him or her in a residential placement or give him other probation, which is the most common outcome. By 2005, 62% of all white delinquents were placed on probation compared to 56% of black delinquents.[85] The greatest disparity exists for drug offenses: 67% of whites that were adjudicated delinquent for drug offenses were given probation as opposed to 57% of black drug offenders.[86] The more lenient disposition is more probable for whites than it is for blacks.[87]

Residential placement may include institutionalization or placement in a camp, ranch, or group home.[88] The likelihood of residential placement for black and Native-American youth was 26%, for white youth it was 21%, and for Asian-American youth it was 22%.[89] Again, the greatest disparity between black and white youth comes with drug offenses. Blacks were given

76 *Id.*
77 Leiber, *supra* note 55, at 14.
78 *Id.*
79 *Id.*
80 *Id.*
81 Puzzanchera & Sickmund, *supra* note 39, at 49.
82 *Id.*
83 *Id.*
84 *Id.*
85 *Id.* at 57.
86 *Id.*
87 *Id.*
88 Taylor, Fritsch & Caeti, *supra* note 60, at 106.
89 Puzzanchera & Sickmund, *supra* note 39.

residential placement 29% of the time compared to 15% of the time for whites. However, while controlling for legal and extra-legal factors, evidence is provided by Leiber that being black is not the only predictor of post-adjudication detention.[90] In fact, black youth were more likely to receive the more lenient outcome of community-based corrections than were white youths.[91]

The outcomes of dispositions vary depending on offense type. According to DeJong and Jackson, offense type has an effect on the results of disposition for youths in Pennsylvania. There, blacks referred for drug offenses are treated more harshly at disposition than blacks charged with other offenses.[92] Whites, however, are no more or less likely to be placed in a secured facility at the time of disposition.[93]

In addition to offense type, there also exist cumulative effects on adjudication and disposition outcomes in the juvenile justice system. For example, being detained before adjudication decreases the likelihood of post-adjudication detention by 46% for all groups.[94] Pretrial detention increases the likelihood of receiving post-adjudication detention by 79% for whites. The trend is similar for blacks, but it is not statistically significant. Pretrial detention also has a positive effect on disposition—it increases the likelihood of receiving residential placement at disposition by 16%. Additionally, being African American decreases the probability of receiving residential placement by 18%.[95]

These trends raise the question of why we see a lower probability of black youth receiving probation and a higher probability of whites receiving residential placement. One study that attempts to explain this relationship focuses on attribution stereotypes as mediating mechanisms in the adjudication of juvenile offenders.[96] Attribution theory explores how internal (individual) and external (environmental) characteristics of juveniles affect delinquency cases.[97] Analyzing 223 narrative reports written by probation officers[98] in three counties in one western state between 1990 and 1991, Bridges and Steen find that the reports of black youth were more likely to include negative internal attributions than reports of whites.[99] Reports of whites were more likely to include negative external attributions than were those for black youth. This shows that probation officers were more likely to describe black and white youth in different lights: blacks

---

90 Leiber, *supra* note 55, at 19; Michael J. Leiber & Joseph D. Johnson, *Being Young and Black: What Are Their Effects on Juvenile Justice Decision Making?*, 54 CRIME & DELINQUENCY, 560 (2008).
91 Leiber & Johnson, *supra* note 90, at 570–71.
92 DeJong & Jackson, *supra* note 49, at 500–01.
93 *Id.* at 500.
94 Leiber, *supra* note 55, at 14.
95 Leiber & Fox, *supra* note 70, at 489.
96 Bridges & Steen, *supra* note 42.
97 Graham & Lowery, *supra* note 42, at 484. *See* SUSAN T. FISKE & SHELLEY E. TAYLOR, SOCIAL COGNITION (2d ed. 1991).
98 These reports are written at the time of disposition, typically following conviction. These reports include the probation officer's assessment of the likelihood of recidivism and recommendation for sentencing using summary information about a youth's social, demographic, and criminal history. Black and white youth were juxtaposed due to the lack of a sizable number of narratives regarding juveniles of other races. Bridges & Steen, *supra* note 42.
99 *Id.* at 562.

were more likely to be seen as innately delinquent, whereas white delinquency was the result of the environment. When it comes to predicting recidivism, probation officers were more likely to describe blacks as having a higher risk of reoffending compared to whites. However, there were no statistically significant differences in sentence recommendations by race.

Bridges and Steen also find that risk assessments and sentence recommendations varied based on case characteristics and social, demographic, internal, and external attributions.[100] Youths with a delinquent history were defined as dangerous enough for pretrial detention, and those who committed more serious, violent offenses were judged to have a higher risk of recidivism. Race, however, was not a significant predictor of this perception of recidivism. Negative attributions overall have strong and significant effects on the assessments of risk, independent of demographic and criminal histories, whereas negative internal attributions have a greater impact on the assessment of risk. Juveniles who are described as incorrigible and personally responsible for their crimes were more likely to be seen as future reoffenders. Race had no direct effect on the assessment of recidivism after controlling for criminal history and attributions made by probation officers.

In a follow-up study to Bridges and Steen, Graham and Lowery examined how police officers and juvenile probation officers perceive and treat juvenile offenders using unconscious racial stereotypes about juvenile offenders.[101] Using an experimental model developed by Devine, a sample of police and probation officers was subliminally primed with words associated with black (a racial prime).[102] Another sample was subliminally primed with words unrelated to race (a neutral prime). The process of exposing a person to a racial prime is believed to activate unconscious racial stereotypes, while the process of exposing a person to a neutral prime leaves them unaffected. The officers exposed to the racial prime are more consciously aware of stereotypes about blacks while those exposed to the neutral prime are not, leaving their biases unaffected by the experimental method. After priming, researchers asked the police and probation officers to read one of two vignettes about a hypothetical adolescent who allegedly committed either a property or personal crime, while omitting the race of the juvenile and leaving the type of offense as ambiguous as possible. They found that police officers exposed to the racial prime judged the hypothetical offenders to be more mature compared to officers exposed to the neutral prime. The probation officers exposed to the racial prime judged the alleged offender to be more mature, more violent, more culpable, more likely to reoffend, and more deserving of punishment. Based on these studies, we can conclude that unconscious stereotyping by juvenile justice officials, as informed by the attribution perspective, can partly explain these racial disparities and the severe punishment of black youth compared to whites.

In sum, evidence of racial disparities in the juvenile justice system exists. Racial and ethnic disparities have been observed in studies at the national, state, and local level. In some

---

100 *Id.* at 564.

101 Graham & Lowery, *supra* note 42, at 484.

102 *See* Patricia G. Devine, *Stereotypes and Prejudice: Their Automatic and Controlled Components*, 56 J. of Personality & Soc. Psychol. 5, 5 (1989) (discussing the experimental model).

instances there are no significant differences between white and minority juveniles in the handling of cases, but in general, there are differences and they range for small to moderate, to quite substantial.

Disparity in the Adult Criminal Justice System

The literature on the adult criminal justice system has not provided consistent and conclusive evidence for obvious discrimination or racial and ethnic bias. The majority of studies indicate that the overrepresentation of African Americans is due to disparate treatment. But even these results vary from weak to strong, depending on both the jurisdictions studied and the decision point focused on by the researchers. Recent scholarship has broadened the conversation to include Latinos, revealing a compounded disadvantage at some decision points due to unique circumstances of some defendants, such as language barriers and legal status.

Traffic Stops

Obviously, the potential for disparity begins with arrest, sometimes connected to ostensibly benign traffic stops. While the majority of stops result in either a warning or a ticket, these interactions can also serve as a gateway to the justice system. For minority racial and ethnic groups, studies have found that they are more likely to be stopped by law enforcement[103] and often for minor infractions.[104] Anecdotal evidence has caused the mainstream media to pick up on the street phrasing "driving while black/brown," assuming that traffic stops are motivated by skin color and not driving behavior.[105] Young African-American and Latino males are seen as the primary targets because they are thought to have a higher proclivity for criminal behavior, by either individual police officers or as a systematic convention within departments.[106] Research finds scant evidence for the differential offending hypothesis. Both qualitative and quantitative

---

103 *See* Gary Cordner, Brian Williams & Alfredo Velasco, Vehicle Stops in San Diego: 2001 (2001), *available at* www.sandiego.gov/police/pdf/stoprpt.pdf; Larry K. Gaines, an Analysis of Traffic Stop Data in the City of Riverside (2003), *available at* www.riversideca.gov/rpd/AGTF/2003%20Final%20Report.pdf; Donna Coker, *Foreword: Addressing the Real World of Racial Injustice in the Criminal Justice System*, 93 J. Crim. L. & Criminology 827, 827–80 (2003); Richard J. Lundman & Robert L. Kaufman, *Driving While Black: Effects of Race, Ethnicity, and Gender on Citizen Self-Reports of Traffic Stops and Police Actions*, 41 Criminology 195, 195–220 (2003); Patricia Warren et al., *Driving While Black: Bias Processes and Racial Disparity in Police Stops*, 44 Criminology 709, 709–38 (2006).

104 Brian R. Kowalski & Richard J. Lundman, *Vehicle Stops by Police for Driving While Black: Common Problems and Some Tentative Solutions*, 35 J. Crim. Just. 165, 165–81 (2007).

105 *See, e.g.*, John Cloud, *What's Race Got To Do With It?*, Time, July 31, 2001, at 42.

106 Robin Shepard Engel & Jennifer M. Calnon, *Examining the Influence of Drivers' Characteristics During Traffic Stops with Police: Results from a National Survey*, 21 Just. Q. 49, 49–90 (2004); Warren et al., *supra* note 103.

evidence has shown that these groups are more likely to be searched, but are less likely to have contraband in their vehicles compared with white men.[107]

Using national survey results, Engel and Calnon investigated the presence of disparate treatment in all phases of driving-related interactions with law enforcement.[108] They found substantial disparities, with African-American and Latino males at increased risk for traffic citations, searches, arrests, and use of force when compared with white males. The odds of receiving a traffic citation are increased by 47% for African Americans and 82% for Latinos. African-American and Latino males are more likely to have their cars searched, an increase of 50% and 42%, respectively, with neither group more likely to be carrying contraband when compared with white drivers. While previous studies have focused almost exclusively on the black/white disparity, current research is addressing the law enforcement experiences of both immigrant and American-born Latinos, often finding that they are detrimentally affected not only by their ethnicity, but also their inability to communicate effectively in English and possible confusion about traffic rules and legal statutes.[109]

In evaluating the differences between law enforcement practices of highway patrol and state troopers in North Carolina, Warren and colleagues found strong evidence of disparities in treatment by state troopers across counties according to the race of the driver.[110] The authors cite the role of the officers' individual—and often subjective—assessments of a traffic violation as a reason for the disproportionate focus on African-America men. However, weak evidence was found for racial disparities in highway stops because such stops are precipitated by an objective assessment of a speeding infraction and an inability to decipher race or ethnicity at higher speeds. Similar studies found that traffic stops exhibit the potential for race-based bias, resulting in moderate disparities in the rate of stops, searches, and arrests.[111] Such findings are important, even with moderate race effects, because traffic stops can represent a first entry point into the criminal justice system; if

---

107 *Id.*; Richard J. Lundman, *Driver Race, Ethnicity, and Gender and Citizen Reports of Vehicle Searches by Police and Vehicle Search Hits: Toward a Triangulated Scholarly Understanding*, 94 J. Crim. L. & Criminology 309, 309–50 (2004); David A. Harris, *Driving While Black: Racial Profiling on our Nation's Highways*, American Civil Liberties Union (Jun. 7, 1999), http://www.aclu.org/racial-justice/driving-while-black- racial-profiling-our-nations-highways.

108 Engel & Calnon, *supra* note 106, at 63.

109 Brian Johnson, *The Multilevel Context of Criminal Sentencing: Integrating Judge- and County-Level Influences*, 44 CRIMINOLOGY 259, 259–98 (2006); Stephen Demuth, *Racial and Ethnic Differences in Pretrial Release Decisions and Outcomes: A Comparison of Hispanic, Black, and White Felony Arrestees*, 41 Criminology 873, 873–909 (2000); Cassia Spohn & David Holleran, *The Imprisonment Penalty Paid By Young, Unemployed Black and Hispanic Male Offenders*, 38 CRIMINOLOGY 282, 281–306 (2000); Darrell Steffensmeier & Stephen Demuth, *Ethnicity and Sentencing Outcomes in U.S. Federal Courts: Who is Punished More Harshly?* 65 AM. Soc. Rev. 705, 705–29 (2000); Marjorie S. Zatz, *The Convergence of Race, Ethnicity, Gender and Class on Court Decision-Making: Looking Toward the 21st Century, in* Criminal Justice 2000: Policies, Processes and Decisions of the Criminal Justice System, 503 (2000).

110 Warren et al., *supra* note 103.

111 Kowalski & Lundman, *supra* note 104; Lundman, *supra* note 107; Lundman & Kaufman, *supra* note 103.

disparities are present here, they set the stage for compounding effects as the individual continues through the system.

Arrests

The research on arrests is limited and the results are divided, with one study of assault and forcible rape charges having shown no disparity between African-American and white defendants,[112] and another study of the decision to arrest for drug-related offenses having found large and substantial race effects.[113] Beckett and colleagues emphasize the interplay between differential policing strategies for racial and ethnic groups and structural and socioeconomic factors that leave citizens vulnerable to detection, while D'Alessio and Stolzenberg assert that any increase in arrests for African Americans is a result of their heightened involvement in criminal activity.[114] In their analysis of the National Incident-Based Reporting System (NIBRS) data on forcible rape, robbery, and assault incidents, D'Alessio and Stolzenberg found that the odds of arrest for white offenders is 22% higher for robbery, 13% higher for aggravated assault, and 9% higher for simple assault when compared with African Americans. The authors conclude that the odds of arrest for white offenders are similar to African Americans, with negligible differences that can be explained by differential involvement in officially reported crimes. Other studies report similar findings,[115] even when expanding beyond law enforcement interactions to further steps in the criminal justice system.[116]

Pretrial Processing

For most arrestees, the first decision point in the criminal justice process is the court's decision to detain the suspect pretrial, release the suspect on his or her own recognizance (ROR), or allow the suspect to post bail in exchange for pretrial release. These decisions are predicated on a number of legal and demographic factors, with research finding that the implementation of seemingly benign decisions results in differences in detention rates for African Americans and Latinos as compared to whites.[117] In this segment of the research, court and community factors are of utmost importance, shaping and shifting how judicial decisionmaking proceeds and the differential effects on African-American and Latino defendants. Reforms that have been enacted in recent decades have limited the discretion of some court actors in an effort to decide cases solely on an offender's legal characteristics, eliminating the possibility of racial or ethnic biases. The research evidence varies with respect to the success of these reforms, but

---

112 Stewart J. D'Alessio & Lisa Stolzenberg, *Race and the Probability of Arrest*, 81 SOC. FORCES 1381, 1393 (2003).

113 Katherine Beckett et al., *Drug Use, Drug Possession Arrests, and the Question of Race: Lessons from Seattle*, 52 SOC. PROBS. 435 (2005).

114 D'Alessio & Stolzenberg, *supra* note 112.

115 Geoffrey P. Alpert, John M. MacDonald & Roger G. Dunham, *Police Suspicion and Discretionary Decision Making During Citizen Stops*, 43 CRIMINOLOGY 407 (2005).

116 Engen & Steen, *supra* note 5.

117 Demuth, *supra* note 109; Schlesinger, *supra* note 6.

TABLE 10.2 Racial Disparities in the Adult Justice System Studies

Study	Jurisdiction	Decision Point	Dependent Variable(s)	Race Relationship Significant?
Spohn & Holleran (2000)	local (Chicago, Kansas City, Miami)	detention	prison sentence (yes/no)	yes
Steffensmeier & Demuth (2000)	federal	detention, length of sentence	prison sentence (yes/no), sentence length	yes
Demuth (2003)	state (75 most populous counties)	bail/pretrial release	eligibility for pretrial release, financial or non-financial release, amount of bail, ability to post bail	yes
Steffensmeier, Ulmer & Kramer (1998)	state (Pennsylvania)	detention, length of sentence	prison sentence yes/no), sentence length	yes
Paternoster & Brame (2008)	state (Maryland)	prison sentence	death sentence (yes/no)	yes
Schlesinger (2005)	state (large urban counties)	bail/pretrial release	decision to deny bail, decision to deny nonfinancial released bail amount, ability to post bail	yes
Bushway & Piehl (2001)	state (Maryland)	sentence length	length of sentence	yes
Johnson (2006)	state (Pennsylvania)	detention, length of sentence	prison sentence (yes/no), sentence length	yes
Albonetti (1997)	federal	length of sentence	sentence length	yes
Engen & Steen (2000)	state (Washington)	charging, detention, length of sentence	prison sentence yes/no), sentence length	no
Steen, Engen, and Gainey (2005)	state (Washington)	detention, length of sentence	prison sentence (yes/no), sentence length	yes
Ulmer & Johnson (2004)	state (Pennsylvania)	detention, length of sentence	prison sentence (yes/no), sentence length	yes
Beckett, Nyrop, Pfingst & Bowen (2005)	local (Seattle)	arrest	drug possession arrest	yes

Study	Jurisdiction	Decision Point	Dependent Variable(s)	Race Relationship Significant?
D'Alessio & Stolzenberg (2003)	federal	arrest	odds of arrest	no
Alpert, Macdonald & Dunham (2005)	Local (Savannah)	arrest	formation of nonbehavioral suspicion, decision to stop and question	no
Engel & Calnon (2004)	federal	traffic stop	citation issued, individual searched for contraband, arrest, threatened or actual physical force	yes
Lundman (2004)	federal	traffic stop	vehicle search, contraband possession	yes
Warren, Tomaskovic-Devey, Smith, Zingraff & Mason (2006)	state (North Carolina)	traffic stop	stops by state troopers, stops by local police	yes
Lundman & Kaufman (2003)	federal	traffic stop	total traffic stops, legitimate reason for stop, perceptions of proper police action	mixed
Kowalski & Lundman (2007)	local ("Midwest City")	traffic stop	traffic stops disaggregated by type	yes

there appears to be a moderate consensus on the continuing influence of judges, especially in the pretrial decision to detain defendants.[118]

Steen, Engen, and Gainey considered the pretrial decision to detain using the racial stereotypes approach, finding a moderate racial disparity in the decision to incarcerate but no race effects for sentence length.[119] The authors contend that African-American defendants are more likely to possess stereotypically dangerous characteristics—being male, having a prior record, having been convicted of a drug felony—and thereby increase their odds of incarceration by 62% when compared with white defendants with similar attributes.[120] The authors argue that judicial perceptions of race did not appear to have a direct effect on sentence length, except in cases of drug distribution offenses that show an increase in sentences for white offenders compared

118 Demuth, *supra* note 109, at 896; Schlesinger, *supra* note 6, at 187; Sara Steen, Rodney L. Engen & Randy R. Gainey, *Images of Danger and Culpability: Racial Stereotyping, Case Processing, and Criminal Sentencing*, 43 Criminology 435, 461 (2005).

119 Steen, Engen & Gainey, *supra* note 118.

120 *Id.* at 451.

to African Americans.[121] Demuth observed that racial and ethnic differences are pronounced in the stages of pretrial processing, resulting in an overwhelming disadvantage for Latino defendants who are less likely to be granted release (50%) than white (67%) and African-American (55%) defendants.[122] Demuth found that Latino defendants face a triple burden in the criminal justice system because they are the most likely to be required to post bail to gain release, they receive the highest bail amounts, and they are most likely to be unable to pay.[123] Only 28% of Latino defendants who are granted bail are released, compared with 40% of African-American defendants and 54% of white defendants.[124] In her multiple jurisdictional investigation, Schlesinger found similar evidence of a racial disparity,[125] most notably during the decision to deny bail, with African Americans being 24% more likely to be denied bail and 21% less likely to be granted non-financial release when compared with white defendants with similar legal characteristics.[126] For Latinos, the disparity widens compared with African Americans: the odds of non-financial release is 15% lower (25% when compared with whites), and when granted bail, the amount is 48% higher.[127] Schlesinger points to the language barrier and citizenship concerns as the source of much of the disadvantage for Latinos in the criminal justice system, compounding any bias that may be based solely on racial and ethnic differences.[128] The disparity for both African Americans and Latinos is even clearer when looking at pretrial decisions for drug offenses, with African-American defendants 80% more likely to be denied bail when compared to white defendants, and Latino defendants 67% more likely to be denied bail compared to whites and 29% less likely to receive non-financial release.[129] Given the concentration of drug offenses during the much maligned War on Drugs, the effects of such disparities, even for minor offenses, could have long-lasting consequences.

Trial/Pleas

The need for efficiency in the justice system has led to a consistent reliance on plea bargaining for quick resolutions in criminal processing, and a possible avenue for bypassing restrictions on judicial discretion. Steen, Engen, and Gainey found that white defendants who pled guilty received a 28% reduction in their sentence while African Americans received only a 13% reduction.[130] However, others have found a slight benefit to the defendant, regardless of race, when a guilty plea is entered.[131] Ulmer and Johnson integrated local and court context variables into their analysis of sentencing outcomes and found that defendants who go to trial are almost twice

---

121 *Id.* at 461.
122 Demuth, *supra* note 109, at 892.
123 *Id.*
124 *Id.*
125 Schlesinger, *supra* note 6.
126 *Id.* at 183.
127 *Id.* at 184.
128 *Id.*
129 *Id.*
130 Steen, Engen & Gainey, *supra* note 119, at 456.
131 Engen & Steen, *supra* note 5, at 1384.

as likely to be incarcerated with a six month increase in sentence length when compared with those who opt for non-negotiated pleas.[132] Other researchers contend that modest effects of race are present in the plea bargaining stage of criminal processing under determinate sentencing reforms, even in the absence of disadvantage in earlier levels of prosecution.[133]

Sentencing Decisions

Based on the reforms made, especially those that limit judicial discretion, decisions and outcomes based on extra-legal factors ostensibly should be eradicated.[134] Guideline systems direct judges to consider only legal factors such as crime type and severity, as well as criminal history, when determining a defendant's detention and sentencing outcomes. Like earlier researchers, Bushway and Piehl differentiated between warranted and unwarranted disparity, with variation due solely to legal factors seen as justifiable (warranted) differences, and unwarranted disparity as the result of the application of extra-legal factors such as race, gender, or income.[135] Researchers make the distinction between these disparity types by examining judicial discretion in sentencing, which may be indicated by deviations from the sentencing guideline recommendations. Such departures are seen most obviously in the pretrial decision to incarcerate and the determination of sentence length, with judges weighing legal factors such as criminal history more heavily against African Americans and Latinos compared with whites with similar legal characteristics.[136]

In their analysis of Washington State Guidelines Commissions data on drug offenses, Engen and Steen found that race effects are not a factor in decisions on sentencing, incarceration, and sentence length.[137] Instead, the severity of charges at conviction changed significantly following changes in legislation that mandated the cessation of judicial discretion and increased the authority of the prosecution.[138] Potentially influential court and community characteristics were not controlled for in the analysis, which may have altered the overall conclusion, especially given contemporary research on sentencing and judicial guideline departures.

Albonetti evaluated the state of disparate criminal justice treatment after the sentencing reforms to determine if non-legal factors continued to be a significant factor in deciding the

132 Jeffrey T. Ulmer & Brian Johnson, *Sentencing in Context: A Multilevel Analysis*, 42 Criminology 137, 159 (2004).

133 Brian D. Johnson, *supra* note 109; John Wooldredge, Timothy Griffin & Fritz Rauschenberg, *(Un)anticipated Effects of Sentencing Reform on the Disparate Treatment of Defendants*, 39 L. & Soc'y Rev. 835 (2005).

134 Celesta A. Albonetti, *Sentencing Under the Federal Sentencing Guidelines: Effects of Defendant Characteristics Guilty Pleas, Departures on Sentencing Outcomes for Drug Offenses, 1991–1992*, 31 Law & Soc'y Rev. 789 (1997).

135 Shawn D. Bushway & Anne M. Piehl, *Judging Judicial Discretion: Legal Factors and Racial Discrimination in Sentencing*, 35 Law & Soc'y Rev. 733, 734 (2001).

136 Albonetti, *supra* note 136; Stephen Demuth, *Racial and Ethnic Differences in Pretrial Release Decisions and Outcomes: A Comparison of Hispanic, Black, and White Felony Arrestees*, 41 Criminology 873 (2004); Steen, Engen & Gainey, *supra* note 119; Steffensmeier & Demuth, *supra* note 109; Darrell Steffensmeier, Jeffery Ulmer & John Kramer, *The Interaction of Race, Gender, and Age in Criminal Sentencing: The Punishment of Being Young, Black, and Male*, 36 Criminology 763 (1998).

137 Engen & Steen, *supra* note 5.

138 *Id.* at 1384.

length of imprisonment for federal drug trafficking cases.[139] She found that extra-legal factors such as gender, race and ethnicity, citizenship status, and education have direct and significant effects on sentence outcomes even when controlling for guideline-defined, legally relevant variables.[140] The probability of incarceration and the length of the sentence were still largely influenced by the type of drug offense; however, race and ethnicity appeared to condition the effect of guideline-mandated factors. Albonetti's work, as well as others, highlighted a moderate level of disparity with the purported protections of sentencing reforms that were designed to limit the discretion of individual judges and deter the use of extra-legal factors in deciding punishments.[141] The supposed objectivity of these pretrial decisions belies processes that, throughout the system, could result in an aggregate disadvantage for African-American and Latino defendants, even if single studies reveal only a minimal or moderate disparity.

IV. Justice and Disparity

This review confirms that racial and ethnic disparities exist in both the American juvenile and adult criminal justice systems. Recent research also confirms that the degree of this disparity varies across jurisdictions, and it appears at different decision points in different jurisdictions. Some studies find moderate to large differences between the ways in which whites, blacks, and Latinos experience justice systems. Others report small differences, some report that they do not uncover evidence of racial and ethnic disproportionality, and still others note disadvantages for whites. Both African Americans and Latinos continue to be overrepresented in prisons, but much of the difference is based on higher levels of involvement by people from these groups in crime. That said, Blumstein,[142] who published the classic paper that concluded that 80% of black/white differences in imprisonment was "warranted" by higher black violent crime rates, has updated that work, looking at crime specific imprisonment rates.[143] He has found great variability; in particular, far less than 80% of black/white differences in imprisonment for drug offenses can be accounted for by behavior differences (in fact, just under 50%). Since so much of America's three-decade imprisonment binge has been fueled by the War on Drugs, we should be more cautious if we conclude that a great deal of imprisonment differences can be accounted for with legally relevant variables.

What is also clear is that, as we expected, research on data gathered in recent decades provides evidence of disparity, and those disparities are far less than was observed earlier in the

139 Albonetti, *supra* note 134.
140 *Id.* at 817.
141 Blumstein, *supra* note 26; Bushway & Piehl, *supra* note 135, at 755; Spohn & Holleran, *supra* note 109; Steen, Engen & Gainey, *supra* note 119, at 460; Steffensmeier & Demuth, *supra* note 109, at 724; Ulmer & Johnson, *supra* note 132, at 166.
142 Blumstein, *supra* note 26.
143 *Id.*

twentieth century.[144] Mann made note of studies that reported gross and large disparities in death penalty and non-death penalty sentences. It is clear that criminal justice practices in the United States have come a long way towards racial and ethnic justice in the past one hundred years. Unfortunately the evidence indicates that we still have distance to travel to reach that "more perfect union."

We did not find support here for the "small effect sizes thesis." The studies that we have reviewed (most published in the past two decades) yield mixed results. Some do not find evidence of a racial disparity, but others do. Among these results are small effects, but there are also studies that report larger, what we have called moderate, racial disparity, and still others found strong evidence of differences in treatment by race or ethnicity. We cannot dismiss, as did Wilbanks, the notion that we still have problems in our criminal justice processing.

We should also take note of the possible accumulating or compounding effects suggested by recent literature. Figures 10.1 and 10.2 display the results, at each stage of the juvenile and criminal justice process, of the studies that we reviewed. At a minimum, these figures display the importance of controlling for selection bias in any of these types of studies. Important decisions are made early in the process, by police, prosecutors, and courts, that determine who is "selected" to proceed to, and under what conditions, the next stage of processing. Failure to account for differential risk of being selected likely leads to biased results. For example, if

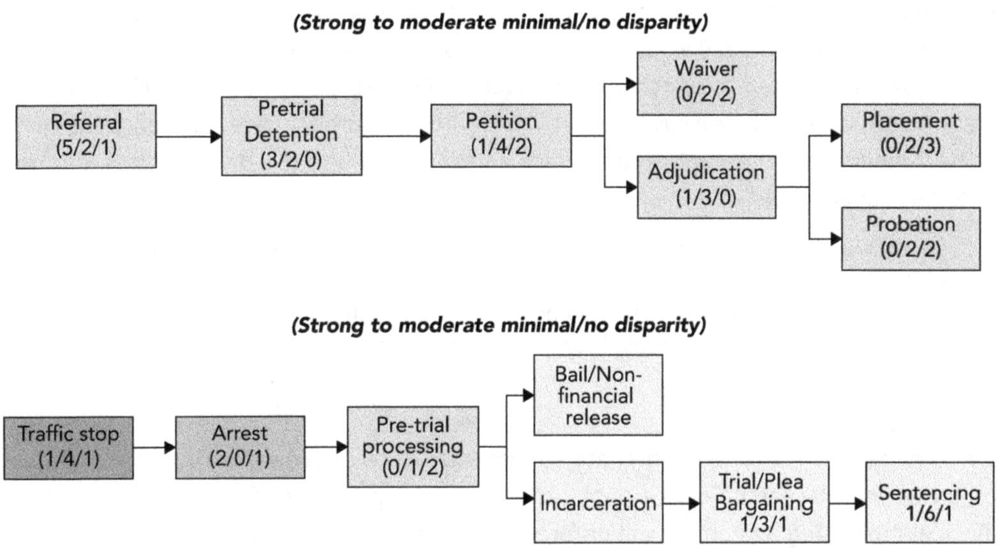

The numbers in the parentheses refer to the number of studies that report a strong and moderate, small or no disparity, respectively, for each level in the criminal justice system.

FIGURE 10.1 AND 10.2

144 For a good review and treatment of this earlier period, see CORAMAE R. MANN, UNEQUAL JUSTICE: A QUESTION OF COLOR (1993).

whites are differentially sorted out prior to sentencing, and then a sentencing study reports no racial difference, we cannot know if there really is no difference between comparable cases, or if minority defendants, of varying types, are being sentenced similarly compared to only the worst of white defendants.

Another consideration highlighted by these figures is the potential for compounding racial differences. Several small differences may accumulate so that the overall differences for people of color and whites going through the justice systems are in total rather substantial. And remember that in these studies, some results indicate not just small racial disparity, but some find moderate and even large differences in the way cases were processed.

Perhaps it is easy for some scholars to conclude that the effect sizes in studies are too small to matter. If so, we ask that they consider two points. First, is the concept of "justice" itself. Can a nation which recites an official Pledge of Allegiance, which includes the words "with liberty and justice for all," reasonably conclude that any statistically significant differences in criminal justice outcomes based on anything but legal factors is acceptable? There are studies that find significant outcomes that are not simply a byproduct of large samples. Such differences run counter to the basic principles upon which the United States was founded, and of which our contemporary leaders are fond of making note in exhortations that we are now a "color blind" society.

If this is too philosophical for the taste of some, we offer a second, perhaps more pedestrian point. What if the small differences reported in these studies affected your son, daughter, father, or mother? What if it was you who was subject to a slightly higher probability of being stopped by police, whose vehicle was searched without real probable cause, who received just a few more days or months in prison? We suspect that you would not dismiss these differences as trivial.

After conducting a thorough study of race and sentencing in the United States, a National Academies Panel wrote:

> [E]ven a small amount of racial discrimination is a matter that needs to be taken very seriously, both on general normative grounds and because small effects in the aggregate can imply unacceptable deprivations for large numbers of people. Thus even though the effect of race in sentencing may be small compared to that of other factors, such differences are important.[145]

This brings us back to the aggregate studies that were discussed earlier.[146] As suggested by the National Research Council panel, the aggregate products of differences observed in individual processing amount to real differences to black and brown populations in the United States. Given the massive increase in American imprisonment that has, in part, been fueled by the War on Drugs, these aggregate patterns, especially Blumstein's more recent work reporting

145 Nat'l Research Council Panel on Sentencing Research, Research on Sentencing: the Search for Reform 92 (Alfred Blumstein et al. eds., 1983).

146 Crutchfield, Bridges & Pitchford, *supra* note 30; Langan, *supra* note 28; Research on Sentencing: the Search for Reform, *supra* note 145.

that only one-half of racial disparities in drug imprisonments can be accounted for by behavior, should be particularly alarming.

There is another problem associated with allowing modest or even small racial disparities to persist without challenge. They add substance to the narrative of injustice; a long held belief by many in black and brown communities holds that rules and fair play do not apply to people of color when they are confronted by the state. People in these communities talk about it, comedians joke about it, and, rest assured, many are convinced of it. When politicians call on young people to believe that they can be whatever they want to be, some will counter with the narrative of injustice. When a people are told that hard work and persistence makes all of the difference, some hear instead the narrative of injustice. And when police departments attempt to explain what looks to the residents of African-American, Latino, Asian, or Native-American communities to be police misbehavior, those explanations are less likely to be accepted because of the persistence of the narrative of injustice. Minimizing the importance of racial and ethnic disparities by the scholarly community only reifies what is believed on the street; that criminal justice in America continues to mean "just us."

CHAPTER 6

Conclusion

Racial disparity refers to a racial group as a whole that consistently receives differential treatment in the system. Racial discrimination refers to an individual that receives unfair treatment due to his or her race. Racial disparity might be a result of accumulated racial discrimination. There is research supporting the existence of racial disparity in criminal justice and there is research refuting it. More research on this topic will be conducted, and the debate conceivably will go on without a consensus. We can join the endless debate, or we can put more emphasis on making sure racial disparity will not be found in the system in the future. To erase racial prejudice is no easy task, and it requires efforts from all parties of interest. On the one hand, we need to change some biased views on race, whereas on the other hand we need to stop doing things that somehow prove certain racial stereotypes to be true. At the same time, we should investigate whether some hurdles are experienced more often by certain racial groups due to their social status and whether such hurdles give them a disadvantage in the criminal justice system.

Discussion Questions

1. Discuss any racial stereotypes you know of. Is there any truth in these stereotypes?
2. Find a crime-related news story in which you believe racial discrimination is evident. What makes you believe the mistreatment is racially motivated? Besides race, what other factors could play a role as well?
3. In the United States, African Americans make up about 13 percent of the general population, but they account for about 50 percent of the prison population. How would you explain this phenomenon?
4. Look up "George Zimmerman" and "Brock Turner" separately. Do you think race was a factor in the sentences they received? Why or why not?
5. Do you think racism is still an issue in today's American society? Give a few examples to illustrate your point.

CHAPTER 7

Drug Policies

Introduction

Recently, some people have warned of an opioid epidemic going on in America. Although not everyone is fond of such rhetoric, there is no denying that drug abuse is a serious problem in our society. It involves both legal and illegal drugs. Some other drugs are not opioids but are still part of the drug problem. Actually, the drug problem is nothing new. It has been a problem for a long time. When the government declared a war on drugs in the 1970s, drug policies became more punitive and more people were found guilty of drug offenses. The purpose supposedly was to reduce drug addiction. Unfortunately, this war on drugs has been deemed a failure by both conservatives and liberals, as it fails miserably to reduce drug abuse, and it is extremely expensive to fight this war. Some organizations, such as the Drug Policy Alliance, have been calling for the end of the war on drugs for years. Despite this, society has not yet come to a consensus regarding what alternative could better deal with the drug problem. As a result, the punitive approach continues to prevail, but more and more law enforcement agencies and prosecutors are making adjustments in terms of allocating resources and seeking punishments in drug-related cases. After all, it is hard not to see the negative and ineffective result of sending people to prison for minor drug offenses.

Alternatively, drug legalization is being promoted as a way to allow the government to better control the drug market and profit from it in terms of taxation. Marijuana legalization in particular has gained considerable traction and has been realized in a few states in the US.

Marijuana has long been considered a drug that is less harmful and less addictive than alcohol or tobacco. Therefore, its legalization seems to be safer for the general public to accept, while other illegal drugs remain doubtful. Advocates believe that by legalizing drugs the violence associated with the turf wars in the black market will decline. Overall, they believe crime rates will drop significantly due to legalization. Opponents are mainly worried that legalization will lead to more addiction and abuse, and some of them are opposed simply because they do not like the idea of legalizing a behavior that is deemed morally wrong.

Drug policies do not have to choose between a war on drugs and legalization, fortunately. There are other approaches. For example, policies can put more emphasis on rehabilitation rather than on punishment. Policies can view drug abuse as a health issue rather than a crime issue. The government can spend more resources on providing medical assistance and social support to the addicts instead of spending billions of dollars on law enforcement and incarceration. Nevertheless, if we cannot reduce the number of people abusing drugs, it could turn into a bottomless hole financially and still fail to solve the drug problem. Hence, drug policies should not become another ideological debate. It is not about which path fits our ideology. It should be about which path can lead to better outcomes, such as reduced drug addiction and associated crimes.

The first article, "Deprofitization of Drugs," discusses legalization as an alternative to our current drug policy and how it might lead to better outcomes. The second article, "The Hidden Costs of America's War on Drugs," examines the history of anti-drug legislation and how much the war on drugs has cost without desirable results. It also touches on the relationship between drug policies and racial disparity discussed in the previous chapter. The two articles have one thing in common: they argue what policies may reduce harm by presenting the reasoning as to why the current drug policies fail to reduce such harm. These are goal-oriented arguments. You may not agree with their goals and conclusions, which is fine; however, if you disagree, you should try to propose your own goal and reasonable argument regarding why current policies can better achieve the goal. Of course, you may propose your own alternative policy as well.

READING 11

Deprofitization of Drugs

James Gray

One major pitfall in the discussion of our current drug policy and alternative options is that people do not define their terms. It is, regrettably, quite common for one person not to know specifically what another person is talking about, and this naturally leads to a great deal of miscommunications and misunderstandings. If people would take care to define their terms, we would make a lot more progress. In this chapter I discuss several options available to deprofitize what are now illicit drugs, taking care to define and explain my terms and to show that many of these alternative approaches are working in other countries. During the discussion, we should all keep in mind that just because these drugs would no longer be illegal for adults, that does not at all mean that we condone or even encourage their use.

Legalization

> *There is just so much money to be made that the slim chance of being caught is always worth the risk. Believe me, after 20 years as a prosecutor and judge, I can assure you that we only catch the stupid ones.*[1]
>
> Magistrate Judge Ronald Rose,
> U.S. District Court, Santa Ana, California

The "legalization of drugs" is an oft-heard phrase. People who favor maintaining the status quo routinely and misleadingly characterize everyone who favors some form

1 Matt Lait, "Make Drugs Legal, U.S. Judge Says," *Los Angeles Times*, April 25, 1992, Orange County ed.: A25.

of change as drug legalizers. It is almost never spelled out what that actually means, but the term connotes—and is designed to connote—that the drug legalizer doesn't feel that dangerous drugs are any big deal and, further, doesn't care if someone sells cocaine to your twelve-year-old child on the street corner across from her school. The U.S. Congress may have had this mental image of the legalization of drugs when it said in the Anti-Drug Abuse Act in 1988, "The Congress finds that legalization of illegal drugs, on the federal or state level, is an unconscionable surrender in a war in which, for the future of our country and the lives of our children, there can be no substitute for total victory."[2]

This reflection was followed by the proclamation that "it is the declared policy of the United States to create a Drug-Free America by 1995."[3] But it is highly important that people define what they mean by "legalization"; otherwise, misunderstandings inevitably arise and impede the progress that could be made in this discussion if people would only define their terms. Drug-free indeed! To begin with, does that mean that we will no longer have aspirin or penicillin? Or if they mean mind-altering and sometimes-addicting drugs, does Congress want to abolish Vicodin and similar pain relievers, since they also fit that definition? In other words, what Congress was talking about was undefined, unrealistic, naive—and silly.

With a legalized product, the price (in this case, drugs that are currently illegal) would be set by the free market, without any restrictions on advertising, brand names, or price. Picture a situation in which a young man who is seventeen years old goes to his local supermarket to buy some groceries. He puts into his cart some frozen lemonade, chocolate chip cookies, aspirin, grapes—and a six-pack of cocaine. A friend had recommended the Big Kick brand of cocaine, and the store is having a special sale that he heard advertised on the radio: six hits for the price of four. In this scenario, all of the products in this man's cart are sold in a legalized, free market.

Under such a program, the Food and Drug Administration would ensure the cleanliness and purity of all of these products and see to it that they were labeled accurately for their contents and strength. This is how the FDA regulates the sale of aspirin, a fully legalized drug in this country. If the manufacturer or vendor were to misrepresent the cocaine or violate the health conditions of its sale, users could sue the manufacturer or vendor in civil court, just as they can for any other product.

The obvious defect in this policy is that cocaine and other dangerous drugs would be pushed to people through advertising and otherwise made glamorous and much too easily available, including to children. People who believe in the legalization of drugs as I have defined it are what I would call pure free marketers.

There are not very many free marketers like this around, of course, though drug warriors like Barry McCaffrey like to pretend that this is what is meant when people speak of legalizing drugs. Most people who advocate the legalization of drugs actually mean something quite different. Often they are talking about programs involving rehabilitation and treatment, medicalization, decriminalization, regulated distribution, or a combination of one or more of these options.

---

2 Public law 100–690, §5011 (1988).

3 Ibid., at section 5252 B. Of course, this date later came and went without further political comment.

That was probably the meaning intended by Abigail Van Buren when she responded, in her Dear Abby column, to a letter from a Mr. Pottratz, an attorney in Minnesota:

> Just as bootleggers were forced out of business in 1933 when Prohibition was repealed, making the sale of liquor legal (thus eliminating racketeering), the legalization of drugs would put drug dealers out of business. It also would guarantee government-approved quality, and the tax on drugs would provide an ongoing source of revenue for drug-education programs. An added plus: There would be far less crowding in our prisons due to drug-related crimes. It's something to consider.[4]

It was also probably the meaning intended by Edward Ellison, the former head of Scotland Yard's Anti-Drug Squad, who said:

> As a former drugs squad chief, I've seen too many youngsters die. I'm determined my children don't get hooked—which is why I want all drugs legalized.
>
> Seven years of my life was spent in Scotland Yard's anti-drugs squad, four as its head. I saw the misery that drug abuse can cause. I saw first-hand the squalor, the wrecked lives, the deaths. And I saw, and arrested when I could, the people who do so well out of drugs: the dealers, the importers, the organizers. I saw the immense profits they were making out of human misery, the money laundering, the crime syndicates they financed. We have attempted prohibition. All that happened was that courts became clogged with thousands of cases of small, individual users, and a generation of young people came to think of the police as their enemies. There were no resources left to fight other crime. I say legalize drugs because I want to see less drug abuse, not more. And I say legalize drugs because I want to see the criminals put out of business."[5]

Since the repeal of Alcohol Prohibition, most states have made liquor available for sale under programs of regulated distribution. It is likely that Ms. Van Buren and Mr. Ellison were recommending a similar program for other mind-altering and dangerous drugs—or maybe they had another option in mind.

Some of the many other well-known and concerned people who have called for the legalization of drugs, without defining what they meant by the term, are former U.S. Secretary of State George Shultz,[6] former Colombian Attorney General Gustavo de Greiff,[7] the late author and syndicated columnist William F. Buckley, Jr.,[8] former New Mexico Governor Gary Johnson, and Judge Robert W. Sweet of the U.S. District Court for the Southern District of New York.[9] In fact, as we saw earlier, the term "legalization" of drugs is not really accurate. The more precise

4 Abigail Van Buren, "Attorney Makes His Case for Legalization of Drugs," Dear Abby, *Orange County Register*, May 3, 1994: Accent 5.

5 Edward Ellison, *London Daily Mail*, March 10, 1998.

6 Stanley Meisler, "Interest in Prestigious Circles," *Los Angeles Times*, November 20, 1989, Orange County ed.: A3, 18: "We need at least to consider and examine forms of controlled legalization of drugs."

7 James Brooke, "A Captain in the Drug War Wants to Call It Off," *New York Times*, July 8, 1994, http://www.nytimes.com/1994/07/08/world/bogota-journal-a-captain-in the-drug-war-wants-to-call-if-off.html.

8 William F. Buckley, Jr., "Awash in Drugs, U.S. Wars on Itself, Only Legalization Can Stop the Futile Battle," *Orange County Register*, October 25, 1989.

9 "U.S. Judge Urges Legalization of All Drugs," *Orange County Register*, December 13, 1989: A7.

term would be "re-legalization" of drugs, because before the passage of the Harrison Narcotics Act in 1914, and a couple of state and local statutes before it, there were no illegal drugs in the United States.

One of the few scholars, to my knowledge, who would take us back to those times is Thomas S. Szasz, a true libertarian free marketer who favors "free trade in drugs for the same reason the Founding Fathers favored free trade in ideas: in a free society it is none of the government's business what ideas a man puts into his mind; likewise, it should be none of its business what drug he puts into his body." Szasz is such an extreme free marketer that he equates government prohibition of drug sales with government prohibition of roadside sales of corn or tomatoes, and he even sees government intervention in this matter as equivalent to state laws about the practice of religion: he finds it unconstitutional and unjustifiable. But not even Mr. Szasz advocates removing age restrictions from drug sales. "Kids," he remarks. "Merrill Lynch can't sell stocks and bonds to children. A real estate agent can't sell houses to children. We are not talking about children. Children do not have any rights. They don't have a right to freedom of religion; they have to follow their parents. We are talking about adults."[10]

Even Nobel Prize–winning economist Milton Friedman, whose pivotal work *Free to Choose: A Personal Statement*,[11] which he wrote with his wife Rose, underscores the crucial link between the free-enterprise system and a free society, would not legalize drugs in the free-market manner in which I defined it above. He would "legalize drugs by subjecting them to exactly the same rules that alcohol and cigarettes are subjected to now. ... Television advertising is forbidden today for alcohol ... for hard liquor. And I say treat this the same way as you would treat alcohol. So, presumably such ads would be forbidden for this."[12]

There is no reason why we cannot adopt one option for one substance and another option for others. For example, why not legalize hemp? Nothing could be easier than to accomplish this simple goal, with a regulation that would read, "Any *Cannabis sativa* plant that has a THC [marijuana's chief intoxicant] content of 0.3 percent or less is legal to cultivate, possess, and sell in the United States of America." These plants could then be raised and harvested without any more state interference than exists for raising cotton or soybeans. The same would be true for the products manufactured from the seeds and fibers of the plant. Right now, farmers in Canada and England are legally raising hemp for commercial purposes. Why can't we? A THC amount of 0.3 percent or less would have no use at all for marijuana smokers. If the THC content were above that limit, those plants would be governed by whatever the laws and regulations were in place for marijuana. By adopting this approach, we could reclaim an entire profitable industry.

To give a sense of the potential magnitude of the commercial market we are talking about, farmers can get the same amount of paper pulp from one acre of hemp as they can from four acres of trees, and it takes twenty years to grow the trees but only one season to grow the hemp.

---

10 Milton Friedman and Thomas S. Szasz, *On Liberty and Drugs* (Washington, D.C.: Drug Policy Foundation Press, 1992), 122, 159, 160.

11 Milton and Rose Friedman, *Free to Choose: A Personal Statement* (New York: Avon Books, 1981).

12 Friedman and Szasz, *On Liberty and Drugs*, at 76–77.

This means that in addition to again using hemp in the making of rope, paper, cloth, and sails for boats, newer products could be produced on the open market. As stated in *U.S. News and World Report*, "Modern-day hemp products include cosmetics, carpets, salad oil, and snacks, as well as construction materials and biodegradable auto parts. Hemp fibers are used in the trunk and door panels of the German-manufactured 5 and 7 series BMW, and Ford is studying their potential for use in radiator grills."[13] U.S. farmers are attempting to get the federal government to allow them to compete once again in this historic and potentially lucrative market, and the government should listen.

I am reminded of the joke about the man who, as a part of his therapy, was shown a number of inkblots and was asked by his therapist to describe what he saw. To each one he answered that he saw "a man and a woman having sex." Finally the therapist told the man that he was obsessed with sex, to which the man replied, "Me? You're the one with all of the dirty pictures!"

There is a similar dynamic at work in the War on Drugs. No matter what substance is being addressed, drug warriors see only a picture of prohibition and prison. Given that a person could not get any more reaction from smoking 0.3 percent *Cannabis sativa* than she could get from smoking this page you are reading, isn't it time we start considering each of these substances separately, on the basis of their potential harm to the user and the society at large?

So where is the harm in legalizing products from industrial hemp? Actually, as a practical matter, both medical marijuana and the hemp industry are virtually legalized already! For example, medical marijuana caregivers and suppliers have formed increasingly large and organized alliances and collectives, with tens of thousands of clients, and hemp products have already become a major economic resource.[14] This was starkly brought home to me when I made a presentation to medical marijuana conferences at both the Los Angeles and Orange County Convention Centers. At these gatherings attended by thousands of people, I was amazed to see entire floors of these cavernous buildings taken up by hundreds of booths selling books, magazines, newspapers, pamphlets, and art objects dealing with marijuana; medical and legal services; hydroponics, heat lamp systems, and other marijuana growing equipment; marijuana rating services; and a wide variety of clothing and edibles made from hemp. In other words, marijuana is already a big and mainstream industry, such that the Cato Institute published information stating that repealing Drug Prohibition would save governments about $41.3 billion a year in law-enforcement costs and generate about $46.7 billion in tax revenue. In fact, just regulating marijuana itself would save about $8.7 billion per year and generate another $8.7 billion in taxes.[15]

---

13 Elise Ackerman, "The Latest Buzz on Hemp, U.S. Farmers Want the Ban on Cultivating the Plant Lifted," *U.S. News and World Report*, March 15, 1999:50. See also Craig Turner, "New Hemp Isn't Meant for Smoking," *Los Angeles Times*, May 16, 1994, Orange County ed.: A1, 10; and Dan McGraw, "Hemp Is High Fashion," *U.S. News and World Report*, January 20, 1997:54, 56.

14 See John Geluardi, *Cannabiz: The Explosive Rise of the Medical Marijuana Industry* (Sausalito, Calif.: PoliPoint Press, 2010); Ed Rosenthal and Steve Kubby, *Why Marijuana Should Be Legal* (Philadelphia: Running Press, 2003); and Roger Parloff, "How Pot Became Legal," *Fortune*, September 28, 2009:142–61.

15 Eve Conant, "Pot and the GOP," *Newsweek*, November 1, 2010:30–35.

Some people argue that legalizing hemp would make the detection of marijuana more difficult because it could be grown within the hemp field. But it is unlikely that marijuana growers would actually do this. Why? Because the hemp would cross-pollinate with the marijuana, and that would lower the THC content of the marijuana plants. Even so, there are solutions to that potential problem—if people are really afraid it could become a problem. For one thing, we could require farmers to register their hemp crops, which would make detection easier. And field kits can quickly measure the plants' THC content. Growing and manufacturing hemp presents almost no risks at all, and it has enormous beneficial potential as an industry. So let's consider legalizing hemp and allowing it to be raised and sold on the open market.

Hypodermic needles are another item that we could consider legalizing for adults, perhaps in combination with the type of needle-exchange program discussed earlier. Studies have shown that needle-exchange programs do not increase the use of drugs. Moreover, deposit-and-refund programs for the recycling of bottles and cans have successfully removed tons of those items from our communities—maybe a tax on needles would encourage their recycling. Freely available clean needles would, as we have seen, decrease the transmission of HIV, hepatitis B, hepatitis C, and other infectious diseases and would also decrease the chance that we or our children accidentally stick ourselves by stepping on a contaminated needle lying in the street, a park, or a vacant lot.

But opposition to proposals like these is ferocious, and so far it has prevailed, in spite of massive evidence that our current policies are complete and utter failures, flawed at their very core. As Walter Wink, a Quaker and a professor of biblical interpretation at Auburn Theological Seminary in New York City, said, "The drug war is over, and we lost. We merely repeated the mistake of [Alcohol] Prohibition. The harder we tried to stamp out this evil, the more lucrative we made it, and the more it spread. Our forcible resistance to evil simply augments it. An evil cannot be eradicated by making it more profitable."[16]

With the exceptions of hemp, hypodermic needles, and medical marijuana, I think it is unlikely that most currently illegal drugs will ever be re-legalized in this country. My purpose is not to advocate legalization or any particular option but is instead to encourage a free and open discussion of our options. So now let us turn now to another one of these—decriminalization.

Decriminalization

> *Whether or to what degree drugs should be decriminalized in the United States is one of the central issues of our times. What is highly disturbing to me is the lack of national debate on the subject and the intransigence of practically all decision-makers to open the subject to examination. What is presently held as true is the belief that the war on drugs is winnable if only we tried harder. Few people are willing to test the proposition in a public arena.*
>
> Judge Phyllis W. Beck,
> Superior Court, Bala Cynwyd, Pennsylvania

16 Walter Wink, "Getting Off Drugs: The Legalization Option," *Friends Journal*, February 1996:13.

In 1976 the Dutch adopted a formal policy of pragmatic nonenforcement for violations involving the possession or sale of up to thirty grams of marijuana, which is enough for about sixty marijuana cigarettes. In 1995 because of international political pressure, that amount was reduced to five grams, or enough for about ten cigarettes. Being realists, the Dutch understood that a ban on marijuana was futile, and since people were going to use it anyway, it was better to have the transactions out in the open rather than in the shadows and to govern behavior instead. In an attempt to steer a middle course between the futility of Drug Prohibition and the unknown perils of drug legalization, Holland thus began its program of *gedogen* ("tolerance") and decriminalization of drugs.

Under a program of decriminalization, the possession, use, and sale of street drugs are still illegal. But as long as people stay within certain well-known guidelines and do not otherwise commit any crimes, the police are instructed to look the other way and not enforce the drug laws. Coffee houses have been established in Dutch cities where patrons can get coffee, tea, and sandwiches—as well as marijuana and hashish. Alcohol and harder drugs are not sold, there is no advertising, sales to minors under seventeen are prohibited, and the sellers at the coffee houses are not allowed to make a nuisance of themselves by hawking passersby on the streets. But if those rules are followed, the sellers and the patrons are left alone.[17]

Hard drugs are treated in a similar manner. Dutch policy attempts to lessen the problems that accompany drug use instead of decreasing drug use itself. Even though the police have strong powers that they can use against hard drugs, as of 1985 the Ministry of Justice instructed them not to use them. The government was persuaded that enforcement would simply turn a health problem into a crime problem. One senior policeman explained the reasoning behind this approach: "If we kept chasing grass or hashish, the dealers would go underground, and that would be dangerous."[18] And so in Holland, sellers and users of hard drugs have been tolerated, as long they do not violate any other laws, do not make a general nuisance of themselves, and keep quantities within widely recognized public guidelines.

Nevertheless, the nonenforcement of the drug laws for small-scale transactions tells only a part of the story about the Dutch approach. The Dutch are really quite intolerant of drug abuse, but they oppose it not in itself but because of the harm it does. Harm reduction is pursued both by aggressively using medical programs, such as drug treatment and needle exchange, and by educational programs rather than criminal crackdowns. With these programs the Dutch government is trying to keep the drug users alive and healthy until they seek their own cure, which is the equivalent of saying that if you must play football, at least wear pads and a helmet. At the same time, Dutch parents are saying to their children that, even though drugs are available through their peers or other sources, this does not mean that it is right, or smart, to use them.

---

17 See E. Leuw and I. Haen Marshall, eds., *Between Prohibition and Legalization: The Dutch Experiment in Drug Policy* (Amsterdam: Kugler, 1996); "Holland's Drugs Policy: War by Other Means," *The Economist*, February 10, 1990:50; Stephen Chapman, "Drug-Tolerant Netherlands Not Suffering," *Colorado Springs Gazette Telegraph*, November 10, 1995: B11; and William F. Buckley, Jr., "In the 'Coffee Shops' of Amsterdam," *Orange County Register*, June 17, 1996: Metro 5.

18 "Holland's Drugs Policy," 50.

At a 1999 conference of police chiefs at Stanford University, the chief of police of a midsize city in New England echoed the Dutch message when he said, "I burned out being a narc, and I grew up when I became a father. I would not arrest my child for drug possession or usage—and would not want anyone else to either. We are doing it wrong. Putting them in jail is the worst thing we can do. That punishment is not banishment from the tribe, which is to say that they will come back. And when they do, they will come out worse. Instead, take the kids to their parents. The parents care if their kids are doing drugs."

Harry Belafonte, honorary chair of the Citizens' Commission on U.S. Drug Policy, which took testimony at the University of Southern California in May 1999, reached similar conclusions on the basis of his own experiences and observations:

> Having grown up in Harlem during the Great Depression, I knew that the real roots of drug abuse and addiction had more to do with poverty, alienation and despair than crimes of malice. Most of the violence associated with drugs stems from our policies of prohibition—just as the notorious gangsters of my youth derived their wealth through bootlegging alcohol. Together we must find a more compassionate and effective drug control policy. As President Jimmy Carter said in 1977, "Penalties against possession of a drug should not be more damaging to an individual than the use of the drug itself."[19]

The Dutch have carefully constructed a program that tries not to do more damage than the use of the drugs themselves, and the results show that their approach is working. Holland has a lower per capita marijuana usage ratio for people at 15 to 64 years old (3.3 percent), than France (4.8 percent) and England (6.2 percent), even though those countries have much tougher laws. Holland also has a lower rate than we do in the United States (5.8 percent), for both teenagers and adults. In fact, use of marijuana by teenagers in Holland is roughly half of what it is in the United States.[20] As Eddy Engelsman, the former Dutch Drug Czar, put it, "We succeeded in making pot boring."[21]

Even more importantly, in Holland between 1979 and 1994, "for the generation under 22 years of age, the percentage using hard drugs went down from 15 percent to 2.5 percent," according

---

19 Institute for Policy Studies, "The War on Drugs: Addicted to Failure—Recommendations of the Citizens' Commission on U.S. Drug Policy," May 2000, at 3. For a copy, write to IPS at 733 15th Street NW, Suite 1020, Washington, DC 20005, or visit http://www.ips-dc.org.

20 See The European Monitoring Centre for Drugs and Drug Addiction at http://www.emcdda.europa.eu/stats08/gpstab12. And compare the study by J. P. Sandwijk, P. D. A. Cohen, S. Musterd, and M. P. S. Langemeijer, "Licit and Illicit Drug Use in Amsterdam II, Report of a Household Survey in 1994 on the Prevalence of Drug Use Among the Population of 12 Years and Over" (Amsterdam: Department of Human Geography, University of Amsterdam, 1995), with the study of the National High School Drug Use Survey conducted by the Institute for Social Research, University of Michigan, on behalf of the National Institute on Drug Abuse, for 1996. About 2.3 percent of Amsterdam's twelve- to fifteen-year-olds and 10.9 percent of its sixteen- to nineteen-year-olds had used marijuana in the previous thirty days, compared to 11.3 percent of fourteen-year-olds, 20.4 percent of sixteen-year-olds and 21.9 percent of eighteen-year-olds in the United States. See also a comparison of a SAMHSA, Office of Applied Studies, Washington, D.C., study and a study by the University of Amsterdam, which shows that drug usage in the United States is five to ten times higher than in the Netherlands. Visit http://www.DrugSense.org.

21 Ethan Nadelmann, "Europe's Drug Prescription," *Rolling Stone*, January 26, 1995:38.

to Dirk H. van der Woude of the Municipal Health Service. "And the average *age* of hard-drug users has gone up from 26.8 years in 1981 to 34.2 years in 1993."[22] This means that younger people are not becoming addicted to these drugs, which results in an average increase in age each year for narcotic drug addicts. Similarly, in 1987 only 1.7 percent of adults in Amsterdam said that they had taken cocaine during the past year, while about 6 percent of the adults in New York said that they had used cocaine in the past six months. And finally, although cocaine users are frequently psychotic, Holland has no cocaine-related crime and no cocaine-related deaths.[23]

Even though powder cocaine is available in Holland for people who want it, there is little crack cocaine to be found. Why? Not because it is difficult to manufacture—because any user knows that powder cocaine can be turned into crack by adding baking soda and water and cooking it in a microwave oven. But crack cocaine is much riskier than powder because of its potency, and users know that, too. So as long as they can afford to purchase powder cocaine, they have no interest in crack. This strongly supports the conclusion that the United States brought the crack epidemic on itself as a result of its prohibitionist policy on powder cocaine. In other words, this was not a drug problem but a Drug Prohibition problem.

For all of its successes, the Dutch have also had some problems with their approach. For example, the people who sell the small amounts of marijuana and other drugs must still obtain their supply from illegal underground dealers, which continues to engender some corruption and violent crime. In addition, since Holland is a small country, fully a third of the people who use and abuse drugs inside its borders are foreigners who come "to have a good time." The Dutch have not yet solved this problem, a variation on Switzerland's Needle Park problem, and they may not be able to solve it on their own. But if other countries adopted the Dutch approach, the problem, obviously, would evaporate, since there would be no need for drug users to crowd into one country or one area. And each country that reformed its policies along Holland's lines would reap the same internal benefits of a drop in drug-related crime and a drop in drug use itself. And as we have seen, some other European countries are moving in that direction, although international reaction to Holland's domestic drug policy has been mixed. The majority of German states are gravitating toward the Dutch harm-reduction and normalizing approach with both marijuana and the harder drugs. Holland has taken some political heat, however, from France and Sweden—not to mention the United States—since Holland's liberal approach runs contrary to several international conventions and also results in a greater flow of drugs into neighboring countries.[24]

The pragmatic Dutch have no intention of formally withdrawing from these conventions that outlaw the sale and use of these drugs; they simply ignore them. The fact that their drug use rates are lower than ours, that their drug addicts are living longer and healthier lives than ours, that fewer young people are using drugs, and that Holland has no cocaine-related crime or deaths

---

22 Georgie Anne Geyer, "The Dutch Can Teach Us About Drug Programs," *Orange County Register*, July 11, 1994: Metro 7.

23 "Holland's Drugs Policy."

24 Leuw and Marshall, *Between Prohibition and Legalization*, at x–xi.

all combine to justify the continuation of their practical, realistic, and effective harm-reduction approach. We would do well to learn from their experience.

One country that has followed the Dutch experience is Portugal—and Portugal's movement has been enormously successful. Why our media have not publicized to the rafters what Portugal has done is truly baffling. In 2000 Portugal realized that they had one of the worst problems with drug addiction in the European Union. So they did something really intelligent: they impaneled a commission of *nonpolitical* experts to investigate the situation and come back with recommendations.

This group less than a year later reported that Portugal had two sizable problems. First, people who were drug-addicted were afraid of their own government. Why? Because if they brought their problems to the government, they would be punished. Consequently, they took their drug problems underground, with all the crime and misery that entailed. Second, the government was spending so much money and effort in investigating, prosecuting, and incarcerating nonviolent drug offenders that it didn't have enough money left for drug treatment.

So in 2001 Portugal decriminalized the possession of up to a ten-day supply of all drugs. Instead of people being arrested if they were found by police to possess or be using drugs, they were referred to "regional committees for the dissuasion of addiction." These "dissuasion committees" had the power to impose warnings or administrative sanctions, including fines, restrictions on driving permits, and referral to treatment. But in a majority of the cases, they gave only a provisional suspension of proceedings—in effect, no punishment—except for those who continued to make a nuisance of themselves on multiple occasions.

What happened? After studying the results for 2001 to 2007, the Cato Institute released a study showing that drug usage nationwide basically remained the same. This statistic in itself shows that those people who argue that if we were to change our drug policy, we would become a nation of drug zombies are simply wrong, if not insulting. In fact, you could give it away for free on every street corner and bless it by every religious leader in town, and I am still not going to jam cocaine up my nose! And I expect that almost everyone else feels the same way. (And those who do not are probably using cocaine already.)

But critically enough, *problem drug usage* in Portugal went down by 50 percent! What caused this drop? Just like the commission found, now that problem drug users were no longer afraid of their own government, they came forward and requested drug treatment in large numbers. And of equal importance, the statistics showed that young people in Portugal were not beginning to go down the road of drug use and abuse in as many numbers. Why? Because of the thought, "Why should I take drugs and go see a doctor? That's no fun!" So according to most people, including the researcher who pored over the evidence, "judged by every metric, the Portuguese decriminalization framework has been a resounding success."[25]

---

25 Glenn Greenwald, "Drug Decriminalization in Portugal: Lessons for Creating Failed and Successful Drug Policies," Cato Institute, 2009: 1. See also Caitlin Elizabeth Hughes and Alex Stevens, "What Can We Learn from the Portuguese Decriminalization of Illicit Drugs?" *British Journal of Criminology* 50, no. 6 (July 2010): 999–1022; Barry Hatton and Martha Mendoza, "Portugal's Drug Policy Pays Off: US Eyes Lessons," Associated Press, December 26, 2010.

And now this approach has spread. On August 21, 2009, Mexico officially decriminalized the possession and use of small amounts of marijuana, cocaine, heroin, and all other drugs.[26] Legislation for this was presented the previous June by Mexican President Felipe Calderon, saying that it makes sense to distinguish between small-time users and big-time dealers, and this approach was also supported by Rafael Ruiz Mena, secretary general of Mexico's National Institute of Penal Sciences, who said, "The important thing is ... that consumers are not treated as criminals. It is a public health problem, not a penal problem."[27] In addition, personal possession of any drug is no longer illegal in Spain, Italy, the Czech Republic, and the Baltic States and some areas of Germany, Switzerland, and Australia have also relaxed their laws for drug possession.[28] And just as in Portugal and Germany, all of the reports so far show positive results.

Regulated Distribution

> *I have viewed and experienced our federal drug laws in action since their serious inception about 1973. The war on drugs is lost for the same reasons that national prohibition of alcohol consumption failed in the '20s and early '30s.*
>
> *Education, legalization with governmental control and not prohibition can solve our drug problem.*
>
> Senior Judge Edward J. McManus,
> U.S. District Court, Cedar Rapids, Iowa

Let us look a bit more closely at alcohol. Today most U.S. states allow the sale of this dangerous and sometimes-addictive drug through a program of regulated distribution. This means that the sale of this mind-altering drug is controlled through regulations and restrictions. In effect, regulated distribution constitutes a recognition that, just as we cannot effectively eliminate air or water pollution by banning automobiles or sewage, we can best reduce and control the harms associated with alcohol by a program of public management and control. A further encouraging thought is that, of all the twenty-seven amendments to the U.S. Constitution, the Eighteenth, which implemented Alcohol Prohibition, is the only one explicitly directed at restricting people's freedom—and it is also the only one that has ever been repealed. Maybe that can establish a precedent.

The approach of regulated distribution is fundamentally based on the realization that *it is much easier to control, regulate, and police a legal market than an illegal one.* While abuses and harms will still occur, at least there are some controls in place. Of course, there are no controls

26 Alan W. Bock, "In Drug-Ravaged Mexico, a New Approach," *Orange County Register*, August 30, 2009: Commentary 1, 5; Tracy Wilkinson and Richard Marosi, "Mexico Shifts Tactics in the Drug Battle," *Los Angeles Times*, August 23, 2009: A21.

27 Quoted in Tracy Wilkinson, "Mexico Moves Quietly to Decriminalize Minor Drug Use," *Los Angeles Times*, June 21, 2009. http://www.latimes.com/features/health/medicine/la-fg-mexico-decriminalize21–2009jun21,0,6336338.story.

28 "A Toker's Guide," *The Economist*, March 7, 2009:34.

at all on illegal drugs under our current policy of Zero Tolerance—except those implemented by drug dealers. But by regulating alcohol in the marketplace, we have virtually eliminated the problems of alcohol impurities in drinks like "bathtub gin" and there is virtually no trafficker-related crime or corruption. Furthermore, no one hands out free samples of alcohol on high school campuses, just as no students are selling Jim Beam bourbon or Marlboro cigarettes to each other on their campuses, both because these markets are effectively policed and because there is no money in it.

Furthermore, we must understand that mind-altering and sometimes-addicting drugs have been around since humankind first walked the face of the earth, and there must be some benefits in their use, because otherwise no one would take them. For example, until I began to have problems controlling my weight as I have grown older, I would use my drug of choice, which is alcohol, almost every day, without problems. Similarly, when I was in Cambodia I asked how customary the use of marijuana was in their society. The reply was that it was common and mostly found in soup. The same thing is true for chewing coca leaves and drinking coca tea in the mountainous regions of Ecuador, Peru, Bolivia, and many other of the higher regions of South America, without any problems for the people greater than turning their teeth purple. But it helps to keep the people warmer. So most of those products are used legally, and their sales are mostly regulated and controlled by the governments—with virtually no problems. Making these drugs illegal in these places would not make them unavailable, it would just create a lot of violence and impure drugs in the marketplace and make lots of racketeers and other thugs obscenely wealthy. Similarly, states with legal lotteries see a marked reduction in the numbers rackets. Thus these approaches verify the practical observations made long ago by Winston Churchill, who said, "If you destroy a free market, you create a black market."

One alternative possibility to prohibition would be to allow the purchase of heroin, cocaine, and marijuana *by adults* at state-licensed package stores. Dosage units of drugs that are now sold on the street for about $10 would be sold for about $2.50 at these package stores, which would eliminate the profitability of illegal sales at one simple stroke. Higher-strength doses would cost more money. The dosages would be plain wrapped, with the dosage amount and strength clearly marked, and the package wrapper would contain appropriate warnings. The drugs would *never* be advertised and would *never* go on sale at a reduced price. Along with the dose, the package would contain a sterile disposable needle (when appropriate), educational material about the dangers of using drugs, and the addresses and telephone numbers of organizations that could assist the user in getting off drugs.

The FDA would monitor and ensure the quality of the drugs, just as it now does our foods and prescription medicines. But the sale, transfer, or furnishing in any manner of any quantity of these drugs to a minor would be severely punished. Laws dealing with driving a motor vehicle under the influence, using or being under the influence in public or in the workplace, assaults while under the influence, and so on, would not be changed.

The unlicensed sale of heroin, cocaine, or marijuana would remain a violation of law. Importantly, however, if the practice continued to any material degree, the price at the government package store would be lowered to reduce further the financial incentive to make such illegal sales. Using this ultimate control of setting the price, society would have the clear means of putting virtually every drug dealer in the country out of business.

Of the approximate purchase price of $2.50, about 75¢ would go to the grower-packager, who would be on a low-bid contract with the government, and about 75¢ would go to the retailer, who would also be on a low-bid contract with the government. The remaining $1 would take the form of a tax, which would be used expressly and solely for education about and treatment of drug abuse.[29]

The only thing we cannot say for certain, under such a policy, is whether the use of currently illegal drugs would increase or decrease in the short run or increase or decrease in the long run. Studies and experiments in England, Switzerland, Holland, Portugal, and elsewhere suggest that drug use would decrease in the long run, but we cannot predict the same result with any certainty. We would have to attempt this new approach to find out.

Many things would affect the outcome. But we can say that implementing a program of this kind for adult use of these drugs would not necessarily result in an increase in their use. It is currently estimated that about 20 million people in the United States use marijuana to some degree, but only 500,000 use heroin. Both of these drugs are widely and readily available from drug dealers, and the disparity in the number of users of the two drugs reflects personal preference rather than availability or even price. But if 20 million people demanded heroin, the illegal market would surely supply it, just as the enormous demand for alcohol was met during Alcohol Prohibition.

Remember too that heroin and cocaine were legal in this country before 1914 but were not widely used. And 100-proof alcohol is widely and legally available now to adults, but it is far less popular than 86-proof. And finally, many people began using drugs because they were enticed into it by drug dealers. Taking the profit motive out of these drugs would virtually eliminate that dynamic. Drugs would literally be deprofitized.

There is no denying that a program of regulated distribution could result in some increased drug use, and I believe that, at least in the short run, it would. Furthermore, the law clearly makes a statement about what is unacceptable in a society, and there is no question that many people abstain from certain forms of conduct because they are illegal. But there would also be incentives for decreased drug use. Just as increased awareness and education have led many people to move away from or at least reduce their use of alcohol and tobacco, we could reasonably expect to see the same thing with other drugs. And more money would be available, thanks to the drug tax, for education and treatment of drug abusers, which would certainly

29 This proposed program is taken directly from the notes I wrote and distributed at the news conference I held behind the courthouse in Santa Ana, California, on April 8, 1992, which were published in James P. Gray, "We Cannot Win the War Against Drugs: A Legal Brief for Decriminalizing Use of Heroin, Cocaine, and Marijuana," *Orange County Register*, April 10, 1992: B13; and James P. Gray, "Proposed Plan for Regulated Distribution of Heroin, Cocaine and Marijuana," *State Pen, Newsletter of the California Chapter of the American Correctional Health Services Association* 13, no. 3 (Fall 1993): 1, 7, 10. For a discussion of similar suggestions, see Dirk Chase Eldredge, *Ending the War on Drugs* (Bridgehampton, N.Y.: Bridge Works, 1998), 166–73. See also http://www.judgejimgray.com.

reduce overall usage. The ban on advertising is also a crucial feature of this plan, but since the government, not private companies, would control and regulate the sale of these drugs, no one could legitimately complain about First Amendment free speech issues. Not only would the glamour of these drugs be substantially reduced by removing their forbidden status and black market influences, there would be no brand names, billboards, or media ads at all—not even posters on the walls at the package stores. Just mundane, plain-wrapped packages stamped with the name and strength of the product. How boring. The quality and variety of the drugs, particularly marijuana, would have to be maintained, but the financial incentives to push any of these drugs from a merchandising standpoint would be virtually eliminated.

With the exception of possible increased usage, *every* other result of this program would be beneficial. Crime would be materially reduced. Even if someone still had to steal to pay for his drug habit, he would steal three-quarters less than under our current system. Even allowing for possible increased usage, burglaries would still be reduced, and there would be much more room in the criminal justice system to investigate, prosecute, and incarcerate those offenders. Funding for gangs and terrorist groups here and all around the world would be substantially reduced, while funding for education about and treatment of drug abuse would be substantially increased. Treatment of drug abuse, moreover, would be less encumbered because the drug-addicted people would not be automatically regarded as criminals. No new taxes would be needed for jail or courthouse construction. Prison overcrowding due to convictions for drug possession and use would be a thing of the past. In fact, it is likely that we would be able to close some existing prisons. And our police departments and courts would once again be available to address society's other pressing needs. In short, the program of regulated distribution I have described would cost the taxpayers nothing, but it would reduce expenses and at the same time raise appreciable amounts of money for drug treatment and educational programs.

Such a program would take the profit out of the drug business, which would substantially decrease the potential for corruption of public servants here and abroad. The pressures created by the War on Drugs for ever-more desperate measures—using the military in domestic affairs, continually increasing criminal penalties, increasing restrictions on the individual rights of our people, and so on—would be virtually eliminated. The work ethic for our youth and many of our older people could be revitalized. Lower-income areas could be reclaimed from drug sellers. Farmers in the world's developing countries would switch from illicit drugs to more economically productive crops. Our country's balance-of-payment problems would be significantly reduced. The spread of HIV and hepatitis from contaminated needles would be significantly reduced. Appreciably fewer overdoses from impure or unknown strengths of drugs would occur.

Whether this program would be expanded to drugs other than heroin, cocaine, and marijuana would be left for the future. There is evidence that marijuana is actually the drug of choice for many users of harder drugs, and therefore there is reason to hope that many of these would revert "down the ladder" to marijuana if it were no longer illegal. It is also possible that under this program users of synthetic drugs like PCP, methamphetamines, and LSD would revert to the organic drugs so that there would be less need to increase the number of drugs sold at package stores. Of course, if the black market for synthetic drugs continued to prosper, expansion of the program could be considered.

Would we put the police, courts, and prisons out of business? Of course not. We will certainly always need the criminal justice system, regardless of our drug policy, but we could once again emphasize the areas in which that system works most effectively: *holding people accountable for their conduct.*

One of the first things that I realized as a judge of the municipal court in Orange County, California, was that the prosecution of defendants charged with driving motor vehicles while under the influence of alcohol (DUI) presented probably the most severe problem area faced by that court. I began to study this area in an attempt to see what could be done other than simply "moving the cases along" through the court system. After about six months of personal interviews, educational seminars on alcohol abuse, and other research, I reached several conclusions about the nature of the problem and how to deal with it. Then, with the assistance and guidance of several others, a majority of judges on our court joined me in initiating a pilot program for screening and sentencing first-time DUI defendants. The results were gratifying, and the statistics showed that we were successful in keeping about 65 percent of these problem drinkers off alcohol for nine months, which was as long as we were able to keep statistics. Among other things, this experience convinced me that a mind-altering, dangerous, and sometimes-addictive drug does not have to be illegal for the criminal justice system to reduce its use by problem users.[30]

The program began on December 17, 1984, and specified that all defendants who had an alleged blood-alcohol level of 0.15 percent or above or who refused to take a blood-alcohol test would be considered "high-risk problem drinkers." That is, in the absence of further information, these defendants were considered likely to become recidivists or repeat offenders. We offered these defendants a fairly severe first-time sentence, which included ten days in jail, a fine, and a suspension of their driver's licenses for six months. Their other option was voluntarily to provide further information to the court as to their alcohol status, in which case a court-sanctioned screening process was immediately available to them. The screening process was designed so that a report was provided to the court within one hour of the referral. Then, as a result of the screening process, if a defendant was found not to be a high-risk problem drinker after all, he or she was offered the same, less severe sentence offered to defendants with lower blood-alcohol levels, which was typically a ninety-day restriction of their driver's license, in addition to a fine and completion of a first-offender educational program.

To defendants still considered high-risk problem drinkers after the screening process who were willing to show by future conduct that they merited extra consideration, we still offered the less severe probationary sentence but with several additional conditions. These strictly enforced conditions were that the defendants completely abstain from ingesting any alcohol for as long as they were on probation, attend meetings of Alcoholics Anonymous, and have a medical doctor

30 This section is condensed from James P. Gray, "Non-traditional Sanctions," in *Drunk Driving Laws and Enforcement: An Assessment of Effectiveness* (American Bar Association, Criminal Justice Section, 1986), 143–46.

interpret their blood test to see if they had alcohol-related medical conditions. They also had to accept alcohol counseling, report back to the court with proof of enrollment, and complete the program, among other things. Basically, we instituted a "drug court." And it worked.

As judges in the criminal justice system, we are in a unique position to give problem alcohol and other drug users some motivation to start them on the way to the realization that they have a problem. Jail is not a cure for the problem, but the threat of jail can go a long way toward helping defendants take the critical step of stopping their drug use so that they can begin to see the damage they are doing to their lives and to the lives of those around them. Jail must, however, be more than a threat: it must be used fully as the punishment it was meant to be for those who choose not to engage in self-evaluation or who substitute excuses for actual performance.

Of course the hope is that once users enroll in a drug-abuse program, the coercion represented by jail will be replaced by legitimate self-concern. Instead of the threat represented by a person in a black robe, they may be moved to reform their behavior when a person in a white smock tells them that their liver is failing because of alcohol or their heart and lungs have been damaged. Maybe a defendant will get the message when an AA meeting shows her by example and by a refusal to accept excuses that stability and a satisfying life are once again possible through sobriety. Perhaps it will be the improvement of a defendant's own family, social, or professional life, when forced by the criminal justice system to remove these dangerous drugs from her life, that will provide the genuine motivation to begin a meaningful recovery. Or perhaps it will be a drug counselor who will be able by her insight and industry to break through to a particular defendant.

Since beginning my duties as a judge, I have discovered that I have the power, one way or another, to help put a substance abuser on the path to productive sobriety. I have received letters from the wives of abusive alcoholics I have sentenced to drug rehab telling me that since their husbands stopped drinking the beatings and abuse had stopped, and they were hopeful that the marriage could be saved after all. I also have heard favorable stories from employers about the regained productivity of many employees who had been sentenced to our program. I have seen slovenly defendants return to court thirty days later looking clean and presentable. Once I sentenced a young man with a large tattoo of a marijuana leaf on his forearm. When he returned thirty days later, I noticed that the tattoo was different, and I asked him about it. He said he did not have enough money to have the tattoo removed, so instead he had the tattoo redesigned as a peacock. I considered that a genuine sign of progress. Professor Mark A. R. Kleiman, an author and professor of policy studies at UCLA in the School of Public Policy and Social Research, has written about the benefits of using the criminal justice system in the manner for which it was designed: holding problem drug users accountable for their actions.

> The key to controlling illicit drugs is to focus on the fewer than 4 million hard-drug addicts. This relatively small group accounts for about 80 percent of the total consumption of cocaine, heroin and methamphetamine. They create problems out of any proportion to their numbers. They suffer enormously and cause suffering around themselves.
>
> Of the conventional tools of drug policy, only treatment has much relevance to controlling the problems of this group. A mountain of data shows that treating a hard-core addict, even

> if with only partial success, creates very large benefits. Although long-term cessation is a highly desirable goal, even imperfectly successful treatment episodes greatly reduce drug consumption and drug-related harm, both while treatment lasts and for some time thereafter. These gains are more than adequate to cover the cost of treatment.
>
> Getting hard-core, hard-drug users into treatment and keeping them there remains a major problem. This is the group least likely to enter treatment voluntarily, most expensive to treat and least likely to succeed by the standard of total abstinence. Many prefer drugs to treatment, as long as they can get the drugs.
>
> The choice, however, need not be left entirely up to the addicts. Sooner or later, most wind up under the jurisdiction of the criminal-justice system. About three-quarters of all heavy cocaine users, for example, are arrested in the course of a year. The criminal-justice system can become a powerful tool for changing drug-taking behavior.[31]

We know that our criminal justice system can coerce *problem* drug users into meaningful and productive sobriety or, if necessary, can remove *problem* drug users from society for long periods of time if they are violent or do not take their recovery seriously. So why do we persist with our failed drug policy, which imprisons weekend pot smokers? If a person uses or even abuses one of these illicit drugs but is not a problem drug user to anyone but himself or herself, let us try to educate that person away from this pattern of self-harm and provide treatment on demand. If users are a harm to other people, they will find their way into the criminal justice system, and judges like me will hold them accountable for their actions, even to the point of removing them from society if need be. But if we would change our approach, we would seriously reduce street crime, violence, corruption, poor community relations, overly aggressive policing, the coercion of our children into lifestyles of drug usage and selling, and even terrorism. Why? Most drug users are not violent; they simply want to be left alone to enjoy their relaxation. It is the drug sellers who terrify neighborhoods and invite rivals to attack. This program of strict regulation and control has worked effectively in combating alcohol abuse and all of these other serious harms, and it can be just as effective for these other mind-altering drugs as well. And it all starts by focusing on people's conduct rather than their drug selections.

31 Mark A. R. Kleiman, "Middle Ground," *UCLA Magazine*, December 1998:10–11. See also Mark A. R. Kleiman, *Against Excess, Drug Policy for Results* (New York: Basic Books, 1992).

The Hidden Costs of America's War on Drugs

Joseph D. McNamara

The Cause of Crime

In 1870, an Italian physician, Cesare Lombroso, sometimes referred to as the father of criminology, concluded that there was a "criminal type." Lombroso, after studying the inmates of an Italian Army penitentiary, hypothesized that it was possible to identify lawbreakers by inherent physical characteristics (Friedman, 1993, p. 141). Ever since Lombroso advanced his premise of "Atavistic Anomalies," countless behavioral scientists have theorized on the causes of crime.

Despite the abundance of conjecture, it is possible in the United States to identify the literal cause of crime—an act or omission prohibited by law and punishable by fine, imprisonment, or death (Black, 1968, p. 444). The United States, unlike many other nations, embraces statutory law. In other words, the crime must be defined in writing by a legislative body of elected officials and endorsed (rather than vetoed) by an executive member of government, who is usually also elected. Thus, the government, by defining certain acts, such as assaults, thefts and murders, or omissions, such as refusing to pay income taxes or failing to obtain a license before driving a motor vehicle, as illegal, causes crime. All fifty states have lengthy penal codes classifying various behaviors as crimes. In addition, counties, municipalities, towns, and villages also label certain activities as illegal. In general, however, federal law preempts decrees of subordinate jurisdictions, subject to certain provisions of the national Constitution, as adjudicated by federal courts (Friedman, 1993, p. 55–58; 297–300).

I was a policeman for 34 years of the last century. As a beat officer in New York's Harlem, and as police chief in Kansas City, Missouri, and San Jose, California, I caused many drug users to be locked up. I have come to believe that jailing people simply because they put certain chemicals into their bloodstream is a gross misuse of the police and criminal law. This article examines some of the reasons why.

Joseph D. McNamara, "The Hidden Costs of America's War on Drugs," *Journal of Private Enterprise*, vol. 26, no. 2, pp. 97-115.

The History of Drug Criminalization in the U.S.

As medical historian Professor David Musto (1987) of Yale has reported, the drug war started roughly 100 years ago. Protestant missionaries from the U.S. working in China and other American religious groups joined with temperance organizations in convincing Congress that drugs were evil and that drug users were dangerous, immoral people. These groups often exhibited xenophobic and religious bias and mistakenly believed that drug use was a habit of foreigners. Some reformers candidly viewed it as the white man's burden to Christianize the yellow (Chinese) heathen. Some were disgusted by the thought of white women being with "Chinamen" in opium dens. Others perceived the drug problem as causing Negroes in the South to attack and murder whites. In addition, many saw drug use as the habit of degenerate Mexicans. The religious groups predominately believed these foreign drug habits to be a moral threat to native-born Americans. Still others were humanely concerned with the obvious damage that this "sinful, depraved and immoral behavior" caused among the "inferior races." The reformers' mistaken biases (most drug use in America was by native-born Caucasians) swayed Congress (Musto, 1987; McNamara, 1973b; Hofstadter, 1955, p. 177–85).

The Progressive drug reform efforts certainly did not solve the drug problem, but they did give birth to unanticipated social damage.

This process of legislating criminal behavior is vital in analyzing America's war on drugs. Given the intensity of emotions surrounding the drug war, the overwhelming majority of Americans, including police officers, let alone residents of other nations, would be surprised to learn that for roughly the first 140 years of this Republic, the sale or possession of certain drugs that today might result in a life sentence in prison was legal. Even children were free to enter a pharmacy or general store to purchase morphine, opium, cocaine, cannabis, and other nostrums that today trigger heavy criminal penalties for possession and sale. In those days, the popular soda beverage Coca-Cola contained cocaine, and most over-the-counter cough medicines included morphine.[1]

In 1914, a government publicly advocating the reduction of crime passed legislation creating unknown millions of additional crimes. Overnight, the U.S. government turned hundreds of thousands of previously law-abiding drug users, ex post facto, into criminals. Historian David Musto (1987, p. 65) describes the Harrison Act as: " ... a routine slap at moral evil"; drugs had to be outlawed because "Cocaine raised the specter of the wild negro, opium the devious Chinese, morphine the tramps in the slums."[2] Furthermore, this legislation, the Harrison Anti-Narcotics Act, represented a sea change in interpreting Constitutional restrictions on the federal government's right to interfere in police powers previously reserved to the states. The Congress that passed the Harrison Act brooded over whether it was violating the Congressional principle that powers not enumerated in the Constitution were reserved to the states (Musto, 1987, p. 21–23). Congress finessed this issue by referring to the Harrison Act as a revenue measure affecting opium, cocaine, and other drugs, because raising revenue and regulating interstate commerce

1 See McNamara (1973a, p. 16–59) and Lindesmith (1965, p. 3) for a fuller discussion.
2 See also McNamara (1973b).

were among the federal powers authorized by the Constitution. Thus, the Harrison Act of 1914 became the cornerstone of American criminal drug control policy, which has continuously expanded the drug war.

Constitutional uneasiness similar to that experienced during the passage of the Harrison Act of 1914 also afflicted Congress when it outlawed cannabis in the 1937 "Marijuana Tax Act," which also eventually received federal court approval as a penal statute. In contrast, federal prohibition of alcohol from 1920–1933 was achieved by the far more formal and cumbersome process of amending the Constitution through the 18th Amendment. When the nation decided that the "noble" experiment of criminal alcohol prohibition had done more harm than good, it was repealed by the 21st Amendment to the Constitution. Some legal scholars thus raise the question as to whether the federal drug laws, which have been legislated by Congress as opposed to being approved through the prescribed process of Constitutional amendment, exceed the authority of Congress (Pilon, 2000, p. 23–40; Duke, 2000, p. 41–60).

Health Care Costs of the Drug War

The Harrison Act contains the sentence: "That nothing contained in this section shall apply (a) To the dispensing or distribution of any of the aforesaid drugs to a patient by a physician, dentist, or veterinary surgeon registered under this Act in the course of his professional practice only: ... with the appropriate practice of medicine" (Harrison Anti-Narcotics Act, 1914, Ch 1, 38 Stat. 785). However, this was not to be the case. The 1938 Food, Drug and Cosmetic Act (U.S. Code Title 21) and the Federal Drug And Control Act (sec. 201[g][1]), the enabling statutes for the Food and Drug Administration, define drugs by their intended purpose, as "(a) articles intended for use in the diagnosis, cure, mitigation, treatment, or prevention of disease ... and (b) articles (other than food) intended to affect the structure or any function of the body of man or other animals." It is self-evident that the broad scope of these definitions means that hundreds of thousands of pharmacological substances are labeled as drugs. It is also true that a modest alteration of molecules can transform a chemical from a legal medicine into a prohibited substance. Furthermore, distribution of non-prohibited substances can result in federal or state prosecutions well beyond the average or even wealthy person's ability to mount a legal defense. Some doctors are now being prosecuted as drug traffickers after federal agents and prosecutors decided that their prescription practices were not "appropriate." Expensive legal fees and the possibility of a life sentence if the verdict goes against the defendant provide a powerful incentive for most physicians to plead guilty to a lesser charge in return for a reduced sentence.

The United States Supreme Court, under its judicial review function, vacillated on the nature of the Harrison Act. Federal Treasury Department agents arrested a number of physicians who had been prescribing narcotic drugs to treat drug addicts and other patients with chronic pain. The doctors' defense that they were practicing medicine was successful in some cases. In 1915, the Supreme Court hardened its position when Justice Holmes wrote in a majority opinion that in passing the Harrison Act:

> Congress meant to strain its powers almost if not to the breaking point in order to make the probably very large proportion of citizens who have some preparation of opium in their possession criminal or at least prima facie criminal, and subject to the severe punishment made possible by S.9. It may be assumed that the statute has a moral end. (U.S. v. Jin Fuey May, 241 U.S. 394, [1915]).

In the 1925 Linder Case (Linder v. U.S. 268, U.S. 5, [1925]) the Supreme Court temporarily wavered by deciding that drug addiction was a disease, not a crime, and therefore subject to medical treatment. But the sum of all these and subsequent opinions, known as "the Doctor Cases," was that prescription of narcotics to help addicts was a violation of criminal law.

In recent years the federal government has begun a new wave of doctor cases. This campaign owes its origin to frequent, embarrassing accusations that the drug war cannot be won because the majority of drug use is by ordinary citizens using legally manufactured, albeit potentially dangerous, prescription drugs. It appears, in the opinion of federal authorities, that these legal medicines are being "abused" to an even greater extent than illegal drugs. The current "doctor" cases differ from those immediately following the Harrison Act in that accused physicians now face federal charges as racketeers distributing drugs as well as a multitude of other felonies, thus exposing them to harsh minimum mandatory sentences up to and including life in prison.[3]

Criminal accusations against doctors can arise in several ways. Commonly, undercover agents of the Federal Drug Enforcement Agency (DEA) visit doctors' offices complaining of severe pain. If the physician prescribes pain medication that is excessive, the physician prescribes without sufficient medical scrutiny to prove that patients' pain complaints are legitimate in the opinion of the police agents and prosecutors, or the authorities believe alternative, nonaddictive drugs might be as effective, the physician may be charged with a multitude of crimes. Law enforcement authorities may also ask patients who are disgruntled or have been apprehended for illegally possessing or trafficking in drugs to complain of chronic pain, in attempts to get physicians to prescribe drugs in quantities or a manner deemed to be criminal by the authorities. Some of the bogus patients are facing long prison terms that can only be mitigated by "cooperating" with authorities. Their testimony and actions frequently lack credibility due to their motives, history of questionable personal drug use, and other crimes they've committed. Nevertheless, defense attorneys often feel compelled to recommend to their physician clients that they plead guilty in a plea bargain promising lesser punishment rather than risk the draconian penalties if they lose at trial. In addition, attorneys facing well-financed prosecutors and law enforcement agencies must advise their clients that mounting a defense, which may or may not succeed, can cost more than a million dollars.

Consequently, many doctors under-prescribe or avoid prescribing pain relievers out of fear of prosecutions that can lead to large fines, defense costs they cannot afford, and decades-long sentences or, indeed, life in prison. Accused physicians also routinely face the loss of their state

3 In 2004, the federal government convicted William E. Hurwitz, M.D., on charges of conspiracy and drug trafficking for prescribing OxyContin and other painkillers in his Virginia clinic. Dr. Hurwitz, who is facing a sentence of 25 years to life, is appealing (Tierney, 2007).

permits to practice medicine and their DEA licenses to prescribe drugs. Non-profit organizations have formed to advocate for patients suffering pain from terminal or chronic diseases who are unable to locate doctors willing to prescribe legal pain medications during treatment. The drug war has shredded the traditional confidentiality of doctor–patient relationships, with doctors testifying against patients, and real and fake patients testifying against doctors.

Furthermore, the rigid labeling of some drugs as being without medical value has hindered research experiments designed to test their value and danger. Although opium, cocaine, and marijuana have been used for centuries by many different cultures for medication or rituals, they have, ipso facto, been placed into Schedule I, a category that the federal government says has no accepted medical use. The government's rigid position that many drugs are too dangerous to have any legitimate medical use has prevented valuable research on the impact of a number of psychotropic substances.

Another hidden cost of drug prohibition is the lack of appropriate supervision over the manufacturing, distribution, and use of drugs, as well as lost tax revenue. Once users turn to the illegal black market, their drug use becomes more dangerous. One of the most disastrous examples is the prohibition of hypodermic needles. Because in most jurisdictions mere possession is a crime, intravenous drug users commonly share needles and in so doing contaminate each other with HIV, hepatitis, and other life-threatening infections. These potentially lethal diseases are easily transmitted to the law-abiding, non-drug using population through sexual intercourse or other interactions. Several studies have shown that cities providing sterile needle exchanges have reduced the spread of HIV infections without incurring an increase in heroin use and addiction.[4]

The Harm of Drugs

Some time ago, in a televised discussion of the U.S. Drug War, a respected friend and former chief United States prosecutor astounded me by declaring that these drugs (the illegal ones) were bad not because they were illegal, but they were illegal because they were bad. Were this true, it would lend a degree of legitimacy to the argument for criminalizing the more dangerous drugs, although it obviously ignores the crucial issue of prohibition and the costs it presents in terms of violence, corruption, financing of illicit enterprises, and disrespect for law and civil rights, not to mention the demonstrated danger of undermining fledgling democracies. In addition, making certain chemical substances illegal makes them more dangerous because it removes their production and use from protective professional and government oversight.[5]

---

4 See McVay's (2007, p. 176–84) discussion of Pain Management for information on syringe exchanges, and p. 146–58 for an excellent and extensive review of the problems of illegal syringes and pain treatment.

5 See Friedman (1972) for a comprehensive description by Nobel Laureate Milton Friedman of the various hidden costs of drug prohibition, such as corruption, violence, unethical and illegal use of informants, diversion of law enforcement resources from essential duties, the undermining of other nations' sovereignty, and other economic predictions that have come to pass because of the nation's wrongheaded war on drugs.

TABLE 12.1 Approximations for Annual Causes of Deaths in the United States in 2000

Cause	Number of Deaths
Tobacco	435,000
Poor diet and physical inactivity	365,000
Alcohol	85,000
Microbial agents	75,000
Toxic agents	55,000
Adverse reactions to prescription drugs	32,000
Suicide	30,632
Incidents involving firearms	29,000
Motor vehicle crashes	26,347
Homicide	20,308
Sexual behaviors	20,000
Illegal drug use, direct and indirect	17,000
Anti-inflammatory drugs such as aspirin	7,600
Marijuana	0

Source: McVay (2007, p. 10)

Furthermore, much of the federal government's own data and data from government-financed research financed contradict the contention that relative danger was the basis for outlawing certain substances. As shown in Table 12.1, the most lethal substances are legal. Unfortunately, under the spell of protecting public health and morals, Congress couldn't foresee these contemporary mortality rates when it passed the Harrison Act.

Increasing Crime

By passing the Harrison Act, the United States federal government, publicly committed to crime prevention, created untold millions of new crimes by overnight criminalizing widespread behavior that had been legal. In effect, the government transformed somewhere between hundreds of thousands and millions (estimates at the time varied widely from 100,000 to 4 million) of individuals into de facto criminals (Black, 1968). In contrast to the mala-in-se (wrong in themselves) crimes such as murders mentioned above, it is impossible to determine with any precision the number of drug crimes because they are consensual transactions between both buyers and sellers who are breaking the law. Actually, the only drug crime data estimates collected and published by the government are those recorded subsequent to drug arrests. One may only speculate how many drug crimes have been committed by those not arrested, as well as the number of past drug crimes committed by those who have been apprehended.[6]

No similar reputable efforts are made to capture the total number of drug crimes because of their secretive and consensual nature. There are data focusing on the supposed number of users of various drugs, the level of international drug production, the quantity of drugs seized, and the health problems and deaths they cause. However, as Peter Reuter, the highly respected analyst, then with the Rand think tank and now a professor at the University of Maryland, put it:

> Official estimates of such things as the number of heroin addicts and the total income from heroin sales were: "a class of 'mythical numbers" that is becoming the routine product of government agencies. The statistics were gathered by very questionable, but unquestioned data collection (Reuter, 1984, p. 136–37).

In short, no one has any idea of the total number of drug violations committed in the United States.

In 2001 a subcommittee of the National Academy of Science compiled a report on the efficacy of U.S. Drug Control Policy. The chair of this subcommittee (Manski, 2001) testified, "We found that the nation lacks the necessary information to gauge the effectiveness of current [drug] enforcement activities. For a program of this magnitude, that is simply unconscionable." In essence, the subcommittee was critical that a program costing hundreds of billions of dollars, incarcerating millions of Americans, being inundated with violence and corruption, and frequently failing in its stated objectives to significantly reduce drug production, importation, use, and the resulting dangers to users, had failed to document the consequences of various changes in government methodology and philosophy through the years. Amazingly, the committee's report received little media attention and no Congressional action.

Fiscal Costs

U.S. drug control policies evoke considerable differences of opinion. Yet, there is consensus that America's drug problems have not been resolved despite enormous increases in government efforts. One indicator of the difficulties inherent in preventing illegal drug use is in the growth of federal spending on drug control. After passing the Harrison Act in 1914, Congress appropriated $150,000 for the Treasury Department, thus maintaining the fiction that the Act was a revenue

6 The federal government does provide two longitudinal annual indices of crimes reported by victims or witnesses. *Crime in the United States*, Uniformed Crime Reports, published by the Federal Bureau of Investigation since 1927, compiles yearly totals of various offenses reported to local and state police agencies. The other index, *Crime Victimization Studies,* begun in 1972, enumerates, through telephone surveys, individual reflections of someone in the household (approximately 77,600 households) as to victimization. Homeless people and those without telephones or who refuse to participate are not included. There are numerous limitations on the research methodology of both indices, not the least of which is that they measure different phenomena. The annual FBI report, although labeled "uniform," nevertheless contains some inevitable cultural reporting differences among the nation's 17,000-plus police agencies. Furthermore, there is general consensus that for a variety of reasons most crime is not recorded in either index.

measure. In 1972, when President Richard Nixon called for a war against drugs, the federal drug war budget was roughly $101 million. In 2011 President Obama's requested budget for "Federal Drug Control" is a record $15.5 billion (Executive Office of the President of the United States, 2010).[7] In addition, the states are estimated to have spent at least $30 billion each year on justice-related drug war expenses since 1998 (CASA Press Release 2000).

The magnitude of the increase is further illustrated by comparing the average 1972 monthly Social Security payment of $177 with the growth of drug control spending. If Social Security benefits had increased at the same rate, current monthly Social Security payments would be in the range of $30,444 rather than approximately $900 now. Similarly, the average 1972 weekly salary of $114 would have soared to roughly $19,608, and a mortgage payment of $408 would have grown to as much as $68,000 per month.[8] It is noteworthy that these comparisons take into account only federal spending. If state and local drug control expenditures are considered, the total cost estimates are approximately $30 billion per year.

Despite this growing expenditure of taxpayers' money, this decade has seen a doubling of opium production in Southeast Asia and a one-third increase in cocaine production in Central and South America. Eighty to ninety percent of illegal drugs shipped to this country arrive undetected (Office of National Drug Control Policy, 1999). More than two decades ago the United States Congress proclaimed, "It is the declared policy of the United States to create a Drug-Free America by 1995" (Anti-Drug Abuse Act of 1988), but the United States, indeed the world, is still awash in illegal drugs that are purer and more potent than ever.

The vast profits resulting from prohibition—a markup as great as 17,000 percent—have led to worldwide corruption of public officials and widespread violence among drug traffickers and dealers that endanger whole communities, cities, and nations. The United Nations reports that there is a $500 billion international black market in drugs. It is beyond the scope of this paper to consider foreign policy costs of the drug war, although Milton Friedman's contentions on the subject are compelling (Friedman, 2005, pp. 77–80). In the U.S., drug-related overdose deaths and emergency room visits have increased. Half of all high school seniors surveyed report having used an illegal drug (Johnston et al., 1996), and 85 percent of them say that illegal drugs are easier to obtain than legal, but regulated, beer (National Center for Addiction and Substance Abuse at Columbia University, 1996).

Presidents William Clinton and George W. Bush assured us that we are winning against drugs, as did their predecessors. Yet people in law enforcement and local communities are unconvinced, for good reason. Although casual illegal drug use appears to fluctuate and may have declined in recent years, regular use has not. People young and old seem to use drugs according to unfathomed fads. Dire government warnings about the newest dangerous trends describing "the most dangerous drug threat ever—heroin, marijuana, cocaine, rock cocaine, ice, date rape

---

7 These are the official figures, but Gaver (2009) argues that the true figures are each at least $8 billion higher.

8 Statistics compiled from the White House, Office of National Drug Control Policy 1999, U.S. Social Security Reports 1973 and 1998, and Statistical Abstract 1972.

drugs, methamphetamine, morphine, oxycontin ..." only confuse matters further. Actually, such warnings are themselves an indication that the drug war is unwinnable. Production sources, smuggling techniques, purity, price, and use patterns have changed throughout the years in the dynamic drug market as the government has made claims of progress, but the war begun in 1914 has no end in sight.

Moreover, the decline in casual drug use may be unrelated to the war on drugs. Cigarette smoking and consumption of hard liquor and high cholesterol food—all as dangerous as illegal drug use—declined because of greater awareness of health dangers, not because consumers were jailed or because the government reduced the supply of these substances by waging a criminal justice war.

Costs to Law Enforcement

In 2008, The Federal Bureau of Investigation reported a total of 14,005,615 arrests in the United States. The number of arrests made by American law enforcement officers in that year for drug abuse violations was 1,702,527 (12% of all arrests) and was more numerous than for any other crime (Federal Bureau of Investigation, 2009). However, jailing drug users does not persistently lessen drug use in society at large, or for that matter in prisons themselves, where illegal drugs are available. Incarceration for mostly minor drug offenses usually destroys the person's life and does immense harm to families and neighborhoods. Justifying jail sentences by claiming that users would likely commit other crimes if they remained free is a flagrant rejection of a fundamental American right—the presumption of innocence.

Certainly, many people who commit crime are also users of illegal drugs. However, there is a vast difference between correlation and causation. Studies of prison populations indicate that inmates have a multitude of questionable behaviors in their past, many times even before venturing into illegal drug use. For example, high percentages of those convicted of crime are illiterate or otherwise uneducated, have poor histories of employment, come from dysfunctional families and neighborhoods, lack positive role models and mentors, received inadequate medical care, and generally lack the social skills that enable most of society to live wholesome lives. Drug use is no more a conclusive explanation of their criminal behavior than these other characteristics; instead, drug use may simply represent another factor that makes these people high-risk candidates for criminality. On the other hand, the illegality of certain drugs inflates their price and may well lead some individuals to commit crimes to obtain drugs. Some users are undoubtedly drawn into the underworld by their necessary contact with drug-dealing criminals, and many non-drug users are attracted to the illegal drug market by the opportunity to earn large sums of money and to gain status among their peers.

There are, however, vast differences in the difficulty that drug crimes pose for the police than other offenses. For example, as has already been mentioned, the police do not routinely resort to use of informants, unlawful searches, or morally and physically dangerous undercover tactics in dealing with the vast bulk of crime. Because drug transactions are consensual, the police do not have the victims, witnesses, and physical evidence that help them solve crimes such as murder, assault, robbery, rape, and burglary. Under the Fourth Amendment, the police, with few exceptions, are not allowed to search people or their homes without a warrant. Yet, last year, state and local police in the United States made close to a million and a half arrests for illegal possession of drugs. Overwhelmingly, these were minor arrests and rarely involved a court-approved warrant.

The inescapable conclusion is that in hundreds of thousands of cases, police officers violated their oath to uphold the Constitution and often committed perjury so that the evidence would be admitted in court. The practice is so prevalent that the term "testilying" is sometimes substituted in police jargon for "testifying." The injury that unlawful searches and perjury by the police does to the credibility of our justice system is immeasurable.

It is also crucial to realize that when the police arrest an armed robber, rapist, or habitual thief who is then imprisoned, another criminal does not quickly move in to fill the void. There is no demand for so many murders, rapes, robberies, or assaults that must be filled. In contrast, the law of supply and demand is operative in the illegal drug market. When the police succeed in destroying a major drug ring [this is rare; most of the 1,702,527 annual drug arrests by state and local police are for minor drug crimes, including approximately 800,000 for marijuana (Federal Bureau of Investigation, 2009), by far the most for any drug], the demand for illegal drugs seems fairly constant, and other "entrepreneurs" quickly fill the void, even before their predecessors are sentenced.

Aside from the considerable cost of conducting years-long investigations of major dealers, other hidden costs arise. The larger drug operations grew because they utilized superior market strategies or employed greater violence against competitors. When the police eliminate the more successful drug organization, rivals commonly usurp other drug entrepreneurs by violence, endangering innocent citizens as well as harming the quality of life in the area. Rival drug dealers do not sue each other. They employ extraordinary violence against not only competitors, but also witnesses they suspect of informing the police of their activities. Indeed, even within their organization, individuals seeking leadership or suspected of "ratting out" to authorities are killed. Moreover, there is greater inclination toward dishonest behavior in illegal industries than in lawful enterprises, which are deterred, at least to some extent, by threat of lawsuits. In the drug underworld, failing to deliver the merchandise or money triggers more violence. Despite the disruptions, the level of drug use in the neighborhood rapidly rises to its previous level, or at most is displaced to nearby locations. In some cases, disruptions in the drug market lead users to other, more dangerous drugs that remain available.

A good question to ponder is, when was the last time a Budweiser beer distributor was gunned down in a drive-by shooting? Most of the crime committed by drug users is not so much the effect of the altered mental state resulting from drug ingestion as the result of the product's illegality. This leads to the further question of why the police, courts, and correction and other government agencies are investing huge sums in the drug war at the cost of diverting scarce resources from pursuing other crimes. At least part of the answer is that government is a monopoly not subject to going bankrupt as a result of failure. Thus, police and criminal justice agencies' performance is measured in terms of process—the number of drug arrests, the number of people incarcerated, and the quantity of drug seizures—rather than goal achievements, such as reducing illnesses and deaths among drug users or keeping the local economy healthy and peaceful enough to provide employment so that families, schools, and neighborhood associations can function well enough to establish and maintain conditions contributing to a prosperous and law-abiding society.

Drug War Costs Related to Racial Inequality

Non-whites have borne the brunt of the punishment for drug crimes even though most drug use is by whites. Alfred Blumstein (1993), former president of the American Society of Criminologists, described the drug war as "an assault on the African-American community." Police on patrol make most drug arrests by simply confronting people on the street, usually without any legal basis for an arrest. Needless to say, members of minority groups resent what they regard as racial profiling by the police, which is itself a violation of law in the United States. Yet, uniformed and plainclothes officers are most often confronted with anonymous buyers and sellers of drugs. Officers necessarily must act more on hunches than evidence. The result is not only a public relations quandary but also a legal one because the Fourth Amendment prohibits warrantless searches in most cases.

The current protests over racial profiling by the police are a reflection of the damage that an ill-conceived law enforcement war against drugs has on the ability of the police to win the cooperation that they need to do their basic job of protecting life and property. Resentful citizens are unlikely to dial 911 to report a burglary in progress or other crime if they view the police as adversaries. It is also true that the average citizen who identifies a drug seller to the police is taking a considerable risk of physical harm from the defendant and his colleagues.

Gangster Cops

Even more damaging is the destruction of trust that follows the exposure of gangster cops who have robbed drug dealers, sold drugs, and framed people in the communities that they swore to protect. Police perjurers far outnumber those cops who are predatory drug criminals; still, there have been thousands of drug-related police crimes since the 1972 declaration of a drug war.

The prevailing opinion of Americans is that drug corruption is a serious problem in countries producing drugs, serving as a conduit for drug smuggling or helping to launder the immense profits from the illicit drug trade, but only a negligible issue in the United States. Yet, data collected from the 1970s to the present lead me to speculate that United States police officers across the nation have committed more than a million serious drug felonies. Some degree of police corruption has been an inherent problem ever since the establishment of the first professional police force in London in 1829. However, because fairly low-paid officials are able to accumulate tax-free fortunes due to the enormous black market profits ensuing from drug prohibition, no nation is free from police drug crimes. In contrast to the traditional police corruption in which police take bribes from gangsters to "look the other way" rather than enforce the law, thousands of American police officers become drug gangsters.

Drug corruption has also penetrated all services of the U.S. military, as they have been given increasing responsibility for drug enforcement. Perhaps the most revealing example is the 2000 conviction of Lieutenant Colonel James C. Hiett, a 24-year Army veteran, who was the United States Army Group Commander heading American military forces in Colombia. The colonel's wife shipped $700,000 worth of cocaine and heroin through the U.S. Embassy in Bogota and sold it in the U.S. He pleaded guilty to laundering some of the money into United States banks (Associated Press, 2000).

There is no way to assess the fiscal cost when neighborhoods become convinced that police officers are part of drug distribution, but it is enormous. Without public trust in the integrity of law enforcement officers, police departments cannot be effective. Citizens will not report crimes to the police, testify during prosecutions, or as jurors believe police officers' testimony. The whole fabric of a civilized society is endangered, if not destroyed.

Conclusion

The United States has been unable to face the failure of its drug policies and to examine alternatives that would lessen dangerous drug use. We are still captive to the myths about drug use and the false stereotypes of drug users created a century ago by religious zealots, xenophobic native-born Americans, and Progressive reformers. Some of the same religious fervor remains. Timothy Lynch (2000, p. 4), Director of the Cato Institution's Project on Criminal Justice, writes of supporters of the drug war talking of drug immorality and drugs destroying users' souls.

Once we are beyond the emotional straightjackets imposed by the Harrison Act's original lobbyists, we can study how we and other countries can minimize the harm of drugs. There is no panacea, but it is clear that continuing to do more of what has not worked in the past century is not the way to start a new millennium. Although all criminal laws are in a sense moralistic, the First Amendment to the United States Constitution calls for a separation of religion and government, especially government coercion favoring certain religions. Those who wrote the Declaration of Independence and the Constitution did not intend that the enormous police power of government should be used to establish public morality and to "save souls." It would benefit America and the world to leave the protection of health and salvation of souls to health professionals and clergy, and to insist that police, courts, and prisons concentrate on protecting life and property from criminals.

Throughout history, mankind has used psychoactive substances for a variety of purposes. Whether we like it or not, drugs will prove attractive to some people. The invisible hand that Adam Smith described as controlling the marketplace exists in the drug market as well. As long as there is a demand for drugs, someone will find a way to supply them. As economically and militarily powerful as the United States has grown, it cannot suspend the law of supply and demand, either domestically or globally. It is not sound public policy to defend America's world war on drugs merely by advancing the argument impervious to empirical proof, namely that things would be even worse without the drug war. Pushing aside unrealistic moralizing, it is arguable that the drug war is causing more harm than the drugs. The challenge to the world is to confront the true costs of U.S. drug control efforts in order to maximize the healthy utility of these substances and to minimize the harm they, and wrongheaded criminal prohibition, cause.

References

Associated Press. 2001. "Colonel Fired For Laundering Cash: Gets No Military Pension And Can't Appeal Decision." *CBS News*, November 6.

Black, Henry C. 1968. *Black's Law Dictionary*. Revised Fourth Edition. St. Paul, MN: West Publishing.

Blumstein, Alfred. 1993. "Making Rationality Relevant—The American Society of Criminology Presidential Address." *Criminology*, 31(1): 1–16.

Duke, Stephen. 2000. "The Drug War and the Constitution." In *After Prohibition: An Adult Approach to Drug Policies in the 21st Century*, ed. Timothy Lynch, 41–60. Washington, D.C.: Cato Institute.

Executive Office of the President of the United States. 2010. National Drug Control Strategy: Fiscal Year Budget Summary. Washington, D.C.: The White House.

Federal Bureau of Investigation. 2009. *Crime in the United States 2008*. Washington, D.C.: Federal Bureau of Investigation.

Friedman, Lawrence M. 1993. *Crime and Punishment in American History*. New York: Basic Books.

Friedman, Milton. 1972. "Prohibition and Drugs." *Newsweek*, May 1, 104.

Friedman, Milton. 2005. "There's No Justice in the War on Drugs." In *Drug War Deadlock*, ed. Laura Huggins, 77–80. Stanford: Hoover Institution Press.

Gaver, John. 2009. *Drug War Cost Clock Updated for 2009*. Houston: Action America.

Hofstadter, Richard. 1955. *The Age of Reform*. New York: Knopf.

Johnston, L.D., P.M. O'Malley, and J.G. Bachman. 1996. *National Survey Results on Drug Use from the Monitoring the Future Study, 1975–1995. Volume I: Secondary School Students*. (NIH Publication No. 96–4139). Rockville, MD: National Institute on Drug Abuse.

Lindesmith, Alfred. 1965. *The Addict and the Law*. New York: Vintage Books.

Lynch, Timothy. 2000. "Tabula Rasa for Drug Policy." In *After Prohibition: An Adult Approach to Drug Policies in the 21st Century*, ed. Timothy Lynch, 3–12. Washington, D.C.: Cato Institute.

Manski, Charles F. 2001. "Testimony." National Research Council Committee of the National Academy of Sciences, April 13, Washington, D.C.

McNamara, Joseph D. 1973a. Organizational Decision Making and Public Policy, An Analysis of Police Drug Enforcement Strategy. PhD diss. Harvard University.

McNamara, J.D. 1973b. "The History of the United States Anti-Opium policy." *Federal Probation*, 5(37): 15–21.

McVay, Douglas (ed). 2007, *Drug War Facts*. Lancaster, PA: Common Sense for Drug Policy.

Musto, David. 1987. *The American Disease: Origins of Narcotics Control*. New York: Oxford University Press.

National Center for Addiction and Substance Abuse at Columbia University, 1996. *National Survey of American Attitudes on Substance Abuse II: Teens and Their Parents*. New York: National Center for Addiction and Substance Abuse at Columbia University.

Office of National Drug Control Policy. 1999. *Drug Policy Perspectives*. Washington, D.C.: The White House.

Pilon, Roger. 2000. "The Illegitimate War on Drugs." In *After Prohibition: An Adult Approach to Drug Policies in the 21st Century*, ed. Timothy Lynch, 23–40. Washington, D.C.: Cato Institute.

Reuter, Peter. 1984. "The (Continued) Vitality of Mythical Numbers." *Public Interest* 75: 135–47.

Tierney, John. 2007. "Trafficker or Healer? And Who's the Victim?" *New York Times*, March 27.

CHAPTER 7

Conclusion

Drug addiction often disrupts employment and interpersonal relationships, which could lead to many more social issues than just crime. Hence, drug policies are related to other social problems in addition to affecting the law and law enforcement. Given the limited resources we have, it is imperative for the government to be wise about how to deal with the drug problem and yield the best result with the least cost. Those who had a legitimate reason to start taking drugs and, unfortunately, became addicted should be able to obtain the help they need without the stigma. For those who never had a legitimate reason to begin with, we should be wondering, "Why do we have so many people who willingly poison their own body? What is the reason that makes these people feel they need to turn to drugs to have fun, to escape from reality, or to impress others?"

Discussion Questions

1. Do some research on the states that have legalized marijuana. What has happened to them in terms of crime rates and economy?
2. How much money has been spent on the war on drugs? What has this war accomplished? Could we have spent the same money in a different way and achieve better results?
3. Some people argue the war on drugs unfairly targets racial minorities. Is this true? Support your answer with facts.
4. What is the opioid epidemic? What is the solution?
5. Are you for prohibition or legalization? Which one do you believe can reduce drug abuse and the cost associated with it? Why?

CHAPTER 8

Mass Incarceration

Introduction

We discussed drug policies in the previous chapter, and we mentioned that current drug policies bring about few positive effects in terms of stopping the drug abuse epidemic. Not only did these drug policies fail to reduce drug abuse and addiction, but they have also contributed to a serious problem faced by the criminal justice system: prison overcrowding. Overcrowding happens when we put too many people in a facility that was not designed to hold so many people. We might be able to find room to place these extra bodies, but these are humans, not products. They need more than just a place for sleeping or standing. The "warehousing" approach does not apply well to humans.

Overcrowding can be observed across the country in most prisons and jails. Until recent years, the crime rates overall were declining for more than twenty years. It implies we have had fewer criminals. However, during the same period, the prison population did not shrink. Many criminologists believe the war on drugs was to blame. While the drug laws became tougher and less flexible in dealing with drug offenders, many people would be sentenced to prison for otherwise minor drug offenses, such as possession of a small quantity of marijuana. Without the drug war mentality, these offenders would probably have received an intermediate sentence or probation. Other than the drug war, the "tough on crime" ideology popular in the 1980s and 1990s called for longer sentences for criminals and thus also contributed to a ballooning prison population.

There are probably other factors that account for the overcrowding issue. In this chapter, we are not going to look to the past and point fingers. Instead, we are looking at the issue that is currently staring at us and trying to figure out what to do next. It is fact that prison overcrowding is an issue that not only creates inhumane conditions for inmates, but also threatens the safety of corrections officers. It is fact that overcrowding makes rehabilitation a fantasy in our correctional system due to limited resources. It is fact that the United States incarcerates more criminals than any other country in the world in terms of both the sheer number and percentage. Given these facts, there are a few questions for students to think about. How do we reduce the prison population and still make sure criminals get the punishment they deserve? Should we build more prisons to accommodate all these criminals, and how much will that cost? Is incarceration the only effective method to serve justice, and what alternatives should be considered or created? More importantly, why do we have so many criminals?

In this chapter, the article selected is not intended to answer all these questions, but it should help students better understand the impact of mass incarceration by addressing the devastating effect that mass incarceration could have on the family that has one or more members being incarcerated. It is important to note that when we put a person in prison, the implication is more than just putting a criminal behind bars. It also means we are removing a person from a family and the absence of this person in the family, especially in the long run, might have consequential effects on other family members, and such effects could, in turn, become a fostering force for criminality or other social problems.

The Long Arm of the Law

The Concentration of Incarceration in Families in the Era of Mass Incarceration

Christopher Wildeman and Sara Wakefield***

Introduction

The dramatic increase in the American imprisonment rate since the early 1970s[1] and the concentration of imprisonment among young minority men with low educational attainment living in the poorest neighborhoods[2] has profoundly altered the life-course for marginalized men and their families. While imprisonment was once uncommon for even the most disadvantaged men, it is now a common event for such men, with upwards of 70 percent of African American men who did not finish high school expected to experience imprisonment by their early 30s.[3] The dramatic risks of imprisonment also have important implications for children since many of the men who cycle through the prison system are also fathers.[4] Indeed, estimates

*Associate Professor of Sociology, Yale University.
**Assistant Professor of Criminal Justice, Rutgers University-Newark.

1 *See* BRUCE WESTERN, PUNISHMENT AND INEQUALITY IN AMERICA 12–15 (2006) (showing how the imprisonment rate has grown since the 1970s, including relative to other developed democracies).
2 For a discussion of how the cumulative risk of imprisonment is concentrated by race and education and how this risk has changed over time, see Becky Pettit & Bruce Western, *Mass imprisonment and the Life Course: Race and Class inequality in U.S. imprisonment,* 69 Am. Soc. Rev. 151 (2004). For a discussion of how highly concentrated imprisonment is in the poorest neighborhoods, see Robert J. Sampson & Charles Loeffler, *Punishment's Place: The Local Concentration of Mass Incarceration,* 139 DAEDALUS 20 (2010).
3 For one recent estimate of the cumulative risk of imprisonment, see Bruce Western & Christopher Wildeman, *The Black Family and Mass Incarceration,* 621 Annals Am. Acad. Pol. & Soc. Sci. 221 (2009).
4 *See* CHRISTOPHER J. MUMOLA, U.S. DEP'T OF JUSTICE, INCARCERATED PARENTS AND THEIR CHILDREN (2000), *available at* http://www.bjs.gov/content/pub/pdf/iptc.pdf.

suggest that over half of all African American children born in 1990 whose fathers dropped out of high school had their father imprisoned at some point between their birth and their 14th birthday.[5]

In light of the concentration of paternal imprisonment among the most marginalized children and the consequences of having ever been incarcerated for adult men's earnings,[6] marital status,[7] and health,[8] researchers have become keenly interested in the consequences of mass imprisonment for childhood inequality. In that vein, most research has focused on the effects of paternal incarceration on individual children,[9] finding that paternal incarceration is associated with a host of negative outcomes ranging from early childhood[10] through adolescence[11]

---

5 Christopher Wildeman, *Parental imprisonment, the Prison Boom, and the Concentration of Childhood Disadvantage, 46* DEMOGRAPHY 265, 273 (2009).

6 *See* Devah Pager, *The Mark of a Criminal Record,* 108 AM. J. SOC. 937 (2003). *See also* Bruce Western, *The Impact of Incarceration on Wage Mobility and Inequality,* 67 AM. SOC. REV. 526 (2002). For a review of this literature, see Sara Wakefield & Christopher Uggen, *incarceration and Stratification,* 36 Ann. Rev. Soc. 387, 394–96 (2010).

7 Although most research on the consequences of incarceration for the probability of marrying suggests fairly small effects, research finds that incarceration dramatically increases the risk of union dissolution. For three excellent analyses in this regard, see Robert Apel, Arjan A.J. Blokland, Paul Nieuwbeerta & Marieke van Schellen, *The Impact of imprisonment on Marriage and Divorce: A Risk Set Matching Approach,* 26 J. QUANTITATIVE CRIMINOLOGY 269 (2010); Leonard M. Lopoo & Bruce Western, *incarceration and the Formation and Stability of Marital Unions,* 67 J. MARRIAGE & FAM. 721 (2005); Michael Massoglia, Brianna Remster & Ryan D. King, *Stigma or Separation? Understanding the Incarceration-Divorce Relationship,* 90 SOC. FORCES 133 (2011).

8 For an application to infectious and stress-related diseases, see Michael Massoglia, *Incarceration as Exposure: The Prison, Infectious Disease, and Other Stress-Related Illnesses,* 49 J. Health & Soc. Behav. 56 (2008). For an application to self-rated health, see Michael Massoglia, *Incarceration, HEALTH, and RACIAL DISPARITIES in Health,* 42 L. & Soc. Rev. 275 (2008). For an application to mental health, see Jason Schnittker, Michael Massoglia & Christopher Uggen, *Out and Down: Incarceration and Psychiatric Disorder,* 53 J. HEALTH & SOC. BEHAV. 448 (2012) and Kristin Turney, Christopher Wildeman & Jason Schnittker, *As Fathers and Felons: Explaining the Effects of Current and Recent Incarceration on Major Depression,* 53 J. HEALTH & SOC. BEHAV. 465 (2012).

9 *See* Christopher Wildeman & Christopher Muller, *Mass Imprisonment and Inequality in Health and Family Life,* 8 ANN. REV. L. & SOC. SCI. 11 (2012).

10 For three of the most recent and rigorous analyses in this literature, see Amanda Geller, Carey E. Cooper, Irwin Garfinkel & Ronald B. Mincy, *Beyond Absenteeism: Father Incarceration and Child Development,* 49 DEMOGRAPHY 49 (2012); Sara Wakefield & Christopher Wildeman, *Mass Imprisonment and Racial Disparities in Childhood Behavioral Problems,* 10 Criminology & Pub. Pol'y 793 (2011) (testing for effects on racial inequality but also presenting estimates of the effects of paternal incarceration on children's behavioral problems using data from the Project on Human Development in Chicago Neighborhoods); and Christopher Wildeman, *Paternal Incarceration and Children's Physically Aggressive Behaviors: Evidence from the Fragile Families and Child Wellbeing Study,* 89 SOC. FORCES 285 (2010).

11 For three of the most rigorous studies considering effects in adolescence to date, see Holly Foster & John Hagan, *Incarceration and Intergenerational Social Exclusion,* 54 SOC. Probs. 399 (2007); John Hagan & Holly Foster, *Intergenerational Educational Effects of Mass Imprisonment in America,* 85 SOC. EDUC. 259 (2012) (presenting an estimate of the direct effects of paternal incarceration on children's educational outcomes, as well as evidence of the indirect effects of going to a school where many children have ever had their father incarcerated on children's educational outcomes); and Michael E. Roettger & Raymond

and even into adulthood.[12] Research that tests for effects on inequality paints an even more negative picture, suggesting not only that mass imprisonment has dramatically increased racial disparities in children's levels of behavioral and mental health problems, as well as their risks of infant mortality and homelessness, but also that the effects of mass imprisonment on childhood inequality are substantially larger than its effects on inequality among adult men.[13]

Important as these contributions are, existing quantitative research on the consequences of mass imprisonment for family life is still limited because it almost never considers the broader concentration of incarceration in families. This oversight is stymying for two reasons. First, qualitative research on the families of incarcerated men shows that most families experiencing incarceration are experiencing the incarceration of not just one family member, but multiple family members.[14] Second, new research suggests that family member incarceration, broadly defined, has implications for women's wellbeing.[15] Taken together, these two bodies of research suggest that paternal incarceration and the incarceration of other family members likely significantly overlap and that this overlap has profound implications for family life.

In this article, we use data from the Project on Human Development in Chicago Neighborhoods (PHDCN) to fill this pressing gap in research on the consequences of mass imprisonment for family life in three stages. In the first stage, we show, consistent with other research in this area,[16] that the families that experience paternal and maternal incarceration also experience many other disadvantages (unrelated to the criminal justice system) even prior to experiencing that event. In the second stage, we rely on a unique series of questions asking about family members' incarceration to show that families experiencing parental incarceration also experience significantly more incarceration in their broader family networks than children without incarcerated parents (although we also show high levels of family incarceration for these children). In the third stage, we use propensity score models, which allow us to compare families identical on all characteristics except parental incarceration, in order to further demonstrate that incarceration

---

R. Swisher, *Associations of Fathers' History of Incarceration with Sons' Delinquency and Arrest Among Black, White, and Hispanic Males in the United States,* 49 CRIMINOLOGY 1109 (2011).

12 *See* Joseph Murray & David P. Farrington, *Parental Imprisonment: Effects on Boys' Antisocial Behaviour and Delinquency Through the Life-Course,* 46 J. CHILD PSYCHOL. & PSYCHIATRY 1269 (2005); Joseph Murray & David P. Farrington, *Parental Imprisonment: Long-Lasting Effects on Boys' Internalizing Problems Through the Life Course,* 20 DEV. & PSYCHOPATHOLOGY 273 (2008).

13 *See* SARA WAKEFIELD & Christopher WILDEMAN, CHILDREN OF THE PRISON BOOM: MASS INCARCERATION AND THE FUTURE OF INEQUALITY (2013); Wakefield & Wildeman, *supra* note 10.

14 For three qualitative studies in this vein that will be discussed in greater detail later in this article, see DONALD BRAMAN, DOING TIME ON THE OUTSIDE: INCARCERATION AND FAMILY LIFE IN URBAN AMERICA (2004); MEGAN COMFORT, DOING TIME TOGETHER: LOVE AND FAMILY IN THE SHADOW OF THE PRISON (2008); AND ANNE M. NURSE, FATHERHOOD ARRESTED: PARENTING FROM WITHIN THE JUVENILE JUSTICE SYSTEM (2002).

15 *See* Hedwig Lee, Christopher Wildeman, Emily A. Wang, Niki Matusko & James J. Jackson, *A Heavy Burden? The Cardiovascular Health Consequences of Having a Family Member Incarcerated,* Am. J. Pub. Health (forthcoming 2014) (showing that having a family member incarcerated leads to worse cardiovascular health for women but not men, suggesting potentially broad effects on women's health).

16 *See* Geller, Cooper, Garfinkel & Mincy, *supra* note 10, at 57–58 (showing that children with previously incarcerated fathers are disadvantaged relative to children who did not experience that event on a host of background characteristics ranging from parental finances to drug abuse).

runs in families. The notion that incarceration, like crime, concentrates in particular families, social groups, and places is not new[17]—but the implications of such concentrations are much more consequential in an era of mass incarceration. Moreover, while criminologists have long been interested in the intergenerational transmission of crime[18] and punishment, the focus in quantitative research has usually been restricted to parents, neglecting larger kinship networks that qualitative researchers have repeatedly identified as important.[19] By incorporating the concentration of incarceration in families beyond parents, we greatly extend the conversation about the effects of mass imprisonment on the most marginalized modern families.

Mass Incarceration and Family Life

Paternal Incarceration and Child Wellbeing

Researchers have long had interest in the consequences of parental incarceration for children, and an early wave of research, primarily appearing in psychology and social work journals starting in the 1970s, demonstrated a strong association between parental incarceration and poor child outcomes.[20] Although scholars in psychology, social work, and related disciplines continue to hold great interest in understanding the consequences of parental incarceration for children, a new wave of research in criminology, demography, and sociology has sprung up in just the last five years.[21] Consistent with previous research on the consequences of parental incarceration and contemporary work in psychology,[22] much of this research suggests that children of incarcerated

---

17 For two examples of how crime and incarceration run in families, see John Hagan & Alberto Palloni, *The Social Reproduction of a Criminal Class in Working Class London, Circa 1950–1980,* 96 Am. J. Soc. 265 (1990); David P. Farrington, Jeremy W. Coid & Joseph Murray, *Family Factors in the Intergenerational Transmission of Offending,* 19 Crim. Behav. & Mental Health 109 (2009). For a classic example of the implications of inequality for crime, see Judith R. Blau & Peter M. Blau, *The Cost of Inequality: Metropolitan Structure and Violent Crime,* 47 Am. Soc. Rev. 114 (1982).

18 *See* Hagan & Palloni, *supra* note 17.

19 *See* Carol Stack, All Our Kin (1974).

20 *See* Joyce A. Arditti, Parental incarceration and the Family: Psychological and Social Effects of Imprisonment on Children, Parents, and Caregivers (2012); Megan Comfort, *Punishment Beyond the Legal Offender,* 3 Ann. Rev. L. & Soc. Sci. 271 (2007); John Hagan & Ronit Dinovitzer, *Collateral Consequences of Imprisonment for Children, Communities, and Prisoners,* 26 Crime & Just. 121 (1999); Joseph Murray & David P. Farrington, *The Effects of Parental Imprisonment on Children,* 37 Crime & Just. 133 (2008).

21 *See* Foster & Hagan, *supra* note 11; Geller, Cooper, Garfinkel & Mincy, *supra* note 10, at 57–58; Wakefield & Wildeman, *supra* note 10.

22 *See, e.g.,* Arditti, *supra* note 20; Danielle H. Daillaire, Anne Ciccone & Laura C. Wilson, *Teacher's Experiences with and Expectations of Children with Incarcerated Parents,* 31 J. Applied Dev. Psychol. 281 (2010) (showing in a brilliant experiment that teachers have lower expectations for children with an incarcerated mother); Joseph Murray, Rolf Loeber & Dustin Pardini, *Parental involvement in the Criminal Justice System and the Development of Youth Theft, Marijuana Use, Depression, and Poor Academic Performance,* 50 Criminology 255 (2012).

parents struggled from a host of deficits before experiencing parental incarceration, many of which were made worse as a result of parental incarceration.[23]

These consistently negative effects of parental incarceration on child outcomes make good sense in light of emerging research linking paternal (and, albeit to a lesser degree, maternal) incarceration with significant downturns in family functioning. Specifically, research in this area demonstrates that families experiencing incarceration show declines in household income,[24] driven partially by the increases in union dissolution[25] that result from incarceration and partially by the reductions in earnings that also result from this event.[26] At the same time, these families also experience increases not only in costs as a result of keeping in touch with an incarcerated family member[27] but also legal debt as a result of their conviction and incarceration.[28]

When the financial consequences of paternal incarceration are joined by the often-drastic consequences of this event for the current and former romantic partners these men leave behind, it becomes more transparent why paternal incarceration is so strongly linked with poor child outcomes. Women who share children with incarcerated men tend to withdraw from their social networks as a result[29] in order to hide the stigma of incarceration,[30] potentially making them

---

23 *See, e.g.*, Geller, Cooper, & Garfinkel, *supra* note 10. Results on the effect of maternal incarceration on children's outcomes are somewhat more inconsistent than are results on the effect of paternal incarceration on children's outcomes, with some rigorous research suggesting negative effects and other similarly rigorous research suggesting null effects. *See* John Hagan & Holly Foster, *Children of the American Prison Generation: Student and School Spillover Effects of Incarcerating Mothers,* 46 L. & Soc'y Rev. 37 (2012); Rosa Minhyo Cho, *The Impact of Maternal Imprisonment on Children's Educational Achievement: Results from Children in Chicago Public Schools,* 44 J. Hum. Resources 772 (2009).

24 *See* Amanda Geller, Irwin Garfinkel & Bruce Western, *Paternal Incarceration and Support for Children in Fragile Families,* 48 Demography 25 (2011).

25 Leonard M. Lopoo & Bruce Western, *Incarceration and the Formation and Stability of Marital Unions,* 67 J. Marriage & Fam. 721 (2005); Massoglia, Remster & King, *supra* note 7; Apel, Blokland, Nieuwbeerta & van Schellen, *supra* note 7.

26 *See* Western, *supra* note 6.

27 For the most systematic estimate, see Olga Grinstead, Bonnie Faigeles, Carrie Bancroft & Barry Zack, *The Financial Cost of Maintaining Relationships with Incarcerated African American Men: A Survey of Women Prison Visitors,* 6 J. Afr. Am. Men 59 (2001) (showing that even women whose household incomes are less than $20,000 annually expend a significant amount of money keeping in touch with incarcerated family members).

28 *See* Alexes Harris, Heather Evans, & Katherine Beckett, *Drawing Blood from Stones: Legal Debt and Social Inequality in the Contemporary United States,* 115 Am. J. Soc. 1753 (2010).

29 For a new quantitative test of this relationship, see Kristin Turney, Jason Schnittker, & Christopher Wildeman, *Those They Leave Behind: Paternal Incarceration and Maternal Instrumental Support,* 74 J. Marriage & Fam. 1149 (2012).

30 For a powerful example, see Braman, *supra* note 14, at 171, where the author argues that [p]erhaps the most significant consequence of stigma among families of prisoners, then, is the distortion, diminution, and even severance of these social ties. Stigma related to incarceration is powerful, in part, because the families know that the same relationships on which they have come to depend can be turned against them, as social networks that provide resources are transformed into social networks of approbation. It is little wonder, then, that many family members carefully guard information about incarceration.

less able to deal with stressful situations that result from the incarceration. They also suffer from marked decreases in mental health,[31] which might also affect their parenting strategies.[32]

Yet reductions in the economic resources available to children and the well-being of their mothers are not the only ways in which paternal incarceration could indirectly influence children, as the incarceration experience also profoundly changes fathers in ways antithetical to high-quality parenting.[33] Especially for fathers residing with the mothers of their children prior to incarceration, incarceration leads to marked declines in the level of cooperation between parents and the quality of paternal interactions with children.[34] Paternal incarceration does not lead solely to declines in the quality of parenting, but also the quantity of paternal involvement.[35] And since fathers who experienced incarceration also struggle with mental health problems as a result of that experience,[36] all of which make them less prepared to parent than they were before experiencing incarceration, it is clear how the combination of reduced financial resources, worse maternal well-being, and worse paternal involvement would harm children.

Broader Research on Family Incarceration

Although much of the research in this area in recent years has considered the effects of parental incarceration on children, the extensive qualitative literature on incarceration and family life suggests that many families struggling with the incarceration of a parent may simultaneously be struggling to manage their households while another close relative is also incarcerated. Donald Braman's *Doing Time on the Outside*[37] and Megan Comfort's *Doing Time Together*[38] provide insight into how common experiencing the incarceration of multiple kin members simultaneously is for the most marginalized families. Consider the case of Pammy, for instance, eloquently described in Braman's pathbreaking work on incarceration and the family.[39] Pammy's father is currently incarcerated. Yet none of her other family members is currently incarcerated. So of her thirteen living relatives (two siblings, two parents, four aunts, and five uncles), only her father was

---

31 Christopher Wildeman, Jason Schnittker & Kristin Turney, *Despair by Association? The Mental Health of Mothers with Children by Recently Incarcerated Fathers,* 77 Am. Soc. Rev. 216 (2012).

32 For one example of how maternal depression shapes parenting behaviors, which are some of the key drivers of child well-being, see Kristin Turney, *Labored Love: Examining the Link Between Maternal Depression and Parenting Behaviors,* 40 Soc. Sci. Res. 399 (2011).

33 For an especially compelling discussion of how incarceration promotes negative change in parenting styles, see NURSE, *supra* note 14, which shows that the prison environment encourages inmates to adopt a highly controlling style of parenting in which children's "infractions" are dealt with swiftly and severely.

34 Kristin Turney & Christopher Wildeman, *Redefining Relationships: Explaining the Countervailing Consequences of Paternal Incarceration for Parenting,* 78 Am. Soc. Rev. 949 (2013).

35 Amanda Geller, *Paternal Incarceration and Father-Child Contact in Fragile Families,* 75 J. Marriage & Fam. 1288 (2013).

36 Schnittker, Massoglia & Uggen, *supra* note 8; Turney, Wildeman & Schnittker, *supra* note 8.

37 Braman, supra note 14.

38 Comfort, supra note 14.

39 Braman, *supra* note 14, at 42 fig. 7.

incarcerated.[40] Contrast this situation with the situation of Renika.[41] Renika's father Arthur is currently incarcerated, but so is her paternal uncle Billy, meaning that she has not one but two close relatives currently incarcerated, which may have important implications for her well-being because it means that both her mother and her aunt must simultaneously struggle to maintain their households in the absence of their husbands.[42]

In a similar vein, Natasha, one of the research subjects in Megan Comfort's *Doing Time Together,* whose boyfriend is currently incarcerated, recounted her experiences visiting prison:

> My sister, she was visitin' her boyfriend, so I was visitin' my boyfriend ... and then I have a friend, her boyfriend was in there, and we'd go up there together, you know, I see people there that I know, I see a whole ton! When I was goin' to Santa Rita, I seen all these people that I know! I was like, "God!" I was like, "What are you doin' up here?" They was like, "What you doin' up here?" It was a whole buncha people. I seen my cousin up there: "I didn't know that he was up here!" "Girl, yeah, he been up here for *a while.*"[43]

Taken together, these examples illustrate just how pervasive family incarceration experiences are for poor families in an era of mass incarceration, suggesting the need to further consider family member incarceration alongside other stressors that the urban poor disproportionately face.[44]

Although very little quantitative research on the consequences of mass imprisonment for families considers these broader consequences of family member incarceration—because, as we mentioned earlier, the emphasis in quantitative research has to date overwhelmingly been the consequences of parental incarceration for children—emerging research in public health suggests that this event may have severe repercussions for the women left to manage their households while a family member is incarcerated. Specifically, research links having a family member incarcerated with health problems including being obese, being in fair or poor health, and having ever had a heart attack or stroke.[45] If broader experiences of family member incarceration are common, as qualitative research suggests they are, and harmful to family members left behind, then the overemphasis on parental incarceration may have led quantitative research to significantly underestimate the impact of mass imprisonment on family life. Braman's work

---

40 *Id.* at 66 fig. 8; 136 fig. 12.
41 *Id.* at ll4 fig. 11.
42 *Id.*
43 Comfort, *supra* note 14, at 152 (emphasis in original). For a parallel discussion, although with a significantly more somber tone, see also *id.* at 152 n. 11.
44 For a similar argument along with greater discussion of the mechanisms through which family member incarceration could compromise women's health, see Hedwig tee & Christopher Wildeman, *Things Fall Apart: Health Consequences of Mass Imprisonment for African American Women,* 40 Rev. Black Pol. Econ. 39 (2013).
45 *See* Lee, Wildeman, Wang, Matusko & Jackson, supra note 15 (showing that having a family member incarcerated leads to worse cardiovascular health for women but not men, suggesting potentially broad effects on women's health). These findings parallel research showing that the incarceration of a family member also has substantial negative effects on the civic engagement of the women left behind. *See* Hedwig Lee, Lauren C. Porter & Megan Comfort, *Consequences of Family Member Incarceration: Impacts on Civic Participation and Perceptions of the Legitimacy and Fairness of Government,* 651 Annals Am. Acad. Pol. & Soc. Sci. 44 (2014).

provides a compelling account of how the incarceration of multiple family members imperils the well-being of women left behind, as Lilly,[46] who has two adult sons incarcerated says:

> It seems like I'm always rippin' and runnin' these days, just to make ends meet. I've got my back and my blood pressure, but I still have to get out to the church to get my groceries to help feed these kids. They have all kinds of expenses, medical bills, shoes. ... But it's a burden like you a parent all over again, but you're ready to retire and you watching your money go. My money's all gone now. I thank God for the church with those groceries. But living week to week, it just keeps you stressed out.[47]

Situations like Lilly's make it clear just how much the concentration of incarceration in family networks may damage the life-chances of the family members left behind, both young and old.

Our Contribution

In order to bring the rigorous quantitative research on paternal incarceration and children's outcomes and the rich qualitative research on mass incarceration and family life more in line with each other, we rely on data from the Project on Human Development in Chicago Neighborhoods (PHDCN) to show how concentrated family member incarceration is among families that have also experienced the incarceration of a parent recently. In so doing, we substantially add to research on the consequences of mass imprisonment for modern families.

Data, Measures, and Analytic Strategy

Project on Human Development in Chicago Neighborhoods

We rely on data from the PHDCN. The PHDCN followed roughly 6,000 children under age 18 living in Chicago over three waves of data collection, spanning the period 1994 to 2002. The goal of the study was to consider how neighborhoods, families, and schools affect child and adolescent development, as well as to provide a descriptive portrait of the social environments experienced by Chicago children.[48]

Measures

We rely on three types of measures of children's family situations: (1) their family background characteristics; (2) their experiences with paternal and maternal incarceration; and (3) their experiences with family member incarceration more broadly. We discuss each in turn.

---

46 For a complete description of Lilly's family life, see Braman, *supra* note 14, at 114 fig. 11.

47 *See id.* at 128. For further discussion of how this family has struggled, see *id.* at 113–34.

48 For a more detailed description of the PHDCN, see Felton J. Earls, et al., *Project on Human Development in Chicago Neighborhoods (PHDCN),* Inter-university Consortium for Political & Soc. Research (2002), http://www.icpsr.umich.edu/icpsrweb/PHDCNZ. For a more detailed description of the benefits of these data for considering the consequences of incarceration for family life, see Wakefield & Wildeman, *supra* note 13.

Our measures of family background characteristics include the following: the child's father's and mother's age (in years); the child's race (Black, White, Hispanic, Other); the child's father's and mother's educational attainment (less than high school, high school only, some college, or attainment of a bachelors degree[49]); a series of measures of family structure (including whether the mother was the primary caregiver, whether the father was the primary caregiver, whether the parents are married, and whether the primary caregiver is single); the per capita yearly income of the household the child was living in (in dollars); public assistance receipt; primary caregiver full-time employment; the socioeconomic status of the neighborhood the child was living in (low, medium, high); and the ethnic composition of their neighborhood (>70% Black, >70% White, >70% Hispanic).[50]

The measures of paternal, maternal, and family member incarceration we rely on come from the same section of the PHDCN (Family Mental Health and Legal History) for each of the three waves of data we analyze, so we discuss them together. At Wave 1, interviewers asked respondents if any of their relatives, including their mother or father, had ever had any trouble with the law (including being stopped by the police or arrested). If any of their relatives had ever been arrested or stopped by the police, respondents were then asked to identify how they were related to the person, if that person had ever accumulated a criminal record, and if that person was currently in jail.[51] Respondents were asked a similar battery of questions of the Wave 2 and 3 interviews, although the items did change in two key ways between Wave 1 and the final two waves.[52] First, rather than being asked if the family member was currently incarcerated, as in Wave 1, respondents in Waves 2 and 3 were asked if the family member had been incarcerated at any point since the last interview.[53] Second, respondents were now given the option of identifying up to 12 members of their family who had recently had a legal problem, a rise from 8 in Wave 1.[54]

By using these unique measures, we are able to come up with (1) four parental incarceration categories (no parental incarceration, paternal incarceration only, maternal incarceration only, both paternal incarceration and maternal incarceration), (2) a measure of the total number of family members experiencing incarceration in roughly the last five to six years,[55] and (3) a pre-

---

49 Very few of the parents we focus on here attained a college degree so we combined this category with those who took coursework after high school but did not graduate. The results are substantively similar, irrespective of the categorization procedure for this variable.

50 For information of the coding for these variables, please contact the authors.

51 Earls, et al., *supra* note 48.

52 *Id.*

53 *Id.*

54 *Id.* Although the number of relatives increased from eight to twelve between Wave 1 and Wave 2, our analyses suggest that this change had virtually no effect on the distribution of incarceration in families between families, as few families had even eight individuals in their family experience incarceration over the course of the survey period.

55 Unfortunately, we cannot distinguish between repeated incarcerations of one family member (who could be incarcerated up to three times, one for each wave, assuming he or she was incarcerated at Wave 1, released and reincarcerated between Waves 1 and 2, and released and reincarcerated between Waves 2 and 3) and first incarcerations for an identical family status (two brothers, for instance). This means that we likely slightly overestimate the number of family members who experience incarceration during

cise indication of who each of those family members were. For each measure, we consider not point-in-time estimates of family member incarceration, but the high estimate of the number of family members incarcerated over the PHDCN study period.

Although many datasets make it possible to measure parental incarceration, the PHDCN dataset is, to our knowledge, the single large, broadly representative dataset that makes it possible to not only estimate how many family members experience incarceration over a specific period of time, but also who those family members are, greatly advancing research on modern families.

Analytic Strategy

Our analysis proceeds in three stages. In the first stage, we present descriptive statistics on the family background characteristics of children who had (1) neither their father nor their mother incarcerated, (2) only their father incarcerated, (3) only their mother incarcerated, and (4) both their mother and their father incarcerated over the study period. In this stage, we also provide two-sample t-tests of statistical significance. We see this step as an important first step because it lets us show how disadvantaged these children were in domains unrelated to family incarceration.

In the second stage of our analysis, we present descriptive statistics on the broader family member incarceration experiences of children who had (1) neither their father nor their mother incarcerated, (2) only their father incarcerated, (3) only their mother incarcerated, and (4) both their mother and their father incarcerated over the study period. Specifically, we start by comparing the average number of family members these children have had incarcerated over the study period before moving on to show how the distribution of the number of family members incarcerated differs across these groups, and close by showing how these groups differ in terms of which family members experienced incarceration. In this stage, we also provide two-sample t-tests of significance. In so doing, we take a step toward considering how the family incarceration experiences of children differ for children who do and do not experience parental incarceration. In the final stage of our analysis, we again consider differences in the family member incarceration experiences between these same four groups of children. But rather than showing descriptive differences between children who do and do not experience parental incarceration, we now use propensity score modeling,[56] which allows us "to compare apples and apples" by matching children who do and do not experience incarceration on all the family background characteristics we showed in the first stage of the analysis. Although the statistical basis for propensity score

---

this period. The bias in these estimates should be fairly small, however, as most of the incarceration experiences were not for individuals (one brother and one uncle, for instance), making us confident that the estimate we provide here is a high-quality one.

56 For a classic description of propensity score models, see Paul Rosenbaum & Donald Rubin, *The Central Role of the Propensity Score in Observational Studies for Causal Effects,* 70 Biometrika 41 (1983). For a newer text that discusses counterfactuals more broadly, see Stephen Morgan & Christopher Winship, Counterfactuals and Causal Inference: Methods and Principles for Social Research (2007). For probably the most transparent application of propensity score models to incarceration, see Michael Massoglia, *Incarceration as Exposure: The Prison, Infectious Disease, and Stress-Related Illnesses,* 49 J. Health & Soc. Behav. 56 (2008).

matching is complex, and we do not belabor the details here,[57] we think this stage is especially important because it lets us show how family member incarceration varies across matched children who do and do not also experience parental incarceration in this period. In so doing, we show just how concentrated incarceration truly is in modern families.

Results

Descriptive Differences in Disadvantage

Before showing how concentrated family member incarceration is, we first show that disadvantaged children with incarcerated parents are exposed to a host of background factors other than incarceration relative to children who have neither parent incarcerated. To this end, Table 13.1 compares children with only a father incarcerated, only a mother incarcerated, and both parents incarcerated to children who have neither parent incarcerated on a host of background characteristics including paternal and maternal age, the child's race, paternal and maternal education, and family structure.

Consistent with previous research on parental incarceration,[58] these descriptive results provide support for the idea that children with incarcerated parents were far worse off than other children—even if differences between children with both parents incarcerated and neither parent incarcerated are not always statistically significant because of small sample sizes. Children with incarcerated parents have significantly younger parents, their parents have significantly less education, they are less likely to grow up with married parents, and they are more likely to be a minority and less likely to be White than children with neither their mother nor their father incarcerated at any point during this study period.

Table 13.2, which shows the differences in the economic resources available to children, whether the family received public assistance, whether the primary caregiver was employed full-time, and the characteristics of the neighborhoods children grow up in further buttress the case that even if children with incarcerated parents did not experience additional bouts of family member incarceration, they are still a marginalized population. Their families on average make significantly less money, are significantly more likely to rely on public assistance, and are significantly more likely to live in neighborhoods that are disproportionately Black than are children with neither parent incarcerated, to highlight just some of the key differences.

---

57 For all of the propensity score analyses, we use kernel matching, which has the benefit of weighting control cases that are closer to treated cases more heavily. Full details of the analysis are available upon request from the authors, although the results were robust to a host of alternative matching algorithms. For a full description of the different variants of propensity score matching techniques, see Sasha O. Becker & Andrea Ichino, *Estimation of Average Treatment Effects Based on Propensity Scores,* 2 STATA J. 358 (2002). For a systematic analysis of how using alternate first and second-stage matching procedures affects results, see MORGAN & WINSHIP, *supra* note 56, at 113 tbl. 4.6.

58 *See* Geller, Cooper, Garfinkel & Mincy, *supra* note 10, 57–58 tbl. 3.

TABLE 13.1 Demographic Characteristics by Maternal/Paternal Incarceration, PHDCN

	Paternal (N=299)	Maternal (N=55)	Paternal and Maternal (N=28)	Neither (N=5,593)
Father Age	31.95*	33.15*	35.14	36.02
Mother Age	28.83*	30.47*	30.77	32.97
Child Male	.52	.33*	.52	.50
Child Race				
Black	.57*	.80*	.67	.32
White	.07*	.04*	.07*	.15
Hispanic	.32*	.15*	.26*	.49
Other	.04	.02	.00	.04
Maternal Education				
Less than HS	.47	.54*	.60*	.44
HS Diploma	.09*	.10	.08	.14
More Than HS	.44*	.37*	.32*	.42
Paternal Education				
Less Than HS	.55*	.49	.64*	.45
HS Diploma	.21*	.22	.23	.18
More Than HS	.23*	.29	.14*	.37
Family Structure				
Primary Caregiver is Bio Mom	.90	.69*	.56*	.88
Primary Caregiver is Bio Dad	.03*	.02	.00	.07
Parents are Married	.17*	.15*	.11*	.49
Primary Caregiver is Single	.60*	.56*	.70*	.30

*Notes: * indicates statistically significant difference between children with an incarerated parent and children who did not experience parental incarceration in the PHDCN at the .05 level.*

Descriptive Differences in Family Incarceration

Having shown substantial, statistically significant, differences between children with an incarcerated parent and other disadvantages, we now move on to the main goal of our analysis: showing how highly concentrated family incarceration is. In Table 13.3, we begin this task by showing how children with an incarcerated parent compare to other children in this key regard.

The descriptive results are highly consistent with our expectations, as children with only an incarcerated father, only an incarcerated mother, and both parents incarcerated all have significantly more other family members incarcerated than do children whose parents do not experience incarceration over this period. Children with neither parent incarcerated have, on average, about .29 additional family members incarcerated over this period, which is just over one-half as many family members as we found for children who experience only paternal incarceration (at .56), just

TABLE 13.2 Economic and Neighborhood Characteristics by Maternal/Paternal Incarceration, PHDCN

	Paternal (N=299)	Maternal (N=55)	Paternal and Maternal (N=28)	Neither (N=5,593)
Salary				
<5,000	.21*	.18	.23*	.12
5,000–9,999	.19*	.12	.19	.12
10,000–19,999	.24*	.33*	.27	.21
20,000–29,999	.13	.14	.23	.17
30,000–39,999	.10	.14	.04	.13
40,000–49,999	.04	.04	.04	.09
>50,000	.08*	.06*	.00*	.16
Per Capita Yearly Income	4,343*	4,271*	3,176*	6,172
Family Receives Public Assistance	.59*	.77*	.65*	.33
Primary Caregiver Full-Time	.47	.58*	.50*	.46
Neighborhood Socio-Economic Status				
Low	.47*	.57*	.44	.36
Medium	.38	.30	.44	.40
High	.15*	.13*	.11*	.24
Neighborhood Ethic Composition				
70%+ Black	.33*	.59*	.41*	.18
70%+ White	.08*	.04*	.15	.14
70%+ Hispanic	.06*	.11*	.04	.13

*Notes: * indicates statistically significant difference between children with an incarerated parent and children who did not experience parental incarceration in the PHDCN at the .05 level.*

under one-half as many family members as found for children who experienced both paternal and maternal incarceration (at .71), and roughly one-third as many family members as children who experience only maternal incarceration (at .85). The final estimate bears special mention, as it indicates that children with only incarcerated mothers have, on average, an additional .56 other family members incarcerated compared to children with no parent incarcerated, providing strong initial support for our argument that incarceration travels in families even more than existing quantitative research in this area has to this point suggested.

Looking further down the table, we find that children with an incarcerated parent are significantly more likely to experience the incarceration of an additional family member than were children with neither parent incarcerated. Indeed, while only 18% of children with neither parent incarcerated could expect to have some other family member incarcerated, children with a parent incarcerated had a 32% chance of having another family member incarcerated (for children with both parents incarcerated) and a 42% chance of having another family member incarcerated (for

TABLE 13.3 The Concentration of Incarceration in Families

	Paternal (N=299)	Maternal (N=55)	Paternal and Maternal (N=28)	Neither (N=5,593)
Number of Incarcerated Relatives	.56*	.85*	.71*	.29
Distribution of Incarcerated Relatives				
0	64.88*	58.18*	67.86*	81.99
1	24.08	14.55	17.86	11.70
2	5.35	12.73	3.57	3.96
3	2.68	12.73	7.14	1.19
4	1.67	1.82	3.57	.27
5 or More	1.32	—	—	.53
Proportion with Any Non-Parent Relative Incarcerated	35.12*	41.82*	32.14*	18.01*

*Notes: * indicates statistically significant difference between incarerated and non-incarcerated population at the .05 level.*

children with only their mother incarcerated). This, again, suggests that children dealing with the incarceration of a parent are far more likely to also be dealing with the absence of some other member of their kin network due to incarceration simultaneously than children with neither of their parents incarcerated. Thus, children adjusting to parental incarceration may be doubly disadvantaged because they have fewer kin supports to rely on when they may need it most.

Of course, the logical counterargument to the findings presented in Table 13.3 is that everyone has a distant relative incarcerated whose incarceration matters for their life not at all. After all, we all have that third cousin we haven't seen in years. We address this possibility in Table 13.4, where we show how the number of close blood relatives—defined as immediate family, grandparents, uncles, aunts, first cousins, siblings, and half-siblings—and parents' partners incarcerated compare to other more distant family members for children who do and do not have a parent incarcerated. The results from these analyses suggest that differences are much more pronounced for close family members and, albeit to a lesser degree, parents' partners than more distant relatives. Interestingly, these differences are most pronounced for having no close relatives incarcerated, where those with no recent parental incarceration are significantly more likely to have no close relatives incarcerated (77%, as compared to 67, 64, and 62% of children with incarcerated parents), and for having two close relatives incarcerated, where those with recent maternal incarceration are far more likely to have two close relatives beyond their mother incarcerated (at 13% and 14%) than children with no recent parental incarceration (at 4%). Differences for parents' partners are small and insignificant, with the exception of children experiencing both paternal and maternal incarceration. Most interestingly, our results suggest that children with no recent parental incarceration are actually significantly more likely to have

TABLE 13.4 Reported Incarcerated Relatives by Paternal and Maternal Incarceration Experience, PHDCN

	Paternal (N=299)	**Maternal (N=55)**	**Paternal and Maternal (N=28)**	**Neither (N=5,593)**
Close Blood Relative Not Parent				
0	.67*	.62*	.64*	.77
1	.25	.20	.21	.18
2	.06	.13*	.14*	.04
3	.01	.05	.00	.05
Partner of Mother or Father				
0	.98	.96	.89*	.99
1	.02	.04	.11	.01
Other Reported Distant Relative				
0	.80	.78*	.79*	.88
1	.20	.22	.21	.12
2	.00	.00	.00	.01

*Notes: * indicates statistically significant difference between children with an incarerated parent and children who did not experience parental incarceration in the PHDCN at the .05 level.*

a distant relative incarcerated at some point, further indicating that the differences in family member incarceration we saw in Table 13.3 are not driven by second and third cousins, but by close blood relatives whose incarceration is relevant for children.

Family Incarceration in Matched Samples

To this point, the results have suggested that children with incarcerated parents differ markedly in their experiences of family member incarceration from children whose parents are not incarcerated. In the final section of this analysis, we sought to further refine this finding by seeing how the family incarceration experiences of children matched on all characteristics save parental incarceration compared using propensity score matching. The results from this exercise are shown in Table 13.5, which shows the average difference between these matched groups in terms of levels of broader family incarceration. In reading this table, the key rows to focus on are the "effect" of treatment row, which shows the difference in the average number of other incarcerated relatives, and the T row, which can be converted to p-values in order to show statistical significance. (T-values above 1.96 for these analyses suggest statistical significance.)

Consistent with the other results presented in this article, results using matched samples again suggest substantial, statistically significant differences in the average number of family members incarcerated for children who do and do not have an incarcerated parent. Children with an incarcerated father have, on average, about .15 more family members incarcerated than children who do not have either parent incarcerated. And the differences in family member

TABLE 13.5 Mean Comparison Using Matched Samples, PHDCN

	Paternal		Maternal		Paternal and Maternal	
	Treatment	Control	Treatment	Control	Treatment	Control
Average Number of incarcerated Relatives	.51	.36	.93	.33	.94	.29
"Effect" of Treatment	.150*		.597*		.645	
T	2.355		3.261		1.733	
N	299	5,593	55	5,593	28	5,593

*Notes: * indicates statistically significant difference between children with an incarerated parent and children who did not experience parental incarceration in the PHDCN at the .05 level based on propensity score models using kernal matching. For just paternal and maternal incarceration, the propensity score model included paternal (maternal) age, paternal (maternal) race, paternal (maternal) educational attainment, and whether the primary caregiver was (1) single and (2) on public assistance. For both paternal and maternal incarceration, the propensity score model included both paternal and maternal age, both paternal and maternal race, maternal educational attainment, and whether the primary caregiver was on public assistance. Contact the authors for further information.*

incarceration for children who have only a mother incarcerated (relative to neither parent) and both parents incarcerated (relative to neither parent) are even more pronounced. For children with incarcerated mothers, the average number of other family members incarcerated was between .597 and .645 family members greater than for children with neither parent incarcerated, a substantial—if statistically insignificant for children experiencing both paternal and maternal incarceration because of small sample size—difference. Taken together, the findings from our matched samples suggest that even when we "compare apples and apples" by matching children identical on other background disadvantages, children with incarcerated parents still have more additional family members incarcerated than do children whose parents were not incarcerated.

Conclusion

The dramatic increases in the American imprisonment rate that have taken place over roughly the last 40 years and the concentration of the risk of imprisonment among young minority men with low levels of educational attainment living in the poorest neighborhoods have made incarceration a common stage in the life-course not just for these marginalized men, but also for the women and children attached to them.[59] This heavy concentration of incarceration among the most marginalized families has spawned a sizable literature on the consequences of incarceration for family life, much, although certainly not all, of which has considered the effects of paternal imprisonment on children's wellbeing from childhood into adolescence and adulthood.[60]

59 *See generally* Pettit & Western, *supra* note 2; Sampson & Loeffler, *supra* note 2; Wildeman, *supra* note 5.
60 For four of the most comprehensive reviews on this topic, see Arditti, *supra* note 20; Comfort, *supra* note 20; Hagan & Dinovitzer, *supra* note 20; and Murray & Farrington, *supra* note 20.

Largely missing from the quantitative research in this area is a recognition that children with incarcerated parents are also likely to experience the incarceration of other family members simultaneously, a fact that has been strongly noted by some qualitative researchers working in this field.[61] The goal of this article was to extend quantitative research in this area by showing just how highly concentrated family incarceration is among the families also experiencing parental incarceration using data from the PHDCN, a dataset uniquely suited to this task.

Consistent with the qualitative literature, the results from our analyses showed large, statistically significant differences in family member incarceration between children who already had a parent missing due to incarceration and children who did not. Across the different variants of parental incarceration—father only, mother only, and both—children with incarcerated parents had, on average, about one-half more family members incarcerated than did children whose parents were not incarcerated. They were also at least twice as likely to have at least one family member incarcerated than were children with no parent incarcerated, again suggesting that the kin networks that could provide the support these children need during this trying time may be too heavily taxed from their own struggles with incarceration to provide the help required of them.

Although the questions we sought to answer were fairly straightforward and the methods we used to answer them simple enough, these results nonetheless have at least three critical implications for scholars of modern families. First, they suggest that incarceration is even more concentrated in families than often thought, which means that the modern families drawn into the penal state experience the incarceration of their kin and kith in an even more profound way than most quantitative, although not qualitative, research suggests. Second, on an empirical level, they imply that the massive literature considering the effects of parental incarceration on children may have been picking up not solely a direct effect of parental incarceration, but a combined effect of parental incarceration and broader family member incarceration. Although this does not invalidate results from these studies—as the studies were still picking up incarceration effects, after all—they do call out the need for greater attention empirically to the overlap between parental incarceration and the incarceration of other family members. Third, and maybe most importantly, since family member incarceration is an important stressor in its own right[62] that is highly concentrated in families, mass imprisonment may have implications for family inequality in a way that previous research has not fully wrestled with. Thus, future research on modern families would do well to attend not just to the consequences of paternal incarceration for child well-being, but also to the broader consequences of the incarceration of other members of kin networks—composed of brothers, sisters, uncles, aunts, and cousins—on family life.

---

61 Braman, *supra* note 14; Comfort, *supra* note 14.

62 *See* Lee & Wildeman, *supra* note 44; Lee, Wildeman, Wang, Matusko & Jackson, *supra* note 15.

CHAPTER 8

Conclusion

As mentioned, putting a criminal behind bars sounds like justice, but its impact is more than serving justice to one person. If we are fostering criminals while incarcerating criminals, then mass incarceration does not seem to be the best solution. When we discuss the issue of mass incarceration, we are not trying to be "soft on criminals." It is not being suggested that we should just let criminals walk free. As stressed several times in this book, criminologists need to look at these issues from a standpoint that takes social cost into consideration. Politicians can afford to say whatever helps them win votes, and that is easy to do as long as they play the ideology card carefully. It means they only need to say what people like to hear. Criminal justice professionals, on the other hand, need to be concerned about what really works and at what cost. Some people might argue mass incarceration works because the crime rates were declining. If this makes sense, then we still need to consider the next question. What is the cost? This would be a good time to revisit the issues discussed in previous chapters in this book because they are all connected.

Discussion Questions

1. How many criminals are currently incarcerated in the United States? How many criminals are being incarcerated worldwide? What do you see when you look at these two numbers?
2. What kinds of criminals deserve to serve time in prison, and what kinds should receive alternative sanctions? Be specific about your criteria.
3. If the Supreme Court orders you to release prisoners immediately to reduce overcrowding in a prison you are in charge of, how would you decide who should be released first?
4. Conduct some research on private prisons. How do private prisons factor into the issue of mass incarceration?
5. Do you believe we should be tough on crime? How can we be tough on crime without overusing incarceration as the punishment?

www.ingramcontent.com/pod-product-compliance
Lightning Source LLC
LaVergne TN
LVHW070321160125
801287LV00007B/37
9781793519320